A Theory of the Executive Branch

A Theory of the Executive Branch

Tension and Legality

MARGIT COHN
The Hebrew University of Jerusalem

OXFORD
UNIVERSITY PRESS

OXFORD
UNIVERSITY PRESS

Great Clarendon Street, Oxford, OX2 6DP,
United Kingdom

Oxford University Press is a department of the University of Oxford.
It furthers the University's objective of excellence in research, scholarship,
and education by publishing worldwide. Oxford is a registered trade mark of
Oxford University Press in the UK and in certain other countries

First Edition published in 2021

Impression: 3

Published in the United States of America by Oxford University Press
198 Madison Avenue, New York, NY 10016, United States of America

British Library Cataloguing in Publication Data

Data available

Library of Congress Control Number: 2020947996

ISBN 978–0–19–882198–4

DOI: 10.1093/oso/9780198821984.001.0001

Printed and bound by
CPI Group (UK) Ltd, Croydon, CR0 4YY

Acknowledgements

This book is the product of a longstanding interest in the executive branch. Parts of it draw on several publications. A book on general unilateral powers in Israel inspired this project and drew the first scheme for the comparative exercises, and several articles offered a basis for the arguments found in Chapters 2–5.

Parts of the book were presented at several seminars and discussions groups. Chapters 1–3 were discussed in a seminar hosted by the UK Constitutional Law Association; at the IX Congress of the International Association of Constitutional Law; at a joint research workshop, held by the Hebrew University and the University of Melbourne law faculties; at the Public Law Discussion Group, UCL London; the Oxford Public Law Discussion Group; the Law School Research Workshop, Trinity College Dublin; and presented as a Barton Public Lecture, Carleton University, Ottawa. Early versions of Chapters 4 and 5 were presented at a Faculty Seminar, Columbia Law School; *Juris Diversitas* Annual Conference; and two ICON-S annual conferences. My views on emergency law were presented at the Minerva Center for the Rule of Law under Extreme Conditions, University of Haifa. Versions of Chapter 10 were presented in the Public Law Discussion Group, UCL London, in a Tri.Con research talk, Trinity College Dublin, and at the Faculty Seminar, the Faculty of Law, Hebrew University of Jerusalem. I thank the OUP editorial team, Jamie Berezin, Paulina dos Santos Major, and Mark Ajin, for their work and support.

I thank the innumerable friends and colleagues who helped me along the way. Paul Craig's kind comments kept me on track throughout this journey. Donald Bello Hutt, Alon Harel, Moshe Hirsch, Hailey Hooper, Aileen Kavanagh, Jeff King, Maria Lee, Henry Monaghan, Colm O'Cinneide, Eloise Scotford, and Peter Strauss offered insights and helpful criticism during various stages of writing. Itamar Ben-David, Sima Granovsky, Daniel Levi, and Tal Sticker offered invaluable research assistance that instructed the analyses in Part III, and Adan Arshied was extremely helpful in the research and preparation of the final version of the book. My intrepid editor Diana Rubanenko provided not only superb assistance but was also a source for many a friendly chuckle on the way.

Parts of the book were written during my sabbatical visits at the Columbia Law School and the Faculty of Laws, UCL London: I thank them for their hospitality and support. Most of the time, however, was spent at my home-base, the Faculty of Law at the Hebrew University of Jerusalem, which provided much of everything needed for the writing and completion of this manuscript, including research and travel grants. Funding for the completion and publication of the book was generously provided by the Israel Science Foundation, under grant 54/21. I thank all, and hope we can further develop the study of the executive branch—a field of research that has never lost its relevance and deserves further attention.

Parts of Chapter 2 are based on Margit Cohn, 'Tension and Legality: Towards a Theory of the Executive Branch' (2016) 29 Can J L and Jurisp 321; parts of Chapters 4 and 5 are based on Margit Cohn, 'Non-Statutory Executive Powers: Assessing Global Constitutionalism in a Structural-Institutional Context' (2015) ICLQ 65.

Contents

List of Abbreviations xiii

Introduction 1

PART I. PRELIMINARIES

1. **Preliminaries** 7
   A. Introduction 7
   B. 'The Executive Branch': A Preliminary Definition 8
   C. The Executive Branch Researched: Common Themes and Debates 9
   D. Constitutionalism and Internal Tensions 22
   E. Answering Initial Challenges to General Theory 27
      1. Comparing Parliamentary and Presidential Regimes? 27
      2. 'Core' Executives and Administrative Agencies 31
   F. Concluding Remarks 39

2. **Reaching the Internal Tension Model** 42
   A. Introduction 42
   B. Three Institutional Models Rejected 43
      1. The Subservient Executive Model: The Separation of Powers and the Rule of Law 43
         a. The separation of powers 43
         b. The rule of law 45
      2. The Imperial Executive Model 47
         a. Managerial theories 47
         b. Exception-based theories 49
      3. The 'Bipolar' Model 53
   C. The Internal Tension Model 55
   D. Concluding Remarks 57

3. **Maintaining the Internal Tension Model** 59
   A. Introduction 59
   B. Conceptualizing Fuzziness I: Research Streams 60
      1. Four Research Streams 60
         a. Delegation and discretion 60
         b. 'Soft law' 62
         c. 'Grey holes' 64
         d. 'Fuzzy law' 66
      2. Moving Forward 68

C. Conceptualizing Fuzziness II: Thirteen Forms of Fuzziness 69
1. Fuzzy Legality: A Taxonomy 69
2. Constitution-Generated Fuzzy Legality 71
a. Open-ended constitutional provisions 72
b. Fuzzy powers under an unwritten constitution 73
c. Non-textual, general constitutional doctrines 75
3. Statute-Generated Fuzzy Legality 78
a. Open-ended, interpretable provisions 79
b. Grants of discretion 80
c. Delegation 82
d. 'Patchwork' legislation 85
e. Multiple and indeterminate decision-makers 86
f. 'Lopsided' statute 89
4. Executive-Generated Fuzzy Legality 91
a. Selective enforcement and creative compliance 91
b. 'Pastiche' law 92
c. Extra-statutory parallel arrangements 93
d. Multiple mixed source citation 94
D. Concluding Remarks 97

PART II. CONSTITUTION-GENERATED FUZZY LAW

4. Unilateral, Non-Statutory Executive Powers 101
A. Introduction 101
B. Non-Statutory Powers: A Short Primer 106
C. Bases of Authority 107
1. Constitution-Based Direct Sources 107
a. An unwritten constitution: the UK 108
b. A written constitution: the US 112
2. Constitution-Type Extra-Textual Doctrines 115
a. Political reality 115
b. Sovereignty and nationhood 116
c. Personification 117
d. 'Historical gloss' 121
e. Aggregation of powers 122
D. Legal Constraints on Unilateral Non-Statutory Powers 123
1. The Residuality Doctrine 123
2. Subjection to Judicial Review 127
E. Concluding Remarks 135

5. The Nature and Use of Unilateral Executive Measures: A Comparative Analysis 137
A. Introduction 137
B. The Curious Case of Mixed-Authority Orders in Council, Executive Orders, and Others 139
1. The United Kingdom: Orders in Council and Proclamations 139
a. The forms 139

b. Fuzziness I: multiple and mixed authorities 141
c. Fuzziness II: the legal status of unilateral measures 145
d. Fuzziness III: access difficulties 146
e. Interim conclusion 149
2. The United States: Proclamations, Executive Orders, Memoranda, and Other Measures 149
a. The forms 150
b. Fuzziness I: multiple and mixed authorities 156
c. Fuzziness II: the legal status of unilateral measures 158
d. Fuzziness III: access difficulties 160
C. Comparative Analysis 161
D. Concluding Remarks 163

PART III. LEGISLATION AND EXECUTIVE-GENERATED FUZZY LAW

6. Case Studies: Emergency and Air Pollution, Overviews 167
A. Introduction 167
B. Emergency Law 169
1. General 169
2. Emergency Law in the UK 171
a. General 171
b. Layers of law pertaining to emergencies 173
(1) Customary international law 173
(2) Constitutional law 175
(3) International treaty law and UN measures 176
(4) EU law 177
(5) Domestic primary legislation 179
3. Emergency Law in the US 180
a. General 180
b. Layers of law pertaining to emergencies 181
(1) Constitutional law 181
(2) Customary international law 182
(3) International treaty law and UN measures 184
(4) Federal primary legislation 185
C. Air Pollution Law 186
1. General 186
2. Air Pollution Law in England 188
a. General 188
b. Layers of law pertaining to air pollution 189
(1) International law 189
(2) EU law 190
(3) Domestic primary legislation 192
3. Air Pollution Law in the US 194
a. General 194
b. Layers of law pertaining to air pollution 194

(1) *Constitutional law* 194
(2) *International and transnational law* 195
(3) *Federal primary legislation* 196
D. Concluding Remarks 197

7. Legislation-Generated Fuzziness: Patchwork Legislation 198
A. Introduction 198
B. Piling-up 199
1. General 199
2. Examples 200
a. *UK anti-terrorism law* 200
b. *UK Brexit legislation* 203
C. Dispersion 204
1. General 204
2. Examples 205
a. *US air pollution* 205
b. *US emergency law* 208
D. The Fuzzy Consequences of Patchworking 212
1. Redundancy/Complexity 212
2. Contradiction 216
3. Under-Funding/Denial of Funding 218
E. Concluding Remarks 222

8. Executive-Generated Fuzziness: On the Spectrum of (Non)-Implementation 223
A. Introduction 223
B. From Informal Enforcement to Creative Compliance 225
1. Informal Enforcement 226
a. *General* 226
b. *Example: EPA's Supplemental Environmental Projects (SEPs)* 228
2. Creative Compliance 232
a. *General* 232
b. *Examples* 233
(1) *EPA's first two decades* 233
(2) *Funding the US-Mexico wall* 235
C. 'Pastiche' Law 239
1. General 239
2. Examples 240
a. *Under- or never-implemented statutes* 240
b. *'Floating' statutes* 242
c. *Under-funded law* 247
D. Fuzzy Implementation: The Prices Paid 249
E. Concluding Remarks 251

PART IV. ANALYSIS

9. Fuzzy Legality and the Challenge to Proper Governance 255
A. Introduction 255
B. The Challenges of Fuzzy Legality to Proper Governance 256
1. Introduction 256
2. Arguments from Democratic Theory 257
a. The rule of law discourse 257
b. Participatory/deliberative democratic theory 262
3. The Benefits of Fuzzy Legality? 265
4. Summary 268
C. The Political Economy of Fuzzy Legality 269
1. Introduction 269
2. The Rise and Retention of Fuzziness: Mapping the Explanatory Factors 271
3. Endogenous Reasons for Fuzziness 272
4. Exogenous Reasons for Fuzziness 278
a. Power-accumulation and retention 279
b. Disagreement 282
(1) During the design stage 282
(2) After introduction 284
c. Pressure to act 285
d. Marginalization 285
D. Concluding Remarks 286

10. Keeping the Internal Tension Under Check: The Role of the Judiciary in a Multiple-Fora Participatory/Deliberative Democracy 289
A. Introduction 289
B. In Search of Normative Integrity 293
C. The Role of the Judiciary: A Critical Overview 295
D. Enhancing Judicial Review: Arguments from Democratic Theory 306
1. The Rule of Law 306
2. Participatory/Deliberative Democratic Theory 308
3. But Why the Courts? 312
E. Addressing Counter-Arguments 313
F. Concluding Remarks 319

Conclusion 321

Index 323

List of Abbreviations

CA	Court of Appeal
CAA	Clean Air Act (US)
CCPR	Centre for Civil and Political Rights
CEO	Chief Executive Officer
CEQ	Council on Environmental Quality
CERCLA	Comprehensive Environmental Response, Compensation, and Liability Act
Ch	Chapter
CUP	Cambridge University Press
DOE	Department of Energy
ed	editor
edn	edition
EPA	Environmental Protection Agency
EU	European Union
FPA	Federal Power Act
HL	House of Lords
HRA	Human Rights Act
ICCPR	International Covenant on Civil and Political Rights
ICJ	International Court of Justice
IEECPA	International Emergency Economic Powers Act
n	note
NEPA	National Environmental Policy Act
OUP	Oxford University Press
para	paragraph
s	section
SEP	Supplemental Environmental Project
tr	translator
UN	United Nations
USC	United States Federal Code
vol	volume

Introduction

This book is a treatise on the executive branch. It was written during a difficult period, marked by several global political, economic, and social crises; a period during which a global pandemic marked the ways heads of nations in Western states and beyond shaped their politics, defined and redefined the allocation of powers between government branches; a time in which leaders of seemingly new personality types landed their societies in deep populist waters. At such a period, it would seem, attention to the executive branch could never have been more timely.

Yet similar observations could have been made, and indeed were advanced in modern democracies during the past two centuries. Serially emerging contingencies have led heads of states to address some of the challenges through their own relative aggrandizement; many sets of difficulties and crises led to further enhancement of executive power, which in turn seeped into more mundane areas of government policy.

Still, no general study of the very nature of this branch of government has emerged. Undoubtedly, political philosophers, historians, political scientists, legal scholars, and psychologists, in tandem with journalists, politicians, concerned citizens, and all informed bodies and individuals, have had much to contribute to the ongoing debates over the role of their respective heads of the executive. However, virtually all that growing body of words and works has focused on *national* heads of executives. No general theory has emerged; no informed shared insights were put forward to assist in creating a universal understanding, valid at least in Western democracies, of the nature of this important player in the history, politics, economics, and culture of modern democracies.

The book is an attempt to launch such a universal discourse. It draws on theories and writings from the fields of political science, political philosophy, law, history, and public administration, under the assumption that only the melding of insights from a variety of disciplines concerned with state power and its implications can lead to the development of a well-rounded theory of the nature of the executive.

This project is based on the understanding that the executive branch in Western democracies has been handed a virtually impossible task. Expected to 'imperially' direct the life of the nation through thick and thin, it is concurrently required to be subservient to legislation meted out by a sovereign parliament. How can such a task be accomplished? And what can be done to ensure, as much as possible, that social needs do not justify the abuse of power?

A Theory of the Executive Branch. Margit Cohn, Oxford University Press (2021). © Margit Cohn.
DOI: 10.1093/oso/9780198821984.003.0001

The book offers a distinct model of the executive, based on a general argument from political philosophy and constitutional theory which, rather than adopt hierarchical accounts of power, prioritizes dispersal of power and recognizes the existence of internal tensions under which games of power are played.

In a nutshell, I develop three arguments. First, to grasp the nature of executive power, one should reject hierarchic accounts of the public sphere: searches for the wielder of the final word should be replaced by a model which rests on networks and inter-branch tensions. Secondly, under this 'internal tension' vision of constitutionalism, the executive branch is to be considered as concurrently subservient to law and dominant over it. Finally, much of public law is shaped in ways that enable this seeming contradiction. Drawing on David Dyzenhaus's concept of 'grey holes', or situations under which a façade of legality masks the absence of substantive limitation of power, I offer a taxonomy of thirteen forms of 'fuzzy' law, generated by constitutions, legislators, and executives. Ranging from open-ended or semi-written constitutions to unapplied legislation, these forms of legality span both constitutional and administrative aspects of public law.

The book is divided into four parts. Part I is dedicated to the development of the theory. Chapter 1 concerns preliminary issues. It first offers a working definition of 'the executive', which focuses on the head of this branch as its representative, directing officer. Following it is an overview of the current literature, identifying common themes and recurring debates. Moving to the first basic assumption which feeds the theory offered in the book, the next section identifies the existence of ingrained internal tensions reigning in several aspects of constitutional law, including in theories of the executive. The final section of this chapter clears away challenges to the comparative exercise offered in the book.

Chapter 2 reaches the internal tension model through a discussion of three existing theories of national executives. Rejection of models of subservience and, conversely, complete dominance, a third attempt at carving out two distinct modes of action under a 'bipolar' model is likewise replaced by the model further developed in Chapter 3, based on the notion of internal tension.

After addressing several streams that are conceptually linked to the model of fuzzy legality, the next chapter identifies different nodes of fuzziness that offer executives the possibility of formally acting under law but in a relatively unfettered fashion. All are discussed in the chapter; those that receive further detailed attention in Parts II and III receive no more than a brief mention.

Part II is dedicated to one type of constitutional-generated fuzziness, which emerges through the use of unilateral executive action, broadly reliant on constitutional constructs. Chapter 4 offers a general analysis of this type of governance, found inter alia in the retention of the Royal prerogative in the United Kingdom, and in unilateral action in the United States that relies on its constitution. Chapter 5 focuses on a well-established practice of the issuance of unilateral semi-formal orders and edicts that draw on such constitution-generated fuzzy sources. The comparative analysis of these practices as they have emerged and evolved in the UK and the US shows a surprisingly high degree of convergence, despite the sharp differences in history, regime structure, and legal culture of both systems.

Moving to statute- and executive-generated fuzziness, Part III focuses on examples taken from two fields of legal action, emergency and air-pollution. Following an overview of the complex legal frameworks in both areas, and in both the UK and the US, presented in Chapter 6, Chapter 7 is dedicated to one form of statute-generated fuzziness, that of patchworking, or the practice of compiling multiple legal sources regulating a specific field, often overlapping, sometimes conflicting. Several forms of semi- or non-implementation are discussed in Chapter 8. Both chapters include examples from the two case-studies, as well as critical assessments of the ways these types of fuzziness have impaired proper governance. This part can be skipped by those preferring to proceed directly to the normative discussion contained in the next Part.

Part IV's first chapter offers a political and normative analysis of the findings provided in the previous chapters. First, I pick up the critical arguments against the reliance on fuzziness, strewn across earlier chapters, to show the ways fuzziness challenges the values embedded in two families of democratic theory—democracy as the rule of law, and participatory/deliberative democracy. Fuzzy law, it is argued, severely hampers the meting out of justice and fairness, and the maintenance of equality, obstructs the clarity and accessibility so vital for the proper operation of law, and thwarts the proliferation of forms of accountability and review. The chapter then offers an analysis of the political economy of fuzziness, defining reasons for the retention of fuzziness that are classified, under a distinction between endogenous and exogenous factors, all leading to the inevitability of fuzziness.

The final chapter advances arguments supporting enhanced review by the judiciary, presented on two levels. Firstly, judicial review of fuzzy law is justified in light of the special problems attached to reliance on such powers. The chapter then links to the general normative debate over the propriety of active judicial review of the executive (and legislation), which again draws on the theoretical constructs relied upon in Chapter 9. In a nutshell, the judiciary is presented as an important, but never a supreme, player, opening channels of deliberation and participation, especially important for those who have limited access (if any) to government corridors.

The modular structure of the book offers readers a choice of focusing on their respective interests. Those mainly interested in political philosophy and theory can direct their attention to Parts I and IV; constitutional theorists may also consider Part II, while those who wish to be informed about the detailed ways in which fuzziness is designed and applied, either due to their interest in public administration and law, or due to their wish to further understand the workings of the advanced theory, can further focus their attention on Part III.

Following the multidisciplinary nature of this exercise, the readership of the book is not limited to any single discipline, and is important to all interested in a variety of aspects of public law and policy, ranging from political philosophy, public law, public policy, to regulatory theory. The book is also likely to interest general legal theorists interested in the nature of law, due to the detailed analysis offered of the ways law enables executives to formally act under law without being substantively limited by it.

Year 2020, the year of completion of this book, was an exceptionally turbulent year, marked in the UK by its withdrawal from the EU, in the US by a continuing (quasi)-crisis concerned with fears of the impact of immigration on the nation (and xenophobia), and, in both, the events and effects of the Covid-19 pandemic; all links to web sources were last accessed on 30 August 2020. I have done my best to ensure that, despite the whirlwind of political and legal events in the past years, the facts and the state of the law discussed in the book all reflect the state of affairs in August 2020. The details, political, social, and legal, will surely change in the future, but I am certain that one of the central elements of these realities, the fuzziness of law, will remain constant. This fuzziness, as I claim, will ensure the continued dominance of the executive, hopefully without further sliding in the future into the realm of non-legality (of the latter, no one can be sure). A premium should hence be given to the development and enhancement of review mechanisms, including review by the judiciary.

PART I
PRELIMINARIES

1
Preliminaries

A. Introduction 7
B. 'The Executive Branch': A Preliminary Definition 8
C. The Executive Branch Researched: Common Themes and Debates 9
D. Constitutionalism and Internal Tensions 22
E. Answering Initial Challenges to General Theory 27
1. Comparing Parliamentary and Presidential Regimes? 27
2. 'Core' Executives and Administrative Agencies 31
F. Concluding Remarks 39

A. Introduction

This chapter introduces the setting for the study of the executive branch and sets aside several issues that may be considered as challenges to the project. A short section on the definition of 'the executive branch' is followed by an overview of the literature on the executive, showing that the immense body of research is almost entirely system-based, and contains limited theoretical and comparative analysis; in conclusion, to date, no general theory, or model of the executive branch, can be found in the current academic literature. An exposé of the central analytical concept used in this book—that of the 'internal tension' element of constitutionalism, leads to the discussion and rejection of two challenges to the project, which draws on the law and political practices of the United States and the United Kingdom. The first focuses on the alleged incomparability of comparisons between parliamentary and presidential regimes, the second on the so-called 'breaking down' of the executive branch and the devolution of many of its functions to bodies placed outside the 'core executive'. Variations do exist, but sufficient similarities, the existence of complex structures that do not follow simple binary divides and the de facto dominance of the executive in both systems, fully support the analyses presented in the book.

A Theory of the Executive Branch. Margit Cohn, Oxford University Press (2021). © Margit Cohn.
DOI: 10.1093/oso/9780198821984.003.0002

B. 'The Executive Branch': A Preliminary Definition

This book is on 'the executive branch': but what does this term mean? Does it refer to the head of the 'core' executive, the prime minister or president, or, collectively, to the departments or ministries that direct the political life of a nation? Alternatively, should a discussion of the 'executive branch' include all bodies that perform actions which are loosely considered to be 'executive'—executive agencies, perhaps also local authorities? But then, what type of action is 'executive'?

None of these questions has a simple answer. In their introduction to one of the very few studies that offer a comparative analysis of the executive branch, Professors Craig and Tomkins find that the difficulties of definition, within (and, it should be added, alongside) constitutions pertain both to functions and institutions.[1] Indeed, any attempt to capture the nature of 'executing' must grapple with the existence of myriad ways in which executives legally wield their powers of policy-making and its application. Institutionally, administrative agencies are well-recognized components of the 'administrative state' in the US, and the debate over their de facto independence, and the normative value of (non)independence is still raging, while attention to these, and to more far-reaching privatization schemes, are found elsewhere. Craig and Tomkins, then, do not ascribe to a single vision or interpretation of the executive, nor do others.[2] I do not attempt to proffer a plain definition—in my case, in line with my faith that fuzziness is the best form of depiction of the nature of complex things, which is applied throughout this book, and my reliance on political interaction rather than on formalistic definitions. For my purposes, the term 'the executive' is chiefly applied to the head of the executive branch, who, as amply shown in the rich literature, is the key wielder of state power in the political sphere; often, but not always, she is able to direct the legislature, but even when this political setup is (temporarily?) unavailable, the head of the executive retains dominance as the maker of policy and its implementer. Other bodies, such as administrative agencies and bodies organized outside of the core executive, are not excluded from the analysis when their impact on the public sphere is substantive, as in the case of the EPA, the US agency authorized to regulate the environment.[3]

[1] Paul Craig and Adam Tomkins (eds), *The Executive and Public Law* (OUP 2006) 5. This unique study within public law addresses eleven legal systems. See further below.

[2] See the review of studies of national executives, Part B.

[3] Questions of 'independence' are dealt with towards the end of this chapter, in other chapters of this book, and, to a great length, by successive generations of scholars and judges. I submit that some control of such agencies by the head of the executive is almost universally maintained, with the possible exception of Central Banks.

C. The Executive Branch Researched: Common Themes and Debates

The study of the executive branch is stupendous, but is lacking in at least two ways. First, following the classical distinction between constitutional and administrative law, two streams of legal research exist, the first mainly dedicated to the role of the head of the executive branch and its powers, the second focused on the so-called 'administrative state', essentially public bodies at large, or agencies in the United States' parlance. Still directed to various extents by the head of the executive branch, such agencies, government departments, and other regulatory bodies attract a different type of consideration by their analysts, largely divergent from the concerns raised by constitutionalists who address the nature and legitimacy of concentrated power. The following survey traces the lines drawn by both streams, noting those that have worked to break down the boundary between the constitutional and the administrative and forge a vision under 'public law'.

Secondly, the hundreds of studies of the executive branch, both in law and political science, are almost entirely system-based. Comparative analysis, and, more importantly in our context, the general theory of the executive branch, remain severely underdeveloped.[4]

By far, the richest bodies of research in all existing disciplines and sub-disciplines—constitutional law, administrative law, political science—are US-based. This overview focuses on the modern presidency, often marked by the year 1933 (the commencement of the first presidency of Franklin Roosevelt and the nascent New-Deal era) as the date of birth of the *real* modern presidency,[5] although earlier works on the presidency are not rare.[6]

[4] For comparative research and edited country surveys see Richard Rose and Ezra Suleiman (eds), *Presidents and Prime Ministers* (American Enterprise Institute for Public Policy Research 1981); Ludger Helms, *Presidents, Prime Ministers and Chancellors* (Palgrave Macmillan 2005); Thomas Poguntke and Paul Webb (eds), *The Presidentialization of Politics* (OUP 2005); Craig and Tomkins (n 1). Some studies, essentially limited to the study of a single executive, dedicate a few pages to reference from abroad. Posner and Vermeule's, for example, is admittedly sketchy: Eric A Posner and Adrian Vermeule, *The Executive Unbound: After the Madisonian Republic* (OUP 2011) 170–74 (located in a chapter that is mainly concerned with the impact of international law on the US). The study of leadership and its psychological traits (text to n 20) offers an exception: in the tradition of comparative politics, studies sometimes span dozens of persons in different leadership positions from a variety of systems, but this research body is not focused on the executive as such.

[5] See Fred I Greenstein, 'Nine Presidents: In Search of a Modern Presidency' in Fred I Greenstein (ed), *Leadership in the Modern Presidency* (Harvard University Press 1988) 296 (the post-New Deal era was marked by the growth of domestic Federal power, as well as by the rise of the US president as the 'leader of the free world'); David Mackay, 'Leadership and the American Presidency' in RAW Rhodes and Paul 't Hart, *The Oxford Handbook of Political Leadership* (OUP 2014) 439, 448.

[6] For studies dating from the late-nineteenth and the early- twentieth centuries see eg Adolphe de Chambrun, *The Executive Power in the United States: A Study of Constitutional Law* (Madeleine Vinton Dahlgren trans., Inquirer Printing and Publishing Company 1874); John H Finley and John F Sanderson, *The American Executive and Executive Methods* (The Century, 1908); William Howard Taft, *Our Chief Magistrate and His Powers* (Columbia University Press 1916).

Apart from generally agreeing on aggrandizement, many analysts of national executives construct their studies around the notion of ambiguity. This is evident in US textbooks, such as Laurence Tribe's classic textbook on American Constitutional Law, in which the chapter on the US President carries the title 'The Puzzle of the Presidency: Its Uneasy Truce with Constitutionalism'.[7] Alluding to debates old and new, Tribe concluded that '[w]hether imperial or simply magisterial ... the American Presidency will never be easy to locate within our constitutional framework'.[8] Other US scholars fully agree.[9]

The British study of the executive shares the US insight about the undefinable nature of the executive branch.[10] So does the study of other legal systems. In the introduction to their edited book on the executive, Professors Craig and Tomkins conclude that all eleven systems analysed 'have found executive power to be a difficult and testing matter', and that '[a]n uneasy ambivalence about executive power may be detected in all of the chapters'.[11]

Very much like their colleagues from law, political scientists have identified the ambiguity of the office. For Cronin and Genovese, who, like most Americans, focus on the United States, this was intentional.[12] This may be a working hypothesis for analysis of the formative years of the US, but, as mentioned above, comparative study has shown a shared pattern of this type of ambiguity that extends well beyond

[7] Laurence H Tribe, *American Constitutional Law* (3rd edn, Foundation Press 2000) 630.

[8] ibid 631.

[9] For a few examples see Henry P Monaghan, 'The Protective Power of the Presidency' (1993) 93 Colum L Rev 1, 5 (noting the absence of 'an adequate legal conception of administrative authority'); Martin S Flaherty, 'The Most Dangerous Branch' (1996) 105 Yale LJ 1725 (addressing the tension between the rise of executive power and its uneasy relationship with the principle of the separation of powers); Saikrishna Prakash, 'The Essential Meaning of Executive Power' [2003] U Ill L Rev 701 at 706 and *passim* (positing 'two narrow conceptions of the executive power', the 'non-executive' thesis, under which the constitution does not empower the president to control federal law execution, and the 'chief overseer' thesis, which recognizes the exercise of influence and monitoring powers, but no authority to execute laws or direct agencies, with the 'chief executive' thesis, under which the Executive Power Clause 'vests the president with control over federal law execution'); Saikrishna Bangalore Prakash, 'Imperial and Imperiled: The Curious State of the Executive' (2009) 50 Wm and Mary L Rev 1021; Peter L Strauss, '"Overseer", or "The Decider"? The President in Administrative Law' (2007) 75 Geo Wash L Rev 696; Michelle Belco and Brandon Rottinghouse, *The Dual Executive: Unilateral Orders in a Separated and Shared Power System* (Stanford University Press 2017).

[10] See eg Adam Tomkins, 'The Struggle to Delimit Executive Power in Britain' in Craig and Tomkins (n 1) 16, 16.

[11] Craig and Tomkins (n 1) 14. See also, in the same vein and linked with the discussion of the executive in the UK, Thomas Poole, 'The Executive in Public Law' in Sir Jeffrey Jowel and Colm O'Cinneide (eds), *The Changing Constitution* (9th edn, OUP 2019).

[12] Thomas E Cronin and Michael A Genovese, *The Paradoxes of the American Presidency* (OUP 1998) 2–3 ('the founders purposely left the presidency imprecisely defined. This was due in part to their fears of both the monarchy and the masses, and in part to their hopes that future presidents would create a more powerful office than the framers were able to do at the time. They knew that at times the president would have to move swiftly and effectively, yet they went to considerable lengths to avoid enumerating specific powers and duties in order to calm the then widespread fear of monarchy'). See also MA Fitts, 'The Paradox of Power in the Modern State: Why a Unitary, Centralized Presidency May Not Exhibit Effective or Legitimate Leadership' (1996) 144 U Pa L Rev 827 (reviewing visions of weakness and dominance).

informed more recent studies of presidential action.[22] History, unilateral measures (with a rise of interest in memoranda and signing statements), and, most prominently, particular presidencies are the most common issues analysed; however, the abovementioned research methodologies may open other channels of discussion.

Legal scholarship, which is just as rich, likewise relies on a variety of several methodologies. As in other aspects of US constitutional law studies, the debate on the presidency opens with a focus on the written Constitution, interpreted/constructed through well-known 'methods', ranging from historical to prudential.[23] These methods/modalities have been used to support series of normative debates over the proper ordering of all features of constitutional law, supporting opposing normative visions; the executive, with which we are concerned here, has not been neglected in this context, as the following paragraphs show.

The propensity of legal scholarship towards the normative is not absent from this field of research. In the US, the debate over the power of the presidency has usually been conducted under a shared vision of the dominance of the US president. This dominance has been normatively assessed by two opposing camps.

The decades-long normative dispute in the academic scholarship can be presented as a series of sub-debates. Some of them were context-specific: in a way, the addressed issues were used a proxies for the general question of the proper nature and extent of the executive branch, headed by the president.

[22] For examples see, respectively, Michael A Sollenberger, 'Presidential Studies, Behavioralism, and Public Law' (2014) 44 Pres Stud Q 758; Bryan Anderson, 'Tweeter-in-Chief: A Content Analysis of President Trump's Tweeting Habits' (2017) 8 Elon Journal of UR in Comm 36; Matthew D Montgomery, Natalie C Rogol, and Justin T Kingsland, 'Presidential Rhetoric and US Supreme Court Rulings: The Effect of Going Public on Citizen Evaluations of Institutions and Policy' (2019) 49 Pres Stud Q 870. Those, and others, are likely to lead to the development of new insights regarding the nature of the executive and executive powers.

[23] For the distinction between 'interpretation' and 'construction', maintained by some constitutional law scholars (and political scientists studying the constitution), see Keith E Whittington, *Constitutional Interpretation: Textual Meaning, Original Intent, and Judicial Review* (University Press of Kansas 1999) 5–14; Lawrence B Solum, 'The Interpretation-Construction Distinction' (2010) 27 Const Comm 95.

Constitutional scholars have recognized six/seven main methods of judicial reasoning involving the application of the constitution in their decision-making. Philip Bobbit's distinction between historical, textual, structural, doctrinal, ethical, and prudential 'modalities' is sufficient for our purposes, although these have been added onto, and dissected into, sub-methods (Philip Bobbitt, *Constitutional Fate—Theory of the Constitution* (OUP 1982)). Originalism and intentionalism could be considered as synonymous to, or perhaps sub-methods of, the 'historical' modality. Some variants of 'the living constitution' family could have also be considered as belonging to this modality, only turning to post-constitution events: even Bruce Ackerman's 'constitutional moments' theory could be considered historical, although it is clearly based on an entirely different understanding of the constitution and of history, and has been presented as anathema to originalism (Bruce Ackerman, *We the People: Foundations* (Belknap Press 1993)). Robert Post's 'responsive' theory of interpretation (presented alongside the doctrinal and historical methods in Robert E Post, 'Theories of Constitutional Interpretation' (1990) 30 Representations 13), could be considered synonymous, or at least related, to the prudential modality. Other modalities, such as 'equitable' (or 'ethical'), and 'natural' are also viewed by some as distinct modes of reasoning and decision-making. See eg Lackland H Bloom, Jr, *Methods of Interpretation: How the Supreme Court Reads the Constitution* (OUP 2009).

One of the earlier mid-twentieth-century strands of research focused on the relationship between the president and the so-called 'independent agencies'. Aspects included presidential removal power of heads of agencies or their high officers, an issue directly linked with the power of presidents to direct such agencies,[24] and analyses of the constitutional status of these agencies, sometimes discussed as belonging to a 'fourth branch of government'.[25] The Second World War, the Cold War, and the Vietnam War raised interest in emergency powers, which generated a collection of analyses of presidential emergency and war powers an aspect that has only flourished further since 9/11.[26]

In the 1990s, the question of the propriety of dominance revolved around the debate over the 'unitary' nature of the executive branch. Essentially, the issue was whether the president had (or should have—unclear in the original) direct influence, or direct control over law execution and the administration-at-large. Such authority could emerge from the appointment and removal powers and from other points of empowerment, under law (by congressional grant), by the adoption of administrative measures (such as reporting requirements set by the White House), and through politics (by all means of influence and coercion). 'Unitarists' not only found proof for presidential control of the entire executive branch, they also generally found this power- structure optimal for better governance. 'Non-unitarists', on the other hand, revealed an opposite reality that was the best of all worlds: arguing

[24] See eg Edward S Corwin, 'Tenure of Office and the Removal Power under the Constitution' (1927) 27 Colum L Rev 533; CB Cross, 'Removal Power of the President and the Test of Responsibility (1954) 40 Cornell LQ 81; Reginald Parker, 'The Removal Power of the President and Independent Administrative Agencies' (1960) 36 Indiana L Rev 63; Jonathan L Entin, 'The Removal Power and the Federal Deficit: Form, Substance and Administrative Independence' (1986) 75 Kentucky LJ 699; Stephen L Carter, 'The Independent Counsel Mess' (1988) 202 Harv L Rev 105 ; Jonathan L Entin, 'Synecdoche and the President: The Removal Power as Symbol' (1997) 47 Case W Res L Rev 1595. The seminal cases include *Shurtleff v United States*, 189 US 311 (1903) (General Appraiser could be removed by president despite statute authorizing removal for cause); *Myers v United States*, 272 US 52 (1926) (Statute granting Congress power in the context of removing postmasters from office found unconstitutional); *Humphrey's Executor v United States*, 295 US 602 (1935) (invalidating the removal of member of the 'independent' Federal Trade Commission not for cause under statute); *Wiener v United States*, 357 US 349 (1958) (invalidating presidential removal at will of War Claims commissioners appointed by Congress, exercising an adjudicatory function judicial); *Bowsher v Synar*, 106 S Ct 3181 (1986) (excessive authority of Congress over removal of the Comptroller General, as the office is part of the executive branch); *Morrison v Olson*, 487 US 654 (1988) (majority upheld the constitutionality of the Office of Independent Counsel, despite the removal power granted to the Special Division, a dedicated court created by Congress; act expired in 1999). For pre-twentieth-century history see eg Entin ibid 714–27.

[25] Peter L Strauss, 'The Place of Agencies in Government: Separation of Powers and the Fourth Branch' (1984) 84 Colum L Rev 573.

[26] Arguably the most influential contribution is historian Arthur M Schlesinger Jr's *The Imperial Presidency* (Houghton Mifflin 1973). For mere examples see Charles A Lofgren, 'War-Making Under the Constitution: The Original Understanding' (1972) 81 Yale LJ 672; John Hart Ely, *War and Responsibility* (Princeton University Press, 1993); Harold H Koh, *The National Security Constitution: Sharing Power after the Iran-Contra Affair* (Yale University Press 1990); Louis Fisher, *Presidential War Power* (3rd edn, University Press of Kansas 2013); David J Barron and Martin S Lederman, 'The Commander-in-Chief at the Lowest Ebb—Framing the Problem, Doctrine, and Original Understanding' (2008) 121 Harv L Rev 689 (2008); Matthew C Waxman, 'The Power to Wage War Successfully' (2017) 117 Colum L Rev 613.

that the role of the president was more limited, they extolled the dispersion of power within the federal administration. And both camps relied on the same 'modalities/methods' of constitutional theorizing: the text of the constitution, the original intent of the founding fathers, and, for many, also the practice of subsequent centuries. Thus, text, original intent, and subsequent history were all enlisted in support of two opposing normative visions.[27]

Other non-textual, functional/political arguments include the recognition of powers that are 'inherent' to the presidency, drawing on diverse sources such as theories of 'stewardship', and the status of the United States as a member of the family of nations, paired with the power of the president to represent the nation.[28] And, moving to history, the well-established judicial doctrine of 'historical gloss', which offers yet another source for aggrandizement, remains part of the academic debate.

In *Midwest Oil* (1915), the Supreme Court upheld the decision to temporarily deny access and use of oil-rich public lands due to a shortage of natural sources, contrary to a statute that enabled free use of land. The court relied on decades of practice, never challenged by Congress, to uphold this practice.[29] The decision does

[27] For some of the unitarist literature see Steven G Calabresi and Kevin H Rhodes, 'The Structural Constitution: Unitary Executive, Plural Judiciary' (1992) 105 Harv L Rev 1155 (1992) (strong emphasis on constitutional text and structure); Steven G Calabresi, 'The Vesting Clauses as Power Grants' (1994) 88 Northwestern U L Rev 1377 (1994) (focus on constitutional text, especially the vesting clauses; Article I's vesting clause ('[a]ll legislative powers herein granted shall be vested in a Congress of the United States') and Article III's vesting clause ('[t]he judicial power shall extend to' ...) both precede a closed list of powers, while Article II's vesting clause ('[t]he executive power shall be vested in a President of the United States of America') that may be interpreted as an open list, leading to a fierce debate over the constitutional legitimacy of 'non-enumerated powers'.); Steven G Calabresi and Saikrishna B Prakash, 'The President's Power to Execute the Laws' (1994) 104 Yale LJ 541 (textualism, considering several clauses of the constitution, and historical understanding); Steven G Calabresi and Christopher S Yoo, *The Unitary Executive: Presidential Power from Washington to Bush* (Yale University Press 2008) (historical overview of the presidency from George Washington to George W Bush); Lawrence Lessig and Cass Sunstein 'The President and the Administration' (1994) 94 Colum L Rev 1 (refuting originalist and historical proof for unitarism, finding it a modern construct). On the non-unitary side see eg A Michael Froomkin, 'In Defense of Administrative Agency Autonomy' (1989) 96 Yale LJ 787 (combining textual, structural, and historical analysis); Peter M Shane, 'Independent Policymaking and Presidential Power: A Constitutional Analysis' (1989) 57 Geo Wash L Rev 596, 596–97 (refuting textualist and originalist arguments for the unitary thesis, moving to modern history); A Michael Froomkin, 'The Imperial Presidency's New Vestments' (1994) 88 Northwestern U L Rev 1346 (refuting Calabresi and Rhodes' structural analysis and offering an alternative structuralist argument). For an attempt at synthesis see Fitts (n 12) 836–37.

[28] Justice Sutherland's recognition of the President's war and foreign affairs powers drew on the nature of the United States 'as a member of the family of nations' and the argument that 'the President alone has the power to speak or listen as a representative of the nation' (*US v Curtiss-Wright*, 299 US 304, 318 (1936)). See, eg David M Levitan, 'The Foreign Relations Power: An Analysis of Mr. Justice Sutherland's Theory' (1946) 55 Yale LJ 467. On non-statutory, inherent-based executive powers see, eg Louis Fisher, 'Invoking Inherent Powers: A Primer' (2007) 37 Pres Stud Q 1 (opening a special issue titled 'Invoking Inherent Presidential Powers'); Henry P Monaghan, 'The Protective Power of the Presidency' (1993) 93 Colum L Rev 1.

[29] *United States v Midwest Oil*, 236 US 459 (1915) (recognition of the legality of executive orders issued for the withdrawal of mineral-rich public lands from private access 'dates from an early period' and found 'known to Congress, as principal, and not in a single instance was the act of the agent disapproved. Its acquiescence all the more readily operated as an implied grant of power in view of the

not contain the term 'gloss', but is the forerunner of subsequent decisions, the best known of which is *Youngstown* (1952). Justice Jackson's second of three 'practical situations' concerns 'a zone of twilight in which he [the President] and Congress may have concurrent authority, or in which its distribution is uncertain;'[30] in such cases, acquiescence and other modes of congressional inertia may 'enable, if not invite' independent presidential action.[31] This was supported by Justice Frankfurter's dictum that

> a systematic, unbroken, executive practice, long pursued to the knowledge of the Congress and never before questioned, engaged in by Presidents who have also sworn to uphold the Constitution, making as it were such exercise of power part of the structure of our government, may be treated as a gloss on 'executive power' vested in the President by S.1 of Art. II.[32]

Moving away from context-specific studies that seemed to be used as proxies for a more general analysis, Eric Posner and Adrian Vermeule in one camp and Bruce Ackerman in the opposing camp shared a similar point of departure: the president (of the United States) has become *the* dominant player in national politics.[33] The normative arguments brought forth in their books could not be more different. Posner and Vermeule depict an administrative state in which the executive enjoys 'enormous power'.[34] 'The executive' is defined as 'the gigantic complex of national political institutions that are not part of either the legislative or the judicial branch'.[35] The link between the executive agencies and the president is directly drawn: various modes of presidential control of the agencies, both legal and political, ensure continuous control, even over so-called 'independent agencies'.[36] Ideologically and politically, this state of affairs reflects the demise of the traditional liberal legalism model; in its simplest version, 'representative legislatures

fact that its exercise was not only useful to the public, but did not interfere with any vested right of the citizen').

30 *Youngstown Sheet and Tube v Sawyer*, 343 US 579, 637 (1952).

31 ibid 637.

32 ibid 610–11. See also *Dames & Moore v Regan*, 453 US 654 at 678–83 (1981) (Executive Order 12294, suspending claims following the settling of the Iran hostage crisis found to be 'implicitly approved' by the linked statutes and by the history of Congressional acquiescence); '[w]e cannot ignore the general tenor of Congress' legislation in this area ... Congress cannot anticipate and legislate with regard to every possible action the President may find necessary to take'. Congressional failure to specifically delegate authority does not, 'especially ... in the areas of foreign policy and national security', imply 'congressional disapproval' of action taken by the executive'). See, generally, Curtis A Bradley and Trevor W Morrison, 'Historical Gloss and the Separation of Powers' (2012) 126 Harv L Rev 411.

33 Bruce Ackerman, *The Decline and Fall of the American Republic* (Belknap Press 2010) eg 32; Posner and Vermeule (n 4) eg 3, 11.

34 Posner and Vermeule (n 4) 3.

35 ibid 5.

36 ibid 6.

govern and should govern, subject to constitutional constraints, while executive and judicial officials carry out the law'.[37] Instead, a competing model emerged, that of presidential primacy, under which 'the legally constrained executive is now an historical curiosity'.[38] In the modern administrative state, 'massive delegation to the executive and frequent crises threaten to relegate legislatures and courts to the sidelines'.[39] Linked with Carl Schmitt's theory, presented as an argument that the other branches fail to answer exigencies as they arise and cannot react with sufficient speed to crises,[40] the authors claim that this state of primacy is unavoidable.[41] Congress has generally abdicated its role as check, both in emergency and normalcy.[42] Courts cannot promise much: by their nature, they can only decide *ex post facto*, and thereby cannot effectively cabin the president; they tend to be intrusive only when the popularity and credibility of the president are at a low ebb; and, under US administrative law, deference is the norm, under and beyond the APA.[43] Against this background, the primacy of the president, 'subject to legal constraints that are shaky in normal times and weak or nonexistent in time of crisis',[44] is not to be feared. Although Posner and Vermeule do not explicitly celebrate such powers, they find that 'because their presence is inevitable, there is no point condemning them; to do so is quixotic'.[45] Politics and public opinion operate as sufficient checks against abuse of power.

In a way, the elevation of social and political, rather than legal forces, links with the 'personality' stream of research discussed previously. Posner and Vermeule argue that election processes, the party system, and the political culture of the US sufficiently cabin presidents from overusing their powers. Presidents must retain popularity and align themselves with popular preferences, not only to be elected but to preserve their leadership; to retain their credibility they opt to apply 'signaling' devices, inter alia by self-restraining (formally and informally, for example by issuing executive orders and rules), making public promises and other declarations directed to appease concerns, and appointing independent commissions and agencies.[46] The public concern that a legal framework could lead to de

[37] ibid 3.

[38] ibid 4.

[39] ibid 3.

[40] ibid 4, 19, 32–34. This theme is further developed in the context of US crises, 34–61, and in the context of legislating authority and US administrative law, 84–112. See also Adrian Vermeule, 'Our Schmittian Administrative Law' (2009) 122 Harv L Rev 1095).

[41] ibid, eg 14–15: 'Our contrary thesis is that executive-centered government is inevitable, and that law cannot hope to constrain the modern executive.'

[42] ibid, eg 41–42, 57–58, 139.

[43] Dispersed in the book, and developed further in Vermeule's subsequent *Law's Abnegation* (Harvard University Press 2016). For critique, and for the normative discussion on the role of the judiciary see ch 10.

[44] ibid 5.

[45] Posner and Vermeule (n 4) 5, 92.

[46] ibid 4, 113–53. For an analysis of the nature and use of executive orders and other president-made measures see ch 5.

facto tyranny deters abuse: 'tyrannophobia', a central theme in US political discourse, has kept the public aware of possible moves towards non-democratic regime changes, thereby keeping the presidents under check.[47]

Except for his recognition of presidential aggrandizement, Ackerman's vision is the exact opposite. For him, the dynamic evolution of the institution that is the presidency towards an extremist wielder of power is 'a serious threat to [US] constitutional tradition'.[48] The current state of the US republic is far removed from any version of original intent; balance of powers has been replaced by a 'executive constitutionalism', a form of governance under which the Office of the Legal Counsel and the White House Council provide polished legal support for presidential initiatives, expanding the presidency's 'destructive capacities'.[49] Under this structure, political and legal legitimations may well draw the judiciary to the margin, as it becomes more politicized and less likely to intervene.[50] In this climate, presidential legitimacy relies on personal charisma, the media, public opinion polls, and unilateral decision-making, which are all supported by legal advice generated by the presidential 'branch'.[51]

The next wave (and latest, to date) in this series of heated conversations on executive power in the US focuses on administrative law, in US-speak, 'the administrative state' as reflected in government action of administrative agencies.[52] This debate is much more than an echo of the earlier body of research on the status of independent agencies,[53] and is explicitly linked to libertarian ideology and politics. These views, shared by some influential judges, do not necessarily target the president, but a strong leaning towards presidential dominance is evident.[54]

Indeed, although the arguments against the administrative state seem neutral, drawing on arguments from theories of the constitution and democracy, in fact the arguments about excessive intervention, undue bureaucracy, and limitation of freedom are highly politicized. The call for limiting agencies actually targets 'left'-leaning agencies. Had all agencies striven towards market liberalization, the campaign would have lost much of its force, or faded away altogether.

[47] ibid 176–205.

[48] Ackerman (n 33) 4.

[49] ibid eg 68, 87–116, 119.

[50] ibid eg 40, 185.

[51] ibid eg 184.

[52] Jack Beermann usefully identifies six structural features of the 'administrative state', a concept that is essentially concerned with the role of administrative agencies: Congress delegates agencies discretionary authority (by legislation); agencies enjoy different degrees of independence and insulation from complete presidential control; their actions combine rule-making, execution, and adjudication; they have authority to inspect premises and require information; adjudication is initially conducted within the agencies; and judicial review of agency action operates under a deferential stance. Jack M Beermann, 'The Never-Ending Assault on the Administrative State' (2018) 93 Notre Dame L Rev 1599, 1602.

[53] Text to n 25. See also the studies on the president's role as chief administrator, Lessig and Sunstein (n 27); Elena Kagan, 'Presidential Administration' (2001) 114 Harv L Rev 2245.

[54] A good example is Gary Lawson, 'The Rise and Rise of the Administrative State' (1994) 107 Harv L Rev 1231.

Philip Hamburger recently reignited this debate over the legality/constitutionality/propriety of the administrative state.[55] In *Is Administrative Law Unlawful?* (2014), his stance is avowedly libertarian: the administrative state, the 'state within the state', carries 'burdens on economic and personal freedom', tending to 'interfere with our elected government'.[56] This attack on the administrative state, alike others, is thus driven by a particular vision of unconstitutional aggrandizement. The argument is linked with deregulation and the removal of 'regulatory burdens', central to Republican presidents, most recently and notably President Trump.[57]

For Hamburger, alongside 'lawful' executive action that applies binding rules made by the legislation and the judiciary, current 'administrative law' is essentially the making of rules that bind and coerce—powers granted under the constitution only to the other branches.[58] The premise that administrative law emerged in the late nineteenth century in order to answer the needs of the administrative state, committed to the regulation of large-scale industries, is false. In fact, argues Hamburger, searchers for the origins of administrative law must hark back to the infamous era preceding England's Glorious Revolution of 1688–89, still relevant to the United States due to its common-law heritage.[59] The British monarchs' invocation of unchecked prerogative powers to the detriment of law and citizens echoes, for Hamburger, the current state of administrative law, under which unfettered agencies act under broad rule-making delegations. These agencies are only marginally checked by courts. Hamburger's discussion of 'extralegal adjudication'[60] (that is, outside courts) first considers the ill-famed English Star Chamber and other forms of adjudication by prerogative courts; the former was dismantled in 1640 by an Act of the Long Parliament, and the latter gradually reshaped themselves under law. The equivalent, in Hamburger's view, is found in the rise of administrative adjudication, which is not that different functionally from prerogative adjudication.

All of this leads to Hamburger's denigration of the state of affairs in which administrative law is 'extralegal, supralegal, and consolidated, and thus a version of

55 Philip Hamburger, *Is Administrative Law Unlawful?* (University of Chicago Press 2014). For a condensed argument see Philip Hamburger, *The Administrative Threat* (Encounter Intelligence 2017). But see Gary Lawson's 1994 diatribe against the administrative state, considered as flagrantly unconstitutional (ibid.).

56 Hamburger, *The Administrative Threat* (n 55) 1.

57 For a report on massive removal of frameworks introduced during President Obama's presidency, as well as general large-scale deregulation see eg Simon F Haeder and Susan Webb-Yackee, 'The Trump administration might be deregulating more than you know (or could know)' *Washington Post* (24 August 2018) < https://www.washingtonpost.com/news/monkey-cage/wp/2018/08/24/the-trump-administration-might-be-deregulating-more-than-you-know-or-could-know/?noredirect=on>). See also the self-congratulatory report of the President's success in this direction: 'President Donald J Trump is Delivering on Deregulation', White House website, <https://www.whitehouse.gov/briefings-statements/president-donald-j-trump-delivering-deregulation/>. Critical comments, and those that argue that no substantive deregulation has in fact occurred, are set aside. All links to web sources in this book were last accessed on 30 August 2020.

58 ibid 2–5.

59 For the English Royal prerogative see ch 4, and, summarily, n 68 below.

60 Hamburger, *The Administrative Threat* (n 55) 129.

absolute power'.[61] For him, a strong link with German law and scholarship, which, alike other continental systems, emphasizes absolutism, has contributed to the processes discussed, as did the US public sphere's emphasis on a tradition of necessity and its link with modernity.[62] The result, he argues, is a form of governance under absolute power that 'runs contrary not only to the Constitution but also to the nature of lawful and constitutional government in Anglo-American society'.[63]

To ensure departure from this problematic state of affairs, Hamburger calls the judiciary to rise from its torpor, expressed in and generated by the doctrine of deference, and follow the English judge Lord Coke. Coke's decision-making in the early years of the seventeenth century challenged royal supremacy, and influenced the reshaping and restraining of the Crown at the end of his century, and, quite possibly, the development of British public law from the end of that century onwards. He finds that Coke's valiant battle against Crown absolutism is just as relevant in current-day United States.[64]

The British study of the executive is smaller in volume and carries lesser political zeal. In 1998, Daintith and Page marked legal scholarship of the executive in the past century as dominantly descriptive and limited in volume.[65] These general tendencies have not changed since. Embarking on a project that was mainly dedicated to an analysis of the inner workings of the executive, Daintith and Page offered explanations for the limited interest of legal scholars; for the authors, the main culprit is the traditional suspicion of the rise of state power (an earlier version, perhaps, of the current wave of mistrust of the administrative state in the US?), which has led to the 'neglect' of the executive.[66] However, mistrust and distaste do not necessarily lead to inattention; other explanations can be forwarded.[67]

The Royal prerogative, probably the most popular alternative focus, may have operated as a proxy for the analysis of the executive branch.[68] The propriety of

[61] ibid 12, and *passim*. For a discussion of 'consolidated power', that is, the consolidation of enforcement power in a single pair of hands, or a single branch, see ibid chs 17–21.

[62] ibid chs 23, 24.

[63] ibid 412; see also esp ch 22.

[64] eg ibid 45–47, 319–20.

[65] Terence Daintith and Alan Page, *The Executive in the Constitution: Structure, Autonomy, and Internal Control* (OUP 1998) 15.

[66] ibid 10.

[67] The neglect of general analyses of the executive may be linked with the constant attention to the prerogative, discussed below, or to the attention to ongoing particular events, such as the war on terror, or more recently, the politics of Brexit. Alternatively, as in other systems, this neglect may be the result of the rise of other preferred fields of research, inter alia constitutional law and human rights on one side, and economics, quantitative studies, and law and society on the other.

[68] The prerogative is discussed in detail in ch 4. For a small sample of twentieth-century literature see Thomas Inskip, Viscount of Caldecote, 'The King's Prerogative' (1941) 7 Cam L J 310; BS Markesinis, 'The Royal Prerogative Revisited' (1973) 33 Cam L J 207; TRS Allan, 'Law, Convention and Prerogative' in TRS Allan, *Law, Liberty and Justice: The Legal Foundations of British Constitutionalism* (Clarendon Press 1993) 237; David Gladstone, 'What Shall We Do with the Crown Prerogative?' (1998) 4(3) J Legis Stud 1; Sebastian Payne, 'The Royal Prerogative' in Maurice Sunkin and Sebastian Payne, *The Nature of the Crown: A Legal and Political Analysis* (Clarendon Press 1999) 77; Margit Cohn, 'Medieval Chains, Invisible Inks: On Non-Statutory Powers of the Executive' (2005) 97 OJLS 118; Thomas Poole, 'The United Kingdom: The Royal Prerogative' (2010) 8 ICON 146.

discussing this 'historical residue' is not only inextricably linked with a key challenge in British constitutionalism—the legitimacy and future of the Monarchy, that is, the very nature of its structural polity; it also remains the focus of discussion of executive powers, as this source still enables government to act in the absence of statute. The normative debate is thus overly, but understandably, concerned with the propriety of the retention of the prerogative, rather than on the question of the nature of executive powers. Still, an obvious price has been paid: the prerogative does not encompass the broader mechanisms of executive action and their implications, and attention to this single aspect of executive powers deflects attention from the other ways of power aggrandizement, and to the development of all-encompassing understandings of the nature of the executive branch. Supporters of reform of the prerogative (that is, for its abolition) at least imply that the time for unfettered executive action which draws on non-legislated rules is over: again, though, the impact of this future transformation to the understanding of the executive is yet to be understood.[69]

Beyond classic discussions of prerogative power, the growing scholarship concerned with unilateral government powers that cannot (or should not) be linked with the historical prerogative powers offers an alternative path for assessment but, once again, has yet to reach full fruition in the form of a general thesis of the executive.[70]

Another direction in British legal scholarship on the executive tends to address structural and organizational issues. Here, analysis focuses on the main players—the prime minister, the cabinet, other ministers, and, sometimes, semi-independent bodies (agencies, in US parlance).[71] Highly valuable for the understanding of the executive today, for now, this stream sets aside general models and theories.

Alongside British political scientists who offer general analyses of the UK executive,[72] some have addressed issues of structure, with special attention granted to

[69] Under previous and current politics, complete abolishment is not forthcoming; instead, piecemeal changes, effected by the legislation of several fields previously left to the prerogative, have been gradually introduced. The most recent reform, the Constitutional Reform and Governance Act 2010, regulates the civil service and legislates the Ponsonby rule, the constitutional convention under which most international treaties are to be laid before Parliament prior to their ratification. For earlier legislative reform see ch 4.

[70] In this stream of research, scholars identify certain types of action that have never been part of the prerogative, and usually reject attempts at the expansion of this essentially problematic source of power. Proposed alternatives range from downright rejection of any unrecognized unilateral power, to a tentative recognition of a so-called 'third source' of power that may, or may not, be upheld judicially. See T Daintith, 'Regulation by Contract: The New Prerogative' (1979) 32 CLP 41; George Winterton, 'The Prerogative in Novel Situations' (1983) 99 LQR 407; BV Harris, 'The "Third Source" of Authority for Government Action' (1992) 108 LQR 626; Maurice Sunkin and Sebastian Payne (eds), *The Nature of the Crown: A Legal and Political Analysis* (OUP 1999); Cohn (n 68) esp 107–108; BV Harris, 'The "Third Source" of Authority for Government Action Revisited' (2007) 123 LQR 225.

[71] Daintith and Page (n 65); Tomkins (n 10).

[72] For general analysis see eg Anthony King (ed), *The British Prime Minister* (2nd edn, Duke University Press 1985); Richard Heffernan and Paul Webb, 'The British Prime Minister: Much More than "First Among Equals"' in Poguntke and Webb (n 4) 26.

the interaction between the prime minister and the cabinet.[73] Attention to personality is also evident, echoing the US 'personal presidency' research, but presented on a smaller scale.[74]

The literature review above is dedicated to the study of UK and US executives, written by researchers operating in those systems. Some comparative work has been mentioned in passing in these bodies of literature, but, again, they were mainly focused on these two systems.[75] To reach a complete understanding of the ways executives are academically treated around the (democratic) world, a full consideration of global studies of executives is required, but this is beyond the scope of a book dedicated to theory, its application, and the role of checking mechanisms. Indications may be drawn from the literature surveyed: most helpfully, the majority of the contributions to Craig and Tomkins' edited volume reflect the shared themes identified here: no clear vision of the executive branch exists; this branch of government has grown to be, or better said has always been, a formidable power in democratic polities based on the general ethos of constitutionalism; and its head, president or prime minister, enjoys unparalleled dominance over the political arena.[76] It is time, then, to move to a discussion of the basis for the theory that explains this dominance despite the seemingly subservient role of this branch in the democratic set-up.

D. Constitutionalism and Internal Tensions

In the absence of general, universal theorizing of the executive, the rich system-based body of research still offers a supporting backbone for developing such a theory. But, being a central issue to the constitution of any democratic system, the starting point should be its central ethos: that of constitutionalism.

This most suitable starting point for the development of a theory of the executive branch in Western democracies is a vague concept: competing notions of the rule of law, process-oriented theories, populist theories, theories that either celebrate or denigrate extensive judicial review, and any other discussion on the nature

[73] See RAW Rhodes and Patrick Dunleavy (eds), *Prime Minister, Cabinet and Core Executive* (St Martins Press 1995); Martin Burch and Ian Holliday, *The British Cabinet System* (Prentice Hall 1996); Martin J Smith, *The Core Executive in Britain* (Macmillan 1999); Stephen Buckley, *The Prime Minister and Cabinet* (Edinburgh University Press 2006).

[74] See eg Anthony King, 'Margaret Thatcher: The Style of a Prime Minister' in King (n 72) 96; Kaarbo and Hermann (n 20); RAW Rhodes, 'Blair and Governance' in Rainer Koch and John Dixon (eds), *Public Governance and Leadership* (Springer 2007) 95; Stephen Benedict Dyson, *The Blair Identity: Leadership and Foreign Policy* (Manchester UP 2009); Kevin Theakston, 'Gordon Brown as Prime Minister: Political Skills and Leadership Style' (2011) 6 Brit Politics 78.

[75] Kaarbo and Hermann (n 20) represents studies from comparative politics; Craig and Tomkins (n 1), comparative law.

[76] Craig and Tomkins (n 1). Evident in the chapters on Canada, Australia, New Zealand, Scotland, France, and Germany.

of constitutional regimes, are all adorned by the title 'constitutionalism'.[77] In all its variants, constitutionalism extends beyond the merely formal requirement for a written document, which is, as well known, is not entirely universal (although, currently, the UK is the single outlier), and must be positively implemented.[78] It consists of two elements: an underlying moral-political value-base and a structure that ensures some form of people-representation. The value-base is addressed later in this book; suffice here to note its variants: its thick and the thin versions rely on key concepts such as the rule of law, 'equal respect and concern', liberty, and dignity, or on a more extensive set of defined liberties.[79] All of these can, and do, serve as the substantive basis of the institutional organization, justifying, and fortifying its elements.

As for the institutional-structural element: too often, this aspect of constitutionalism is presented as combining two components: supremacy (of the constitution and, often, of the judiciary as final interpreter of the constitutional text)[80] and entrenchment (the insulation of the constitution from so-called 'normal politics' by requiring special, onerous amendment processes).[81] As such, classical constitutionalism draws on hierarchical thinking: essentially, the constitutional structure is viewed as organized around a supreme force that retains its supremacy, at least during mundane political periods.

[77] See eg AW Bradley, Katja S Ziegler, and Denis Baranger, 'Constitutionalism and the Role of Parliaments' in Katja S Ziegler, Denis Baranger, and AW Bradley (eds), *Constitutionalism and the Role of Parliaments* (Hart 2007) 1–7; CP Patterson, 'The Evolution of Constitutionalism' (1947–48) 32 Minn L Rev 427 ('constitutionalism is only the name of the trust which man reposes in the power of a document as a means of controlling the government'); A Sajó, *Limiting Government: An Introduction to Constitutionalism* (Budapest: Central European University Press 1999) at xiv ('constitutionalism is the set of principles, manners, and institutional arrangements that were used traditionally to limit government'); 'Constitutionalism', *Stanford Encyclopedia of Philosophy*, available <http://plato.stanford.edu/entries/constitutionalism/#BM1>; Mark Tushnet, 'A New Constitutionalism for Liberals?' (2003–2004) 28 NYU Rev L and Soc Change 357, assessing various 'grand theories' of constitutional law.

[78] For the distinction between formal and substantive constitutionalism, see eg Bradley, Ziegler, and Baranger (n 77); Walter F Murphy, 'Constitutions, Constitutionalism, and Democracy' in D Greenberg and others (eds), *Constitutionalism and Democracy: Transitions in the Contemporary World* (OUP 1993) 3, 5; HWO Okoth-Ogendo, 'Constitutions without Constitutionalism' in Greenberg and others, 65; Bruce Ackerman, 'The Rise of World Constitutionalism' (1997) 83 Va L Rev 771.

[79] For discussions see eg Bradley, Ziegler, and Baranger (n 77) 6–7; Murphy (n 78) 14–17; for a normative discussion that addresses this in passing see ch 10.

[80] For most constitutionalists, and in most written constitutional structures, it is the judiciary that is entrusted with the role of final constitutional interpreter and protector of the values enshrined in the constitution. These constructs are evident in modern constitutions and are central to some mid-twentieth century theory (eg CH McIlwain, *Constitutionalism: Ancient and Modern*, revised ed (Cornell University Press 1947) ch 1); to Ronald Dworkin's theory of the constitution, ostensibly limited to the American system but applicable and discussed in the context of other Western polities (Ronald Dworkin, *Taking Rights Seriously* (Duckworth 1977) chs 5, 6; Ronald Dworkin, 'Introduction: The Moral Reading and the Majoritarian Premise' in *Freedom's Law* (OUP 1996) 2–19); and to other eminent constitutional theorists, for example TRS Allan and Aharon Barak (TRS Allan, 'Constitutional Dialogue and the Justification of Judicial Review' (2003) 23 OJLS 563; Aharon Barak, *The Judge in a Democracy* (Princeton University Press 2008)). See also WP Murphy, 'Constitutions, Constitutionalism, and Democracy' in Greenberg and others (n 78) 3, 14–17; Bradley, Ziegler, and Baranger (n 77) esp 6.

[81] See eg Cass R Sunstein, 'Constitutionalism and Secession' (991) 58 U Chi L Rev 633 (considering the values and utilities of entrenchment).

While the supremacy of the constitution is clearly central to constitutionalist structures, and courts are indeed granted powers that can transform existing structures, supremacy, or the absolute rule of a single body or value, does not tie in with politico-legal reality, nor should a supremacy-based structure be considered normatively superior, as discussed below.

The rejection of hierarchical and binary analysis draws on a general body of research that spans the nature of ideas, social constructs, and natural phenomena. In his systems theory, Lotfi Zadeh argues that dichotomies should be replaced by gradually transforming continuums. Sets and realities comprise components and concepts that are not neatly divided by sharp dichotomous lines. Rather, concepts (such as 'age') bear gradually transforming meanings (such as 'not too young', 'quite old', etc). The 'principle of incompatibility' stresses a departure from clear-cut constructs: the more complex and varied the set, the less accurate its analysis.[82]

Similarly, the rejection of dichotomies is a universal element in Kelso and Engstrøm's *The Complementary Nature*. Kelso and Engstrøm offer a rich range, over history and across disciplines, of oft-viewed conflicting opposites that range from Heraclitus' permanence and change in the sixth century BC to the late twentieth-century biologist Stephen Gould's distinction between gradualism and saltationism (law is singly represented by Gandhi's discipline/ obedience).[83] For them, contraries and dichotomies should be reconsidered as 'complementary' and simultaneous.[84]

The affinity between hierarchical and dichotomous thinking is clear: both are attempts to present sharp, mono- or bi-dimensional visions of natural phenomena and concepts. Furthermore, the bi-dimensional quality of dichotomies may be only a preliminary step: dichotomies are often used to point towards a normative choice of a single, proper, and supreme meaning, and in institutional contexts such as the one I am concerned with, one supreme body.

In law, these arguments fit well with British public law theorist Martin Loughlin's 'sceptic' or interpretative method, that

> differs from the liberal interpretative method ... by adopting a 'pluralising' rather than 'singularising' hermeneutics. Rather than seeking the one correct reading, it traces the various meanings within the texts and, through the exercise of relating language to experience and being attentive to the instabilities of meanings, seeks

[82] Lotfi A Zadeh, *Fuzzy Sets and Applications: Selected Papers* (Wiley 1987).

[83] JA Scott Kelso and David A Engstrøm, *The Complementary Nature* (MIT Press 2006). For condensed representations see ibid at 36–37, 257–62 (law is still missing in the latter longer list; several pairs pertaining to politics are listed, none are directly relevant). I thank Oren Perez for directing me to this source.

[84] ibid at 64.

> understanding by relating parts to the whole and vice versa in what can be called a 'fusion of horizons'.[85]

Rather than merely providing a multi-dimensional reading of constitutionalism, I offer the 'internal tension' model as an explanatory tool for many a legal/political construct. Under this model, constitutionalism is constituted of several self-contradicting tensions, which are constantly played out by several competing forces. Tensions between the need to grant power and the need for its constraint and between supremacy and representation are played out in various ways. For example, the entrenchment of a constitution, and more so eternity clauses that prohibit amendment of its clauses, stand in tension with the ideas of progress and pluralism, which imply change rather than stability, and are central to modernity; the supremacy of the constitution or of any other designated body directly challenges pluralistic citizen representation via a variety of bodies; the grant of the 'last word' to the judiciary is confronted by the principles of representation as employed in the 'democratic deficit' arguments; and, finally, arguments regarding the nature of the executive branch seem to oscillate between visions of legal subservience and political dominance, a tension central to this book.

Recognition of the ways such internal tensions operate is key to better understanding of realities. For some, the departure from monodimensionality has even more promise: for Kelso and Engstrøm, complementarity ties in with harmonious coexistence: '[r]econciliation means a harmonizing, a bringing together of that which has previously been considered incommensurate'.[86] Aspirations for the achievement of a harmonious public sphere are, unfortunately, just as misjudged as the retention of hierarchies and dichotomies, but the replacement of dichotomous and hierarchical ordering with a recognition of multi-dimensional dynamics carries several benefits. Analyses under this template do not merely offer more accurate depictions of government-in-action; they tie in with theories of participatory and deliberative democracy and enable the development of better-tuned formulations for a more than sub-optimal husbandry of political life.

Calls for a hierarchical analysis are evident in some constitutional contexts, most prominently in the context of the voluminous scholarship on judicial review and the role of the judiciary in constitutional structures. The space between the two opposing normative schools, calling for either supremacy of the judiciary or the exit of courts from social and political decision-making, is by

[85] Martin Loughlin, 'The Pathways of Public Law Scholarship' in Geoffrey P Wilson (ed), *Frontiers of Legal Scholarship* (Wiley 1995) 184. [Spelling follows the original].
[86] Kelso and Engstrøm (n 83) 63.

now densely populated.[87] Similarly, the focus on constitutional amendment by formal mechanisms only has been challenged by studies of 'living constitutions' and 'constitutional moments'.[88]

The study of the executive branch lacks similar sophistication. It is often split between two opposing normative camps, the first advocating executive supremacy, the second calling for its full subjection to law. Some remedy can be found in these pages, dedicated to detailed discussion of this tension, and offering case-studies that expose the ways this tension operates in two public-political spheres.

In sum, attempts at resolving any of the internal tensions by constructing a hierarchical structure should be replaced by the recognition that precarious balancing acts are unavoidably and constantly performed under the label 'constitutionalism'. Multidimensional models that accept ingrained tensions and are built around competing conceptual bases provide better templates for analysis of public law and its ever-evolving expressions in policy-making and implementation. In such pluralist theoretical arenas, several vectoral forces, pulling in different directions, provide complex answers to complex situations. Such models tie in with the social sciences, where top-down, hierarchical models of decision-making have long been rejected in favour of pluralist, network, and other theories which focus on the multiplicity of political forces in the socio-political spheres.[89] On the normative level, they are also better-tuned with theories that enhance participation as an optimal form of governance.

The case of the executive, analysed in this book, provides a detailed example of the workings and benefits of reliance on the internal tension model. In this

[87] At least three strands of research can be discerned: scholars who advocate participatory and deliberative democracy through the image of 'dialogue', those who require judicial 'deference' to other departments, and those who link the degree of constraint with the existence of other modes of hearing of grievances. For mere examples see, in the first school, Peter Hogg and Allison Bushell, 'The Charter Dialogue between Courts and Legislators (Or Perhaps the Charter of Rights Isn't a Bad Thing after All)' (1997) 35 Osgoode Hall LJ 75 at 79; Christine Bateup, 'The Dialogic Promise: Assessing the Normative Potential of Theories of Constitutional Dialogue' (2006) 71 Brook L Rev 1109; Margit Cohn, 'Sovereignty, Constitutional Dialogue and Political Networks' in Richard Rawlings, Peter Leyland, and Alison Young (eds), *Sovereignty and the Law: Domestic, European and International Perspectives* (OUP 2013) 236. For the second school, which can be subdivided into arguments for deference and to arguments for weak forms of review, see, eg, Aileen Kavanagh, 'Deference or Defiance? The Limits of the Judicial Role in Constitutional Adjudication' in G Huscroft (ed), *Expounding the Constitution: Essays in Constitutional Theory* (CUP 2008) 184; Alison L Young, 'In Defence of Due Deference' (2009) 72 Mod L Rev 554; Stephen Gardbaum, 'Reassessing the New Model of Commonwealth Constitutionalism' (2010) 8 Int'l J Const L (I·CON) 167. For the third school see Alon Harel and Adam Shinar, 'Between Judicial and Legislative Supremacy: A Cautious Defense of Constrained Judicial Review' (2012) 10 Int'l J Const L (I·CON) 950.

[88] See David A Strauss, *The Living Constitution* (OUP 2010); Ackerman, *We the People* (n 23); Bruce Ackerman, 'The Living Constitution' (2007) 120 Harv L Rev 1737.

[89] These theories cannot be addressed here in detail. For neo-pluralist and network theories see eg Robert A Dahl and Charles E Lindblom, *Politics, Economics, and Welfare* (Harper 1963); David Marsh and RAW Rhodes, *Policy Networks in British Government* (Clarendon Press 1992).

context, I replace efforts to identify a single explanatory basis for the exercise of executive power with a vision of a volatile fusion of submission and dominance.

E. Answering Initial Challenges to General Theory

Among the several possible reasons for the paucity of general theorizing of the executive branch, two seemingly strong justifications can be summarily rejected. First, it may be argued that attempts to introduce theories that are valid in both parliamentary and presidential systems are exercises in 'comparison of incomparables', due to the insurmountable differences between these regime types. The second issue focuses on the argument that in today's 'regulatory state', the central government has been virtually replaced, in most matters of social and economic policy, by independent agencies that are directly authorized by statute to design and implement policy without being directly answerable to the executive; in this climate, so this argument goes, any discussion of the 'core executive' misses the mark. Both arguments are considered here on two levels: the structural and the political.

1. Comparing Parliamentary and Presidential Regimes?

At first glance, the different structures of these two regime families should indeed deter comparison between their respective executives.[90] Under the main variant of this argument, presidential regimes are designed to grant the head of the executive a stronger claim for power. Being directly elected by the people, presidents enjoy a unique political status and are directly accountable to the people, not to other government branches; the limited power of their removal (usually by impeachment only) further insulates presidents from the legislature; and, finally, presidents carry an institutional ability to direct government, which draws not only on their insulation from parliament but also on the constitutional grant of direct powers that do not need to rely on statute. In comparison, this argument usually goes, prime ministers are indirectly elected, and thus enjoy lesser political legitimacy; are reliant on parliament when introducing major policy, which renders them politically weaker;

[90] I set aside premier-presidentialism, or semi-presidentialism, the mixed regime created in the Fifth French Republic, as unnecessary for the coming analysis, which breaks down the dichotomy on the basis of function and politics. Under the analysis offered in this section, this sub-type of presidentialism can be placed on the offered continuum of relative powers, alike 'purer' regimes, according to relative power politics. On this regime type see Maurice Duverger, 'A New Political System Model: Semi-Presidential Government' (1980) 8 European J Political Res 165; Matthew Soberg Shugart and John M Carey, *Presidents and Assemblies: Constitutional Design and Electoral Dynamics* (CUP 1992) 23–24.

and are constantly under the threat of removal by a non-confidence vote in parliament, a force that sets an irremovable constraint on their power.

Although the recognition of differences between the two regime types is obviously not incorrect, this classic argument grants excessive attention to too few elements or variables. Essentially, support for non-comparability focuses on two variables—election and removal of the head of the executive, although richer lists of categories have been forwarded.[91] Still, the degree of direct access by the executive to the legislative body has not been generally considered. Singly considered, this factor seems at first glance to offer a second argument for non-comparability: prime ministers have direct access to parliament, rendering them politically stronger than presidents, who must rely on political channels to advance their agendas in Congress.

In fact, none of these factors should lead us to the incomparability conclusion. To demonstrate that parliamentary and presidential regimes do not fall neatly into two categories of relative executive power, I rely on George Tsebelis's influential 'veto player' theory.

For Tsebelis, a veto player is 'an individual or collective actor whose agreement ... is required for change of policy'.[92] Institutional veto players, government bodies operating in the political sphere under the constitution, may affect the heads of executive branches' ability to forward their agendas. Political parties can operate as veto players: for example, in coalition governments, heads of governments must acquire the agreement of all parties that are member of the coalition before moving ahead.

The interaction between the executive and the legislature in the context of the partisan composition of both branches suffices to show that parliamentary and presidential regimes do not fall neatly into two categories. On a spectrum based on the combination of structure with partisan politics, the strongest executive would be a prime minister who enjoys an absolute, or decisive, majority in parliament. In this political climate, the removal power by a no-confidence vote is virtually eliminated politically.

The ensured majority in parliament is but one element. Prime ministers are the heads of the largest party in parliament, and sometimes serve as members of

[91] For some of the salient work see Douglas V Verney, *The Analysis of Political Systems* (Compton Printing Works 1959) 17–56; Arend Lijphart, *Democracies: Patterns of Majoritarian and Consensus Government in Twenty-one Countries* (Yale University Press 1984) 68–74; Matthew Soberg Shugart and John M Carey, *Presidents and Assemblies: Constitutional Design and Electoral Dynamics* (CUP 1992); Juan J Linz, 'Presidential or Parliamentary Democracy: Does it Make a Difference?' in Juan J Linz and Arturo Valanzuela (eds), *The Failure of Presidential Democracy: The Case of Latin America*, Vols 2, 3, 6 (John Hopkins University Press 1994); Arend Lijphart, 'Presidentialism and Majoritarian Democracy: Theoretical Observations (1994)' in Arend Lijphart, *Thinking about Democracy* (Routledge 2008) 141.

[92] George Tsebelis, 'Decision Making in Political Systems: Veto Players in Presidentialism, Parliamentrism, Multicameralism and Multipartyism' (1995) 25 Brit J Pol Sci 289, 301. See also George Tsebelis, *Veto Players: How Political Institutions Work* (Princeton University Press 2002).

parliament; they thus have direct access to the speaker's chair and to the ongoing business of parliament. Furthermore, no-confidence votes usually lead to the dissolution of parliament itself and are therefore less attractive than envisaged. Hence, this structure offers the executive the strongest relative power.

Second on this spectrum of relative institutional dominance stands the president governing during shared-government terms. Presidents who enjoy a majority in both houses of the legislature are often presumed to hold the strongest relative power, but the insulation of the presidency from the legislature, which serves to buttress the office from undermining parliamentary forces, is also a constraint on the president's ability to directly interfere in the parliamentary process. Prime ministers' institutional access to parliaments, enabling them to direct parliament's agenda, is missing. Therefore, this variant should be placed second in the spectrum of relative power.

Next on this spectrum are parliamentary and presidential bicameral regimes in which the executive enjoys a majority in one of the houses. The structural constraints emerging under this configuration depend on the relative powers held by each house. In this context, presidential regimes that grant the president a veto power over an opposing house, and further insulate the office from removal by a no confidence, naturally offer more relative power than regimes which lack these features or at least the first feature, as in the case of parliamentary systems.

Further down the line are presidents that enjoy no majority in the legislature, as in the case of Bill Clinton's presidency between 1995 and 2001. Under this configuration, the legislature(s) are active and influential veto players. The head of the executive may invoke his veto power, if that tool is available, and can still rely on the legitimacy garnered from direct elections, but his dominance is obviously hindered by the extent of negotiations required to pass most initiatives through the legislature.[93] At their extreme, such contingencies have led to more

[93] Compare, eg President Obama's political ability to pass reforms through Congress during the 111th, 112th, and 114th Congresses. President Obama enjoyed a majority in both houses of the 111th Congress, a majority that enabled, inter alia, the passing of the health-care reform law. Although the process was far from easy, with opposition within the Democratic party not only lengthening the process, but also transforming some of its elements, when compared to the trials the President has encountered in the current Congress, this reform practically sailed through. Four major policy crises represent the hardships facing a president who has lost the majority in one of the houses of Congress. All were resolved at the eleventh hour, or beyond, by compromising on the original programmes: the passage of the six-month 2011 federal budget, the increase of the nation's public debt, the 'fiscal cliff' near-debacle, and the resolution of the October 2013 government shutdown. (On these events see Sheryl Gay Stolberg and Robert Pear, 'Obama Signs Health Care Overhaul Bill, with a Flourish', *NY Times* (23 March 2010); Carl Hulse, 'Budget Deal to Cut $38 Billion Averts Shutdown', *NY Times* (8 April 2011); Jennifer Steinhauer, 'Divided House Passes Tax Deal in End to Latest Fiscal Standoff', *NY Times* (1 January 2013); Jonathan Weisman, 'Republicans Back Down, Ending Crisis over Shutdown and Debt Limit', *NY Times* (16 October 2013).) Throughout, and more so during the two-house Republican Congress, President Obama's extensive reliance on unilateral measures (executive orders, memoranda, and policy statements) presents yet another twist on the complexity of power politics.

than twenty 'government shutdowns', gaps in the continuing appropriation of Federal funding, the longest one to date being the thirty-five-day 2018–19 government shutdown during Donald Trump's presidency.[94]

This configuration still offers better options for executive dominance when compared to the weakest configuration, a parliamentary set-up under which the prime minister's party, despite being the largest in parliament, has no majority, and relies on either a multi-party coalition or, in the most extreme version, heads a minority government. In such a case, the threats of a successful no-confidence motion, and, more likely, the regularity of mundane failures in passing reforms through parliament, are compounded by the constant threat of defection by one or more coalition parties. In the context of the cabinet, the prime minister may have limited control over his secretaries of state or ministers, since in such government coalitions, some ministers, often the more central ones, will necessarily belong to a coalition party rather than to the main party. The possible absence of negative repercussions would derive from the endemic weakness of such a government, and, decisively, by the constant threat of the overturning of government by a no-confidence motion.[95]

In sum, as far as structure goes, the power sources and veto points that lead to domination differ across regime types, but power configurations cut across political regimes. Structurally, presidents are indeed more insulated politically than prime ministers, and are usually granted veto powers, but prime ministers are ensured direct access to parliament and domination of its processes. Thus, comparison cannot be rejected on simple structural grounds. More sensitive analyses are required, replacing the simplistic distinction between parliamentarism and presidentialism.

Should the breaking-down of the distinction into a spectrum of power-structures lead to the final rejection of any type of comparison? While possible, the retention of comparison is justified by the findings of sufficient similarities in the politics of both regime types. The democratic climate and structure, the similar function and logic of government branch action,[96] and the evident phenomenon of executive dominance in both presidential and parliamentary regimes, expressed inter alia in titles such as 'the Blair presidency',[97] all justify the continuation of such comparison. My analysis of the executive branch, then,

[94] For analysis see Clinton T Brass, 'Shutdown of the Federal Government: Causes, Processes and Effects', Congressional Research Service 2013.

[95] On the political dynamics of coalition veto players see Tsebelis, 'Decision Making' (n 92) 302–305; George Tsebelis, 'Veto Players and Law Production in Parliamentary Democracies' in Herbert Döring (ed), *Parliaments and Majority Rule in Western Europe* (Palgrave Macmillan 1995) 83.

[96] For just a few see Tsebelis, 'Decision Making' (n 92) 292; Christoph Möllers, *The Three Branches* (OUP 2013) 111, 114.

[97] See Michael Foley, *The British Presidency: Tony Blair and the Politics of Public Leadership* (Manchester University Press 2000); Graham Allen, *The Last Prime Minister: Being Honest About the UK Presidency* (2nd edn, Imprint Academic 2002); Rhodes (n 74) 96. On this phenomenon in the UK and beyond see Poguntke and Webb (n 4).

spans both regime families, with full recognition of the possible variations of relative executive power.

2. 'Core' Executives and Administrative Agencies

A second challenge to the development of general theory of the executive concerns the so-called 'breaking down' of the executive branch. Usually discussed by administrative law scholars, the focus is on the role of independent agencies in policy-making and implementation. The opening words of Article II of the American constitution, '[t]he executive power shall be vested in a president of the United States of America', seem to imply that the president is the only titular of the executive power; similarly, other constitutions define the head of government as the embodiment of the executive branch. Yet regulatory agencies are granted extensive powers under law in 'the regulatory state', key to the analysis of all modern Western polities.[98] Agencies have been viewed as the rising pattern of governance,[99] simultaneously viewed as constitutionally problematic, 'a fourth branch' that is relatively independent from the other three.[100] Under this template, if agencies are indeed independent, and are granted extensive powers heretofore considered executive in nature, could a theory of 'the executive' as such make any sense?

The response to this challenge is once again both structural and political. Measuring the structural independence of agencies is not a simple matter. No clear definition exists in the legislature.[101] For some, including some members of the

[98] See eg Giandomenico Majone, 'The Regulatory State and Its Legitimacy Problems' (1999) 22(1) West Eur Pol 1; Giandomenico Majone, 'The Rise of the Regulatory State in Europe' (1994) 17(3) West Eur Pol 77.

[99] See, eg, Jacint Jordana, David Levi-Faur, and Xavier Fernández i Marín, 'The Global Diffusion of Regulatory Agencies: Channels of Transfer and Stages of Diffusion' (2011) 44 Comp Pol Stud 1343.

[100] See, eg, Peter Strauss, 'The Place of Agencies in Government: Separation of Powers and the Fourth Branch' (1984) 84 Colum L Rev 573; Adrian Vermeule, 'Conventions of Agency Independence' (2013) 113 Colum L Rev 1163; 'Symposium, the Uneasy Constitutional Status of the Administrative Agencies' (1986) 36 Am U L Rev 277–601; *Free Enterprise Fund v Public Company Accounting Board*, 561 US 477 (2010), 130 S Ct 3138 at 3151–63, 3148 (2010) (citing the parties' agreement that the Board was 'part of government' for constitutional purposes).

[101] The closest to a definition in the US is found in the 1980 Paperwork Reduction Act (94 Stat 2812, 44 USC §§3501–21). In its current version, 'agency' is defined as 'means any executive department, military department, Government corporation, Government controlled corporation, or other establishment in the executive branch of the Government (including the Executive Office of the President), or any independent regulatory agency'; 'independent agencies' are mainly enumerated: the term means 'the Board of Governors of the Federal Reserve System, the Commodity Futures Trading Commission, the Consumer Product Safety Commission, the Federal Communications Commission, the Federal Deposit Insurance Corporation, the Federal Energy Regulatory Commission, the Federal Housing Finance Agency, the Federal Maritime Commission, the Federal Trade Commission, the Interstate Commerce Commission, the Mine Enforcement Safety and Health Review Commission, the National Labor Relations Board, the Nuclear Regulatory Commission, the Occupational Safety and Health Review Commission, the Postal Regulatory Commission, the Securities and Exchange Commission, the Bureau of Consumer Financial Protection, the Office of Financial Research, Office of the Comptroller of the Currency, and any other similar agency designated by statute as a Federal independent regulatory agency or commission'. 44 USC §3502(1), (5).

judiciary, an agency is assured independence when its head is removable by the President only for the causes listed in the statutory framework, not by presidential will.[102] This is, of course, an important feature of independence, but scholarship identifies additional factors. Formal structures may set limits on the choice of appointees or on their removal; structurally place the agency within or outside a government department; deny independent authority to litigate within the agency; establish accountability mechanisms to different external players; set procedural rules (for example, requirements for consultation and rule-making processes); make rules regarding budgetary autonomy, the length of term, the structure of leadership (single head or board), and, in case of leadership by a board or commission, the existence of staggered terms of appointment. Lastly, oversight by the 'core' executive, introduced by statute or otherwise, may be part of the formal framework.[103]

In the United States, a system which, it is argued, puts a premium on agency independence,[104] three structural mechanisms raise serious challenges to this very feature of regulatory governance (the political factors contributing to presidential dominance are mentioned above and discussed further below). First are the appointment and removal processes of heads of the so-called 'independent agencies'. These processes have received ample judicial and academic attention in the US, especially the removal power: since the political nature of appointments is central to US culture, the emphasis has thus generally moved to the question of grounds of removal, with free, not-for-cause presidential removal being challenged for its implications on independence—or to cases in which Congress is actively involved

[102] The origin of this equation is arguably *Humphrey's Executor v United States*, 295 US 602 (1935) (Congress's determination to create an agency that would be independent from any department equalled its freedom from executive control; the statutory requirement of removal only by cause thus did not enable removal for any other non-enumerated cause). The ruling does not imply that this feature is the only one to be considered in measuring independence, but this conclusion was fully embraced by Judge Kavanaugh in *PHH Corporation v Consumer Financial Protection Bureau*, 839 F3d 1 (DC Cir 2016) 5 ('[a]n agency is considered "independent" when the agency heads are for cause, not at will') (The decision found that a for-cause clause in a statute that created an agency headed by a single person and not by a board or commission was unconstitutional). The decision was vacated and redecided en banc by the same court in 2018 (*PHH Corporation v Consumer Financial Protection Bureau*, 881 F3d 75 (DC Cir 2018). Judge Kavanaugh, now on the Supreme Court, is not likely to change his views). For the more recent literature following this direction see eg Marshall J Breger and Gary J Edles, 'Established by Practice: The Theory and Operation of Independent Federal Agencies' (2000) 52 Admin L Rev 1111, 1138; Jacob E Gersen, 'Designing Agencies' in Daniel A Farber and Joseph O'Connell (eds), *Research Handbook on Public Choice and Public Law* (Edward Elgar 2010) 333, 347; Lisa Schultz Bressman and Robert B Thompson, 'The Future of Agency Independence' (2010) 63 Vand L Rev 599, 610.

[103] Factors collected from Möllers (n 96); Rachel Barkow, 'Insulating Agencies: Avoiding Capture through Institutional Design' (2010) 89 Tex L Rev 15; Kirti Datla and Richard L Revesz, 'Deconstructing Independent Agencies (and Executive Agencies) (2013) 98 Cornell L Rev 769, 784–812; Jennifer L Selin, 'What Makes an Agency Independent?' (2015) 59 Am J Pol Sci 971; David E Lewis and Jennifer L Selin, 'Political Control and the Forms of Agency Independence' (2015) 83 Geo Wash L Rev 1487. See also Adrian Vermeule, 'Conventions of Agency Independence' (2013) 113 Colum L Rev 1163.

[104] The first agency credited as 'independent' was the Interstate Commerce Commission, established by the Interstate Commerce Act 1887. For a list of independent agencies and useful links see <https://pitt.libguides.com/usgovinfo/independentagencies>.

under legislation.[105] The outcome of the series of decisions concerned with removal powers is generally one that supports presidential dominance over agencies which exercise an 'executive function'.[106]

The second mechanism, the oversight over agencies by the presidential Office of the Management of the Budget in the Office of the White House (OMB), is sometimes not based on statute, but rather on executive orders issued by the president and presented as unilaterally made in the absence of statute.[107] Earlier executive orders that targeted only agencies within government were replaced in 1993 by President Clinton's Executive Order 12866, substantially amended since by all incoming presidents.[108] Under this regime, all agencies, including those considered independent, are subject to duties that fall short of direct control but affect their autonomy: requirements concerning the content and volume of regulations, reporting duties, and OMB authority to 'review' regulations and return them to their sender, are more than mere recommendations.[109] These orders are careful to add

[105] For references to jurisprudence and scholarship see above (n 24). For example, the Administrator of the Environment Protection Agency (EPA), considered a prime example of the independent agency and discussed throughout this book, is appointed by the President upon the advice and consent of the Senate, a process that is likely to enable the President, as long as the Senate majority remains in his party's hands, to influence, to a certain extent, the subsequent politics of the agency.

For a short mention of the unique status of the RPA see Susan Bartlett Foote, 'Independent Agencies under Attack: A Skeptical View of the Importance of the Debate' [1988] DUKE LJ 223, 224 n 7. For executive oversight over the agency see eg Robert V Percival, 'Checks without Balance: Executive Office Oversight of the Environmental Protection Agency' (1991) 54 L and Contemp Problems 127. See below on the evolving role of the OMB.

[106] For a summary see Legal Information Institute, Cornell Law School, 'The Removal Power' <https://www.law.cornell.edu/constitution-conan/article-2/section-2/clause-2/the-removal-power>.

[107] For these, and other such measures (proclamations, memoranda, and signing statements) see ch 5.

[108] The two first Executive Orders, numbered 10244 and 12174 (23 March 1978, 30 November 1979, respectively, 43 FR 12661, 44 FR 69609) set requirements for regulation-making of executive agencies. The first required agencies, inter alia, to submit 'significant' regulations to a 'regulatory analysis'; a report of the criteria was to be submitted and approved by the OMB. Among other exemptions, the order explicitly excluded 'independent regulatory agencies', without defining this category. The second focused on the reduction of the number of regulations, under the slogan 'paperwork minimizing', a term that remains central to the discourse, evident inter alia in the title of the Paperwork Reduction Act 1980 (n 101). Executive Order 12291 (17 February 1981, 46 FR 13193) relied on the definition of 'agency' and independent agency' in the Paperwork Reduction Act, and subjected executive, non-independent agencies to a more robust oversight regime, including the preparation of regulatory impact analysis prior to the making of 'major rules' and their submission to the OMB, submission of notices of all planned rules, and the grant of some review powers to the OMB.

[109] Revoking early orders, Executive Order 12866, *Regulatory Planning and Review*, 30 September 1993 (58 FR 51735) requires all agencies to prepare a regulatory agenda of regulations that will undergo review and a regulatory plan of the significant regulations to be issued in the forthcoming year. The agency is required to state the relation between its objective and the President's; the plan should provide justification for the promulgation of each such regulation; state the alternatives, the estimated costs and benefits, and the need for the action. The plan is to be submitted annually to the Office of Information and Regulatory Affairs (OIRA), established in 1980 and operating within the OMB; the OIRA administrator may notify an agency if she finds that a planned regulatory action is inconsistent with the President's priorities, after which consultation between the Vice President and the targeted agency may be initiated. All agencies (unless exempted by OIRA) must provide OIRA with a draft of the regulatory action, assess its costs and benefits, explain its consistency with the statutory mandate, and, 'to the extent permitted by law', its promotion of the President's priorities and its avoidance of 'undue interference' with state, and other public bodies' exercise of their government function. Additional

provisos that emphasize that their authorizations apply 'to the extent permitted by law' and other such terms,[110] but the message to all agencies is clear.[111]

cost-benefit and other analyses are required for 'significant' regulations, as determined by OIRA, who can review these regulations and return unsuitable or otherwise suspect ones to the agency for further consideration. Unresolved disagreements would be settled by the President or the Vice President with the agency involved, resulting in 'recommendations' issued by the President. These provisions, applying to all but exempted agencies, are the central provisions of the order (EO 12866, Sections 4(b), 4(c), 6, 7). A subsequent Executive Order, issued by President George W Bush in 2007, subjecting 'substantive' agency guideline documents to the same regime, was revoked by President Obama in 2009 (EO 13422, 72 FR 2763; EO 13497, 74 FR 6113, revoking also President Bush's EO 13258, which essentially removed the involvement of the Vice President). President Obama did not however remove OIRA's involvement: in 2011 he 'reaffirmed' EO 12866, adding some participatory values and extending them to independent agencies in EO 13563 and EO 13579 (76 FR 3821, 76 FR 41587), and a year later, further emphasized the value of participation, requiring regular reporting to OIRA (EO 13610, 77 FR 28469). President Trump's executive orders in 2017 and 2018 only tightened the OMB's control of agencies, 'executive' and 'independent' alike. Ordering all agencies to repeal at least two regulations for each introduced, Executive Order 13771 requires reporting to the OMB and authorizing the OMB to provide guidance and identify the total sum of incremental costs allowed in issuing new regulations and repealing regulations (Executive Order 13771, *Reducing Regulation and Controlling Regulatory Costs*, 82 FR 9339). Another executive order submits all agencies to the 'regulatory reform agenda', inter alia requiring them to designate an official as a Regulatory Reform Officer (EO 13777, 82 FR 12285). See also, in the context of environmental law, Executive Order 12088, *Federal compliance with pollution control standards*, 2.11.10, 43 FR 47707; Executive Order 13432, *Cooperation Among Agencies in Protecting the Environment With Respect to Greenhouse Gas Emissions From Motor Vehicles, Nonroad Vehicles, and Nonroad Engines*, 14.5.07, 72 FR 27717.

Other executive orders set written policies in defined fields, which have an effect, if indirectly, on agency action. For example, during his first two years in office, President Trump addressed, inter alia, the fields of energy, collective bargaining, and environmental review in infrastructure projects (EO 13783, 82 FR 16093; EO 13807, 82 FR 40463; EO 13836, 83 FR 25329). Only the second is limited to agencies within government.

[110] See eg EO 12866, Sections 1(b), 2(b), 6(a)(3)(B)(ii), 7 ('to the extent permitted by law'); EO 13563, Section 6(b) ('consistent with law and its [the agency's] resources and regulatory priorities').

[111] Two examples concerned with the Environmental Protection Agency (EPA) may suffice to show the impact of such orders. Both belong to the Trump presidency, but similar events have occurred earlier. Part of President Trump's agenda of rolling back stringent regulation of emissions, the President issued a memorandum directed to the EPA, requiring the agency to continue its programmes, designed to protect the environment, while reducing 'unnecessary impediments to new manufacturing and business expansion essential for a growing economy'. Inter alia, the EPA was required to process in a timely manner state implementation plans (NAAQs), consider the impact of emissions generated internationally in assessing states' attainment, and provide flexibility to states in the context of identifying and achieving offsets. These, and all other requirements, were to be 'implemented consistent with applicable law and subject to appropriations'. Less than two months later, an EPA memorandum issued by the Administrator to his Assistant Administrators set five principles for future review of NAAQs, citing the President's memorandum, under a general commitment to go 'back to basics' and, while applying the laws, sustain a level of risk that sufficiently protects public health without reaching for zero-risk levels. For the memoranda see <https://www.whitehouse.gov/presidential-actions/presidential-memorandum-administrator-environmental-protection-agency/>, later published as Memorandum, *Promoting Domestic Manufacturing and Job Creation—Policies and Procedures Relating to Implementation of Air Quality Standards*, 83 FR 16671 (12 April, 2018); *Back-to-Basics Process for Reviewing National Ambient Air Quality Standards*, 9 May 2018 <https://www.epa.gov/sites/production/files/2018-05/documents/image2018-05-09-173219.pdf>. For a critical assessment see EELP, *Subverting the Process of Setting Health-Based Air Quality Standards: EELP Interviews Janet McCabe*, 26 June 2018 <https://eelp.law.harvard.edu/2018/06/subverting-the-process-of-setting-health-based-air-quality-standards-eelp-interviews-janet-mccabe/>. The legality of another measure is still contested in court: a broad duty set by President Trump in Executive Order 13771, requires all agencies to repeal at least two existing regulations for each new regulation issued. *Reducing Regulation and Controlling Regulatory Costs*, 30 January 2017, 82 FR 9339. Answering a challenge to the

The final mechanism has received lesser attention, certainly beyond the US. Annual appropriations acts, which authorize government expenditure, consistently contain policy riders that set constraints on action, usually by setting limits on expenditure on action rendered undesirable, but sometimes by directly prohibiting or authorizing government preferred policy.[112] Such riders, discussed in detail in Chapter 7 and mentioned in Chapters 3 and 8, have traditionally shaped g overnment policies, despite Senate Rule XVI, which severely constrains the use of riders in appropriations bills to transform legislation or its application. Legislated in Congress, these riders may represent a presidential agenda that targets agency action, although they are often the result of consistent pressure from interest groups. An example of the latter type of rider is the repeated inclusion of the following rider annual appropriations since 2010

> Notwithstanding any other provision of law, none of the funds made available in this Act or any other Act may be used to promulgate or implement any regulation requiring the issuance of permits under title V of the Clean Air Act (42 U.S.C. 7661 et seq.) for carbon dioxide, nitrous oxide, water vapor, or methane emissions resulting from biological processes associated with livestock production.[113]

constitutionality of this order, based on separation of powers arguments, the DC District Court granted the White House order to dismiss the case for lack of standing, setting a date for further hearings towards a final judgment (Civil Action No 17-253 *Public Citizen, Inc v Donald Trump* (RDM) (DDC 19 Dec 2019)). The order is found inter alia in the EPA's website <https://www.epa.gov/laws-regulations/executive-order-13771-reducing-regulation-and-controlling-regulatory-costs>.

For some examples of the literature on this topic, in addition to the scholarship on the 'unitary presidency' (n 27) and Kagan's influential work (n 53) see eg Cary Coglianese, 'Presidential Control of Administrative Agencies: A Debate over Law and Politics' [2010] U Pa J Constl L 637; Robert V Percival, 'Who's in Charge? Does the President Have Directive Authority over Agency Regulatory Decisions?' (2011) 79 Fordham L Rev 2487; Peter Ketcham-Colwill, 'Presidential Influence over Agency Rulemaking through Regulatory Review' (2014) 82 Geo Wash L Rev 1622.

[112] On this feature see eg Sandra Beth Zellmer, 'Sacrificing Legislative Integrity at the Altar of Appropriations Riders: A Constitutional Crisis' (1997) 21 Harv Envtl L Rev 457; Zachary S Price, 'Funding Restrictions and Separation of Powers' (2018) 71 Vanderbilt L Rev 357. For a stronger emphasis on the implications for Congress see eg Jack M Beermann, 'Congressional Administration' (2006) 43 San Diego L Rev 61; Richard J Lazarus, 'Congressional Descent: The Demise of Deliberative Democracy in Environmental Law' (2006) 94 Geo LJ 61; James Wallner, 'How to Spot Policy Riders in Appropriations Bills', 22 August 2018 <https://www.legbranch.org/2018-8-22-how-to-spot-policy-riders-in-appropriations-bills/>.

[113] For this provision as enacted between 2010 and 2020 see Interior Department and Further Continuing Appropriations, Fiscal Year 2010, PL 111-88, §424 ('2010 Appropriations Act'); Consolidated Appropriations Act 2012, PL 112–74, §426; Consolidated Appropriations Act, 2014, PL 113–76, §420; Consolidated and Further Continuing Appropriations Act, 2015, PL 113–235, §419; Consolidated Appropriations Act, 2016, PL 114–13, §417; Consolidated Appropriations Act, 2017, PL 115–31, §417; Consolidated Appropriations Act, 2018, PL 115–41, §416; Consolidated Appropriations Act, 2019, PL 116–6, §416 (2019 Appropriations Act); Further Consolidated Appropriations Act, 2020, HR 1865, PL 116–94, §437; Further Consolidated Appropriations Act 2020 §437. During budget crisis years, for which achievement of a federal budget was especially problematic politically, continuing temporary acts extended the application of the former budgets, hence this provision as well. See, in 2011, initially by the Continuing Appropriations Act, Fiscal Year 2011, PL 111–242, HR 3081, Sec 101(5), finally by the Department of Defense and Full-Year Continuing Appropriations Act, 2011, PL 112–10, HR 3081, §§1101(a)(4), further provisions Secs 1734–39; similarly, in 2013, initially by the Continuing

The consistent inclusion of this rider through several presidencies, at least one of them committed to energy reform, may remove some responsibility from some of these presidents, but at least in cases in which accord between the president and Congress exists, this tool further enables presidents to impact on agencies policies and action.

The British structural set-up has not given ground to similar complexity. Stronger formal links between agencies and central government result in a spectrum of relative independence that is much more skewed towards dependence. Furthermore, the debate over the independence of agencies, 'arm's-length bodies' in British idiom,[114] is far less politically laden.

Beyond core government departments, the British government operates through three other types of bodies: executive agencies (in British parlance, units within government departments that enjoy some budgetary independence), non-departmental public bodies (which are not part of government, hence 'at arm's length') and non-ministerial departments (operating 'similarly to normal government departments').[115] A fourth group of bodies, defined as 'public corporations' in government accounts, contains several bodies usually recognized as performing a regulatory function (such as the Bank of England, the Civil Aviation Board, and the Financial Conduct Authority); these enjoy the highest degree of formal autonomy.[116]

Yet all degrees of autonomy are structurally limited by a variety of mechanisms. Inter alia, the Cabinet Office scrutinizes the action of all bodies belonging to the first three groups, conducting 'functional' and 'tailored' reviews under guidance documents detailing the in-depth extent of such review.[117] Statutes, including

Appropriations Act, Fiscal Year 2011, PL 112–75, HJres 117, §101(7), further provisions in Secs 1404, 1406–407, finally by the Consolidated and Further Continuing Appropriations Act, 2013, PL 113–6, HR 933, §1101(a)(3), further provisions §§1405–407. For another example of this type see ch 9.

[114] See eg Cabinet Office, *Public Bodies 2018–2019* (Cabinet Office, undated) 31 <https://assets.publishing.service.gov.uk/government/uploads/system/uploads/attachment_data/file/786952/6.5040_CO_PublicBodies2018-19.PDF>; Cabinet Office, *Classification of Public Bodies: Guidance for Departments* (Cabinet Office, undated) < https://www.gov.uk/government/publications/classification-of-public-bodies-information-and-guidance>. For links to other guidance documents see <https://www.gov.uk/government/collections/public-bodies-information-for-departments>.

[115] *Public Bodies 2017* (n 114) 53. 'Next Steps' agencies, named under government policy introduced in 1988, are now considered 'executive agencies'; although the original rationale was to unpack service-givers from central government, bodies such as the Competition Service, the Equality and Human Rights Commission, and the Environment Agency clearly function beyond this rationale. See eg Efficiency Unit, *Improving Management in Government: The Next Steps* (HMSO 1988); Diana Goldsworthy, *Setting Up Next Steps* (HMSO 1991); Colin Turpin and Adam Tomkins, *British Government and the Constitution: Text and Materials* (7th edn, CUP 2011) 432–36.

[116] See HM Treasury, *Whole of Government Accounts, —Year Ended 31 March 2019*, HC 2164 (2019). These annual reports consolidate the financial statements of thousands of bodies in the public sector. A list of bodies is provided in Annex 1. For a survey of all types of such bodies, organized in seven layers, see Matthew Flinders, *Delegated Governance and the British State* (OUP 2008) 99–138 (classified according to organizational distance from the core executive).

[117] For a short guidance, with links to detailed guidance documents, see Cabinet Office, *Public Bodies* <https://www.gov.uk/guidance/public-bodies-reform>.

those that establish regulatory public corporations, offer additional modes of subjection to central government. In addition, for a of five-year period ended in 2017, ministers were authorized to abolish or merge agencies, modify their structure, or transfer the functions of a large number of listed regulatory bodies. Such changes now require legislation.[118] In his study of delegated governance, a consideration of the variety of British bodies discussed above, Matthew Flinders identifies 'six dimensions of autonomy and control'. Ranging from the ability to make unilateral policy decisions, to reporting requirements, these do not differ substantively from the formal indicia developed in the US.[119]

In these two systems, then, complete structural independence cannot be found. Even the usual example of central banks as the epitome of the independent agency should be contested: few, if any, central banks operate, for example, without requirements for prior consultation with the treasury or other government bodies prior to the adoption of certain measures and policies.[120] Here, too, on a spectrum of structural independence, the independence of an agency can range from virtually full autonomy, strong autonomy, semi-autonomy (for example, when an agency is part of a ministry but its budget is appropriated separately, or when its employees are free from some of the restrictions set on civil servants), and, at the extreme pole of dependency absence of structural autonomy, evident in the

[118] Public Bodies Act 2011.

[119] Flinders (n 116) 142–45. Organized as six pairs of mechanisms of autonomy on the one side and control on the other, these 'dimensions' are: managerial (managerial autonomy, reflected in the existence of decision-making competences/ex ante government control of decisions through the issuance of rules and approval requirements; policy (the ability to decide policy processes, when policy is set externally, and the setting of targets/ex ante control of processes and performance); structure (appointment of an agency head and the accountability of an agency head to external bodies, with appointment of these taken into account/ hierarchical and accountability structures that effect control); financial (budget and direct receipt of income generated from agency outputs/control through change of budget); legal (agency's legal status preventing altering competences/change of legal statues or the dissolution of the body); interventional (freedom from ex post reporting requirements and from government sanctions of threats when deviation occurs/reporting requirements, auditing, and sanctions or direct intervention in case of noncompliance). Summarized ibid 144.

[120] Suffice to note some of the different modes of Treasury participation in the workings of the Bank of England (BoE). Under the Bank of England Act, substantially amended in the Bank of England and Financial Services Act 2016, the Treasury may add or remove a seat on the Court of Directors (Section 1A); the issuance of a code of practice for the Monetary Committee or its change require consultation with the Treasury (Schedule 3, para 13(B)(4)); may initiate a review, by a person independent from the Bank of England, of the economy, efficiency and effectiveness with which the BoE has used its resources in discharging its functions as the Prudential Regulation Authority, although the review 'is not to be concerned with the merits of the Bank's general policy or principles in pursuing the Bank's objectives' (Section 7F); and, regarding the duty of the BoE to comply with certain EU directives, the Treasury may direct the Bank to desist from action that appears to the Treasury incompatible with obligations of the United Kingdom (section 30C). These are mere examples of a general trend. For nuanced studies on the independence of central banks (considering, in addition to de jure independence, also political and empirical aspects, the latter discussed separately below) see Vittorio Grilli and others, 'Political and Monetary Institutions and Public Financial Policies in the Industrial Countries' [1991] Econ Policy 341; Marco Arnone, Bernard J Laurens, and Jean-François Segalotto, 'The Measurement of Central Bank Autonomy: Survey of Models, Indicators, and Empirical Evidence' (2006) IMF Working Paper WP/06/227.

case of departments of a government ministry. Independence, then, is a matter of degree—and the argument for the complete dismantling of central government cannot be fully supported.[121]

Moving, now, to politics, or to 'de facto independence' in both systems: as some scholars have noted, formal independence (if such exists at all) is neither a necessary or sufficient condition for independence. Formally dependent agencies may exercise strong autonomy from intervention, and, conversely, agencies structured to be highly independent may subject themselves to central government (or be captured by interest groups, another element altogether).[122] The variety of elements that can, and have, granted heads of executive political power over so-called 'independent agencies' include the choice of appointee as head of an agency, appointment turnover and frequency, 'voluntary' resignation after losing presidential or prime ministerial support, the existence of veto players, the age of the agency, the frequency of revolving door events and of ad hoc contacts, government influence on the agency's budget, the weight of partisan membership on board members' nominations, submission to advice and other pressures or contacts with the 'core' executive, personal connections—in short, all things political.[123] In addition, the degree of agency independence can, and does, change over time, not only due to formal transformations and reforms—an obvious element that further challenges rigid classifications.[124] Finally, courts have been receptive to the inclusion of government agencies and government corporations as part of the government, in different contexts.[125] Clearly, then, the degree of agency independence is not easy to assess: the interplay between the multiple features, structural and political, leads to the understanding that independence, too, is potentially a matter of degree.

Most of these studies present concrete evidence of executive control over so-called 'independent agencies'.[126] While degrees of control vary in politics just as

[121] On the idea of a spectrum, or continuum of independence, see Datla and Revesz (n 103) 825.

[122] See Adrian Vermeule, 'Conventions of Agency Independence' (2013) 113 Colum L Rev 1163, esp 1174–81 (emphasizing the role of 'conventions', or followed understandings, a useful concept that is however unnecessary for the current discussion of independence); for a similar argument beyond the US see Martino Maggetti, *Regulation in Practice: The de Facto Independence of Regulatory Agencies* (ECPR Press 2012), esp 45–47 (supporting the argument of variable independence with the analysis of sixteen bodies operating in the fields of finance and competition in several European countries).

[123] Indicia of political variables collected from eg Terry Moe, 'Regulatory Performance and Presidential Administration' (1982) 26 Am J Pol Sci 197; Neal Devins and David Lewis, 'Not-So Independent Agencies: Party Polarization and the Limits of Institutional Design' [2008] BU L Rev 459; Maggetti (n 122); Datla and Revesz (n 121) 812–24.

[124] For studies of formal structural changes over time see eg Selin (n 103); Lewis and Selin (n 103) 1512–14.

[125] See *Lebron v Nat'l Railroad Passenger Corp*, 513 US 374 (1995) (AMTRAK, created by law as a federal corporation to further governmental objectives, was part of the government for the purposes of the First Amendment); *Free Enterprise Fund v Public Company Accounting Board*, 561 US 477 at 419–513 (2010) (relying on the parties' agreement that the PCAOB was 'part of government' for constitutional purposes).

[126] See eg Moe (n 126) (in three central independent agencies, regulatory performance has changed on the change of administration); Devins and Lewis (n 123) (focusing on commissioner tenure in twelve agencies up to, and including, George W Bush's administration); Maggetti (n 122) (research of sixteen agencies regulating financial services, competition and telecommunications in ten European

much, if not more, than in structure, executive control is an accepted fact. For example, and once again in the context of the regulation of pollution, the strong political ties between presidents and their appointee administrators of the EPA, considered the prototype of an independent agency, is evident not only in the fact that the administrators usually end their terms with the end of a presidential term, if not sooner, but is also reflected in the fact that their policies do not substantially deviate from their president's agenda.[127] Not surprisingly, commentators have advanced the argument that the president has the power to control the EPA, and, by extension, similar agencies.[128] In Elena Kagan's words, published a few years before her appointment to the US Supreme Court, 'we live today in an era of presidential administration'.[129] A similar claim applies to the UK, with the obvious changes applied.

Supplementing these analyses, a final insight on the nature of agencies leads to their inclusion in the executive branch in its broad sense. The function of agencies as policy-makers under organic statutes is essentially executive in nature. The classical emphasis on agency 'multitasking'—agencies have been described as exercising all three government functions, rulemaking, implementation, and adjudication—is in fact typical to the core executive just as much as it is relevant to agencies: executive action essentially involves all three functions. Although insulation from the executive may exist to different degrees, the prevalence of executive oversight and the functional similarity between the core executive and administrative agencies both lead me to consider in this article the executive, the core government, and agencies as comprising the executive branch in the broad sense.

F. Concluding Remarks

This chapter was designed to address three preliminary issues. Following an initial definition of the 'executive', which focuses on the head of this branch of

Countries; summary plan and results at 50–51, 170–71); Datla and Revesz (n 121) (classifying a large number of agencies, using their proposed indicia).

[127] For example, EPA enforcement patterns show distinct results that tally with the presidents' environmental policies. Collecting data from the EPA, New York Times' reporters found variations in the number of cases filed by the agency during the first 266 days of GW Bush, Obama, and Trump (2,600, 2,900, and 1,900 cases, respectively) and in the setting of civil fines for environmental repairs (amounting to 2.6, 10.1, and 1.3 billion Dollars, respectively). Eric Lipton and Danielle Ivory, 'Under Trump, EPA Has Slowed Actions Against Polluters, and Put Limits on Enforcement Officers', *NY Times* (New York, 10 December 2017) < https://www.nytimes.com/2017/12/10/us/politics/pollution-epa-regulations.html>. See also eg Eric Schaeffer and Tom Pelton, *Less Enforcement: Communities at Risk* (Environmental Integrity Project 2019) <https://www.environmentalintegrity.org/wp-content/uploads/2019/02/EIP-Enforcement-Report.pdf>.

[128] On the EPA see Joshua K Westmoreland, 'Global Warming and Originalism: The Role of the EPA in the Obama Administration' (2010) 37 Env Affairs 225.

[129] Kagan (n 53) 2246.

government, the review of the body of research on the executive in two disciplines, political science and law, reveals several common themes. First, to date, there is virtually no study of the office as a universal element in all democracies; discussions of the nature and operation of the executive branch in national systems abounds, but the need to provide general theory, or at least some insights that are valid beyond specific domestic borders, is still unanswered. The literature however shares several understandings. The executive branch is commonly considered a powerful, if not the most powerful, branch of government. In addition, commentators note the ambivalence surrounding the nature of the executive. The use of terms such as paradoxes and puzzles, as we shall see in Chapter 2, all point to a shared vision of the branch as one that is not easily explained.

Moving to methodologies and, further, to normative stances about the relative power of the executive, the chapter first identified several streams in political science studies. The chronologically organized overview began with the personal presidency group of theories, which gained centrality in the second half of the twentieth century; other emerging foci included the application of public choice, institutionalism, organization theory, and reaching to the current interest in behaviouralism and experimental studies, while history has remained a central focus of research, more so in law.

Beyond history, normative studies, offered by public law scholars and philosophers, have contributed to the rich body of research. Both sides of the ongoing academic dispute over the proper extent of executive power have been amply represented; as in most cases of normative debates, the debate is still open.

To provide a complete introduction to the following chapters, I continued by addressing the general feature of all discussions of aspects of constitutionalism, the internal tension ingrained in all such aspects. In the context of the executive, the starting point of the analytical structure offered in Chapters 2 and 3 is the existence of an internal tension between the need to empower executives in order to enable swift action in different contingencies, and the need to constrain these powers due to the ingrained risk of abuse of power.

Concluding this chapter, I addressed two issues that can be raised to support arguments against the foci offered in the book. First, as the book considers theory and practice in the US and the UK, one may argue that comparing executives in presidential and parliamentary regimes is due to fail, since the regimes are so fundamentally different in this respect. Here, I offered a novel distinction between these two regime families, which focused on the existence of different permutations of the interaction between the legislature and the executive in the two regimes. The factors taken into consideration, namely the existence of direct access to parliament and the majority enjoyed in parliaments, place both regimes in different places on a spectrum of relative power. Under this scale of relative power, executives in parliamentary systems who maintain a strong, stable majority in parliament, enjoy the highest level of political power due to their direct access to parliament; the weakest executive in this spectrum would be a president whose party holds no majority in both houses of parliament. Strewn across this spectrum are other cases of relative power. This breaking-down of the so-called 'clear dichotomy' between presidential and parliamentary regimes, as well as the political fact of dominance in both regimes, justified the continued attention to these two regimes. The comparative analyses offered in most of the following chapters vindicates this methodological decision: much of the convergence, and, indeed, the differences in structure and attitudes, found in this book, have little to do with the regime-type.

The final hurdle set before the leap into the model of the executive, the existence of so-called 'independent agencies' as a bar for the attempt to address the executive as such, has been likewise dealt with. Administrative agencies have indeed taken over a large portion of policy- and rule-making away from the core executive. Yet, even in the US, the home of the independent agency, subjection to the White House remains constant, to some extent, and appointments often ensure political affinity between the president and at least some of these agencies; other forms of dominance, such as setting bars on expenditure, have further encumbered so-called 'rebellious agencies'.

Having dealt with these preliminary issues, entry into a discussion on the nature of the executive is now open. Chapter 3 opens the analysis by considering different institutional models of the executive, and ends with my selection of the model that informs the rest of the book.

2

Reaching the Internal Tension Model

A. **Introduction** 42
B. **Three Institutional Models Rejected** 43
  1. The Subservient Executive Model: The Separation of Powers and the Rule of Law 43
    a. The separation of powers 43
    b. The rule of law 45
  2. The Imperial Executive Model 47
    a. Managerial theories 47
    b. Exception-based theories 49
  3. The 'Bipolar' Model 53
C. **The Internal Tension Model** 55
D. **Concluding Remarks** 57

A. Introduction

In Chapter 1, I showed that studies of the executive branch are typically system-based and normative. The propensity towards normative analysis, expressed in those studies, is characteristic to legal research, but the robustness of any normative study depends on the existence of a strong theoretical basis. Such a basis is absent from studies of executive powers: competing normative arguments are not supported by a general explanatory model of the executive that extends beyond the methodologies of particular texts and histories. At their best, descriptive accounts have been based on simplistic recognitions of the key role of the executive, supplemented by references to 'paradoxes' and 'puzzles'.[1] Such accounts do not amount to a general model of the executive branch.

This chapter sets aside the normative element, and develops a model that weds observations of reality with legal theory. I reject rushing into normative argumentation over the proper extent of powers and the justifiable modes of review of state powers by courts and other bodies. Bypassing general theory is likely to lead to unsubstantiated results; a workable depictive model must first be developed to support the normative analysis. In other words, the descriptive must precede the normative.

Based on the internal tension model, governing constitutionalism-at-large, I submit that the executive is best viewed as straddling the line between subjection

[1] Laurence H Tribe, *American Constitutional Law* (3rd edn, Foundation Press 2000) 630; see also Thomas E Cronin and Michael E Genovese, *The Paradoxes of the American Presidency* (OUP 1998).

A Theory of the Executive Branch. Margit Cohn, Oxford University Press (2021). © Margit Cohn.
DOI: 10.1093/oso/9780198821984.003.0003

to law and dominance beyond law. This is no 'paradox:' embodying one of the tensions ingrained in constitutional law, the executive draws on an irresolvable tension between its role as executor of law, under the separation of powers ideal, and its function as manager, or dominant decision-maker in the political sphere, in which it acts above and beyond the law. Under the internal tension model, normative theory can be better expounded, and the extent of required constraints over excessive power can be better addressed.

In this chapter I discuss and reject three models of the executive branch, all of which are based on hierarchical and dichotomous thinking. The subservient executive model connotes full supremacy of the constitution and legislation over the executive; the imperial executive model draws on a vision of executive supremacy; and the third, bipolar model offers a vision of alternating modes of operation. All are rejected in favor of a model that recognizes the internal tension which underlies executive action.

B. Three Institutional Models Rejected

1. The Subservient Executive Model: The Separation of Powers and the Rule of Law

Arguments for the subservience of the executive to law are supported by two key values of modern democracy—the separation of powers and the rule of law. Both fail as single depictive accounts of the ways executives operate in the social and political spheres, but, of course, should not be rejected.

a. The separation of powers

Under this key element of the democratic ethos, the executive power is granted its traditional function, that of executing the laws enacted by the legislature.[2] Maurice Vile's treatise on the principle and its workings in key Western democracies, which remains the central focused study of the separation of powers ideal,[3] offers two important insights. First, the principle should be deconstructed into two elements: differentiation and separation of functions. The novelty of the principle, famously elaborated by Montesquieu and Locke before it was embedded in modern

[2] This does not mean that modern democratic constitutions cannot advance alternative formal structures. The Constitution of the Fifth French Republic formally grants the executive a residual power to legislate in areas not delineated in the Constitution. The extent to which the Conseil Constitutionnel can prevent statutes from entering 'forbidden' areas is a matter of debate, but the emerging practice tends towards the more traditional allocation of powers, under which the legislature has the upper hand. For the main stepping-stones see CC 82–143, 30 July 1982, *Blocage des prix et revenus*, Rec 57; CC 05-512, 21 April 2005, *Loi d'orientation et de programme pour l'avenir de l'école*, Rec 72; CC 2012-649 DC 15 March 2012, *Simplification du droit*, Rec 142.

[3] Maurice JC Vile, *Constitutionalism and the Separation of Powers* (Clarendon Press 1967).

democracies, lay not in distinguishing different government functions: the differentiation of powers was recognized in antiquity, cited by Aristotle, although the nature and source of legitimacy of state powers were far removed from contemporary understandings.[4] The requirement for separation, on the other hand, is a more recent addition, earliest reflected in Montesquieu's famous declaration that 'there would be an end of everything' if the three functions were to be exercised by the same person or body, and his preceding call for a state of affairs under which 'power should be a check to power'.[5]

Vile's second insight concerns the gap between principle and its application, or myth and reality. Essentially, the principle as presented above is a 'pure' version, 'a stark, extreme doctrine' that has rarely (if ever) been held in practice.[6] Indeed, political and legal realities both assert this, reaffirming the absence of full commitment of democratic polities to the executive-as-executioner. In parliamentary regimes, constant parliamentary support (usually through the maintenance of a majority) is necessary, granting direct access of prime ministers to parliament and guaranteeing executive control.[7] The United States' checks and balances variant refines the pure principle in a more nuanced way,[8] and its Constitution offers readings that do not imply a relatively limited role for the executive, a direction discussed below.[9]

[4] Aristotle recognized 'three elements', or powers, in each 'constitution', referring to 'one element which deliberates about public affairs', another 'concerned with the magistracies', and 'that which has judicial power' (Aristotle, *Politics*, in Richard McKeon (ed), *The Basic Works of Aristotle* (Random House 1941) 1297b–1298a). See also Marsilius of Padua's fourteenth century recognition of similar government functions (still stressing the convergence of all functions in the hands of one absolute ruler). Marsilius of Padua, *The Defender of the Peace* (Alan Gewirth tr, Columbia University Press 1956) 61–62. For discussions of the three functions in pre- and post- modernity see Montesquieu's third version of the principle, Baron de Montesquieu, Charles Louis de Secondat, *The Spirit of the Laws* (Thomas Nugent tr, Batoche Books 2001), book XI, ch 6, 174 (referring to 'those three powers, that of enacting laws, that of executing the public resolutions, and of trying the causes of individuals'. For the two preceding division of powers see ibid 173). But see John Locke, *Two Treatises of Government*, ed by Peter Laslett (CUP 1960), book II, § 143 (concerned only with the separation between the legislature and the executive).

[5] ibid ch 6, 173, ch 4, 172, respectively. Montesquieu's second requirement that 'power should be a check to power' was not explicitly linked with the idea of separation of functions, but has long been fully owned as such, adopted by supporters of the 'checks and balances' version of the principle.

[6] On the 'pure doctrine' see Vile (n 3) 12–13, supported by proof throughout the book.

[7] See eg Vile (n 3) at 53–75; Bruce Ackerman, 'The New Separation of Powers' (2000) 113 Harv L Rev 634; David Samuels, 'Separation of Powers' in Carles Boix and Susan C Stokes (eds), *The Oxford Handbook of Comparative Politics* (OUP 2007) 703.

[8] *The Federalist* Nos 47, 48, 51. The idea is also expressed in Montesquieu's call that 'power should be a check to power' in order to prevent abuse. Baron de Montesquieu, *The Spirit of the Laws* (Thomas Nugent Trans, Hafner 1949) Book XI, ch 4. On the basis of this and other parts of the work, Eisenmann claimed that Montesquieu never preached for separation, rather against concentration of power in one pair of hands. Charles Eisenmann, 'L'Esprit des Lois et la séparation de pouvoirs' in Christian Pfister and others (eds), *Mélanges Carré de Malberg* (Sirey 1933) 165. But see William Gwyn, *The Meaning of the Separation of Powers* (Tulane University 1965) 104 (arguing that Montesquieu expounded a doctrine of separation). See also William B Gwyn, 'The Indeterminacy of the Separation of Powers in the Age of the Framers' (1988) 30 Wm & Mary L Rev 263; Martin S Flaherty, 'The Most Dangerous Branch' (1996) 105 Yale LJ 1725, 1802–10; Vile, *supra* note 6 at 120–21, 153–62.

[9] See text to n 21.

The final blow to the subservient model is, of course, political reality, an aspect I deal with extensively in this book.

Regarding the executive branch, the separation of powers principle connotes subservience of the executive to the legislature, hence its relative weakness. Some type of principal-agent relationship is assumed, where the agent follows the principal's edict. The level of detail of such edict may vary, but the reins remain in the hands of the principal. The flip-side of this is, of course, an exclusive grant of the legislative power to Parliament.

b. The Rule of Law

The second basis for the depiction of a subservient executive is the concept that carries the title 'the rule of law'. Here, too, commentators link the concept to a history that, once again, harks back to Aristotle, and for some, to Plato before him.[10] The modern readings of this vague concept focus on different sets of values that are more sensitive to the complexity of politics, and law may fit well with and support a model of executive subservience: an executive operating under law is necessarily subservient to the central law-maker, the legislature. Yet the vagueness inhering in the evolved concept, as well as its main use as a component of many normative arguments regarding the nature of law in the public sphere render the concept a weak candidate as a depictive model of any part of the polity, including the executive branch of government.

A few words about the well-discussed multiplicity of meanings that the term carries. In the words of one commentator, 'there are almost as many conceptions of the rule of law as there are people defending it'.[11] Analyses classifying its many permutations as 'thick' and 'thin' or 'formal' and 'substantive' abound.[12] Yet for the

[10] Plato's earlier claims in *The Republic* and the *Stateman* that ruling by a Philosopher-King was better than rule under statute were transformed in *The Laws*' call for the supremacy of laws, interpreted by some as a nascent version of the rule of law. See Plato, *The Republic*, ed GRF Ferrari, tr Tom Griffith (CUP 2000) 427A; Plato, *The Statesman*, ed Ramond Klibansky and Elizabeth Anscombem tr AE Taylor (Nelson and Sons 1961) 294–305; Plato, *The Laws*, tr Thomas L Pangle (University of Chicago Press 1988), esp 713c, 715d, 784e–874d. For analysis see George Klosko, *The Development of Plato's Political Theory* (Methuen 1986) esp, regarding the move to the rule by laws, 225–34. Aristotle's maxim that rules should be 'supreme' was nevertheless linked with requirements of justice, reason, and proper decision-making, and spanned all manners of regimes, but is likewise analyzed as a version of 'the rule of law'. For the reference to supremacy see Aristotle, *Politics* (n 4) 1282b. for discussion and further references see Judith Shklar, 'Political Theory and the Rule of Law' in Allan C Hutchinson and Patrick Monahan (eds), *The Rule of Law: Ideal or Ideology* (Carswell 1987) 1, 1–4.

[11] Olufemi Taiwo, 'The Rule of Law: The New Leviathan?' (1999) 12 Can JL and Juris 151, 152. See also Shklar (n 10) (noting that the concept can be easily shown as 'meaningless thanks to ideological abuse and general over-use'). For mere examples of the rich body of research see Robert Paul Wolff (ed), *The Rule of Law* (Simon and Schuster 1971); Brian Z Tamanaha, *On The Rule of Law: History, Politics, Theory* (CUP 2004); Jørgen Møller and Sven-Erik Skaaning, *The Rule of Law: Definitions, Measures, Patterns and Causes* (Palgrave Macmillan 2014).

[12] See eg for the former classification, Allan C Hutchinson and Patrick Monahan, 'Democracy and the Rule of Law' in Hutchinson and Monahan (n 10) 97, 100–02; for the latter, see Paul P Craig, 'Formal and Substantive Conceptions of the Rule of Law: An Analytical Framework' (1997) Public Law 467 (providing a highly useful overview of the different theses of the main scholars addressing the concept).

purpose of this chapter it is unnecessary to decide on the propriety of any of them. First, 'thin' versions suffice to describe the role of the executive as formally subservient to the legislature; secondly, most of these versions, especially those of the 'thick' or substantive varieties, are essentially normative, tracing the minimal (or maximal) requirements for the operation of a proper political structure directed by law. For this chapter, we are seeking something else: a descriptive model that captures the ways executives operate within their political arrangements. Here, and despite its importance as a normative ideal, the force of 'the rule of law' as a single determinant of the nature of the executive is weak.

It would seem that only Dicey's influential late nineteenth- century work on the English constitution was originally designed as a descriptive account. For Dicey, the rule of law was 'a characteristic of the English constitution';[13] he found all the three meanings of the principle embedded in his national constitution: the supremacy of law, as opposed to exercise of arbitrary power; the equal subjection of all to law, including officers; and the primacy of the protection of rights and freedoms.[14] Yet two elements, recognized by Dicey himself, distance his rule of law from reality, in Dicey's time, and more so, beyond. Dicey sought to show that the remaining Crown prerogative powers, or the powers to make law unilaterally exercised de facto by the government of the day, could always be curtailed by the legislature;[15] indeed, prerogative powers remained then, as they do today, a source of power that has little to do with the structural meaning of the rule of law under a model of subservience.[16] Furthermore, Dicey's distinction between continental and English attitudes towards the grant of discretion was likewise questionable at its time, and is clearly out of sync with current reality. Dicey was particularly critical of the penchant of continental systems to grant broad discretion to the monarch and his apparatus. Whatever the validity of his nineteenth-century claim that '[i]n almost every continental community the executive exercises far wider discretionary authority in the matter of arrest, of temporary imprisonment, of expulsion from its territory, and the like, than is either legally claimed or in fact exerted by the government in England',[17] it clearly cannot pass muster in any current Western democracy. On either side of the Channel or the Atlantic, discretion is often broadly granted to authorities in order to address fast-changing and complex issues and to escape the political need to decide in detail in politically sensitive issues.[18]

[13] AV Dicey, *Introduction to the Study of the Law of the Constitution* (8th edn, Macmillan 1915) 110.
[14] ibid 110–21.
[15] ibid eg 282.
[16] See ch 4.
[17] Dicey (n 13) 110.
[18] For the classics see Kenneth Culp Davis, *Discretionary Justice: A Preliminary Enquiry* (Baton Rouge: Louisiana State University Press 1969) at 4; Denis J Galligan, *Discretionary Powers* (Clarendon Press 1986) 1, 7.

In sum, as formal overarching constitutional principles, both absolute separation of powers and rule of law fail to provide a full account of the workings of the executive. However, the liberal democratic ethos on which the modern state is based has never divorced itself from these aspirational values. They flourish on the mythic level and are expressed in constitutional structures. Thus, both ideals cannot be removed from the analysis of the executive and its presentation as subservient to law, but they clearly cannot operate as sole theory bases.

2. The Imperial Executive Model

The second model is based on a view of the executive as dominant in both constitutional and political spheres. The title of this section alludes to Arthur Schlesinger's influential study that warned against the rise of presidential dominance in the 1970s;[19] as a general title, this model has developed in three central directions. The first direction offers little for theory. Being entirely US-based, various sources for analysis—the text of the Constitution, original intent, evolving history, natural law, 'historical gloss', and the like have been relied upon by many scholars of the US presidency, including the participants in the 'unitarian government' debate, discussed in Chapter 1. The other two streams, drawing on the key concepts of management and of emergency, are more promising for the development of an imperial executive theory that reaches beyond the US.

a. Managerial Theories

I begin with the direction that may have lost its relative force with the emergence of the emphasis on emergency powers, but is still central to the understanding of the executive as dominant. Under this group of theories, the presidency is first and foremost a CEO-type office. Its holder possesses the task of steering the social and economic spheres by yielding political power, under a constitutional structure that enables such exercise of authority. Under this framework, power is expressed by directing, rather than merely obeying and executing, and executive action alongside and outside the law is constitutionally allowed or at least tolerated. The richest debate in this vein is US-based, but similar views of the executive are shortly alluded to at the end of this section.

Taking the 'president as CEO' image seriously, Tom Lin has recently dedicated an article to a comparison between presidents and corporation CEOs. Careful not to overemphasize similarities, the article still analyzes the ways in which heads of the executive can dominate government, offering unity, accountability, and effectiveness in exchange of the accumulation of power.[20]

[19] Arthur M Schlesinger Jr, *The Imperial Presidency* (Houghton Mifflin 1974).
[20] Tom CW Lin, 'CEOs and Presidents' (2014) 47 UC Davis L Rev 1351.

Unitarian theory, discussed in Chapter 2, celebrates the president's ultimate power over Congress, the states, and the administration. Rather than focus on the management functions of the president, reliance on history, text, original readings, and the like has supported visions of the US executive's dominance over the organization that is the state, and hence, indirectly support a managerial view, but functional analysis is not central to this stream. Similarly, non-textual, functional/political arguments, and notions of 'historical gloss', further support this view, but are not concerned directly with management.

In comparison, the work of Kagan, Lessig, and Sunstein offers accounts of the president as head of the administration, and are closer to the managerial view and in line with functional analysis.[21]

Moving to arguments for dominance beyond law, Posner and Vermeule's work oscillates between the emergency-based strand, discussed below, and the functional-managerial. For Posner and Vermeule, in the complex modern administrative state, there is a general need to delegate powers to the executive as the only branch that can successfully tackle fast-changing realities: 'the legally constrained executive is now a historical curiosity'.[22] Rather than view this state of affairs with alarm, for them this type of executive government 'is best in the thin sense in that there is no feasible way to improve upon it, under the conditions of the administrative state'.[23]

The study of the presidency in political science which offers similar insights of dominance focus on personality and/or structure. The study of the 'personal presidency', implicitly supported a managerial view. Richard Neustadt's *Presidential Power* created a school of thought; for him, the president operates within a constraining constitutional structure, but his dominance derives from his powers of persuasion and bargaining, both powerful tools in the hands of a person with 'an extraordinary temperament' and the right psychological makeup.[24] The flood of studies offering accounts of personal presidencies—some of them, in the eyes of critics, journalistic and conservative—all attest to one implied assumption. Like any successful manager, presidents use all available resources; charisma and other personality traits are more influential than formal authority derived from law.[25]

Alternatively, following a structural vein, Terry Moe argued that presidential action was a process directed by 'structural choices'. Employing rational choice and new-institutionalism theories, he argued (before somewhat changing his mode of analysis), that the president's unique position draws on the constitutional structure,

[21] Lawrence Lessig and Cass R Sunstein, 'The President and the Administration' (1994) 94 Colum L Rev 1; Elena Kagan, 'Presidential Administration' (2001) 114 Harv L Rev 2245.

[22] Eric A Posner and Adrian Vermeule, *The Executive Unbound: After the Madisonian Republic* (OUP 2011) 4 and passim.

[23] ibid 5 and passim.

[24] Richard E Neustadt, *Presidential Power: The Politics of Leadership* (Free Press 1960, 1990).

[25] See ch 1.

which grants him political advantage over congress through ingrained flexibility and discretion. Thus, the president is 'ultimately responsible for day-to-day governance', able to override Congressional preferences and set the tone in the political arena.[26] This type of analysis, and the subsequent studies that combine personality with structure, similarly refer to toolboxes typically available to managers.

The vision of the head of the executive as a strong manager is not unique to the US, nor is it unique to presidential systems. Titles such as 'the British presidency' and 'the presidentialization of politics' in Europe draw on political realities across Western systems, in which heads of executive branches exert political dominance in all public spheres.[27] Although the concept of 'manager' is not explicitly discussed, the discussed dominance of the heads of the executive branch at least implies the adoption of a managerial view.

b. Exception-Based Theories

This strand of research has early roots, but has taken center-stage in recent decades. Here, the nature and extent of executive power derives from its usage in extreme, rather than normal situations. Much of this literature seems to advance an argument that is limited to emergencies, but some scholars go further to devise a general theory of executive action that draws on emergency power. If the executive is the wielder of power in emergencies, and the decision whether such an emergency is in the executive's hands, either under the formal constitution or politically, the office achieves full supremacy in the political arena. Carl Schmitt's theory of the exception, which has received renewed attention in recent years, has become central to many a theory in this group. Most recently, it has been taken up by Posner and Vermeule, who declare that they, and the constitution they are expounding, have adopted 'a Schmittian view'.[28]

Carl Schmitt's statement that '[s]overeign is he who decides on the exception',[29] a realist ruling on the ultimate power in society, has indeed been twinned in the United States with theories of presidential aggrandizement that peaked during George W. Bush's presidency but were circulated long before 9/11. Some of them were critical historical analyses; Arthur Schlesinger's *The Imperial Presidency*, published just before *US v Nixon* and President Nixon's resignation, traced a history

[26] Terry Moe and Scott A Wilson, 'Presidents and the Politics of Structure' (1994) 57 Law Contemp Probs 1, 22.

[27] For the UK see RAW Rhodes, 'Blair and Governance' in Rainer Koch and John Dixon (eds), *Public Governance and Leadership* (DUV 2007) 95, 96. See also Michael Foley, *The British Presidency: Tony Blair and the Politics of Public Leadership* (Manchester University Press 2000); Graham Allen, *The Last Prime Minister: Being Honest About the UK Presidency* (2nd edn, Imprint Academic 2002); Thomas Poguntke and Paul Webb (eds), *The Presidentialization of Politics* (OUP 2005). For Europe see, generally, Gianfranco Pasquino, 'Governments in European Politics' in José M Magone (ed), *Routledge Handbook of European Politics* (Routledge 2015) 295, 306–07.

[28] Posner and Vermeule (n 22) inter alia 32–34.

[29] Carl Schmitt, *Political Theology: Four Chapters on the Concept of Sovereignty* (George Schwab tr, MIT Press 1985) 5.

of the use of war powers by presidents from independence to the Watergate affair, reaching grim conclusions regarding the Nixon debacle, which had nothing to do with an actual emergency.[30] Others have approached the issue comparatively, in general studies of emergency regimes that focus on the role of the head of the executive.[31]

The force of these path-breaking studies has been almost overshadowed by 9/11 and its aftermath. The (in)famous post-9/11 memos, which embedded extra- and contra-legal presidential action during emergencies in a distinct vision of the US constitution, importantly the Commander-in-Chief clause, are but one representation of the emergency-derived aggrandized presidency argument.[32] Posner and Vermeule's managerialist arguments for executive aggrandizement are twinned with a strong insistence that in emergencies, US presidents (or at least, successful ones) have followed what in fact was a 'Schmittian view', setting aside the notions of legality in favour of active problem-solving.

Those who support this growth of power feed on the same sources to which managerialists turn, but supplementary theories have been developed in this context. Reliance on inherent powers has taken different forms, such as Theodore Roosevelt's 'stewardship' theory and the recognition of inherent powers, expressed most clearly in the field of war powers and foreign affairs.[33] *Youngstown Sheet and Tube v Sawyer*, still considered the central decision in the US that addresses the constitutionality of unilateral presidential power, issued no clear rule against unilateral action during emergencies. The existence of relevant statutory bases for action in the *Youngstown* affair rendered the presidential action unlawful, yet dicta that either recognized or denigrated the use of non-statutory powers in other cases have provided rich fodder for subsequent debates.[34]

[30] Schlesinger (n 19). For a reassessment that considers subsequent events, see Andrew Rudalevige, *The New Imperial Presidency: Reviewing Presidential Power after Watergate* (University of Michigan Press 2005).

[31] Clinton Rossiter, *Constitutional Dictatorship: Crisis Government in the Modern Democracies* (Westport: Greenwood Press, 1948); Mary Sieghart, *Government by Decree* (London: Stevens, 1950).

[32] For an overview, see Jonathan Canfield, 'The Torture Memos: The Conflict between a Shift in U.S. Policy towards a Condemnation of Human Rights and International Prohibitions against the Use of Torture' (2005) 33 Hofstra L Rev 1049 at 1050–55. For a compilation of released memos and other documents concerning post 9/11 government measures, see ACLU, *The Torture Database* <https://www.thetorturedatabase.org/search/apachesolr_search>. See also John Yoo, *The Powers of War and Peace: The Constitution and Foreign Affairs After 9/11* (University of Chicago Press 2005); John Yoo, *Crisis and Command* (Kaplan 2009).

[33] On the 'stewardship' theory, see Theodore Roosevelt, *An Autobiography* (Macmillan 1914) 372 ('My view was that every executive officer, and above all every executive officer in high position, was a steward of the people bound actively and affirmatively to do all he could for the people, and not to content himself with the negative merit of keeping his talents undamaged in a napkin. I declined to adopt the view that what was imperatively necessary for the Nation could not be done by the President unless he could find some specific authorization to do it. My belief was that it was not only his right but his duty to do anything that the needs of the Nation demanded unless such action was forbidden by the Constitution or by the laws.') Justice Sutherland's recognition of the President's inherent powers focused on war in addition to foreign affairs. See *US v Curtiss-Wright*, 299 US 304, 318 (1936).

[34] *Youngstown Sheet and Tube v Sawyer*, 343 US 579, 637 (1952). The case involved a challenge against a Presidential Executive Order to seize a steel factory during the Korean War, after a strike that

Moving to political reality, heads of the executive branch have developed practices that lack direct links with statute or the constitution. In the US, some of these defied the Constitution's allocation of powers between government branches, but were not found invalid at the time of their invocation. President Lincoln's measures during the Civil War, including the suspension of the *habeas corpus*, were validated post factum by Congress and courts;[35] challenges to the constitutionality of executive agreements with foreign states that bypass the constitutionally-required advice and consent of the Senate for the making of treaties, have not fared well in the Supreme Court;[36] applications concerned with repeated cases of engaging the nation in war without obtaining Congressional consent as required by law were likewise rejected, usually not even reaching the Supreme Court, or rejected as non-justiciable.[37]

And there is more: the concept of the emergency is a key element for the understanding of Western polities. Much has been written about the US government's deeply rooted dedication to, if not obsession with, emergencies, high and low, as bases for their aggrandizement.[38] Posner and Vermeule's thesis is closely

effectively shut down the factory. The majority of justices did rule that the seizure was unlawful, since legislation in force granted powers to confront industrial action. Alongside the two justices who rejected all non-statutory emergency power, the other three justices on the majority were ready to accept circumstances in which presidents could invoke powers that extended beyond the existing legislation, effectively joining the three minority judges. Justice Clark, for example, asserted that 'the Constitution does grant the President extensive authority in times of grave danger and imperative national emergency ... In describing this authority I care not whether one calls it "residual," "inherent," "moral," "implied," "aggregate," "emergency" or otherwise' (ibid at 661). The case cannot thus be cited as proscribing invocation of such powers, notwithstanding substantive differences between the judges who were ready to uphold non-statutory emergency powers. On the decision see eg Edward S Corwin, 'The Steel Seizure Case: A Judicial Brick without Straw' (1953) 53 Colum L Rev 53; Michael Paulsen, 'Youngstown at Fifty: A Symposium' (2002) 19 Const Commentary 1.

35 See eg David P Currie, 'The Civil War Congress' (2006) 73 U Chicago L Rev 1131; Andrew Kent, 'The Constitution and the Laws of War during the Civil War' (2010) 85 Notre Dame L Rev 1839 (focusing on Congress and on the courts, respectively).

36 The term 'executive agreement' encompasses three types of transnational agreements: agreements made by the president under statutory authorization; agreements authorized by both Houses of Congress after signature; and purely sole agreements, made by the president in the absence of any congressional participation. For analysis see, eg Oona A Hathaway, 'Presidential Power over International Law: Restoring the Balance' (2008) 119 Yale LJ 140, at 144 n 4. Decisions that upheld executive agreements include *US v Belmont,* 301 US 324 (1937); *US v Pink*, 315 US 203 (1942); *Dames and Moore v Regan*, 453 US 654 (1984).

37 For decisions on challenges to the legality of the Vietnam War see *Berk v Laird*, 317 F Supp 715 (NY DC 1970); *Orlando v Laird*, 443 F 2d 1039 (2d Circuit, 1971); *Massachusetts v Laird*, 451 F (2d) 26 (1st Circuit, 1971) (all three addressed the arguments but rejected the applications under the question doctrine). Later applications concerned with other uses of military force were summarily rejected under this doctrine; see, eg *Crockett v Reagan*, 720 F (2d) 1355 (CA DC 1983) (cert den); *Sanchez-Espinoza v Reagan*, 770 F (2d) 202 (CA DC 1985); *Lowry v Reagan*, 676 F Supp 333 (DDC 1987); *Ange v Bush*, 752 F Supp 509 (DDC 1990); *Doe v Bush*, 323 F (3d) 133 (1st Circ 2003) (the latter decided on ripeness).

38 See eg Jules Lobel, 'Emergency Power and the Decline of Liberalism' (1989) 98 Yale LJ 1385 at 1400 n 68; Oren Gross, 'Chaos and Rules: Should Responses to Violent Crises Always be Constitutional?' (2003) 112 Yale LJ 1011; Kim Lane Scheppele, 'Law in Time of Emergencies: States of Exception and the Temptation of 9/11' (2004) 6 U Pa J Const L 1001. See further text below at nn 44–49.

linked: relying on presidential action in two emergency-type situations, they supplement the extensively-discussed war on terror with references to the 2008 financial crash, arguing for a well-established practice of presidential self-aggrandizement despite of, or in the face of, law and its formal constraints.

Schmitt, Schlesinger, John Yoo, and other participants in this branch of the debate may have focused on emergency needs, either as basis for their descriptive analyses or to enhance a normative argument for either self-containment of power (as per Schlesinger) or presidential aggrandizement (as per Yoo), but these are more than mere theories of the exception. As Schmitt recognized, power held in one type of contingency turns to potential power retained in other contingencies. As such, this strand of argument can support presidential strength that extends beyond emergencies. Steering reaches a new dimension, whether dangerous, welcome, or structurally unavoidable.

How, then, should both groups of arguments for a dominant executive be assessed? Most managerial/exception models were developed under a generally diluted commitment to legality, the linchpin of constitutionality; at their extreme, law as such is not necessarily instrumental. For Posner and Vermeule, the executive, at least in the US, is 'subject to legal constraints that are shaky in normal times and weak or nonexistent in times of crisis', due to both delegation and exigencies. The unavoidable power of the executive, which is essentially divorced from law, offers, in their view, the best version of modern governance, at least when twinned with the political checks they consider sufficient to ensure no extreme abuse of powers.[39]

Criticism of this stance is relevant both on empirical and normative grounds, but this article is concerned with the former. Empirically, it would be grossly incorrect to underestimate the role of legalism in the US. As Richard Pildes argues, law serves as a forceful player in the very system these authors attempt to redefine as one that rejects its pull.[40] Managerialists and exception-based theorists are, however, correct in their descriptive analyses of executive dominance. Indeed, despite the normative calls for self-containment and for the constitutionalization of emergencies and their subjection to robust checks, politics and history repeatedly brings such visions of power to the fore; their rejection is futile. What is needed, then, is a way to accommodate both models.

[39] Posner and Vermeule (n 22) 4 and *passim*.

[40] Richard H Pildes, 'Law and the President' (2012) 125 Harv L Rev 1381. Support of this argument can be found, for example, in analyses of the 'regulatory style' of the US, defined as 'adversarial legalist'. See Robert A Kagan, *Adversarial Legalism: The American Way of Law* (Harvard University Press 2003). On the normative level, the vision of 'the executive as manager', either as CEO or actor-in-the-last-resort, is as problematic as the 'executive as executor' model, but for entirely different reasons. As long as it is divorced from, or only loosely attached to, the concepts of legality and the rule of law, its legitimacy is highly questionable. All modern Western constitutions, even in their 'thinnest' varieties, retain a link with legality. In sum, an argument that cancels the force of this value, in the context of the democratic liberal sphere, is a gross misrepresentation of Western political cultures. For a forceful argument in this vein see David Dyzenhaus, *The Constitution of Law: Legality in a Time of Emergency* (CUP 2006).

3. The 'Bipolar' Model

Rather than wed subservience with dominance, the third model is based on a distinction between two political and legal climates—normality and emergency. Under this model, the executive is indeed relatively subservient in some fields, but in others, his power is no less than imperial. These attempts at retaining the distinction between the exceptional and the mundane wish to settle the puzzle by carving out distinct territories for each of the competing visions of the executive. This model fails as well, and not only due to the impossibility of distinguishing between those climates in today's polities (if it ever could have been upheld).

In *Taming the Prince*, Harvey Mansfield addresses early political philosophers' theories of the executive. His focus on theorists from Aristotle to the Federalists is preceded by an introduction that offers a distinct modern vision of the office. For Mansfield, executives operate in an either/or method, moving from subservience to dominance according to exigencies:

> The ambivalence of the executive ... must be understood less as embodying two rival, contrary conceptions than as the same thing in two phases or aspects ... an ideal executive ... would combine in himself the ambivalence inherent in the office, ducking out of sight and leaping into view when necessary and appropriate.[41]

This distinction between two modes of action is shared by at least two groups of theorists. First are those who study the areas of action in which the executive is prone to be imperial, namely national security and foreign affairs. In this context, setting the contours of powers is aided by distinguishing between those areas and more mundane ones. Hence, for example, Louis Koenig's argument for a 'two-track system', set entirely within his analysis of the role of the president in foreign policy, and Theodore Lowi's subsequent distinction between 'fast' and 'slow' tracks of action.[42] Lowi's analysis, which is already more general, leads us to a second group of theorists, who join Mansfield to identify duality as a feature of executive action at large. Thus, in Dennis Mueller's words, '[t]he president has considerable latitude when it comes to committing the nation to war and foreign affairs, but he can implement his domestic program only with the concurrence of both houses of Congress'.[43]

[41] Harvey C Mansfield Jr, *Taming the Prince: The Ambivalence of Modern Executive Power* (Johns Hopkins University Press 1989) 15.

[42] Louis W Koenig, 'The Modern Presidency and the Constitution' in Martin Fausold and Alan Shank (eds), *The Constitution and the American Presidency* (State University of New York Press 1991) 171, 191–93; Theodore J Lowi, 'Afterword: Presidential Power and the Ideological Struggle Over Its Interpretation' ibid 227, 236–37.

[43] Dennis C Mueller, *Constitutional Democracy* (OUP 1996) 235.

The main weakness of the bipolar model is its implied assumption that two modes of reality essentially exist. Under this model, in any given instance, the executive either 'ducks' or 'leaps'. 'Leaping' is likely to occur in exceptional cases, while 'ducking' should be viewed as the normal state of affairs. Here, then, is another example of binary thinking. Yet, exemplifying the futility of bifurcation, this clear distinction between normality and exception or emergency is untenable.

Of course, some periods can be identified as pure emergency times, and full normality should not be ruled out. Yet the literature on the seepage of emergency into normalcy is especially useful here. In his analysis of the Cold War, Schlesinger argued that at least part of both sides' actions were fed by 'delusions of crisis'. The argument that 'there's no such thing as normal times anymore', made during a Senate hearing in 1973,[44] has been supported, *inter alia*, in Jules Lobel's treatment of the proper constitutional and legal treatment of such powers. Writing in the wake of the Iran-Contra affair, Lobel topped his analysis with an argument that a vision of normality was not part of the American psyche nor of its policies, and his insights have clearly not lost their force since.[45]

Indeed, as Kim Lane Scheppele argues,

> the 'normal' American constitutional order can be seen as thoroughly shot through with emergency law ... America has not in general had a toggle-switch approach to crises, where normal constitutionalism continues until a switch is flipped to stop it, and then the emergency continues until the switch is flipped back.[46]

Further developing this argument, Posner and Vermeule's administrative state is beset with situations that may have earlier been considered as divine punishment or unfortunate supernatural events beyond human control, and have been embraced by the administrative state, to be resolved as best possible. They further argue that the very pace of modern life constantly creates situations that lie on a continuum of events rather than on belonging either to 'peacetime' or 'emergency'.[47]

These cultural and legal tendencies are global. Nicole Questiaux's comparative analysis of the recurring pattern in many democracies to retain emergency executive powers long after, and well beyond, the requirements of a specific

[44] Hearings Before the Senate Special Committee on the Termination of the National Emergency, 93rd Cong, 1st Sess 83 (testimony of Professor G Casper), cited in Lobel (n 38) 1400 n 68.

[45] Lobel (n 38) 1402, 1403 [footnote omitted]. See also Jules Lobel, 'The War on Terrorism and Civil Liberties' (2001) 63 U Pitt L Rev 767 at 770–78 (linking twentieth century history with the current war on terrorism).

[46] Scheppele (n 38) 836, 839.

[47] Posner and Vermeule (n 22) 31–32.

exigency,[48] is supported by Oren Gross and Fionnuala Ní Aoláin's more recent work on emergency periods. On the temporal level, emergency periods worldwide tend to be extended, and powers originally devised to answer exigencies fulfill more mundane government needs. Spatial distinctions between special anomalous zones and controlling territories are broken down, since boundaries are permeable. The distinction between domestic and foreign affairs often fails, leading to a blurring of interests in the era of globalization and interdependence. The separation between 'us' and 'them', justifying distinct treatment of each group, is mainly analysed as dangerous, but can also be viewed as difficult to maintain in a mixed society. Hence, the exception is normalized through entrenchment in time and in institutional structures, supported by a growing acceptance of this process of normalization.[49]

Under such realities, then, the assumption that the executive acts in a bipolar fashion is indefensible. Even under the assumption that the original distinction was originally tenable—an assumption I question, as many constitutions were created in times of crisis—the rise of emergency-based discourse and its seepage into so-called normality render this model unworkable.

C. The Internal Tension Model

In Chapter 2, I have argued that internal tensions are endemic to public law. Recognition of the tension between the necessity of polities to grant power and their need to constrain power in order to avoid its abuse is key to the understanding of public law, and, in the context of this book, to the understanding of the ways executives operate in the modern state. Neither complete submission to the legislature nor imperialism fully characterizes the executive. In the absence of a clear distinction between normality and emergency, it would also be futile to press bi-polar theories on the executive. Yet none of these conclusions should be viewed as a failure of theory. On the contrary: both subservience and dominance of the executive prosper in reality just as much as they are backed by the basic ideals of modern Western democracy.

The multifaceted executive is well recognized in the literature. Writing about the US Constitution, Edward Corwin opined in 1940 that

> … the Constitution reflects the struggle between two conceptions of the executive power: the conception that it ought always be subordinate to the supreme

[48] See eg Nicole Questiaux, *Study of the Implications for Human Rights of Recent Developments Concerning Situations Known as States of Siege or Emergency*, UN ESCOR, 35th Sess, Agenda Item 10, UN Doc E/CN.4/Sub.2/1982/15 (1982).

[49] Oren Gross and Fionnuala Ní Aoláin, *Law in Times of Crisis: Emergency Powers in Theory and Practice* (CUP 2006) 171–243; Gross (n 38) 1069–96.

> legislative power, and the conception that it ought to be, within generous limits, autonomous and self-directing; or, in other terms, the idea that the people are *represented* in the Legislature *versus* the idea that they are *embodied* in the executive. Nor has this struggle ever entirely ceased, although on the whole it is the latter theory which has triumphed. To repeat what was said in an earlier page, "Taken by and large, the history of the Presidency has been a history of aggrandizement."[50]

Corwin's reference to 'a history of aggrandizement' was addressed in Chapter 2. The emphasis here is on the interplay between two visions of the office, recognized by others as well[51]—and easily applied beyond the confines of the US constitutional framework.

Indeed, the rich literature that identifies 'paradoxes' and 'puzzles', deriving from competing visions of the executive, supports the adoption of such a model. The clash between the president as tyrant and the president as clerk, between overseer and decider, the paradoxes ingrained in the office, discussed earlier,[52] provides in fact the basis for a better understanding of the executive branch.

Thus, in the context of the theory of the executive, Mansfield's notion of ambivalence minus his claim for bipolar reality, supplemented by theories of pluralized construction and unresolved tensions, support a model that emphasizes the multidimensional nature of this institution. The tension between legality on the one side and political and social realities on the other side cannot be settled in favour of one of these social interests. Arguably, in some instances, executives fully obey detailed, constraining statutes (hence, are fully subservient to law) or act in blatant contravention of the law (thereby dominating the legal and political spheres). However, more often than not, the executive, entrusted with the role of management of the polity under law, operates as both an 'executor' of law, under its commitment to the rule of law and subject to the political ideal of separation of powers, and as an 'executive', or CEO, entrusted with steering the state in sickness and in health.

[50] Edward S Corwin, *The President, Office and Powers* (NYU Press 1940) 310.

[51] Consider Peter Strauss's observation that while many administrative rules, issued by administrative agencies, 'speak the usual mix of scientific and legal justification for "expert" action ... [and] scarcely allude to the President's participation', the public sees 'actions that are openly political and explicitly presidential'. In the spirit of the 'constitutional puzzle' literature discussed above, Strauss argues that the Constitution does not resolve the tension between the president as tyrant and the president as clerk. Strauss then moves to a normative argument against excessive presidential intervention in agency action; I remain with his observation of the existence of two concurrent and opposing visions of presidential action, and use it as a basis for a general model. Peter Strauss, *Presidential Rulemaking* (1997) 72 Chi-Kent L Rev 965, 966–67, 979–80. See also Thomas E Cronin and Michael A Genovese, *The Paradoxes of the American Presidency* (OUP 1998); Saikrishna Bangalore Prakash, 'Imperial and Imperiled: The Curious State of the Executive' (2009) 50 Wm & Mary L Rev 1021; Peter L Strauss, '"Overseer", or "The Decider"? The President in Administrative Law' (2007) 75 Geo Wash L Rev 696.

[52] See ch 1.

D. Concluding Remarks

Public law theory often leans towards the normative. Important as this direction is, analyses concerned with the executive branch tend to confuse the descriptive with the normative; participants tend to buttress their normative stance by offering historical and textual proof that lean precariously towards their arguments. Hence, the emerging descripto-normative studies in this field tend to be flat; they are insufficiently supported by a general explanatory model of the executive that extends beyond the methodologies of particular histories and texts.

This chapter opts for the development of a representational, depictive model that can be employed as an investigative tool in further studies of the executive branch. Discussions of the nature and powers of the executive branch tend to be held in the constitutional law sphere. This focus is too narrow, as it ignores the ways legislation and executive practice shape and legitimate executive action in novel ways that rely on the constitution only tenuously.

In the field of public law theory, then, I reject hierarchical and binary thinking in favor of multidimensionality. Opting for this general focus on the descriptive, I argue that models which recognize complexity, in law and elsewhere, better represent complex realities. The recognition of the internal tensions besetting constitutionalism, well-identified in some research fields such as judicial review and decision-making, is yet to be further developed in studies of the executive branch. Tracing the main research directions, I have reached a theory of the executive that is better-tuned with political and social realities, setting the ground for optimal designs of constitutional structures.

How can this interplay be sustained without it slipping into abuse and unlawfulness? In the next chapter, I submit that the law offers executives a variety of ways to act both under and beyond law, while remaining within the sphere of legality. Under the rule of law ideal, in any of its forms, law should be fixed, predictable, and accessible. In our context, public law should both define and delineate the ways executives are authorized to act, and offer those who are subject to the law the ability to be prospectively aware of the rules that govern a field of action. Yet, commonly, public law does not offer definitive accounts of executive powers. This feature is not merely an unavoidable outcome of the indeterminacy of text. Public law is often designed, interpreted, and implemented in ways that maintain the tension between legality in its narrow sense and necessity, or political expediency, in their broader sense.

A final note on the descriptive/normative aspects of this model. The internal tension model offered here is descriptive rather than normative. A move to the normative should join the debate between those who celebrate unfettered administrative action and those alarmed by the aggrandizement of the executive branch. A promising direction in my view is the recognition that internal tensions, leading to action in the shadow of the law, are inevitable as much as they are constitutionally problematic, and that all forms of review of executive action should therefore be augmented. In the context of judicial review, the still existing arguments against judicial check due to its so-called supremacy, based on the very type of hierarchical thinking rejected in this book, should be set aside in favour of visions of judicial review as promoting deliberation and participation. This aspect is discussed in the last chapter of this book.

3

Maintaining the Internal Tension Model

A. Introduction 59

B. Conceptualizing Fuzziness I: Research Streams 60

1. Four Research Streams 60
   a. Delegation and discretion 60
   b. 'Soft law' 62
   c. 'Grey holes' 64
   d. 'Fuzzy law' 66
2. Moving Forward 68

C. Conceptualizing Fuzziness II: Thirteen Forms of Fuzziness 69

1. Fuzzy Legality: A Taxonomy 69
2. Constitution-Generated Fuzzy Legality 71
   a. Open-ended constitutional provisions 72
   b. Fuzzy powers under an unwritten constitution 73
   c. Non-textual, general constitutional doctrines 75
3. Statute-Generated Fuzzy Legality 78
   a. Open-ended, interpretable provisions 79
   b. Grants of discretion 80
   c. Delegation 82
   d. 'Patchwork' legislation 85
   e. Multiple and indeterminate decision-makers 86
   f. 'Lopsided' statute 89
4. Executive-Generated Fuzzy Legality 91
   a. Selective enforcement and creative compliance 91
   b. 'Pastiche' law 92
   c. Extra-statutory parallel arrangements 93
   d. Multiple mixed source citation 94

D. Concluding Remarks 97

A. Introduction

This chapter is dedicated to an overview of the ways the internal tension model operates to empower the executive branch, simultaneously under law and beyond its confines. It offers an answer to the questions of how can the internal tension between the need to grant power and the need to constrain it, discussed in the previous chapters, be maintained without tipping the scales towards one of them? How can executives act relatively unfettered while remaining within the zone of legality? The 'fuzzy law' image proffer an initial answer, by pointing at practices under which an authorizing rule may present a façade of legality that derives from its binding formal status, while its content or application offer broad options for action (and possible abuse) which conceals a reality of a-legality.

A Theory of the Executive Branch. Margit Cohn, Oxford University Press (2021). © Margit Cohn.
DOI: 10.1093/oso/9780198821984.003.0004

Beyond general and philosophical studies of the indeterminacy of law,[1] the scholarship in this context has been conducted under four parallel paths. The first emerged from administrative law scholarship, and focuses on delegation and discretion; the second is concerned with so-called 'soft law', originally discussed by international lawyers, but now seeping into analyses of domestic law; a third direction relies on the term 'fuzzy law', which was originally conceived in the context of the study of regulation; finally, the concept of 'grey holes', an analytical tool conceived in studies of law during emergencies, likewise points out indeterminacy under law. In this chapter, I trace the development of these distinct bodies of research, which have yet to be integrated, and organize these concepts under a shared template.

The second part of the chapter is dedicated to an analysis of the *types* of such soft/fuzzy/grey legal constructs, organized according to the identity of their generators—the constitution, the legislature, and the executive. The resulting taxonomy of thirteen different forms of fuzziness offers a basis for the next part of this book, dedicated to case-studies of several such soft/fuzzy/grey measures.

The analysis is based on the assumption that fuzzy law, as such, operates under a shadow. Inevitable and ubiquitous it may be, as much of this book shows, but its pervasive presence in public law should not lead to acceptance or celebration. As Chapter 9 elaborates, reliance on fuzzy law stands in direct contradiction to the rule of law and to all other ideational bases that support the exercise of state power under the liberal-democratic ethos.

B. Conceptualizing Fuzziness I: Research Streams

1. Four Research Streams

The idea that law is indeterminate has attracted much attention in public law scholarship in different contexts and sub-disciplines. The following overview of four research streams is chronologically arranged; to date, very little interaction between these streams can be found.

a. Delegation and discretion

'Delegation' and 'discretion' are often discussed conjointly in the literature. Professor Davis's book, *Discretionary Justice*, includes a chapter on 'the rule of law and the non-delegation doctrine', and others follow the same pattern.[2] Yet these are

[1] See HLA Hart, *The Concept of Law* (Clarendon Press 1961) 121–32; Timothy Endicott, *Vagueness in Law* (OUP 2000).

[2] Kenneth Culp Davis, *Discretionary Justice: A Preliminary Inquiry* (Louisiana State University Press 1969) 27–51. See also, eg, Denis J Galligan, *Discretionary Powers: A Legal Study of Official Discretion* (Clarendon Press 1997); David Epstein and Sharyn O'Halloran, *Delegating Powers: A Transaction Cost*

in fact two separate features of statutory arrangements, which are further discussed below. Suffice here to note the centrality of this stream in both constitutional and administrative law.

Indeed, the study of discretion is not a recent phenomenon. More than a hundred years ago, Albert Kocourek, a Northwestern University professor of jurisprudence, noted that discretion was 'a standing and permanent characteristic of the law, and one of the great levers of legal evolution', and provided the oft-considered explanation that '[s]ome sequences of fact are so complicated ... that the legal rules to govern such cases must unavoidably be stated in terms of discretion'.[3] Definitions of this legal construct can also be found in more recent studies, now classic, as in Kenneth Culp Davis' definition of discretion, equating it with limits set on a public officer's power which 'leave him free to make a choice among possible courses of action or inaction'.[4] Denis Galligan's equally influential *Discretionary Powers* similarly addressed discretion as 'the making of decisions in the absence of previously fixed, relatively clear, and binding legal standards', 'the authority to choose amongst alternative causes of action' and, for him, 'perhaps unfortunately ... autonomy in judgment and decision'.[5] Delegation, on the other hand, is a feature under which a statute-based grant of authority to act or to make rules, originally granted to an officer or administrative body, is transferred, under the authorizing statute or on the basis of established doctrine, to a second actor, often institutionally subordinate to the original bearer of authority, but not necessarily so.

These exercises in definition have served to support different research directions, ranging from the empirical (quantitative analyses of *de facto* grants of discretion and delegations),[6] through the structural/political (analyses of the politics of the interaction between government branches),[7] to the normative (essentially, arguments that excessive discretion and delegation endanger proper modes of rule-making and their *de facto* application).[8] Most of these consider the workings

Politics Approach to Policy Making under Separate Powers (CUP 1999); John D Huber and Charles R Shipan, *Deliberate Discretion? The Institutional Foundations of Bureaucratic Autonomy* (CUP 2002).

3 Albert Kocourek, 'Formal Relation between Law and Discretion' (1914) 9 Ill L Rev 225. See also Ernst Freund, 'The Substitution of Discretion with Rule in Public Law' (1915) Am Poli Sci Rev 666.

4 Davis (n 2) 4.

5 Galligan (n 2) 1, 7, 8.

6 Epstein and O'Halloran (n 2) 86–239; Huber and Shipan (n 2).

7 For the rich body of research that analyses the ways in which government branches interact, with special focus on the retention of control by the legislature despite the statutory grant of discretion and delegation, see eg Epstein and O'Halloran (n 6) 1–86; Mathew D McCubbins, Roger Noll, and Barry Weingast 'Administrative Procedures as Instruments of Political Control' (1987) 3 J Law, Econ and Org 243; D Roderick Kiewiet and Mathew D McCubbins, *The Logic of Delegation* (Chicago UP 1991) esp ch 7; Kathleen Bawn 'Political Control Versus Expertise: Congressional Choices about Administrative Procedures,' (1995) 89(3) APSR 62.

8 See Davis (n 2); Theodore J Lowi, *The End of Liberalism: The Second Republic of the United States* (2nd edn, WW Norton 1979) (presenting his 'abdication' thesis, under which, by inserting such provisions in statutes, Congress abdicates its constitutional role of lawmaking, granting excessive, virtually unchecked, policy-making powers to unelected administrators); Philip Hamburger, *Is Administrative*

of state powers, rather than focusing on the executive as such.[9] The link to the assessment of executive powers under a template of open-endedness is often only implied, but is, however, obvious. The greater the discretion granted, the greater freedom of choice offered to state actors, and the more indeterminate will the law be, still under the aegis of legality. Likewise, each grant of authority to delegate contains a kernel of indeterminacy, but of a different kind; if determinacy denotes, inter alia, the ability of those subject to the law to understand future use of an authorization and to plan ahead accordingly, the very option of dispersion of power fuzzies-up notions of constancy and consistency, challenging reliance on past practices as determinants of future use of authority. Hence my inclusion of discretion and delegation as two forms of fuzzy legality, discussed below.[10]

b. 'Soft law'

The term 'soft law' is sometimes credited to Lord McNair, the British legal scholar who served as judge in the International Court of Justice and was the first president of the European Court of Human Rights.[11] Indeed, the term originally emerged in the context of international law. Richly researched as much as the previous constructs, soft law is classically defined as a written but not formally binding rule. It is either a stand-alone measure or an add-on to formal law as an interpretation or complementary rule, which operates as a strong advisory rule that signals the importance of compliance and impacts on participation in and the behaviour of transnational groups. In Dinah Shelton's work on 'soft law', offered in the context of international law, the term is used 'as a synonym for normative statements contained in instruments that are not legally-binding'; her definition refers to

> … any written international instrument, other than a treaty, containing principles, norms, standards, or other statements of expected behavior. Soft law 'expresses a preference and not an obligation that states should act, or should refrain from acting, in a specified manner'.[12]

Law Unlawful? (University of Chicago Press 2014) esp 473–75 (attacking the modern administrative state characterized as acting under grants of discretion. See further ch 1).

[9] The exception being Hamburger's work (n 8), discussed in detail in ch 1.

[10] See sections C.3.b and C.3.c below.

[11] See discussion in Jean d'Aspremont, 'Softness in International Law: A Self-Serving Quest for New Legal Materials' (2008) 19 Eur J Int'l Law 1075, 1081.

[12] Dinah Shelton, 'Soft Law' in David Armstrong (ed), *Routledge Handbook of International Law* (Routledge 2009) 68, 69. For references to 'soft' international law as indeterminate see also eg Kenneth W Abbott and Duncan Snidal, 'Hard and Soft Law in International Governance' (2000) 54 Int'l Org 421, 422 (identifying three dimensions within the realm of soft law: obligation, precision, and delegation); Andrew T Guzman and Timothy Meyer, 'International Soft Law' (2010) 2 J Leg Analysis 171, 174 (viewed as a broad array of arrangements organized as 'a continuum, or spectrum, running between fully binding treaties and fully political positions').

For some, soft law also applies to vague binding rules. In Shelton's words, the term is sometimes used 'to refer to weak or indeterminant provisions of a binding treaty'.[13] However, the transplantation of the term to analyze binding, albeit open-ended domestic law may obfuscate the understanding of the nature of rules. In comparison to a consensually-based arrangement, an indeterminate provision in a binding arrangement exemplifies an entirely different feature of law, one that is discussed here as 'fuzzy'. Reliance on a rule that is formally binding, if vague, raises entirely different concerns from those arising in the exercise or implementation of a rule that is formally based on consensus and on shared understandings of proper behaviour. The difference may be formal—consent-based frameworks may be more religiously followed than edicts backed by statute—but questions regarding the legitimacy of a rule and the sanctions for its infraction are addressed, and resolved, under different frameworks and sets of principles.

Beyond its application in international law, the term has sometimes been used in the context of domestic, rather than international law. In *Soft Law and Public Authorities*, Greg Weeks adopts the term in the context of regulation, and also conflates between non-binding 'tertiary' rules, a true example of soft law, with discretion/delegation, features found in many statutes—again, types of ambiguity that are distinct from the former type of rule.[14]

Neither of these expanded applications of 'soft law' are categorically incorrect; however, the mix of uses may be one explanation for the laments voiced by some commentators who found the term confusing and unhelpful.[15] In this book, the term 'soft law' is discarded. I am concerned with measures that are formal 'law', or derive from such rules, be they statute-based or constitution-based, yet are open-ended enough to enhance executive power and set few constraints on its exercise. Rules that are semi-formal and binding by consensus only, or presented as binding without the imprimatur of a supporting statute (as in the case of guidance, for example) may have great impact on the public spheres, both transnational and national, but they should not be confused with fuzzy law.

A second reason for the removal of the term is that soft law may be fuzzy in terms of its origin and status, but need not be fuzzy in its content. Consensually-made rules may be highly detailed and religiously followed, two features that can be missing in fuzzy arrangements.

Finally, the retention of the distinction between 'fuzzy' formally-made rules and 'soft' rules that are not formally binding is important. A reference to 'the rule of law' would be in place here. The binding force of formal rules arises from their democratic legitimacy; made by legislatures or under their edicts, authorizations to

[13] Shelton (n 12) 69.

[14] Greg Weeks, *Soft Law and Public Authorities: Remedies and Reform* (Hart 2016).

[15] See eg CM Chinkin, 'The Challenge of Soft Law: Development and Change in International Law' (1989) 38 ICLQ 850, 850 (due to the variety of forms, the term is a 'misleading simplification); László Blutman, 'In the Trap of a Legal Metaphor: International Soft Law' (2010) 59 ICLQ 605.

direct and constrain individuals' action, paired with enforcement powers, are supported by popular will. The inability of individuals to plan their action according to these rules and to foresee the consequences of their choice of action, which are essential features of fuzziness, constitute serious challenges to the legitimacy of these rules, based on the required balance between state power and personal autonomy. On the formal level, soft, directly unenforceable rules present an entirely different challenge, even when they are generally followed.

Before fully rejecting the term, a caveat is still in place. Fuzziness that emerges from an unwritten constitution, as in the case of the UK's recognition of the royal prerogative as a source of executive power, could fall under the definition of 'soft law': it is considered binding despite the absence of a formal backing.[16] This type of fuzziness could indeed be reclassified. For the sake of consistency, nevertheless, I retain the term discussed in this book; this type of indeterminacy is not functionally different from other constitution-derived types of fuzziness.

c. 'Grey holes'

Analysis under this term shares one important feature found in two of the three other frameworks discussed here, that of 'imperfect legality'. Originally conceived in 2006 in the context of human rights and emergency law, David Dyzenhaus identified a pattern under which formal legal frameworks conceal the absence of substantive limitation of the executive under a façade of legality, and distinguished it from earlier discussions of 'black holes', found when action lies completely beyond the reach of law.[17] Subsequent writing, especially Posner and Vermeule's, picked up this term as useful for their analysis of the powers of the US president. As in the case of the analysis of soft law, no attention to the types of such holes exists. The work is normative in nature; Dyzenhaus's warnings about the dangers of the proliferation of grey holes is challenged by Posner and Vermeule's supportive arguments that mitigate, or even eradicate, the dangers inherent to reliance on 'grey holes'.

The metaphor of the hole first appeared in discussions of the total absence of law found in certain aspects of the twenty-first century 'war on terrorism', in the context of the US military Guantánamo Bay base. Originally a military zone, the base was used in the 1990s as a refugee processing centre, and later became the infamous facility housing suspected terrorists, under a legal regime that attracted much attention in the public sphere and in courts. Considering the absence of 'regular' law in the camp, Gerald Neuman found the centre an example of an 'anomalous zone', in which fundamental legal norms are suspended.[18] The term 'black hole' entered the scene later, in the Court of Appeal's *Abbasi* decision (2002). Here, Lord Phillips

[16] See below and ch 4.

[17] David Dyzenhaus, *The Constitution of Law: Legality in a Time of Emergency* (CUP 2006); See also David Dyzenhaus, '*Schmitt v. Dicey*: Are States of Emergency Inside or Outside the Legal Order?' (2006) 27 Cardozo L Rev 2005, 2018.

[18] Gerald L Neuman, 'Anomalous Zones' (1996) 48 Stan L Rev 1197.

cited the term twice, first citing the term used by the applicants in the hearings, then concluding that the applicant was indeed being 'arbitrarily detained' in a 'legal black-hole'.[19] The term was later adopted by Lord Steyn,[20] and formed the basis for Dyzenhaus's study of legality in times of emergency.

'Grey holes', as defined in Dyzenhaus's work, appear in statutes when the statute carries 'the façade or form of the rule of law' but grants no 'substantive protection'.[21] As examples, Dyzenhaus discusses detention regimes designed under statute that appear to grant detainees procedural rights that are, in fact, insufficient to effectively contest the detention—hence the designation of the statute as providing a mere façade of legality.[22] And, 'since such grey holes permit government to have its cake and eat it too, to seem to be governing not only by law but in accordance with the rule of law, they and their endorsement by judges and academics might be even more dangerous from the perspective of the substantive conception of the rule of law than true black holes'.[23] Much of Dyzenhaus's concern revolves around the threat of such 'holes' to the wellbeing of the rule of law, a concept further discussed in Chapter 9. To allay this threat, Dyzenhaus continues, judicial review should not be 'half-hearted' (at best), as is often the case; courts should strive to minimize the breadth of grey holes, if not to obliterate them, in the spirit of ensuring the protection of individuals and the substantive rule of law.[24]

Dyzenhaus's analysis of both types of holes focuses on the availability and depth of judicial review, a stance embedded in the common-law tradition that underlies his work. My book is concerned with grey holes as sources of power, rather than on holes created by the removal of judicial powers that check and constrain the executive, partially or completely. Still, and despite the different foci, Dyzenhaus's image of the 'hole' as a source of power comprises the basis for the development of my model of the executive.

Adopting Dyzenhaus's conceptual framework, *The Executive Unbound* moves from Dyzenhaus's focus on emergency powers and his reliance on substantive rule-of-law values as the directing force for redesigning the dynamics between law, the executive, and the judiciary. Instead, the authors offer an analysis that spans run-of-the-mill administrative law, under a functional argument about the inevitability and possible utility of maintaining grey holes.[25] For them, too, grey holes are found

[19] *R (Abbasi) v Secretary of State for Foreign Affairs* [2002] EWCA Civ 1598, [2003] UKHRR 76, paras 22, 64. On the decision see Dyzenhaus (n 17) 166–70. On the regime see Fleur Johns, *Non-Legality in International Law: Unruly Law* (CUP 2013) ch 3.

[20] Johan Steyn, 'Guantanamo Bay: The Legal Black Hole' (2004) 53 ICLQ 1,

[21] Dyzenhaus, *Constitution of Law* (n 17) 3. See also Dyzenhaus, '*Schmitt v. Dicey*' (n 17) 2018 ('A grey hole is a legal space in which there are some legal constraints on executive action—it is not a lawless void—but the constraints are so insubstantial that they pretty well permit government to do as it pleases').

[22] Dyzenhaus, *Schmitt* (n 17) 2023, 2026.

[23] ibid 2018.

[24] Dyzenhaus, *Constitution of Law* (n 17) 3.

[25] Eric A Posner and Adrian Vermeule, *The Executive Unbound: After the Madisonian Republic* (OUP 2010).

in both legislation and judicial practices. Some are open-ended statutory provisions, such as the APA provision which offers agencies exemptions from notice requirements 'when the agency for good cause finds ... that notice and public procedure thereon are impracticable, unnecessary, or contrary to the public interest'.[26] Other grey holes are judge-made doctrines of administrative law such as the development of a 'softer' review under the arbitrary and capricious standard of review.[27] Normatively, Posner and Vermeule extoll administrative action unfettered by courts; for them, politics and public opinion serve as the best, and sufficient, checks on presidential power—a position rejected throughout this book.

d. 'Fuzzy law'

Rather than rely on the term 'soft law', with its confusing meanings, my earlier study of the indeterminacy of regulatory arrangements involved the coining of a term that initially served to challenge the assumption that most regulatory frameworks relied on a single legislative mandate and operated under its formal arrangements. The term was used before the emergence of the image of the 'hole'. Both terms address action under law that is simultaneously beyond its constraint, hence 'fuzzy' and 'grey' could be interchangeable.

Essentially, the distinction between 'soft' and 'fuzzy law' is based on the formal legal status of the measure. 'Soft law' originally referred to transnational arrangements that have no formal status, hence not directly enforceable, but still considered (softly?) binding by members of the international community, and later infused into administrative law analysis. The expansion of the concept of 'soft law' to open-ended, vague measures, was in fact a move into a different species of law, one that is formally binding, but is nevertheless weak in its ability to define and constrain action.

The starting point of my articles on 'fuzzy law' in the context of regulation[28] was the classic assumption that statute law is the primary source of regulatory frameworks. Although this assumption has been strongly challenged in this subdiscipline, and some definitions of 'regulation' do not include statute as one of their components,[29] the legislative mandate is very often considered an intrinsic part of regulation and the *grundnorm* used for accountability mechanisms and legal oversight.[30]

[26] 5 USC §553(b)(3)(B); Posner and Vermeule, ibid 99–100.

[27] 5 USC §706(2)(a); Posner and Vermeule, ibid 97–99.

[28] Margit Cohn, 'Fuzzy Legality in Regulation: The Executive Mandate Revisited' (2001) 23 L and Policy 469; applied in Margit Cohn, 'Fuzzy Legality and National Styles of Regulation: Government Intervention in the Israel Downstream Oil Market' (2002) 24 Law and Policy 51.

[29] Philip Selznick's influential definition of regulation as a 'sustained and focused control exercised by a public agency over activities that are valued by the community' does not expressly require control by statute. Philip Selznick, 'Focusing Organizational Research on Regulation' in Roger Q Noll (ed), *Regulatory Policy and the Social Sciences* (University of California Press 1985) 363.

[30] On the legislative mandate as the basis for proper regulation see Robert Baldwin and Christopher McCrudden, *Regulation and Public Law* (Weidenfeld and Nicolson 1987) 33; Robert Baldwin, *Rules and*

One could use the term 'legislative mandate' as simply meaning any statutory provision that heads a regulatory package. A less technical/positivistic definition seems to stand in the background of regulatory discussions, at least as an ideal-type or measuring rod for actual legal arrangements. According to this ideal-type, the legislative mandate is sector specific, detailed, and inclusive, doubly empowering, and limiting. Ideally, a legislative mandate is a tight set of rules applying to a well-defined sector and tailored to fit particular policy objectives. As a complete set of rules, it both empowers and limits, containing both power grants and restrictions to be laid on the exercise of these powers.

Under this ideal-type, an all-encompassing statute is introduced through participatory legislative processes to provide a visible and accessible set of rules that defines and structures regulators' behaviour, enables the regulated to plan future action, and serves as a yardstick for judicial and other checks on regulatory action. In the tradition of preference for statute-law, the legislative process promotes participation of a variety of interest groups; strengthens accountability, as checks provided by other authorities and external interest groups use this statute as the ground on which they can base challenges to the framework of its application. Furthermore, penal, fiscal, and other constricting provisions require statute; most regulatory regimes do grant regulators such powers, therefore reliance on statute is but another benefit.

The fact that most legislative mandates depart from this ideal is of course no novelty,[31] but none of the important studies of flexible regulation identified the variety of forms in which actions purported to be 'perfectly legal' concealed a reality of virtual lawlessness. My articles addressed practices 'that cannot be considered illegal, but in fact frustrate(s) law's function as creator of visible and accountable rules'.[32] The term 'fuzzy legality' was borrowed from 'fuzzy set' theory, introduced as an alternative to binary thinking and applied in diverse fields such as bioinformatics, computer studies, linguistics, and psychology.[33] The insight that concepts (such as 'age') bear gradually transforming meanings (such as 'not too young' and 'quite old'), fit perfectly with the idea of law as one that rejected 'crisp' and clear-cut

Government (Clarendon Press 1995). On the assumption that the legislative mandate is, empirically, the basis of government action see Cohn (n 28) 471.

[31] In addition to delegation and discretion, addressed above, see studies that identify regulatory action 'in the shadow of the law'. For focus on enforcement tactics that use law as a 'last resort,' a 'benign big gun' that operates as a threat, supporting less forceful enforcement, see Keith Hawkins, *Environment and Enforcement: Regulation and the Social Definition of Pollution* (Clarendon Press 1984) ch 10; Ian Ayres and John Braithwaite, *Responsive Regulation* (OUP 1992) ch 2. See further discussion in section C.4 below.

[32] Cohn (2001) (n 28) 471.

[33] See eg Lotfi Zadeh, 'Fuzzy Sets' (1965) 8 Information and Control 338; Lotfi Zadeh, *Fuzzy Sets and Applications: Selected Papers* (Richard M Tong (ed), Wiley 1987); Bart Kosko, *Fuzzy Thinking: The New Science of Fuzzy Logic* (Hyperion 1993).

dichotomies—in this case the dichotomy between legality and illegality; this theoretical basis remains central to this book.

My early articles identified six forms of fuzzy legality: action in the 'absence' of law (in the absence of a legislative mandate, other constitutional sources, statutes, and private law measures offering some form of conceived authorization); sweeping statutory delegations; a 'lopsided' legislative mandate (empowering and only nominally restraining, sometimes introduced only if required by law, and containing authorizations to act); exercises of selective enforcement; reliance on extra-statutory parallel arrangements; and 'pastiche', or dead-letter law.[34]

This initial work on the 'fuzziness' of public law focused on regulation, one of the central outputs of executive power, and it did not link the phenomenon of 'fuzziness' with a theory of executive power as such, a task addressed in this book. The taxonomy of these forms of fuzziness, offered in the articles, did however open a path towards this book's development of an analytical, multi-layered investigation of the ways executive branches accumulate and retain power under law without being overly constrained. All the forms of fuzziness, discussed in the earlier work, plus additional forms of legal fuzziness, are succinctly discussed in Part C below.

2. Moving Forward

None of the alternatives to the concept of fuzzy law discussed above offer accounts of the different forms under which indeterminate features of law can appear and flourish. Those concerned with delegation and discretion essentially focus on statutory design, those discussing 'grey holes' are mainly concerned with the role of the courts (in Dyzenhaus's case) and executive powers under and beyond law (in Posner and Vermeule's). In fact, both bodies of research weave their normative accounts around the interplay between two main actors, the legislature and the judiciary.

My study removes the emphasis on the judiciary as a generator of grey holes; rather, as further discussed in Chapter 10, courts may contribute by upholding, or expanding, existing fuzzy nodes of law; rarely will they create new ones. The literature's focus on the judiciary is understandable—these are studies of common law systems, but some grey holes are rarely discussed in courts, and may thus remain unrecognized by the general public. Thus, excessive focus on the judiciary deflects attention from ways executives can, and do, add items to the menu of fuzziness.

Regarding 'menus', a second weakness lies in the absence of an analytical examination of grey holes. Some examples of arrangements under 'a façade of legality'

[34] Cohn (2001) (n 28) 476.

are offered, but a taxonomy of the range of practices that may lead to indeterminacy, or a node of fuzziness, is still missing. My earlier article on the fuzziness of law in the context of regulation[35] offered a nascent typology, which is further expanded in this book to offer the broadest range of ways and means that enable executives to formally act under law but escape at least some of law's potential for constraining power. Table 1 presents fourteen answers to the question 'how does law enable the executive to perform this composite task, to be both subject to law and its master?'

C. Conceptualizing Fuzziness II: Thirteen Forms of Fuzziness

1. Fuzzy Legality: A Taxonomy

Fuzziness, or legality in form but not in substance, can be effected in two ways. First, law may exist, but provide a loose framework that enables extensive powers with limited constraint. This type of fuzziness is at the focus of two of the four schools of study, discussed above: the study of delegation and discretion and the study of 'grey holes'. Another source of fuzziness exists when law is multi-levelled or scattered; in such a case, the difficulty of deciphering the law, and the possibility of adding new law when seen befitting, effectively enables the executive to act under limited constraint. This type of fuzziness has received little attention in the context of discussions of executive power.

Under this taxonomy, some forms of fuzzy legality rely on constitutional texts or understandings, others derive from statute, and some are generated by the executive itself and accommodated by other government branches (Table 1). The taxonomy offered in this part classifies fuzzy nodes by their generator. As mentioned above, my study removes the emphasis on the judiciary as a generator of fuzziness; its role is generally limited to upholding or expanding existing nodes of fuzziness. The detailed case-studies contained in Part II of the book do consider this role, while a normative argument for the transformation of this role to purely corrective is advanced in the last chapter of this book.

The following sections flesh out the contours and content of these nodes of fuzziness, using examples from the UK and the US, the two systems used throughout the book. Three forms of fuzzy law are discussed in detail in Parts II and III and are therefore only briefly analysed in this chapter.

[35] Margit Cohn, 'Fuzzy Legality in Regulation: The Executive Mandate Revisited' (2001) 23 L and Policy 469.

Table 1 Fuzzy Legality: A Taxonomy

Type	Nature	Details and Examples
A. Constitution-generated		
1. Open-ended provisions in a written constitution	Interpretable explicit direct authorization, under some, or limited constraints	US: vesting clause, take-care clause, commander-in-chief clause.
2. Unwritten constitution granting fuzzy powers	Historically or otherwise recognized executive powers.	UK: history, constitutional conventions, Royal prerogative.
3. Constitutional doctrines	Justification of executive non-statutory powers that does not rely on the constitution as such	US: 'stewardship' theory, inherent powers UK: Royal prerogative; personification, in context of 'new prerogative'/'third source' executive powers.
B. Legislature-generated		
1. Open-ended provisions	Broadly interpretable legislative provisions.	Vague, open-ended statutory text.
2. Discretion	Authorization to act granting choice between several alternatives: (1) mandatory authority: duty to act. (2) discretionary authority.	(1) Discretion how to act (choice between alternatives). (2) Two levels of discretion: whether and how to act.
3. Delegation	(1) Statutes delegating rule-making powers. (2) Authorization to sub-delegate.	(1) Authority to make regulations, orders, and other rules (2) Sub-delegation of rule-making or decision-making power. Legal system may require explicit authorization in statute.
4. Patchwork legislation	Multiple layering of sources of power: piling-up, dispersion.	Multiple emergency legislation, multiple authorizations for market regulation, riders in appropriation acts that prohibit funding.
5. Indeterminate or multiple decision-makers	Power not authorized to specified office or body; grant of decision-making power to several officers.	Use of generic general term, eg 'secretary of state'; explicit grant in statute or authorization to sub-delegate.

Table 1 *Continued*

Type	Nature	Details and Examples
6. Lopsided statute	Statute chosen only if necessary by law, or in order to empower but not limit; incomplete regulatory frameworks.	Legislation of criminal penalties and taxation, other powers and constraints deriving from extra-statutory sources.
C. Executive-generated		
1. Selective enforcement and creative compliance	Extensive informal enforcement; law as 'last resort'/ 'benign big gun'.	Negotiated, consensual arrangements employed in lieu of prosecution and other statute-based arrangements.
2. Parallel extra-statutory arrangements	Introduction of parallel schemes outside of statute.	Parallel extra-statutory subsidies; presidential executive agreements (US); governance under contract.
3. Pastiche law	'Dead-letter' law.	Unimplemented statute (possibly enacted under pro-legislation pressure with insufficient subsequent support, or when out of sync with social/political reality).
4. Multiple mixed sources	Secondary legislation/ mixed authority unilateral measures relying on multiple sources of power (multiple statutory sources / mixed statutory and non-statutory).	Secondary legislation/ Executive Orders recitals.

2. Constitution-Generated Fuzzy Legality

In a New York Times op-ed, Professor Geoffrey Stone of Chicago labelled the United States Constitution a 'fill-in-the-blank' constitution, while Professor Vernon Bogdanor, the Oxford political scientist, has been quoted as saying that he 'makes a living out of something that doesn't exist—namely a British constitution'.[36] Whether these quips are fitting or not, no one would deny that constitutions are notoriously fuzzy, and that executives often rely on powers that generate

[36] Geoffrey R Stone, 'Our Fill-in-the-Blank Constitution', *The New York Times*, 13 April 2010 <https://www.nytimes.com/2010/04/14/opinion/14stone.html>; Chris Arnot, 'Interview: Ruling Class', *The Guardian*, 17 February 2009 <https://www.theguardian.com/education/2009/feb/17/vernon-bogdanor>,

directly from the constitution, rather than statutes, relying on features that are far from exact.

The blanks to be filled come in different shades of grey. This section addresses some of these forms of fuzziness that fuel executive power: textual indeterminacy, fuzziness in the absence of a written constitution, and, as a third type of constitution-generated fuzziness, doctrines and forms of reasoning which loosely derive from expanded understandings of the nature of a constitution and the ways it directs the polity. It thus offers an introductory overview of all of these forms of fuzziness, while Chapter 5 is dedicated to an extensive analysis of one of the outcomes of constitutional fuzziness: the ways these nodes of power fuzzily support non-statutory, unilateral executive power.

a. Open-ended constitutional provisions

All legal texts require interpretation; mathematical units and other measurable components are at best marginal to such texts. As a concept, the term 'open-endedness' refers to a degree of fuzziness that extends beyond the natural subjection of text to interpretation, which still retains an element of direction. Consider the power of the US president to grant reprieves and pardons, or to convene Congress 'on extraordinary occasions'. The first power is limited by nature, as it cannot be considered to authorize other types of action, such as sentencing. The second, while open to interpretation, still sets some limits on the invocation of powers through the requirement that the occasions be 'extraordinary'. We're concerned here with provisions that are open-ended enough to support a full range of meanings; the range of possibilities available under such a degree of open-endedness accords the provision a mere façade of legality.

Article II of the US Constitution offers well known examples of this phenomenon; all of those discussed below have been interpreted in opposing ways, supporting either the empowerment or constraint of the president; in other words, none of the clauses, discussed below in the order of their appearance, offers a definite delineation of executive powers. The open-ended vesting clause, heading a seemingly inconclusive list of executive powers, which differs from the vesting clauses of Articles I and III, is concerned with the legislature and the judiciary. Sections 2 and 3 of Article II enumerate a renowned list of powers, including the command of the armed forces, the grant of pardons, the making of treaties under senate advice and consent, and the ambiguous 'take care that the laws are faithfully executed' clause. All are open for interpretation, notably the 'take-care' and commander-in-chief clauses, which have offered promising bases for expansionist visions.[37] These clauses are discussed in detail in Chapter 4. Suffice here to note this most open-ended clause.

[37] For a detailed analysis of these clauses see ch 4. For the twentieth-century debates, especially the unitarist/non unitarist dispute, that inter alia relied on textual evidence, see ch 1.

The clause 'he shall take Care the Laws be faithfully executed', contained in Section 3 and dubbed 'the take-care clause', could have been interpreted as a mere allowance to take measures ancillary to the implementation of laws, but it has supported much more. As Jack Goldsmith and John Manning note in their review of the take-care clause, the clause has been generally endorsed by courts in contexts as diverse as the president's power to remove from office and the exercise of prosecutorial discretion. It has also instructed the scope of standing to sue (derived from the distinct powers granted to the executive branch and the judiciary in the constitution), and has served as one of the bases for the recognition of what the authors call 'presidential completion power'—incidental measures that are considered necessary for the proper implementation of a statutory command.[38] In this category, the authors inter alia referred to Executive Order 12291 and its progenies, unilaterally issued by presidents to impose duties on agencies, including the completion of a cost-benefit analysis prior to agencies' rulemaking. In a published opinion, President Reagan's Office of Legal Counsel found that the power to issue the order derived from this clause.[39]

Despite some rulings that seem to constrain the reliance on the clause, Goldsmith and Manning find the general pattern to be one of judicial expansion of presidential powers, and also note that in doing so, the court did not interpret the clause under its well-established canons of interpretation usually applied when interpreting the constitution; the clause appeared to be self-explanatory.[40]

b. Fuzzy powers under an unwritten constitution

Professor Bogdanor's jest about the nonexistence of the British constitution, cited above, was never intended to reflect the reality of his home system. No operating polity can exist without a set of rules that govern its basic functions. Yet, as is well known, the British constitution is currently the single democracy that does not base its formal structure on some form of supra-statutory structure or a document designated 'constitution'.[41] Instead, the British legal system operates under an amalgam of statutes that contain provisions of a constitutional nature,[42] some case-law, and a collection of unwritten understandings and rules of practice known as 'constitutional conventions'.[43] All these aspects of the structural constitution enjoy

[38] See ch 4.

[39] Jack Goldsmith and John F Manning, 'The Protean Take Care Clause' (2016) 164 U Penn L Rev 1835, 1835–62.

[40] Goldsmith and Manning (n 39) 1853–62. On this clause and its use see further, ch 4.

[41] Note that I do not discuss here bills of rights and other documents designed to protect human rights by limiting the legislature, rather those frameworks concerned with the institutional structure of government-at-large.

[42] The 'usual suspects' are the Magna Carta 1215, Petition of Right 1628, the Bill of Rights 1689, Act of Settlement 1701, Act of Union 1707, Parliament Acts 1911–1947, the European Communities Act 1972, the Scotland Act 1998, the Human Rights Act 1998, the House of Lords Act 1999, the Constitutional Reform Act 2005, and the Constitutional Reform and Governance Act 2010.

[43] For constitutional conventions, see eg Ian Loveland, *Constitutional Law, Administrative Law and Human Rights: A Critical Introduction* (8th edn, OUP 2018) 223–50.

a historical pedigree; even those seemingly governed by a statute of parliament are coloured by past practice.[44]

When a constitutional framework, or field, is unwritten, fuzziness is unavoidable: definite understandings of an unwritten arrangement, even when firmly supported by history and practice, are always susceptible to rereading and manipulation.

Zooming onto the executive, the best-recognized form of an unwritten source of power is the Royal prerogative, which pertains to Crown powers that were not taken away by Parliament. Although extensively discussed in Chapter 4, some attention is due here.

By their nature, prerogative powers are fuzzy. No one, at least since the early nineteenth-century, has dared present a complete list of prerogatives,[45] although recent government and parliamentary reports have offered their versions.[46] Academics provide lists that are carefully supplemented by a caveat such as 'it is not possible to give a comprehensive catalogue of prerogative powers', followed by a discussion of the classically acknowledged ones.[47] The legitimacy of the prerogative remains a constitutional convention, one of the constitutional rules which are considered part of the unwritten constitution of the United Kingdom.

Some prerogatives concern inter-branch matters, such as the power to summon parliament and the power to grant assent to bills passed by parliament. More important for our discussion are prerogatives that pertain to administrative powers. Historically, all prerogative powers were directly linked with the Crown. This link has not been formally severed, but centuries of practice have established, under constitutional conventions, that all prerogatives of an administrative nature are in fact exercised by the prime minister and his government. Some of these, such as coinage, the drawing of territorial waters, and the maintenance and management of the Civil Service have been legislated, the latter only in 2010. The passport regime, powers linked with foreign affairs and national security, the appointment of high-level officers, the power of mercy, and legislation in colonies and overseas territories, are the best-known remaining prerogatives. In these fields, then, the government retains freedom to act, constrained mainly by the possibility of judicial

[44] For overviews of all elements of the constitutional framework, see, in addition to Loveland (n 43) Part One, AW Bradley, KD Ewing, and CJS Knight, *Constitutional and Administrative Law* (18th edn, Pearson 2018) 12–30; Robert Blackburn, *Britain's Unwritten Constitution*, 13 March 2015, British Library Website <https://www.bl.uk/magna-carta/articles/britains-unwritten-constitution>.

[45] Joseph Chitty, *A Treatise on the Law of the Prerogatives of the Crown* (Butterworth 1820).

[46] For such reports see House of Commons, Public Administration Select Committee, *Taming the Prerogative: Strengthening Ministerial Accountability to Parliament*, HC 224, 16 March 2004, 5–12 (concerning prerogative powers exercised by ministers); *The Royal Prerogative*, House of Commons Library Briefing Paper 03861, 17 August 2017, 9–13; Ministry of Justice, *The Governance of Britain, Review of the Executive Royal Prerogative Powers: Final Report* (Ministry of Justice 2009) 31–34. For the reform of the prerogative, see ch 4.

[47] See eg Bradley and Ewing (n 43) 258–65, and further, ch 4.

review and the looming threat of future legislation, all under a recognized, albeit unwritten, element of the constitution.

The fuzziness of the prerogative has enabled governments and courts to squeeze new powers into the existing framework by being rediscovered as 'old' prerogatives. Some of this stretching is rather innocuous—for example, the inclusion of modern warfare and technology within the ancient prerogative of war would attract no criticism.[48] But some judicial reasoning has gone much further, to the extent of reinventing the past, as in the case of the discovery of the 'historical' power to keep the peace of the realm as a well-grounded prerogative, one that enabled the court to approve an extension of police powers beyond statute.[49] Other non-statutory powers currently invoked in the United Kingdom and recognized as 'prerogatives', such as ex-gratia payment schemes (*Lain* 1967) and government dissemination of information (*Jenkins* 1971),[50] were likewise newly recognized prerogatives, but are in fact different, 'third source' powers, discussed in the next section.

c. Non-textual, general constitutional doctrines

This type of fuzziness does not draw on the constitution as such, rather on different constructs that should still be considered as pertaining to the constitutional sphere, through their retention of some link to the constitution. I identify five such doctrines: political reality, the state's sovereignty, the 'personification' of government as holder of powers akin to those of individuals and legal personalities, history as providing a 'gloss' on the constitution or otherwise embedding the recognition of governmental action on past use, and conceptions of 'aggregation', under which the general tenor, and collection, of various sources suffice for the recognition of executive powers. All of these are fuzzy, as none can show a pure pedigree derived directly from the constitution, and therefore their contours are not decipherable. These doctrines are discussed in detail in Chapter 5, in the context of executive exercise of unilateral, non-statutory power. Two linked examples could suffice here: political practice and as 'gloss'.

Justifications drawing on political reality carry a long pedigree. US presidents have justified some of their contested action, especially during emergencies, by referring to urgency and the need to answer crises. The best-known example of such practice is President Lincoln's action during the Civil War, some of which was

[48] See *Re Petition of Right* [1915] 3 KB 649, CA; *A-G v De Keyser Royal Hotel* [1920] AC 508.

[49] *R v Secretary of State for the Home Department, ex parte Northumbria Police Authority* [1987] EWCA Civ 5; *R v Secretary of State for the Home Department, ex parte Northumbria Police Authority* [1989] QB 26 (CA) (power of central government to supply anti-riot equipment to local police stations in the argued absence of such authority in the Police Act. The Court of Appeal found sufficient basis in the statute, but addressing the question of the continued existence of a prerogative to maintain 'the peace within the realm', the court adopted the lower court's reasoning that the Act did not create a 'monopoly' that excluded central government action in this field).

[50] Adjudged in *Criminal Injuries Compensation Board ex parte Lain* [1967] 2 QB 864; *Jenkins v AG* (1971) 115 Sol J 674.

contrary to the Constitution. President Lincoln's message to Congress on 4 July 1861, justifying his unilateral suspension of the habeas corpus due to the exigencies of the rebellion and the need to preserve the nation and the Constitution is often cited as an example,[51] but this speech linked necessity with the ambiguity of the text, in the President's argument that the suspension clause had not explicitly assigned the power to any of the branches. Direct reliance on politics is expressed, for example, in Lincoln's 1864 letter to Albert G Hodges, editor of the *Commonwealth*, regarding his emancipation proclamation:

> ... my oath to preserve the constitution to the best of my ability, imposed upon me the duty of preserving, by every indispensable means, that government—that nation—of which the constitution was the organic law. Was it possible to lose the nation, and yet preserve the constitution? ... I felt that measures, otherwise unconstitutional, might become lawful, by becoming indispensable to the preservation of the constitution, through the preservation of the nation ... I claim not to have controlled events, but confess plainly that events have controlled me.[52]

President Lincoln's actions were ratified after the end of the Civil War,[53] but the spirit of the doctrine has remained, although much of the subsequent extra-statutory emergency action has been at least loosely connected with the text of the constitution or on statute—types of fuzziness discussed above and below.

Political arguments have aided executives in their justification of unilateral powers in broader areas of activity. President Roosevelt's 'stewardship theory' relied on political responsibility rather than authorization by the constitution or Congress. In his autobiography, he famously wrote:

> My view was that every executive officer, and above all every executive officer in high position, was a steward of the people, and not to content himself with the negative merit of keeping his talents undamaged in a napkin ... I acted for the public welfare, I acted for the common well-being of all our people, whenever and in whatever manner was necessary ... I did not care a rap for the mere form and show of power; I cared immensely for the use that could be made of the substance ... I declined to adopt the view that what was imperatively necessary for the Nation could not be done by the President unless he could find some specific authorization to do it.[54]

[51] Goldsmith and Manning (n 39).
[52] ibid.
[53] ibid.
[54] Theodore Roosevelt, *An Autobiography* (Macmillan 1916) 372.

Moving to the second constitutional doctrine, history, past practice, and precedent operate in both systems as generators of fuzziness and have enabled the extension of executive powers beyond textual authorization. The Royal prerogative, still a feature of the British constitution, is essentially historical in nature,[55] but history has supported US presidential power, albeit in an entirely different fashion. Embodied in the doctrine of 'historical gloss', past practice, in the absence of congressional objection, has served in more than a few cases to offer not only a tool for expanded interpretation of the constitutional text, but also as an alternative theory that considers inter-branch interaction over time as a generator of legitimacy. In *Midwest Oil* (1915), the legality of executive orders issued for the temporary withdrawal of mineral-rich public lands from private access was found to be embedded in a practice that 'dates from an early period', 'known to Congress, and as principal, and not in a single instance … disapproved'.[56] 'Gloss' and undisturbed executive practice feature in Justice Jackson's opinion in *Youngstown*, as part of his second category,[57] and in Justice Frankfurter's oft-cited dictum:

> … a systematic, unbroken, executive practice, long pursued to the knowledge of the Congress and never before questioned, engaged in by Presidents who have also sworn to uphold the Constitution, making as it were such exercise of power part of the structure of our government, may be treated as a gloss on 'executive power' vested in the President by S.1 of Art. II.[58]

Since then, the concept has been used by courts and by government to legitimate action that did not derive from a clear statutory authority.[59]

The other four constructs are further elaborated in Chapter 4. Under the first of these, the concept of state sovereignty as a predecessor of the formal constitution has been recognized as a sufficient source for presidential power in the fields of war and foreign affairs.[60] Next is the recognition of a 'third source' of powers, non-statutory powers that are not recognized (or should not be recognized) as prerogative powers in the historical sense but are part of government arsenal of powers.[61] Under the third, several commentators and courts have reverted—some

[55] On the prerogative, see part C.2.b of this chapter.
[56] *US v Midwest Oil*, 236 US 459, 469, 475 (1915)
[57] *Youngstown* (n 13) 637.
[58] ibid, 610–11.
[59] See *Dames and Moore v Regan*, 453 US 654 (1981), 686; *American Insurance Association v Garamendi*, 539 US 396 (2003), 414. Government memoranda that relied on longstanding presidential practice and relied on the 'gloss' doctrine include Caroline D Krass, *Authority to Use Military Force in Libya*, 1 April 2011 <https://fas.org/irp/agency/doj/olc/libya.pdf>; Virginia A Seitz, *Lawfulness of Recess Appointments During a Recess of the Senate Notwithstanding Periodic Pro Forma Sessions*, 6 January 2012 <https://www.justice.gov/file/18326/download>. See, generally, Curtis A Bradley and Trevor W Morrison, 'Historical Gloss and the Separation of Powers' (2012) 126 Harv L Rev 411.
[60] *US v Curtiss-Wright*, 299 US 304 (1936), 317–18. See further Chaps 4, 10.
[61] For the first contribution in this vein see BV Harris, 'The "Third Source" of Authority for Government Action' (1992) 108 LQR 626.

with reservations, some quite happily—to an analogy between the state and the powers of a legal person. In this context, the British government unearthed in 2002 a legal memorandum made in 1945 that, it is argued, has provided a basis of power equivalent to these inhered in an individual or a body corporate. Dubbed the 'Ram Doctrine', it opines that 'a department can do anything that a natural person can, provided it is not forbidden from doing so'.[62] Finally, the fourth construct is the idea of the 'aggregate powers' of the president, found inter alia in Chief Justice Vinson's dissenting opinion in *Youngstown*, which upheld President Truman's order to seize the steel mills on strike during the Korean War. Relying on the longstanding practice of presidential action during emergencies, discussed above, Chief Justice Vinson's main source for this alternative source of authority was a statement written by the then Attorney General Jackson, one of the Justices on the *Youngstown* bench, which found that a proclamation ordering an earlier seizure 'rest[ed] upon the aggregate of the Presidential powers derived from the Constitution itself and from statutes enacted by Congress'.[63]

3. Statute-Generated Fuzzy Legality

Many statutes offer executives broad legal powers without substantively limiting their application. Most, if not all, analyses of such open-ended statutes employ either 'delegation' or 'discretion', or both, as keywords, but there are other ways in which legislators can enable the extension of executive powers without so decreeing. This part is dedicated to an analysis of six types of statute-derived fuzziness.

In addition to its focus on delegation and discretion, much of the existing literature is obsessed with emergency law: the emergency statute is often offered as the essential example of a fuzzy statute. Indeed, emergency conditions require, and thus supply justification for, wide power grants that enable the head of state to promulgate statute-type orders as required by emergency exigencies. These frameworks are often designed to be employed across the system and are limited only by vague general purpose proclamations. Emergency-enabling laws tend to outlive the actual emergencies they addressed, thereby availing governments of extensive powers outside substantive statutory constraints.[64] The focus on emergencies deflects attention from the commonness of the open-ended statute. Obviously,

[62] See *Malone v Metropolitan Police Commissioner* [1979] 1 Ch 344. On the Ram Doctrine see originally Anthony Lester and Matthew Weait, 'The Use of Ministerial Powers without Parliamentary Authority: The Ram Doctrine' (2003) PL 415.

[63] 89 Cong Reg 3992 (1943), 5 May 1943. Cited in *Youngstown* (n 13) 695–96. See further ch 4.

[64] See eg Nicole Questiaux, *Study of the Implications for Human Rights of Recent Developments Concerning Situations Known as States of Siege or Emergency*, UN ESCOR, 35th Sess, Agenda Item 10, UN Doc E/CN.4/Sub.2/1982/15 (1982); Oren Gross and Fionnuala Ní Aoláin, *Law in Times of Crisis: Emergency Powers in Theory and Practice* (CUP 2006); and Part II of the book

sweeping delegations and grants of discretion are much more universal features of legislation, as are the other forms of fuzziness discussed here; the utilities of open-endedness are not exclusively linked with emergency.

a. Open-ended, interpretable provisions

The indeterminacy of all non-mathematical language subjects all legal texts to interpretation. As in the case of constitutions, statutory provisions move into the fuzziness realm when they offer little or no instruction as to the remit of their interpretation.

Consider, first, an example from emergency law. Under Section 26(1) of the British Counter-Terrorism and Security Act 2015, '[a] specified authority must, in the exercise of its functions, have due regard to the need to prevent people from being drawn into terrorism'.[65] 'Specified authorities' are listed in great detail in Schedule 6 of the Act; although the secretary of state is authorized to change the schedule in a statutory instrument, the published list offers at any time sufficient knowledge of the identity of such authorities. The term 'due regard', on the other hand, does exclude cases in which no, or little regard is given, but there is little direction here. The statute does proceed to authorize the secretary of state to issue guidance, to which the authority 'must have regard',[66] but, in the absence of further instruction in the statute, this arrangement leans heavily toward fuzziness.

Moving to non-emergency law and the context of air-pollution law, discussed in Chapters 6–8, consider two examples. §109 of the US Clean Air Act (CAA)[67] was one of the provisions challenged in *Whitman* (2001), a central decision concerning the nondelegation doctrine.[68] The section requires the agency to publish regulations prescribing a national primary ambient air quality standard, defining national primary ambient air quality as a standard 'the attainment and maintenance of which in the judgment of the Administrator, [are] based on such criteria as allowing an adequate margin of safety, are requisite to protect the public health' (§109(b)(1)). The terms 'adequate', 'safety', and 'public health' all required interpretation.

A second example, the Advanced Technology Vehicles Manufacturing Program (ATVM), administered by the US Department of Energy under the Energy Independence Security Act 2007, offers loans to support the development of advanced technology vehicles and their support components. Inter alia, an 'advanced technology vehicle' is defined as a light duty vehicle that meets three conditions; under the third, the vehicle must meet 'at least 125 percent of the average base year combined fuel economy for vehicles with substantially similar attributes'.[69] In both

[65] Counter-Terrorism and Security Act 2015.
[66] Counter-Terrorism and Security Act 2015, Section 29.
[67] 42 USC §7409.
[68] *Whitman v American Trucking Associations*, 531 US 457 (2001).
[69] Energy Independence Security Act, §136(a)(1)(C), 42 USC §17013(a)(1)(C).

provisions, the interpretable terms offer some direction, but still enable the regulators to take a variety of positions.

b. Grants of discretion

As mentioned above, 'discretion' and 'delegation' are often discussed conjointly in the literature. Kenneth Culp Davis's study of discretion includes a chapter on 'the rule of law and the non-delegation doctrine', Denis Galligan's *Discretionary Justice* is laced with references to delegation, and others follow the same pattern.[70] Indeed, the US non-delegation doctrine, discussed below, is concerned with both forms of statutory design. Yet, to fully understand their force in statutory design, these two elements should be discussed separately as two important elements of statutory design that may contribute to fuzziness.

Discretion, well-presented in both Davis and Galligan's analyses, is found in any grant of choice between alternatives.[71] Interpretable provisions obviously require the exercise of discretion, since the central stage of the interpretation process is the choice between possible meanings. But statutes often explicitly grant discretion. Consider for example §110(a)(5)(A)(i) of the CAA, part of the provision regulating state implementation plans:

> Any State may include in a State implementation plan, but the Administrator may not require as a condition of approval of such plan under this section, any indirect source review program. The Administrator may approve and enforce, as part of an applicable implementation plan, an indirect source review program which the State chooses to adopt and submit as part of its plan.[72]

Under this provision, states *may* include an indirect resource review programme in their implementation plans, and the Administrator *may* approve and enforce such plans. In both cases, the statute grants an explicit discretion to decide *whether* to act at all, preceding the decision of the *content* of the plan. Thus, the decision whether to act or not is the first exercise of administrative discretion. The extent of discretion exercised in the second stage is linked with the first type of statute-generated fuzziness, discussed above: it derives from the degree of detail offered in

70 Davis (n 2); Galligan (n 2); Epstein and O'Halloran (n 2); Huber and Shipan (n 2).

71 In his classical study of discretionary justice, Davis finds 'discretion' 'whenever the effective limits on his power leave him free to make a choice among possible courses of action or inaction' (Davis (n 2) 4). Davis offers thirteen examples of government action, all of which refer to situations in which public officers, legally or illegally, choose a course of action from an array of alternative options. Davis's second example concerns a manager of a public housing project who evicts a family on the ground of 'undesirability', assumedly on the basis of the term being a statute-based condition for eviction. This is but one example of the most common feature of legal provisions: their interpretability.

72 42 USC §7410(a)(5)(A)(i).

the statute and the nature of constraints, when these are added onto the authorization to act.[73]

The grant of discretion to an administrative agency passes into the realm of fuzziness when it is sweeping and contains few, loose standards or operating instructions. Losing its substantial content, the statute has nothing much to say on the substantive level and is no longer a valid measuring rod for the administrative action it seems to authorize. And the greater the extent of non-mandatory grants of authority, the fuzzier the arrangement, as the decision of how the power will be exercised remains in the hands of the agency.

Consider, for example, section 3 of the British Environmental Protection Act 1990. Under the title 'Emission etc. limits and quality objectives', its length in words does nothing to limit the discretion granted therein. Only its last subsection, dealing with the publication of regulations, sets a defined duty to act. Not so the substantive powers provided:

> (1) The Secretary of State may make regulations under subsection (2) or (4) below establishing standards, objectives or requirements in relation to particular prescribed processes or particular substances.
> (2) Regulations under this subsection may—
>   (a) in relation to releases of any substance from prescribed processes into any environmental medium, prescribe standard limits for—
>   (i) the concentration, the amount or the amount in any period of that substance which may be so released; and
>   (ii) any other characteristic of that substance in any circumstances in which it may be so released;
>   (b) prescribe standard requirements for the measurement or analysis of, or of releases of, substances for which limits have been set under paragraph (a) above; and (c) in relation to any prescribed process, prescribe standards or requirements as to any aspect of the process.
> (3) Regulations under subsection (2) above may make different provision in relation to different cases, including different provision in relation to different processes, descriptions of person, localities or other circumstances.
> (4) Regulations under this subsection may establish for any environmental medium (in all areas or in specified areas) quality objectives or quality standards in relation to any substances which may be released into that or any other medium from any process.

[73] Compare this authorization with the duty to adopt an implementation plan, as required in §110(a)(1) of the CAA. Under this provision, '[e]ach state shall, after reasonable notice and public hearings, adopt and submit to the Administrator, within 3 years ... a plan which provides for implementation'. Discretion is obviously not absent here, but this discretion is exercised only in the second stage; the adoption of a plan, as such, is mandatory.

(5) The Secretary of State may make plans for—
(a) establishing limits for the total amount, or the total amount in any period, of any substance which may be released into the environment in, or in any area within, the United Kingdom;
(b) allocating quotas as respects the release of substances to persons carrying on processes in respect of which any such limit is established;
(c) establishing limits of the descriptions specified in subsection (2)(a) above so as progressively to reduce pollution of the environment;
(d) the progressive improvement in the quality objectives and quality standards established by regulations under subsection (4) above; and the Secretary of State may, from time to time, revise any plan so made.

(6) Regulations or plans under this section may be made for any purposes of this Part or for other purposes.

(7) The Secretary of State shall give notice in the London, Edinburgh and Belfast Gazettes of the making and the revision of any plan under subsection (5) above and shall make the documents containing the plan, or the plan as so revised, available for inspection by members of the public at the places specified in the notice.

Little more need be said when regulation or plans 'may be made for any purposes of this Part or for other purposes', one of the offerings of this outstandingly loose grant of discretion.[74]

c. Delegation

A system of administrative law may contain an umbrella rule that allows for such passing-on of authority, provided that the delegatee is within the agency, as in continental systems. Once distinguished from discretion, in common-law systems, under the maxim *delegate potestas non potest delegari*, such delegation is possible only when authorized in statute.[75] Under this canon, delegation has been under doctrinal attack, most saliently in the US. I do not aim to trace here the life and probable demise of the US nondelegation doctrine, one of the relatively strongest doctrines designed on its inception to cabin delegation.[76] For our purposes, suffice

[74] Formally repealed by the Pollution Prevention and Control Act 1999 (Schedule 3), the repeal has not entered into force, as no commencement order for that Schedule was issued for England and Wales. The result is the existence of a second type of fuzziness, featured in the repealing act. On this type of fuzziness, 'pastiche law', see below and ch 8.

[75] In the absence of such explicit authorization, executives have interpreted some statutes as thus enabling, and courts have sometimes upheld these readings (as in *Shreveport* 1944). In these cases the fuzziness is co-generated by all three government branches.

[76] On the doctrine see eg Theodore J Lowi, *The End of Liberalism: The Second Republic of the United States* (2nd edn, WW Norton 1979); Cass R Sunstein, 'Nondelegation Canons' (2000) 67 U Chi L Rev 415; Eric A Posner and Adrian Vermeule, 'Interring the Nondelegation Doctrine' (2002) 69 U Chi L Rev

to note that delegation comes in two forms. Under the first type of delegation, a statute authorizes administrative agencies to make regulations and other secondary rules. This type of delegation, which ostensibly places legislative power in the hands of an agency, is extensively discussed as a challenge to the separation of powers.

The second type of delegation occurs within the administration. A statute that grants an officer an original authority to act may empower the holder of the authority to further delegate the power to another person, usually within, but possibly outside of, the agency. All types of decision-making can be delegated in this way, from rule-making to the power to decide on individual cases.

The general authorization to delegate found in §301(a)(1) of the CAA (42 USC §7601(a)(1)) embodies both types of delegation:

> The Administrator is authorized to prescribe such regulations as are necessary to carry out his functions under this Act. The Administrator may delegate to any officer or employee of the Environmental Protection Agency such of his powers and duties under this Act, except the making of regulations subject to Section 307(d), as he may deem necessary or expedient.[77]

Another distinct example, with a far more intricate framework of delegation authorization, is taken from the Environmental Protection Act 1990. These are the first seven out of the twelve subsections of section 4, entitled 'Discharge and Scope of Functions':

> (1) This section determines the authority by whom the functions conferred or imposed by this Part otherwise than on the Secretary of State are exercisable and the purposes for which they are exercisable.
> (2) Those functions, in their application to prescribed processes designated for central control, shall be functions of the appropriate Agency, and shall be exercisable for the purpose of preventing or minimising pollution of the environment due to the release of substances into any environmental medium.
> (3) Subject to subsection (4) below, those functions, in their application to prescribed processes designated for local control, shall be functions of—
> (a) in the case of a prescribed process carried on (or to be carried on) by means of a mobile plant, where the person carrying on the process has his principal place of business—

1721; Keith E Whittington and Jason Iuliano, 'The Myth of the Nondelegation Doctrine' (2017) 165 U Penn L Rev 379.

[77] Section 307(d)(1) (42 USC §7607d)(1)) contains an extensive list of powers under the Act; the list can be supplemented by the Administrator. These powers, then, cannot be delegated. All remaining powers (eg those in §§105(b)(1), 110(h)(2), 113(d)(3)) are delegable.

(i) in England and Wales, the local authority in whose area that place of business is;
(ii) in Scotland, SEPA;

(b) in any other cases, where the prescribed processes are (or are to be) carried on—
(i) in England and Wales, the local authority in whose area they are (or are to be) carried on;
(ii) in Scotland, SEPA;

and the functions applicable to such processes shall be exercisable for the purpose of preventing or minimizing pollution of the environment due to the release of substances into the air (but not into any other environmental medium).

(4) The Secretary of State may, as respects the functions under this Part being exercised by a local authority specified in the direction, direct that those functions shall be exercised instead by the Environment Agency while the direction remains in force or during a period specified in the direction.

(4A) In England and Wales, a local authority, in exercising the functions conferred or imposed on it under this Part by virtue of subsection (3) above, shall have regard to the strategy for the time being published pursuant to section 80 of the Environment Act 1995.

(5) A transfer of functions under subsection (4) above to the Environment Agency does not make them exercisable by that Agency for the purpose of preventing or minimising pollution of the environment due to releases of substances into any other environmental medium than the air.

(6) A direction under subsection (4) above may transfer those functions as exercisable in relation to all or any description of prescribed processes carried on by all or any description of persons (a 'general direction') or in relation to a prescribed process carried on by a specified person (a 'specific direction').

(7) A direction under subsection (4) above may include such saving and transitional provisions as the Secretary of State considers necessary or expedient.[78]

Both types of delegation under statute, a delegation to make rules and the empowerment of power-transfer or power-sharing, contribute to fuzziness, especially when the primary holder of authority retains the original decision-making power together with the delegatee. This delegation enlarges the potential number of decision-makers while also enabling the emergence of several, possibly competing, readings and applications of an arrangement.

[78] Square brackets, referring to subsequent amendments, omitted. For the retention of this section in force despite a 1999 formal repeal see n 74 and ch 8.

An interim observation: the three statute-generated grey holes discussed above are often redundant, and overlap is sometimes inherent to their creation. Grants of discretion and authorizations to delegate often contain open-ended, interpretable provisions; many delegations of rule-making authority are not mandatory, and thus contain two stages of discretionary decision-making: the primary holder of authority retains discretion on whether to delegate at all, and will exercise some discretion when deciding whom to delegate to. Yet, these forms of fuzziness are analytically distinct.

d. 'Patchwork' legislation

This type of fuzziness emerges not due to the absence of statute, but rather due to the proliferation of legislation in a specific area. Attention to this legislative practice has focused on emergency law, but, again, is much more commonplace. Analysed in detail in Chapter 6, the idea that a field of executive action is typically organized in a single, overarching legislative mandate, or is at least easily traceable to a limited set of rules which delineate the contours of action by setting limits and conditions, is challenged through the common use of two patterns leading to fuzziness: piling-up and dispersion.

'Piling up' exists when several arrangements, each of which could singly address the regulated field of action, leads to the existence of a collection of statutes and rules, some overlapping, some at least potentially offering alternative paths for action which may contradict each other. The main issue here is not the only inherent danger of over-expansion of power; fuzziness exists even when a new arrangement is *not* stricter than its precursors, since the executive retains the ability to choose from the existing menu of power sources, or to opt for a novel arrangement.

Under the second form of patchworking, so common that it is rarely considered a fuzzy legislative practice, redundancy is replaced by dispersion. The so-called central legislative mandate, when it exists, is never the sole source of executive authority. The focus here is not on secondary legislation and other executive rules made under the legislative mandate, as they draw their force from the parent statute and can be easily traced. Other legal rules that have no direct link to the so-called legislative mandate are usually in existence. Beyond statutes that pertain to the regulated field, unilateral measures, and, in a federal system, state law, often complement (and possibly contradict) the legal measure considered as the governing rule. Riders in the annual appropriations acts that set substantive limits on the use of appropriated funds or introduce programs not authorized elsewhere, are the least discoverable.[79]

Both forms of patchworking, piling-up and dispersion, create fuzziness. When several routes of executive action are available, executives are granted a choice of

[79] For a detailed analysis of the nature and function of riders see ch 7.

sources, while other players in the public sphere may find it very difficult to plan ahead. In the absence of rules that limit patchworking, such fuzziness may grow in time. Similarly, fuzziness-by-dispersion renders any arrangement difficult to grasp and necessitates trawling through the entire legal system. These common features of the legal system almost always ensure that the deciphering of a legal arrangement requires a high level of legal expertise; even when relied upon, the potential of supplementing the arrangement with additional legislation, when not twinned with a commitment to pare down existing relevant law, remains. Easy reliance on the law, which is required for planning ahead, is thus seriously impaired.

Like other types of fuzziness, both forms are unavoidable, the first for convenience and political reasons, the second simply due to the complexity of realities which law attempts to organize. Both, however, lessen the hold of substantive legality and enhance the executive's freedom to act within formal legality in the absence of easy access to the rules.[80]

e. Multiple and indeterminate decision-makers

The retention of the original power by a delegator is but one example of a broader governance pattern, under which many, or unspecified, holders of authority formally exist. First, a general national practice may allow statutes to merely refer to a generic 'minister' or 'secretary of state', leaving the head of the executive to allocate powers and change these allocations at will. A second version of this type of fuzziness exists when, under a patchwork configuration, several holders of power exist; a third occurs when a statute grants a single power to a multitude of persons or bodies.

The first type of indeterminacy is one of the linchpins of the British cabinet system. In the past, statutes granting powers to act named the office to which those powers were granted, although transfer was not prohibited.[81] This practice is practically obsolete. Instead, the generic term 'Secretary of State' is found in many statutory authorizations, with no specific identification of the authorized officer.[82] Under the Interpretation Act, the term means 'one of Her Majesty's Principal Secretaries of State';[83] the assignation of powers to specific secretaries of state is in the hands of the Prime Minister.[84]

[80] For further discussion see ch 7.

[81] For example, powers in section 34 of the Clean Air Act 1956 were mainly granted to 'the Minister', defined in the statute 'as respects England and Wales, the Minister of Housing and Local Government and, as respects Scotland, the Secretary of State'—the latter representing the pattern that has replaced former specified authorizations.

[82] For example, in the Clean Air Act 1993, which consolidated and repealed several clean air statutes, including the 1956 Act referred to above, the term 'Secretary of State' is used no less than 104 times; no further information about her identity is offered.

[83] Interpretation Act 1978, Ch 30, Sch 1; following the Interpretation Act 1889, Ch 63, sec 12(3).

[84] Under the Cabinet Manual, a non-statute based code of rules that dominates the field in the absence of a statutory framework, 'Most statutory powers and duties are conferred on the Secretary of State; these may be exercised or complied with by any one of the secretaries of state. This reflects the doctrine that there is only one office of Secretary of State, even though it is the well-established practice

The existence of several institutions and officers responsible for administering various aspects of a single field of government action is likely to multiply when the framework is patchworked by dispersion. Consider for example the multiple bodies in charge of the regulation of air pollution in the UK. The statutes grant several governmental bodies a range of powers and responsibilities. These bodies, ranging from government ministries, through a separate agency, to the distinct and separately organized local government, operate alongside non-governmental bodies. The latter are not entrusted with law-making or law-enforcement, but still play a substantive role in the field, if only by raising agendas through public debate and legal challenges, thereby contributing to the design and implementation of policy. The general separation between rule-makers and enforcers contributes to the complexity.

The main government department entrusted with the protection of air quality, the Department for Environment, Food, and Environmental Affairs (DEFRA) operates under its Secretary of State; four other ministerial posts manage and direct this mega-department. Traditionally, one of the Parliamentary Under-Secretaries of State for Environment, is responsible for the regulation of air quality.[85] Other government departments are often involved in policy- and regulation-making in the field. Most importantly, two ministers at the currently named 'Department for Business, Energy and Industrial Strategy' (previously 'the Department for Energy and Climate Change'; other titles existed previously) are granted responsibilities in the field of climate change—a seemingly distinct field that clearly links to the more traditional field of air quality.[86]

to appoint more than one person to carry out the functions of the office ... It is also the well-established practice for each secretary of state to be allocated responsibility by the Prime Minister for a particular department ... and, accordingly, for each Secretary of State, in practice, to exercise only those functions that are within that department. It is for the Prime Minister to determine the various departments'. Cabinet Office, *The Cabinet Manual: A Guide to Laws, Conventions and Rules on the Operation of Government* (1st edn, 2011), secs 3.26, 3.27. Sec 3.26 contains a reference to the current Interpretation Act, adding that this applies 'unless a contrary intention appears', in line with sec 5 of the 1978 Act.

85 Prior to her appointment as Secretary of State for Work and Pensions in 2019, this post was filled by Thérèse Coffey MP. The allocation of this responsibility is currently not available on DEFRA's site. For the department's governance structure see < https://www.gov.uk/government/publications/government-ministers-and-responsibilities >. Note on political offices in Ministries (Departments): generally, there are two type of under-secretary: a Minister of State is considered higher in rank than a Parliamentary Under Secretary of State. See eg Andrew Defty, 'Who governs? Knowing your Secretary of State from your Parliamentary Private Secretary', posted 14 October 2018 <*https://whorunsbritain.blogs.lincoln.ac.uk/2018/10/14/who-governs-knowing-your-secretary-of-state-from-your-parliamentary-private-secretary/*>. For the Under Secretary's responsibilities see Cabinet Office, *List of Ministerial Responsibilities, Including Executive Agencies and Non-Ministerial Departments*, updated and accessible through <https://www.gov.uk/government/publications/government-ministers-and-responsibilities>.

86 According to the government's list of ministerial responsibilities for 2020 (n 85), the Secretary of State heading this Department, and the Minister of State for Energy and Clean Growth, at the same department, are both responsible for issues concerning climate change, but so is the Parliamentary Under Secretary of State for Environment at DEFRA.

Other government departments share responsibility in the field.[87] In addition, the Environment Agency, established in 1996 as an independent body as part of the Conservative Party political manifesto at the time, was to create 'a new Environment Agency which will bring together the functions of the National Rivers Authority, Her Majesty's Inspectorate of Pollution and the waste regulation functions of local authorities'.[88] Not designed to replace DEFRA, despite its main focus on aspects of water pollution, air quality remains one of its areas of responsibility. The agency must be consulted with in a variety of contexts, including the Secretary of State's making of a national air quality strategic plan and regulations under the act, but has little direct powers in the field.[89] Nor is it fully independent: under law, the agency is required to bear in mind DEFRA policy, regulations, and guidelines, and the ministry plays a central role in appointing the agency's highest officers.[90] The framework also grants powers to local authorities, especially enforcement powers, an aspect that is not discussed here in detail.[91] Despite the dominant role of the central government, attention to the contribution of local governments is crucial for the understanding of the regime and its operation.[92]

[87] Under the Cabinet Office list for 2020 (n 85), the following ministers have been defined as holding responsibilities in the context of the environment: the Ministry of Defence (Minister of State for Defence Procurement); Department of International Development (Minister for Pacific and the Environment); Northern Ireland Office (Secretary of State for Northern Ireland); Department for Transport (Parliamentary Under-Secretary of State); HM Treasury (Exchequer Secretary to the Treasury; Minister for Equalities; reference to taxation issues). Agencies and government bodies likewise defined include the driver and Vehicle Licensing Authority, the Driver and Vehicle Licensing Agency, the Planning Inspectorate, and HM Revenue and Customs (concerning taxes).

[88] 1992 Conservative Party General Election Manifesto, *The Best Future for Britain* <http://www.conservativemanifesto.com/1992/1992-conservative-manifesto.shtml>.

[89] Under EPA 1990, local authorities are responsible for the grant of 'authorizations' (permits) for processes and substances prescribed by the Secretary of State, for the monitoring of such activities and serving enforcement and prohibition notices in case of infringement (EPA 1990, Sections 6–14, further detailed in Schedule 1). The Clean Air Act 1993 likewise relegates permit and enforcement powers to local authorities (inter alia, local authorities approve chimneys and furnaces, declare 'smoke control areas' subject to special regimes, require information and initiate enforcement processes). The EA 1995 require local authorities to review the air quality in their areas, to designate the non-achieving areas as 'management areas', and to set 'action plans' requiring improvement by set dates (the 'LAQM' regime) (for the full regime see EA 1995, Sections 82–86. For a DEFRA overview see <https://laqm.defra.gov.uk/public-health/roleforlas.html>).

[90] EA 2005, mainly Part IV, further details in Schedule 11. In a report prepared by the National Archives, designed to assist in deciding which documents to conserve, the relationship between these bodies is described as follows: 'DEFRA sets overall policy on the environment and sustainable development within which the Environment Agency undertakes its work. DEFRA in particular: makes appointments to the Board (with the exception of one member appointed by the WG) and appoints its Chairman sets objectives for the Agency's functions and its contribution to sustainable development approves its budget and payment of Government grant for its activities in England and approves its regulatory and charging regimes'. National Archives, *Operational Selection Policy 58, Environment Agency 1996–2012* (Crown Copyright 2012) 7. In its website, the EA does not refer to any responsibilities in the air pollution field, except by declaring it has responsibilities for 'regulating major industry and waste'. <https://www.gov.uk/government/organisations/environment-agency/about>.

[91] For a short overview see Stuart Bell and others, *Environmental Law* (9th edn, OUP 2017) 127–29.

[92] For analysis of patchworked regimes see ch 7.

Finally, administration by multiple decision-makers, either under an original statutory authorization or through delegation, is an inherent organizational feature of agencies involved in large-scale decision-making. Section 206 of the US Clean Air Act, concerned with the compliance and testing of vehicles, contains a typical enforcement provision of that type:

> For purposes of enforcement of this section, officers or employees duly designated by the Administrator, upon presenting appropriate credentials to the manufacturer or person in charge, are authorized (1) to enter, at reasonable times, any plant or other establishment of such manufacturers, for the purpose of conducting tests of vehicles of engines in the hands of the manufacturer ...[93]

These types of multiple structuring contribute to the fuzziness of statutes. Under the first type, even knowledge about the identity of the authorized person is absent: no wonder that one commentator presented this phenomenon as an example of 'the smoke and mirrors at the heart of the UK constitution'.[94] Linked with patchworking, the existence of multiple bodies, each operating separately or with some co-ordination under separate, sometimes overlapping frameworks, virtually ensures the inability to grasp the intricacies of the ways a single area is regulated. Finally, although multiple authorized officers, such as inspectors, assessors, and other holders of official authority must typically follow the same rules, the discretion essential to much of the decision-making process adds another layer of fuzziness to the existing ones. Once several holders of authority exist, the potential for contradicting decisions grows.

f. 'Lopsided' statute

Under this type of fuzziness, a statute is intentionally limited in coverage. For instance, a statute may address only the aspects that require explicit legislative authorization under the constitution or a constitutional-type rule, such as the setting of criminal penalties and taxes or the grant of franchises, licenses, and other property entitlements, but other aspects that can be applied without specific statutory authorization remain unlegislated.

Consider, for example, the Act of 21 March 1942, enacted less than a month after the issuance of the executive order that authorized the designation of areas that were to be established as internment camps for US citizens of Japanese ancestry. Neither executive order 9066, issued on 19 February that year, nor executive order 9102, issued on 18 March, were made under statute.[95] The Act did not

[93] 42 USC §7542.

[94] Andrew Blick, *The Codes of the Constitution* (Hart Publishing 2016) 154.

[95] Executive Order 9066, *Authorizing the Secretary of War to Prescribe Military Areas*, 19 February 1942, 7 FR 1407; Executive Order 9102, *Establishing the War Relocation Authority*, 18 March 1942, 7 FR 2165. The recital of the first order referred to 'the authority vested in me as President of the United States, and Commander in Chief of the Army and Navy'; the second cited 'the authority vested in me by

replace it; rather, in one paragraph, it set penalties on those who act in contravention of the order or other measures made in this context.[96] The legislative effort, motivated by the need to establish crimes, was unconcerned with all other aspects of the arrangement, first and foremost its very authority: evidently, the executive order was deemed sufficient. The government's intent to enable the enforcement of the orders and measures made under them by legislating was documented, and cited in Chief Justice Stone's decision in *Hirabayashi* (1943).[97]

Such statutes are not made merely during wars and emergencies. Consider, for example, the privatization of a government-owned enterprise. Some aspects of privatization require legislation, for example the equalization of voting rights prior to floating shares on the market, the creation of a government-owned golden share in the privatized concern, and the introduction of sanctions applicable when the enterprise does not willingly co-operate with the privatization process. Other aspects may not need to rely on legislation. A privatization act may lack programmatic expressions of the values to be advanced, provisions outlining the privatization process in detail, or provisions as to the rights of employees of the privatized concern. In such cases, the executive will revert to other fuzzy sources of power, constitution- or executive-generated. Most probably, in addition to constitution-backed powers, gaps will be filled by private law tools, discussed below. For example, the sale can be effected in the market, and other aspects may be regulated under contract, if at all. In such cases, the statute cannot be cited as the sole source of action. This type of fuzziness is generated by the façade of legality offered by the legislative mandate.

the Constitution and statutes of the United States, as President of the United States and Commander in Chief of the Army and Navy'.

[96] PL 77–503, 56 Stat 173. Prior to its repeal in 1976, the Act was first located at 18 USCA § 97a (transferred to § 1383 in 1948). The statute referred to action 'in any military area, or military zone prescribed, under the authority of an Executive order of the President, by the Secretary of War, or by any military commander designated by the Secretary of War, contrary to the restrictions applicable to any such area or zone or contrary to the order of by the Secretary of War or any such military commander'. Those acting under knowledge of the restriction were liable to fines and imprisonment.

[97] *Hirabayashi v US*, 320 US 1375, 1380–82. The statute was also referred to in *Korematsu v US*, 323 US 214 (1944). Indeed, the curfew measures, and later measures that established centres, challenged in these and other court proceedings, were promulgated and applied after the statute was added. Orders made before the introduction of the act were concerned with the designation of large areas as military areas. For the history see eg *Hirabayashi*, ibid 1378–80. Attention to the statute in the literature is limited, and is even less featured in the public knowledge. See eg Wendy Ng, *Japanese American Internment During World War II: A History and Reference Guide* (Greenwood Press 2002) (no mention); Roger Daniels, *The Japanese American Cases: The Rule of Law in Time of War* (University Press of Kansas 2013) (mentioned in passing at 24–25).

4. Executive-Generated Fuzzy Legality

The two previous sections were dedicated to the ways in which the constitution and the legislature can grant executives extensive freedom to act while remaining within the sphere of legality. This section shows how executives can generate further fuzziness. Each of the following four types of fuzziness corrodes the force of statute law as a direct, detailed, and all-encompassing framework.

a. Selective enforcement and creative compliance

Aspects of implementation and enforcement, central to the understanding of the true nature of the operation of any field of executive action, attract much attention in the research fields of administrative law, public policy, and regulation. In these contexts, fuzziness emerges when a substantive gap between the law in the books and the law in action removes the role of formal law as the sole organizer of executive action. Two such fuzzy nodes of legality are discussed in detail in Chapter 8. The first is the result of flexible modes of enforcement. Under the title 'responsive regulation', substantial attention has been granted to the transformation of the legislative mandate from organizer of action to a 'looming threat'. Observing the regulators of water pollution, Keith Hawkins noted that legal sanctions and other statutory powers were used selectively, as a 'last resort', usually preceded by gentler practices such as persuasion and agreement.[98] Likewise, Ian Ayres and John Braithwaite identified the prevalence of the 'enforcement pyramid' model, in which statutory sanctions operate as 'benign big guns', positioned at the top of an escalating series of sanctions, and used only when the softer options are insufficient.[99] Most observers within the regulation discipline have found this model useful,[100] but for our purposes, whatever its utilities, relative agency freedom is ensured by this practice, while clarity and certainty are compromised.

A second type of fuzziness results from the principal-agent problem arising from the congress-agency relationship in the design and implementation of regulatory regimes. Overly zealous legislators may create an arena in which the regulatory agency, in effect, plays the role of creative compliant, simply because the legislation is too ambitious or otherwise impossible to apply in its entirety. Agency noncompliance that undermines statute is achieved in various ways which cannot be classified as pure infraction of the law. These tactics have been recognized to include

[98] Keith Hawkins, *Environment and Enforcement* (1984) 198.

[99] Ian Ayres and John Braithwaite, *Responsive Regulation: Transcending the Deregulation Debate* (OUP 1992) 19–53. See also Eugene Bardach and Robert Kagan, *Going by the Book: The Problem of Regulatory Unreasonableness* (Transaction Publishers 2002).

[100] Hawkins notes that employing sanctions and other statutory powers selectively was viewed, at least by the regulators, as promoting the efficiency of regulatory action as well as its social legitimacy by better conforming with social conceptions of justice (Hawkins 1984, ch 19). Bardach and Kagan's 'good inspector' employs responsive and flexible methods instead of tough 'legalistic' ones (Bardach and Kagan (n 99) 123–51).

'shirking by undersupplying policy outcomes; pursuing policy objectives that are inconsistent with the preferences of elected political officials; or creating new, organized political interests'.[101] In the face of legislative attempts to overcome such practices by laying down procedural mechanisms in lieu of costlier methods of direct monitoring, agencies sometimes retaliate by invoking additional noncompliance tactics; those may include the formulation of directives and guidance rules that circumvent formal statutory constraints.[102] These accounts indicate a cyclic process of creating congressional rules → agency noncompliance → creating additional rules, and so on. These agency noncompliance tactics are not necessarily illegal, but are clear cases of unfaithfulness to the ideal of strict legality.

b. 'Pastiche' law

This type of fuzziness, analysed, as its formers, in Chapter 8, emerges when a statute is ignored, unimplemented, or has not come into force. Much attention has been granted to one type of pastiche law: laws that have lost all touch with current reality and social norms, as in the case of Texas' sodomy law, decided upon in *Lawrence v Texas* (2003);[103] the law had never been enforced against consenting adults acting in private, and is considered as a perfect example of the desuetude doctrine.[104] But pastiche law can be unimplemented or rarely implemented from inception, in several ways.

Overly zealous legislatures, discussed above, may introduce a statute due to political pressure, in the absence of true executive or agency support; in other cases, statutes may simply be set aside by the executive due to their onerous content. A well-known example of this type of fuzzy statute, the War Powers Resolution,[105] is discussed in Chapter 8: essentially, no president has ever followed the exact process required under this joint resolution.

The UK offers an example of a different, common form of pastiche, one that occurs when legislation never enters into force. British legislation often requires that designated provisions enter into force by a commencement order to be made by a Secretary of State or Minister. In the absence of such an order, the legislative framework remains on the books but is no more than a promise for future awakening. Years commonly pass between the legislation date of a statute and its entry into force.[106]

[101] McCubbins, Noll, and Weingast (1987) (n 7) 273.

[102] James T Hamilton and Christopher H Schroeder, 'Strategic Regulators and the Choice of Rulemaking Procedures: The Selection of Formal vs Informal Rules in Regulating Hazardous Waste' (1994) 57 L and Contemp Probs 111; Terry M Moe, 'Delegation, Control, and Study of Public Bureaucracy' (2012) 10 The Forum, Issue 2 Article 4.

[103] 539 US 558 (2003).

[104] Cass R Sunstein, 'What Did *Lawrence* Hold? Of Autonomy, Desuetude, Sexuality, and Marriage' (2003) 55 Sup Ct Rev 27, 30. On this doctrine in the US and its relevance to prosecutorial discretion, see Note, 'Desuetude' (2006) 102 Harv L Rev 2209, esp 2222–25.

[105] 50 USC §§1541–48.

[106] See ch 8.

In all such cases, as in other forms of fuzziness, consideration of the legislation as such does not reflect the actual state of the law. Grasping governing law requires more than a mere study of the law-in-the-books. Expertise, and knowledge of the changing landscape of the law-in-action is required. Moreover, the existence of statute law may contribute to misapprehension by those who take statute law seriously.

c. Extra-statutory parallel arrangements

A different form of fuzziness emerges when statute law is supplemented by a non-statutory arrangement. This may occur when a pastiche law is de facto replaced by a non-statutory arrangement, but can be found even when the statute is applied, simply as a parallel option. In both cases, instead of acting under statute, executives rely on their constitution-generated, inherent, or prerogative powers, discussed above. For example, the executive may establish parallel grant and aid programs and underfund statute-based ones. In the context of US foreign affairs, presidential unilateral signing of executive agreements with foreign entities, under a process that bypasses the advice-and-consent requirement of the Treaty Clause, is a commonly used alternative. The Congressional-Executive agreement receives post-signature congressional approval by simple majority and is now recognized as a second form of international obligation. Further, purely unilateral sole executive agreements that do not benefit from congressional approval are just as common. Both outnumber, by far, the number of treaties signed under the Treaty Clause.[107] Executive agreements have no direct explicit constitutional authority, although some, returning to the fuzzy clauses discussed above, have argued that sufficient authorization can derive from the constitution.[108]

Private law offers an additional source of parallel arrangements. The prominence of government contracting as a governance tool is well recognized.[109] Much of this literature is concerned with outsourcing as a rising governance mechanism in neo-liberal economies, but, beyond this context, government contracts may introduce and enforce policies, at least on parties contracting with the state. The unequal power of the parties is often reflected in government dictation of terms,

[107] See eg Kiki Caruson and Victoria Farrar-Myers, 'Promoting the President's Foreign Policy Agenda: Presidential Use of Executive Agreements as Policy Vehicles' (2007) 60 Political Research Q 631; Anne E Nelson, 'From Muddled to *Medellín*: A Legal History of Sole Executive Agreements' (2009) 51 Ariz L Rev 1035; John Yoo, 'Rational Treaties: Article II, Congressional-Executive Agreements, and International Bargaining' (2011) Cornell L Rev 1; Daniel Bodansky and Peter Spiro, 'Executive Agreements+' (2016) 49 Vand J Transnat'l L 885.

[108] For example, Nelson (n 107) 1038–62.

[109] For literature from the UK see eg Ian Harden, *The Contracting State* (Norman Lewis and Cosmo Graham (eds), Open University Press 1992); Mark Freedland, 'Government by Contract and Public Law' (1994) Pub L 86; ACL Davies, *Accountability: A Public Law Analysis of Government by Contract* (OUP 2001). For literature from the US see eg Jody Freeman, 'The Contracting State' (2001) 28 Fla St U L Rev 155; Jody Freeman and Martha L Minow (eds), *Government by Contract: Outsourcing and American Democracy* (Harvard U Press 2009).

including government-favourable termination clauses. Contracting may be required under a legislative mandate, but this is not necessarily the case. Further, negotiations leading to arrangements made 'in the shadow of the law' can be the backbone of a regulatory framework in-action, despite the absence of explicit authorization in statute.[110]

d. Multiple mixed source citation

Under the classic rules of administrative legality, regulations, orders, and other similar measures are made under statutory authorization that both grants them their binding force and limits their potential extent. Under this accepted understanding, the legality of secondary legislation is to be first and foremost derived from its parent statute; if its provisions cannot be traced to the delegation contained in statute, it will be *ultra vires*. To provide initial information regarding the source of delegation, regulations contain recitals of authority that cite the statutory source.

This type of statute-based fuzziness occurs when a measure cites several sources of authority, often contained in more than a single statute. Sometimes, several separate sources are required in order to legally embed an arrangement. No fuzziness then exists. But the practice of citing multiple sources is often a different type of patchworking or piling-up, an insurance policy to ensure legality when one of the sources is questionable, or when none of them is considered sufficient. Thus, multiple sources are especially useful when no single statutory source seems to provide direct validity to the measure.

Consider, for example, the sources cited in the recitals of executive orders. This form of American presidential measure has attracted extensive academic research, especially in the post 9/11 era, alongside a growing attention to other written measures issued by presidents, such as proclamations, signing statements, and memoranda.[111] Statutes sometimes directly authorize the president to act by executive order,[112] but the most common orders have a lesser link, if any, to statute, and these offer an excellent example of multiple citation. While the fuzziness of the legal force of executive orders and their companions cannot be linked only to the recitals of the orders, the fuzziness of the recitals offers presidents the best legal support in case of challenges to the legality of the order.

Under the accepted understanding, expressed in *Youngstown*, executive orders may either rely on a statute or on the constitution.[113] In the majority of cases, however, the president's power seems to stem from both, at least on the face of the

[110] For the term in the context of UK regulation see Cento Veljanovski, 'The Regulation Game' in Cento Veljanovski (ed), *Regulators and the Market* (Institute of Economic Affairs 1991) 3, 9. See also Ayres and Braithwaite 1992 (n 99); Fiona Haines and David Gurney, 'The Shadows of the Law: Contemporary Approaches to Regulation and the Problem of Regulatory Conflict' (2003) 25 L and Policy 353.

[111] See ch 5.

[112] See Kevin M Stack, 'The Statutory President' (2005) 90 Iowa L Rev 539.

[113] *Youngstown Sheet & Tube v Sawyer*, 343 US 579, 585 (1952).

orders. For example, President Trump's 2018 order that reimposed sanctions on Iran first cites 'the Constitution and the laws of the United States', then proceeds by referring to no less than six statutes as 'included' in the reference to 'the laws of the United States'.[114]

In *Hamdan* (2006) the Supreme Court struck down the arrangement set in the order and in the later legislated Detainee Treatment Act, under which suspected terrorists were to be tried by a specially created military commission. None of the order's cited sources were found sufficient; neither the nebulous reference to the authority granted 'by the Constitution and the laws' nor the cited statutory provisions.[115] A singularity in the context, it should further be noted that the court refrained from deciding whether the president was empowered to unilaterally convene military tribunals in times of controlling necessity, considering it a still open question.[116] Furthermore, the decision did not overrule *Hamdi* (2004), which had considered the AUMF as an activation of the war powers and therefore as a possible source for rulemaking.[117]

This order is far from exceptional. All but three of the thirty-seven measures issued by President Trump in 2018, designated as 'executive orders' and uploaded onto the White House website, cited 'the Constitution and laws of the United States' as their sole source for promulgation.[118] Of the thirty-four remaining executive orders, fourteen supplemented this general reference with a citation of at least one enabling statute.[119] Almost 60% of these orders, then, listed only the general, highly fuzzy source of authority; the others remain just as fuzzy. A historical

[114] Executive Order 13846, *Reimposing Certain Sanctions with Respect to Iran*, 7 August 2018, 83 FR 38939. For the text of the recital of this order, and an analysis of this mixed-authority pattern, see below and ch 5.

[115] *Hamdan v Rumsfeld*, 548 US 557 (2006) 593–95.

[116] ibid 2774 (distinguishing the ruling in *Quirin* (*ex parte Quirin*, 317 US 1 (1942)), under which the predecessor of §821, a congressional authorization for military commissions sufficed to establish the court, viewed as 'controversial,' and concluding that 'even *Quirin* did not view the authorization as a sweeping mandate for the President to "invoke military commissions when he deems them necessary"... Rather, the Quirin Court recognized that Congress had simply preserved what power, under the Constitution and the common law of war, the President had had before 1916 to convene military commissions—with the express condition that the President and those under his command comply with the law of war'.

[117] ibid 2775 (assuming that the AUMF did activate the President's war powers, there was still no authorization to the challenged action).

[118] The two exceptions are orders extending previous declarations of states of emergency, made under earlier executive orders that cited that source of authority, as well as several statutes. The third order was a delegation made under statute, and had no recital but for the reference to the statute. For the texts of these orders see https://www.whitehouse.gov/presidential-actions/executive-order-presidents-continuation-national-emergency-respect-venezuela/; https://www.whitehouse.gov/presidential-actions/executive-order-presidents-continuation-national-emergency-respect-ukraine/ (neither has been numbered, nor can they be found in the American Presidency Project website, an important academic source for all presidential action managed at UC Santa Barbara <https://www.presidency.ucsb.edu/>). For the third, numbered 13,380, see https://www.whitehouse.gov/presidential-actions/executive-order-delegation-authority-approve-certain-military-decorations/. On this pattern of reliance see also ch 5.

[119] Half of these were concerned with the setting or continuation of international economic sanctions.

study of earlier presidential reliance practices, published in 1957, shows an entirely different pattern—about 48% of the compiled orders made between 1945 and 1956 cited only a statute, and only about 10% did not cite any statutory authority.[120] The move towards a wholesale reliance on the clause 'the Constitution and laws of United States' has well preceded President Trump's administration: the clause became standard long before.[121] A similar pattern is evident in some of the President's other forms of unilateral rulemaking, notably in the case of proclamations and memoranda.[122]

One may argue that reference to the 'Constitution and the laws of the United States' is merely declaratory, part of the recital, which in itself is not definitive. Still, the larger the number of sources cited, the more legally embedded the appearance of the order. Multiple citation also operates as a potential insurance against illegality, under the assumption that, when and if a challenge to the legality of the order is made, one of the (possibly) shaky authorizations will emerge to save the order. The reference to 'the Constitution' provides an especially potent source of legality, assuming courts uphold reliance on fuzzy constitutional sources.

Multiple authority citing is not unique to executive orders; regulations and orders made under statute often cite more than one authority. As in the case of multiple sources for action under a patchwork mode, reliance on multiple authorities offers the rule-maker a much better shot at ensuring the legality of the order, concurrently compromising clarity and foreseeability. The existence of multiple rules may also assist executives to clothe their rule-making with a semblance of legality. Consider the case in which a secondary rule seems to lack a clear authority: citation of several sources of power offers a better case of success if that rule is challenged for illegality.

[120] See House of Representatives, Committee on Government Operations, *Executive Orders and Proclamations: A Study of a Use of Presidential Powers*, 85th Congress, 1st Session, Committee Print 89166 (Government Printing Office 1957) 39–40. For another quantitative analysis of executive orders made by several presidents, from Franklin Roosevelt to Bill Clinton, that distinguishes orders according to citation of sources of authority, see Adam L Warber, *Executive Orders and the Modern Presidency: Legislating from the Oval Office* (Lynne Rienner 2006) 89–105 (showing gradual rise of citations with vague authority sources).

[121] To supplement Warber's findings (n 120), a search of executive orders issued in 2011–2012 shows a similar pattern. All fifty-eight executive orders made during this period relied on 'the Constitution and laws'; in fifty-four of them, it was the only source cited. Search, 13 February 2013, of orders then available on the White House website (in previous administrations, historical archives of executive orders issued by previous presidents were directly available through this website. In most recent years, the website does not offer links to historical orders, nor does it present presidential rules, orders, and proclamations according to their classification).

[122] Compare, eg, *Presidential Memorandum for the Secretary of State*, 4 June 2018 (suspension of certain limitations set under statute, relying on 'the Constitution and the laws of the United States' as well on the statute) with *Special Policy Directive—3, National Space Traffic Management Policy*, 18 June 2018 (designated a presidential memorandum, directed to the Vice President. Five Secretaries of State and four officials, setting out in detail the national space traffic policy without citing a source of authority). See further ch 5.

D. Concluding Remarks

This chapter offered a catalogue of the different ways in which constitutions, statutes, and executives can, and have, developed fuzzy forms of legality. Spanning both the constitutional and the administrative aspects of executive action—in this field, especially, retention of a separation between constitutional and administrative law misrepresents the reality of political decision-making—the model offers a useful template for analysis of the tenuous link between power and legality, both in national security/foreign affairs contexts and in more mundane but far from marginal fields of action. At their highest level, these sources stem from broadly penned constitutional structures, or looser constructs that have much more to do with constitutional theory or politics than with law in its narrow sense. Other fuzzy sources are generated by the legislature, while others are developed by the executive itself. All of these are sufficiently embedded in the legal/political structure, inter alia through judicial sanctioning and political realities.

Some of the elements of this taxonomy are well-recognized forms of open-ended executive authority, but have received limited conceptual attention. In addition to the casual use of 'discretion' and 'delegation' as interchangeable modes of statute-design, other forms of fuzziness have not even been identified as such. Citation of multiple sources of authority, unorganized piles of relevant sources of power, and the exercise of extra-statutory powers alongside statute, as well as other forms of limited fidelity to statute, are elements that should not be ignored by theorists of administrative action who wish to address the intricate relationship between power and legitimacy.

PART II

CONSTITUTION-GENERATED FUZZY LAW

4
Unilateral, Non-Statutory Executive Powers

A. Introduction 101
B. Non-Statutory Powers: A Short Primer 106
C. Bases of Authority 107
1. Constitution-Based Direct Sources 107
a. An unwritten constitution: the UK 108
b. A written constitution: the US 112
2. Constitution-Type Extra-Textual Doctrines 115
a. Political reality 115
b. Sovereignty and nationhood 116
c. Personification 117
d. 'Historical gloss' 121
e. Aggregation of powers 122
D. Legal Constraints on Unilateral Non-Statutory Powers 123
1. The Residuality Doctrine 123
2. Subjection to Judicial Review 127
E. Concluding Remarks 135

A. Introduction

This chapter and the following one offer an in-depth analysis of one form of constitution-generated fuzziness. Alongside the freedom offered under open-ended interpretable constitutions, executive action in the absence of a clear authority to act is a similarly ubiquitous feature of public law. The bases of such powers range from historically-embedded sources of power such as the British royal prerogative, through uncontested long-standing practices, to reliance on concepts of sovereignty. The high-level but indeterminate sources of such action typically do not delineate the limits of such action; thus, they essentially guarantee the fuzziness so favoured by executives. As I show in Chapter 5, this fuzziness may be increased when unilateral semi-formal measures are difficult to access, and when the sources of authority are mixed. In this Chapter, I consider in detail all the recognized sources for the continued existence of unilateral non-statutory powers in the two compared systems and address two accepted legal constraints on their application: their subjection to statute, under the doctrine of residuality, and their subjection to judicial review.

The starting point of this analysis is that, like other forms of fuzziness, unilateral, non-statutory executive powers in a democratic society directly challenge the basic democratic principles that justify exercise of force in the social and economic

A Theory of the Executive Branch. Margit Cohn, Oxford University Press (2021). © Margit Cohn.
DOI: 10.1093/oso/9780198821984.003.0005

spheres. Two central values, representation and deliberation, are compromised. We may agree or disagree with the temporary denial of statutory rights to access and use oil-rich public lands due to the depletion of natural sources, with the suspension of claims of US nationals against Iran as part of an agreement to free the US hostages, with the subjection of government contractors to non-discrimination policies, or with the indefinite detention of suspected terrorists.[1] But, fundamentally, in these cases the interests of individuals were initially affected without legislative authorization: in the first example, against its authorization, in the third, against the background of the inability to pass similar policies in congress, and in all the above examples, due to the convenience of reliance on this nebulous source of power.

Indeed, no-one could challenge the extent of executive use of powers sourced from the constitution. During his first two weeks in office, President Trump signed no less than nineteen written measures. Attention is usually granted to executive orders, for good reason—the first four of the seven executive orders issued during this period were concerned with minimizing the effect of the *Patient Protection and Affordable Care Act* ('Obamacare') with a view to its repeal; the setting of constraints on (or 'expediting') environmental review in the introduction of large-scale infrastructure projects; the tightening of immigration policy; and the enhancement of border security inter alia by expediting the building of the border wall.[2] Attention is still due to other measures: during this brief period, the President issued several memoranda, inter alia his memorandum to withdraw from the Trans-Pacific Partnership, to support domestic manufacturing by expediting approvals processes, and to promote the building of two major pipelines.[3]

All the above-mentioned executive orders and memoranda cited as their source of powers the formula 'the Constitution and laws of the United States of America', further discussed in Chapter 5; in all but two executive orders, this was the only citation of authority. Despite the fuzzy reference to 'the laws', it is the Constitution that the president mainly relied on.

These examples are not unique to this president. Despite some comments on President Trump's penchant for using unilateral measures, this practice carries a

[1] Decided, respectively, in *Midwest Oil* (n 15), *Dames & Moore v Regan*, 453 US 654 (1981), *Farmer v Philadelphia Electric Co*, 320 F2d 3 (3d Cir 1964), and *Hamdan v Rumsfeld*, 548 US 557 (2006).

[2] Executive Order 13765, *Minimizing the Economic Burden of the Patient Protection and Affordable Care Act Pending Repeal* (20 January 2017), 82 FR 8351; Executive Order 13766, *Expediting Environmental Reviews and Approvals for High-Priority Infrastructure Projects* (24 January 2017) 82 FR 8657; Executive Order 13768, *Enhancing Public Security in the Interior of the United States* (25 January 2017) 82 FR 8799; Executive Order 13767, *Border Security and Immigration Enforcement Improvements* (25 January 2017) 82 FR 8793.

[3] Memorandum on Withdrawal of the United States From the Trans-Pacific Partnership N*egotiations and Agreement* (24 January 2017), 82 FR 8497; *Memorandum Permitting and Reducing Regulatory Burdens for Domestic Manufacturing* (24 January 2017) 82 FR 8667; *Memorandum on Construction of the Dakota Access Pipeline* (24 January 2017) (82 FR 8662); *Memorandum on Construction of the Keystone XL Pipeline* (24 January 2017) (82 FR 8663).

long history. Nor is unilateral decision-making limited to the US. British prime ministers may have issued a smaller number of unilateral measures, but these can, and have, borne important consequences.

Consider the British *Bancoult* affair, entirely generated by unilateral executive action. The affair concerns the British Indian Ocean Territory, an overseas territory consisting of several islands (also known as the Chagos Archipelago), located halfway between Africa and Indonesia. The archipelago's location at the centre of the Indian Ocean renders it a strategic asset in high international politics. In the 1960s, the British and American governments signed a bilateral agreement concerned with the future of the territory, under which the local inhabitants, of Mauritian and Seychellian origin, were to be removed from the territory to enable the United States to establish defence facilities on Diego Garcia, the largest island. The evacuation of all inhabitants was finalized by 1973; the US facilities on the island, currently named Navy Support Facilities Diego Garcia, were extensively relied upon during the Gulf War and continue to play a role in US military post-9/11 operations and beyond.[4]

All the measures made by the government in this affair were unilateral. No statute directly authorizes the British government to enter into treaties; under the British constitutional structure, this power is exercised by the government in the name of the Crown, as an exercise of the historical Royal Prerogative, the remaining field of unilateral extra-statutory action formally in the hands of the Monarch.[5] Evacuation was originally effected by an ordinance made under the local constitution, and was later ratified under a new constitution that squarely denied the inhabitants' right of abode. The BIOT constitutions, and other constitutions penned by the British for colonies and other protectorates, were introduced by the British government as orders in council, semi-formal written measures made under the Royal prerogative.

Part of the struggle of a group of Chagossians to be reinstated in the territory was fought in courts. The challenge to the legality of the order and the evacuation under a constitution order that denied the right of abode to former inhabitants reached the House of Lords in 2008. Deciding the appeal, the House of Lords was required to rule upon several difficult issues. The question of the government's authority to sign bilateral accords was not one of them, as the British constitutional structure enables this practice; but questions regarding the authority to deny abode

[4] See eg JF Burns, *British Territory Used in 2 Renditions Flights*, New York Times, 1 December 2008; for an argument supporting US interests in the territory see Walter C Ladwig III, Andrew S Erickson, and Justin D Mikolay, 'Diego Garcia and American Security in the Indian Ocean', in Carnes Lord and Andrew S Erickson (eds), *Rebalancing US Forces: Basing and Forward Presence in the Asia-Pacific* (Naval Institute Press 2014) 130.

[5] Part 2 of The Constitutional Reform Act 2010 replaces the constitutional convention best known as the Ponsonby Rule with a requirement to lay certain international agreements before Parliament prior to ratification, but the authority of the government to sign treaties is only implied by the requirement that the process be initiated by a Minister. On the prerogative see below.

by a unilaterally made order in council, and the subjection of this measure to judicial scrutiny, were central to the decision.[6] Developments since then have included a British declaration of the area and beyond as a Marine Protected Area, made under a prerogative-based proclamation, a judicial recognition of the powers exercised in this context, an ICJ advisory opinion calling for the UK to cede sovereignty to Mauritius 'as part of the decolonization process', endorsed by the UN General Assembly, and ongoing appeals against the British government's subsequent actions.[7] None of these still ongoing chapters of this affair have had any impact on the use of the prerogative in this context and in others.

Indeed, US presidents and the British government have exercised unilateral powers in many foreign and domestic fields.[8] British examples that have received

[6] *R (on the application of Bancoult) v Secretary of State for Foreign and Commonwealth Affairs (No 2)* [2008] UKHL 61 (*Bancoult 2* (HL)), overturning decisions in the Divisional Court and the Court of Appeal. For the previous decision on the matter, *Bancoult 1* (2001), see below.

[7] The main stepping-stones since 2008 include, chronologically, the government's decision to designate the area including the archipelago and beyond as a Marine Protected Area (MPA) effected in a prerogative-based proclamation (April 2010); the decision of the UN Arbitral Tribunal operating under the UN Convention on the Law of the Sea, which found no direct jurisdiction over substantive issues of sovereignty, but ruled that the establishment of the Marine Protection Area breached several articles of that convention, and noted several undertakings of the British government concerning the retention of fishing rights, rights for minerals and oil, and the returning of the archipelago when no longer needed for defence purposes (*Mauritius v the United Kingdom*, ICGJ 486 (PCA 2015); the UK Supreme Court decision to uphold *Bancoult 2* (HL) (*R (on the application of Bancoult (No 2)) v Secretary of State for Foreign and Commonwealth Affairs* [2016] UKSC 35); the government's decision to reject resettlement plans, the instatement of a 'support package', and the extension of the UK-US arrangement until 2036 (November 2016), see eg, respectively, <https://www.theguardian.com/world/2016/nov/16/chagos-islanders-cannot-return-home-uk-foreign-office-confirms>; <https://sites.google.com/site/thechagosarchipelagofacts/british-government-policy/non-resettlement-support-package>; <https://www.ft.com/content/abbc879a-ac1d-11e6-ba7d-76378e4fef24>); the UK Supreme Court's decision upholding the MPA (*R (on the application of Bancoult No 3) v Secretary of State for Foreign and Commonwealth Affairs)* [2018] UKSC 3); the Divisional Court decision that rejected arguments against the government's renewed decision against resettlement and its instatement of a 'support package' for Chagossians, denying leave to appeal (*R (on the application of Hoareau and Bancoult) v Secretary of State for Foreign and Commonwealth Affairs* [2019] EWHC 221, 8 February 2019); the ICJ advisory opinion deciding against the UK and ruling that it cedes its administration of the archipelago (Legal Consequences of the Separation of the Chagos Archipelago from Mauritius (ICJ Advisory Opinion No 169, 25 February 2019)); the endorsement of the ICJ opinion by the UN General Assembly (*Advisory opinion of the International Court of Justice on the legal consequences of the separation of the Chagos Archipelago from Mauritius in 1965*, Resolution A/RES/73/295, 24 May 2019); and the UK Court of Appeal's decision allowing appeal on most counts, overturning in this respect the February 2019 ruling (*Hoareau v Secretary of State for Foreign and Commonwealth Affairs* [2019] EWCA Civ 1254, 16 July 2019); appeal to the Court of Appeal in 2020, hearings began in May 2020 (see https://www.judiciary.uk/publications/hoareau-another-v-the-secretary-of-state-for-foreign-and-commonwealth-affairs/). To date, then, the struggle continues. For an overview of the affair up to May 2019 see Jon Lunn, *Disputes over the British Indian Ocean Territory: May 2019 Update*, House of Common Briefing Paper No 6908, 28 May 2019.

[8] Such powers are not unique to the two systems studied in this book, although here I discuss these two systems only. For an earlier analysis that compared the UK and the US with Israel, from which some of this chapter draws, see Margit Cohn, 'Non-Statutory Powers in Three Regimes: Assessing Global Constitutionalism in a Structural-Institutional Context' (2015) 64 ICLQ 65; for constitution-derived unilateral action in the Fourth and Fifth French Republic see eg Margit Cohn, 'Non-Statutory Executive Powers in France: A Comparison between Two Regimes' in Alexis Alabrian and Olivier Morétau (eds), *Comparative Law and . . .* (Presses universitaires d'Aix-Marseille 2015) 51.

judicial and academic attention include, in addition to those invoked in the *Chagos* affair, non-statutory *ex gratia* compensation schemes,[9] the passport regime,[10] contracts and other types of market transactions employed as policy instruments,[11] and dissemination of information.[12] Those from the US include the use of 'executive agreements', international agreements signed by the President in the absence of the advice and consent of the senate, required in Article II's treaty making clause;[13] the incarceration of US citizens of Japanese ancestry during the Second World War, prior to legislation of the matter;[14] and the temporary withdrawal of private use of oil-rich public lands due to the depletion of natural sources.[15]

This chapter considers the different doctrines adopted in both systems for upholding these, and other examples of the exercise of non-statutory powers. In a constitutional monarchy, such powers may rely on historical constructs that are relics of former Crown omnipotence, as in the case of the United Kingdom. In other systems, such as the US, a written constitution may be originally ambiguous, either due to disagreement on the proper extent of executive powers, lack of time, or inattention; in any such case, the constitution provides a fertile, if fuzzy, ground for the growth of non-statutory executive powers doctrines. History and original text are but starting points: the presence of such powers in modern democracies is a-historical, and derives, it is claimed, from several features of the modern state, revolving around the doctrines discussed below. None of these claimed bases of these powers settles comfortably with modern constitutionalism, committed to clarity and accessibility of legislative-made rules. The preference for the unilateral over the statute-based path enables executives to retain a façade of legality, once those powers enjoy some systemic recognition.

The chapter and its immediate follower is not concerned with informal measures issued by executives, such as policy notices and other expressions of intent, although they may have a significant impact upon daily life. I treat only measures that have a 'legislative' effect, that is, measures that impact on the general public, rather than apply as internal administrative guidelines. Excluded measures include appointments of ministers, judges, and other high-level offices, reorganization orders concerned with the internal administration of government departments, orders regarding the operation of churches and parishes (in the UK), the creation of advisory bodies, and proclamations declaring national commemoration

[9] *Criminal Injuries Compensation Board, ex parte Lain* [1967] 2 QB 864.

[10] *R v Secretary of State for Foreign and Commonwealth Affairs, ex parte Everett* [1989] QB 811.

[11] On the non-statutory nature of such powers see Terence Daintith, 'Regulation by Contract: The New Prerogative' (1979) 32 CLP 41; Mark Freedland, 'Public Law and Private Finance—Placing the Private Finance Initiative in a Public Law Sphere' (1998) PL 288.

[12] *Jenkins v AG* (1971) 115 Sol J 674.

[13] See eg PJ Spiro, 'Treaties, Executive Agreements, and Constitutional Method' (2001) 79 Texas L Rev 961; BR Clark, 'Domesticating Sole Executive Agreements' (2007) 93 Virginia L Rev 1573.

[14] See above n 18.

[15] Challenged and approved in *Midwest Oil* (n 1).

days or special periods of awareness to a social phenomenon. In addition to the examples listed above, measures of interest include, in the United Kingdom, orders in council that legislate for British colonies and territories and proclamations that declare the specifications of legal tender. In the United States, such 'legislative' measures include executive orders that block property of belligerent countries, executive orders that subject independent agencies to White House review, and proclamations that apply and amend free trade agreements, the latter ostensibly made under statute.[16]

In Chapter 5, I discuss the nature of such (semi-)formalized measures in a comparative context and show a surprising similarity between those established in the UK and the US, that persists despite the emergence and continued evolution of two distinct regimes. Attention is granted here to their sources of legitimacy.

B. Non-Statutory Powers: A Short Primer

Despite their problematic nature, prerogatives and other constitutionally-based unilateral powers have always been on the menus of executives in democratic Western states—the above are but a few examples. Such powers have gone by different names: prerogative, residual, inherent, autonomous, general, unilateral, presidential ... These titles do not reflect distinctive and separate constructs and are largely interchangeable (subject to necessary national adjustments). In this study of such powers I choose the neutral term 'non-statutory powers' deliberately, as it does not reflect any a priori attitude towards the invocation of such powers, nor does it imply preconceptions about the supremacy of any of the two contesting powers—legislative and non-legislative sources of power.

The arguments for broad and flexible executive power draw on law's limitations and on expediency. Setting aside the normative element, discussed in Chapter 10, scholarship on the 'administrative state' could be interpreted as allowing such a form of governance. As the argument goes, states have broadened and diversified the range of their involvement in the social and economic spheres; additional fields have been added to the repository of state responsibilities, and the volume of action expected has amplified.[17] Against this background, it is argued, executives are

[16] See eg *Executive Order 12866, Regulatory Planning and Review*, 30 September 1993, 58 FR 51735 and ch 1; *Executive Order 13928, Blocking Property of Certain Persons Associated with the International Criminal Court*, 11 June 2020, 85 FR 36139 and ch 5; *Proclamation 10053, To Take Certain Actions Under the United States-Mexico-Canada Agreement Implementation Act and for Other Purposes*, 29 June 2020 < https://www.whitehouse.gov/presidential-actions/proclamation-take-certain-actions-united-states-mexico-canada-agreement-implementation-act-purposes/>.

[17] The literature depicts a transformation from the Minimal State, through the Welfare State to the current Neo-Liberal State. Roughly, this corresponds to visions of the state as peace-keeper, through welfare-advancer, to regulator. See Karl Polanyi, *The Great Transformation* (Rinehart 1944);

best placed to respond to fast-moving, ever-changing realities; legislatures, in comparison, are too burdened by politics to answer pressing challenges. As I show in Chapter 9, such arguments are overrated, if not downright false. The claim for ease and expediency may be justified during times of emergency but has little purchase when considering decades-long practices of reliance on rules made unilaterally by executives, discussed in this chapter.[18]

The flip side of these arguments for utility and ease in governance, calling for the enhancement of unilateral executive power, is the danger of abuse of powers, exacerbated due to the vagueness concerning the legality and accessibility of such powers. Governments are often likely to prefer non-statutory powers to legislation. Informal rule-making bypasses the arduous legislative process that provides potential entry-points for interest groups and other participants in the public sphere. Non-statutory rules, independently formed by executives, are both more pliable and amenable to further change by the same informal measures. Once instated, an unwritten arrangement could be more elusive, rendering review and other modes of accountability more difficult to maintain.[19]

C. Bases of Authority

1. Constitution-Based Direct Sources

This section is concerned with sources that can be directly linked with the constitution of a polity. Other doctrines that have recognized sources for unilateral power which are not derived from statutes are considered in Section 2.

Giandomenico Majone, 'From the Positive to the Regulatory State: Causes and Consequences of Changes in the Mode of Governance' (1997) 17 J Pub Pol 139. In the context of law, see RB Stewart, 'The Reformation of American Administrative Law' (1975) 88 Harv L Rev 1667; Kenneth Culp Davis, *Discretionary Justice: A Preliminary Inquiry* (Louisiana State University Press 1969); DJ Galligan, *Discretionary Powers* (Clarendon Press 1986).

[18] The practice of replacement of orders made during emergencies by statute-law is rare. Consider, for example, the infamous executive order of February 1942, which decreed that all US citizens of Japanese ancestry be interred in camps, an order justified by the government of the day by national security concerns that arose during the Second World War. Less than a month later, Congress enacted an act that introduced penalties for violating the order and measures made under it; rather than providing authorization, the short statute was only concerned with enabling implementation of the order, and was thus a lopsided statute, not truly covering the field (for a discussion of lopsided statute see ch 3). Executive Order 9066, *Authorizing the Secretary of War to Prescribe Military Areas*, 7 FR 1407; PL 77–191, 56 Stat 173. Strongly denigrated, a compensation program introduced in 2001 still could not remove the effects of that case.

[19] For a parallel argument that addresses the 'incompleteness' of law see Katharina Pistor and C Xu, 'Incomplete Law' (2003) 35 Int'l Law and Politics 931, 938–44. See also the discussion on delegation and discretion in ch 3.

a. An unwritten constitution: The UK

The UK may be credited (or defamed) for having the only unwritten Western constitution; although this title is not entirely accurate—a collection of statutes does organize several aspects of the state's governance alongside a set of constitutional conventions—no statute frames the power of the executive branch.[20] Despite its uniqueness, the age of this constitutional framework justifies its discussion before the analysis of non-statutory executive powers under a more common structure, organized around a written, supra-statutory constitution.

From the vantage point of the twenty-first century, the transformation of England from a medieval monarchy to a modern democratic polity headed by a Crown that no longer plays an active part in the political decision-making arena can be viewed as a smooth one, although some of the earlier events were far from peaceful.[21] Under the setting of the Crown into the constitutional framework, with the ascendancy of Parliament, the core of the executive power was gradually transferred to the Prime Minister, but remnants of past Crown sovereignty remain to date in the form of the Royal prerogative, although its shape has changed with the times.[22] This long-standing tenet of the British constitutional framework is the central constitutional source for powers exercised under the constitution and in the absence of statute.

The Prerogative, as defined after the 1688 Glorious Revolution, pertains to those powers retained by the Crown and not taken away by Parliament, and is part of the compromise reached with (or forced on) the Monarchy at the end of the seventeenth century.[23] For centuries, prerogative powers remained strongly tied with the eminence of the Monarch, an attitude echoed in Blackstone's eighteenth-century definition:

> By the word prerogative we usually understand that special pre-eminence which the King hath, over and above all other persons, and out of the ordinary course of the common law, in right of his regal dignity.[24]

[20] See ch 3.

[21] For the classic accounts of English constitutional history see Frederic W Maitland, *The Constitutional History of England* (CUP 1919) (spanning the period up to 1888–1889); William S Holdsworth, *A History of English Law* (Methuen & Co 1924) esp Vol VI. For a modern analysis see eg Ann Lyon, *Constitutional History of the UK* (2nd edn, Routledge 2016).

[22] For this process, emphasizing the ministry of Sir Robert Walpole in 1721, see Elizabeth Wicks, *The Evolution of a Constitution: Eight Key Moments in British Constitutional History* (Hart 2016) 53–64; for a current overview see A Bradley, KD Ewing, and CJS Knight, *Constitutional and Administrative Law* (17th edn, Pearson 2018) 257–8.

[23] See Holdsworth (n 21) Vol VI ch IV. Other types of non-statutory powers, including 'third source' and 'administrative' powers not derived from statute, are discussed in section (2) below, as their link to the constitution as such remains fuzzy.

[24] W Blackstone, *Commentaries on the Laws of England* (8th edn, Clarendon Press 1778) Book I, ch 7, 239. Blackstone's definition more than echoes John Cowell's, printed more than 100 years earlier: in his legal dictionary, prerogative of the King is defined as 'that special power, preeminence or priviledge that the King hath in any kinde over and above the ordinarie course of the common law, in right of

The rise of elected politics and parliamentary power directed Dicey's late-nineteenth-century definition:

> The prerogative appears to be both historically and as a matter of fact nothing else than the residue of discretionary or arbitrary authority, which at any given time is legally left in the hands of the Crown.[25]

Some 'political' prerogatives, pertaining to parliament and legislation, Crown immunities and Crown privileges, are not directly relevant to this book.[26] I focus on prerogatives that are purely executive in nature, for example, the waging of war, the conduct of foreign affairs, the grant of pardon, the administration of the passport regime, and some high-level appointments.

By its nature, then, 'prerogative' refers to a historical list of specific powers, largely acknowledged by courts but not dependent on their recognition. Yet almost no one (at least since Chitty[27]) has dared to present a complete list of prerogatives. Lists are carefully supplemented by a caveat such as 'it is not possible to give a comprehensive catalogue of prerogative powers',[28] followed by a discussion of the classically acknowledged ones.[29] The legitimacy of their exercise remains a constitutional convention, one of the constitutional rules that are considered part of the unwritten constitution of the United Kingdom.

Despite the historical link to the Crown, all 'executive' prerogatives, from war powers via the pardon power to the grant of passports, have been entrusted entirely into the hands of the executive since the nineteenth century; the symbolic assertion of the Crown remains, but the decisions and rules all reflect the choices of the government of the day.[30]

his crown'. John Cowell, *The Interpreter or Booke Containing the Significations of Words* (1607, William Sheares (ed) 1637) (pages unnumbered).

[25] AV Dicey, *An Introduction to the Law of the Constitution* (5th edn, Macmillan 1897) 354.

[26] The Crown officially summons, prorogues, and dissolves Parliament as well as affixes his or her assent to bills passed by Parliament—since 1967, under the Royal Assent Act. For a general overview see eg Bradley, Ewing, and Knight (n 22) 256–74.

[27] Joseph Chitty, *A Treatise on the Law of the Prerogatives of the Crown* (Butterworth 1820).

[28] Bradley, Ewing, and Knight (n 22) 258.

[29] ibid 258–65. But see GS McBain, 'Expanding Democracy—Transferring the Crown Prerogatives to Parliament' (2014) 6 Rev Eur Stud No 1.

[30] Although Dicey addresses prerogative as 'power left at any moment in the hands of the Crown, whether such power be in fact exercised by the Queen herself or by her Ministers' (n 25) 355, he distinguishes between some powers still exercised by the Queen, 'transactions (which are of more frequent occurrence than modern constitutionalists are disposed to admit) in which both the Queen and her Ministers take a real part, and also ... that [a] large and constantly increasing number of proceedings which, though carried out in the Queen's name, are in truth wholly the acts of the Ministry' (ibid 356). As part of the exit of the Crown (as a person) from political affairs, the exercise of these powers by the government is an uncontested convention. See eg *Blackburn v Attorney General* [1971] 1 WLR 1037, 1040; *R (Miller) v Secretary of State for Exiting the European Union* [2017] UKSC 5, eg [45], [48].

Dicey's definition emphasizes one important aspect of the prerogative that has since developed into the well-established rule of residuality. Under this central limitation, no non-statutory powers, even lofty prerogatives, can be exercised when a statute governs the same field. This doctrine is extensively assessed below; suffice to note here that under the schoolbook version, 'if the whole ground of something which could be done by the prerogative is covered by the statute, it is the statute that rules'.[31]

The natural 'shrinking' of the prerogative due to the general expansion of legislation over the past two centuries has been twinned with a strengthened commitment to legality, under the principles of the sovereignty of parliament and the rule of law, all anathema to arbitrary prerogative. Dicey does hint at the problem of retention of the prerogative—it offers the government 'large powers which . . . are constantly exercised, free from Parliamentary control',[32] but he refrains from calling for its removal. Instead, his emphasis is on constitutional conventions that determine, and constrain, the exercise of the prerogative.[33] Harsh twentieth-century criticism of executive discretion under legislation, notably Lord Hewart's influential *The New Despotism*,[34] further strengthened the critical attitude. Under the modernization of public law, current calls for reform have been voiced by academics as well as politicians.[35]

Some prerogatives have indeed been legislated, as in the earlier case of the Crown prerogative of coinage: counterfeiting and other such offences were consolidated in the Coinage Offences Act 1832; the current Coinage Act 1971 replaces the Coinage Act 1870, and places all powers in this field in the hands of the Crown, but under statute. A similar transformation of the setting of the baselines for the measuring of the breadth of British territorial sea was introduced in The Territorial Seas Act 1987.[36] More recently, the regulation of the civil service, previously

[31] *A-G v De Keyser Royal Hotel* [1920] AC 508, 526. On the residuality doctrine in practice see Section D.

[32] Dicey (n 25) 393.

[33] ibid ch XIV.

[34] Lord Hewart, *The New Despotism* (Ernest Benn 1929).

[35] For some reform proposals and reports published under the auspices of Parliament and the government see Public Administration Select Committee, 2004, *Taming the Prerogative: Strengthening Ministerial Accountability to Parliament*, 4th Report of Session 2003–04, HC 422; Ministry of Justice, The Governance of Britain, CM 7170 (July 2007); Ministry of Justice, *The Governance of Britain: Review of the Executive Royal Prerogative Powers: Final Report* (2009); Political and Constitutional Reform Committee, *Role and Powers of the Prime Minister*, First Report of Session 2014–2015, HC 351 (2014). For more recent briefs and surveys see Gail Bartlett and Michael Everett, *The Royal Prerogative*, House of Commons Briefing Paper 03861 (2017); Emily Haves, Prerogative Powers of the Crown, House of Lords Library Briefing, 13 December 2019 <https://researchbriefings.parliament.uk/ResearchBriefing/Summary/LLN-2019-0156. The literature on the prerogative in the twenty-first century ranges from downright denigration (eg David Gladstone, 'What Shall We Do with the Crown Prerogative?' (1998) 4(3) J Legis Stud 1. The Brexit affair, which involved the attempt of the government to rely on the prerogative to unilaterally withdraw from the EU, and the ensuing attempt to introduce a lengthy prorogation period, as an attempt to limit debate on the withdrawal, were both foiled by the judiciary (see below), and have inspired a spate of academic attention, some of it cited below n 123, 125.

[36] Section 3, Coinage Act 1971; Section 11, Coinage Act 1870. The Territorial Waters Jurisdiction Act 1878, which fixed British territorial waters under the three nautical miles rule, was mainly concerned

subject to prerogative-made orders in council, the Ponsonby rule, a convention under which international treaties signed by the state must be laid in Parliament for twenty-one sitting days prior to their ratification, were legislated in 2010.[37] The last in this series of reforms to date, the Fixed-Term Parliaments Act 2011, sets fixed dates for polls for parliamentary general elections.[38] Some other bills introduced in Parliament never reached fruition.[39]

The prerogative remains central in some fields: the passport regime remains prerogative-based, no statute directs decisions on foreign affairs and warfare.[40] The recently declared convention requiring a parliamentary debate and vote prior to committing troops to armed conflict has not fully removed government prerogative in this field.[41]

To summarize, two insights are important. First, despite some whittling down of prerogative powers, some still remain in force. Further, calls making declarations such as 'the death of prerogative' misrepresent the reality of fuzzy law in the UK.[42] Thomas Poole's post-mortem mainly draws on the fact the prerogative-based powers are now likened to statute-based action as far as judicial review is concerned, an aspect I discuss below. However, the remaining prerogatives remain fuzzy and, perhaps more importantly, the continued existence of fuzzy law that

with criminal jurisdiction; the Territorial Seas Act 1987 not only quadrupled the extent, but also legislated the prerogative to change the extent. The power is granted to the Crown, but now under statute.

[37] The Constitutional Reform and Governance Act 2010, Ch 25, Parts I, II.

[38] Fixed-Term Parliaments Act 2011.

[39] For some of these bills see Crown Prerogative (House of Commons Control) Bill 1988 [HC 117]; Crown Prerogatives (Parliamentary Control) Bill 1999 [HC 123]; Prime Minister (Office, Role and Functions) Bill 2001 [Presented at HC as Bill 60]; Armed Forces Deployment (Royal Prerogative) Bill 2016–17 [HL 10].

[40] For recent lists of existing prerogatives see McBain (n 29); Haves (n 35) 13.

[41] Since parliament's vote on the deployment of forces to Iraq in 2003, the government has recognized this convention, expressed inter alia in the Cabinet Manual and reaffirmed in subsequent government representations. The failure of such a vote regarding intervention in Syria in 2013 and the subsequent reversion of government policy have reinforced this substantive political constraint on this prerogative power. See Cabinet Manual (1st edn, 2011) para 5.38; House of Lords Constitution Committee, Constitutional Arrangements for the Use of Armed Forces, 2nd Report of Session 2013–14, HL Paper 46 (July 2013); C Mills, *Parliamentary Approval for Deploying the Armed Forces: An Update*, Commons Library Standard Note SN05908 (December 2013). This important development has yet to lead to legislation, which is not currently forthcoming; the deployment of personnel for non-combat purposes, as in the case of Mali in 2013, remains, under government policy, free from this constraint; and, generally, policy decisions in the field are still made under the prerogative. See eg Gavin Phillipson. '"Historic" Commons' Syria vote: the Constitutional Significance', Parts I and II, <http://ukconstitutionallaw.org/2013/09/19/gavin-phillipson-historic-commons-syria-vote-the-constitutional-significance-part-i/> and <http://ukconstitutionallaw.org/2013/11/29/gavin-phillipson-historic-commons-syria-vote-the-constitutional-significance-part-ii-the-way-forward/>; S Wilks-Heeg, A Blick, and S Crone, 'Despite David Cameron's Defeat in Syria, the UK Parliament Actually Has Relatively Weak War Powers Compared to Legislatures in Other Democracies', <http://blogs.lse.ac.uk/europpblog/2013/08/30/despite-david-camerons-defeat-on-intervening-in-syria-the-uk-parliament-actually-has-relatively-weak-war-powers-compared-to-legislatures-in-other-democracies/>.

[42] Thomas Poole, 'The Strange Death of Prerogative in England' (2018) 43 U Western Australia L Rev 42.

derives from other doctrines such as the recognition of third source powers and the personalization of government action, both addressed below, can only mean, at its best, that prerogative has shrunk but constitution-based fuzziness has not.

b. A written constitution: The US

Article II of the US Constitution, discussed in previous chapters, is a typical example of an extremely open-ended constitutional clause. Its textual ambiguity was not merely the outcome of indeterminacy of text: there is ample evidence of the embedded disagreement between participants at the Philadelphia Convention, and later, regarding the nature and extent of powers to be granted to the president. The shared allegiance to the constitution as the primary element of the new polity, and to the ideal of separation of powers in its checks and balances version was a constant guiding light, but the contours of the constitutional structure were originally fuzzy and remain so.

The Philadelphia Convention's mandate 'to render the Constitution of the Federal Government adequate to the exigencies of the Union'[43] was directed by two forces. Looming in the background was the colonial legacy: in the newly independent nation, popular understandings found any form of monarchy abhorrent. However, the Annapolis resolution was generated by the virtual breakdown of the Confederation structure as a framework strong enough to resolve the problems facing the new nation in the absence of a national executive. The decision to move ahead was thus designed to resolve the domestic problems created by former arrangements.[44]

Accounts of the long, sometimes tortuous weeks that led to the finalization of the text show that initial drafts were in fact starting points for the overturning, reintroducing, and otherwise turning around of key elements of Article II. The framers argued long and hard over the Presidential election process, his enumeration and his removal from office,[45] but the minutiae of Article II powers received far less attention and were finally settled by the Committee of Detail and Committee of Style. One telling example: the final wording of the vesting clauses, to which I return below, was the product of the Committee of Style. The retention of an open-ended Article II could have been explained by the views of certain members who generally supported an 'energetic' executive, but the final version cannot be described as the product of open and detailed reasoning. Gouverneur Morris, the active member of the Committee of Style, holds the main credit.[46]

[43] The Annapolis Convention resolution, text in M Jensen, JP Kaminski, and GJ Saladino (eds), *The Documentary History of the Ratification of the Constitution, Vol. I: Constitutional Documents and Records, 1776–1787* (Wisconsin Historical Society Press 1976) 184.

[44] See eg Max Farrand, *The Framing of the Constitution of the United States* (Yale University Press 1913); CC Thach, *The Creation of the Presidency, 1775–1789* (Johns Hopkins Press 1922); Michael J Klarman, *The Framers' Coup: The Making of the United States Constitution* (OUP 2016).

[45] See Thach (n 44) 76–165.

[46] On the contribution of the Committee of Style in this respect see Thach (n 44) 138–39; William M Treanor, 'The Case of the Dishonest Scrivener: Gouverneur Morris and the Creation of the Federalist

Underlying this seemingly surprising marginalization of the treatment of executive powers lay deep ideological disagreement, discussed in detail in Chapter 9. These disagreements on function and text set the tone for the future, and also revolved around the proper interpretation of Sections 2 and 3 of Article II, which offer a menu of possibilities. These provisions enumerate a list of powers that include, in addition to powers such as the grant of pardons and the making of treaties under Senate advice and consent, two promisingly open-ended clauses.

Section 2 opens with the words 'The President shall be Commander in Chief of the Army and the Navy'—a clause that has supported readings of presidential dominance in the field of national security.[47] Possibly the best relatively recent example of government reliance on this clause is the so-called first torture memo, Jay Bybee's memorandum of August 2002 addressed to the then White House Counsel Alberto Gonzales.[48] Here, the power of the president to wage war, and under that power, to capture, detain, and interrogate detainees, squarely relies on the Vesting Clause and the Commander-in-Chief clause as sufficient sources of this power. The emphasis is on the latter clause. Citing several war-time judicial decisions and previous memos, the author of this memo finds that, embedded in 'the text, structure and history of the Constitution', 'the Commander-in-Chief powers and the President's obligation to protect the nation imply the ancillary powers necessary to their successful exercise'.[49]

The clause 'he shall take Care the Laws be faithfully executed', contained in Section 3 and dubbed 'the take-care clause', could have been interpreted as a mere allowance to take measures ancillary to the implementation of laws, but the clause has supported much more. As Jack Goldsmith and John Manning note in their definitive review of the take-care clause, the clause has been generally endorsed by courts in contexts as diverse as the president's power to remove from office and the exercise of prosecutorial discretion. It has also instructed the scope of standing to sue (derived from the distinct powers granted to the executive branch and the judiciary in the constitution), and has served as one of the bases for the recognition

Constitution' (2019) currently at <https://scholarship.law.georgetown.edu/facpub/2163/> esp 49–53. For the version offered by the Committee of Style that included the vesting clause of Article II see Max Farrand (ed), *The Records of the Federal Convention of 1787* (1911), Vol 2, 591, 597.

[47] For contributions that focus on this clause see, eg David J Barron and Martin S Lederman, 'The Commander in Chief at the Lowest Ebb—Framing the Problem, Doctrine, and Original Understanding' (2008) 121 Harv L Rev 689, 941; Brian Logan Beirne, 'George vs. George vs. George: Commander-in-Chief Power' (2007) 26 Yale L & Pol'y Rev 265. This position has attracted strong criticism, notably in John Hart Ely, *War and Responsibility: Constitutional Lessons of Vietnam and Its Aftermath* (Princeton University Press 1995). See also Ingrid Brunk Wuerth, 'International Law and Constitutional Interpretation: The Commander in Chief Clause Reconsidered' (2007) 106 Mich L Rev 61 (drawing on international law); David Luban, 'On the Commander-in-Chief Power' (2007) 81 S Cal L Rev 478 (taking a philosophical and historical stance).

[48] Jay Bybee, *Memorandum for Alberto R Gonzales, Counsel to the President*, 1 August 2002, https://nsarchive2.gwu.edu/NSAEBB/NSAEBB127/02.08.01.pdf ('torture memo').

[49] ibid 37–38.

of what the authors call 'presidential completion power'—incidental measures that are considered necessary for the proper implementation of a statutory command.[50] In this latter category, the authors also included, inter alia, Executive Order 12291 and its progenies, unilaterally issued by presidents to impose duties on agencies, including the completion of a cost-benefit analysis prior to agencies' rulemaking.[51] Indeed, in a published memorandum, President Reagan's Office of Legal Counsel found that the power to issue the order derived from this clause.[52]

In all of the above contexts, the president's powers were expanded; Goldsmith and Manning also observe that the clause was instrumental in decisions that *de-limited* presidential powers, discussed below in the context of the force of the residuality rule in the US, but these authors find the general pattern to be one of judicial expansion of presidential powers, and also note that in doing so, the court did not interpret the clause under its well-established canons of interpretation usually applied when interpreting the constitution; the clause appeared to be self-explanatory.[53] Critique of the expanded version of this clause was voiced earlier,[54] but the force of this clause has only been strengthened over time; it offers another example of the utility of the open-ended constitutional text for those who wish to exercise extensive power in the absence of clear authorization while seemingly acting under law.

In sum, each and every theory of the role of the US presidency advanced since the ratification of its constitution, from a limited vision of the president as presider/moderator to the full-fledged version of a post 9/11 imperial ruler, have found a basis in the text, in different understandings of original intent, and in constitutional history.[55] Reliance on text, as such, when upheld or found justified (by courts, by politics, or even merely by the president) renders such powers fuzzy, albeit of a particular form of 'non-statutariness'. Powers that derive solely from the

[50] For the history of reliance on this clause see Jack Goldsmith and John F Manning, 'The Protean Take Care Clause' (2016) 164 U Penn L Rev 1835, 1839–48, 1851–53. In the context of the president's removal power see eg James Madison's speech in Congress on 17 June 1789, in *Annals of Congress, House of Representatives, 1st Congress, 1st Session*, <https://memory.loc.gov/cgi-bin/ampage?collId=llac&fileName=001/llac001.db&recNum=259>. For additional relatively recent discussions on this context see Patricia L Bellia, 'PCAOB and the Persistence of the Removal Puzzle' (2012) 80 Geo Wash L Rev 1371, 1383–88; Bruce A Green and Rebecca Roiphe, 'Can the President Control the Department of Justice?' (2018) 70 Ala L Rev 1. For the reliance on the clause in the context of the president's completion power see Jack Goldstein and John F Manning, 'The President's Completion Power' (2006) Yale LJ 2280. For some of the seminal judicial decisions see *Myers v US*, 272 US 52 (1926); *Heckler v Chaney*, 470 US 821 (1985); *Lujan v Defenders of Wildlife*, 504 US 555 (1992); *Free Enterprise Fund v Public Company Accounting Oversight Board*, 561 US 477 (2010).

[51] Goldsmith and Manning (n 50) 2295–96.

[52] Executive Order 12291, Federal Regulation, 46 FR 13193. On this memorandum, and the extensive response, see Goldsmith and Manning (n 50) 2296–97.

[53] Goldsmith and Manning (n 50).

[54] See eg A Michael Froomkin, 'The Imperial Presidency's New Vestments' (1994) 88 Northwestern U L Rev 1346, 1363–65; Curtis A Bradley and Martin S Flaherty, 'Executive Power Essentialism and Foreign Affairs (2004) 102 Mich L Rev 545, 546–53.

[55] See also ch 1.

constitution do not derive from statute, but can (or at least, potentially can) boast a constitutional pedigree that, under general understandings, carries an exalted status. Under traditional accounts, written constitutions can be amended only by the formal processes set in them, and these are typically difficult to achieve, more so the notorious difficulty of amendment of the US constitution; such powers, it may be argued, are therefore also relatively immune from removal.[56]

2. Constitution-Type Extra-Textual Doctrines

Alongside powers that can be found to derive directly from the constitution, several doctrines have served to identify and apply powers that could not be thus slotted. Having no link to a statute, these should all be identified as deriving from the constitutional sphere, broadly defined.

In Chapter 3 I identified five such doctrines: political reality; the state's sovereignty; the 'personification' of government as holder of powers akin to those of individuals and legal personalities; history as providing a 'gloss' on the constitution or otherwise embedding the recognition of governmental action (for example under the construct of the 'common law' that supports recognition due to past practice); and conceptions of 'aggregation', under which the general tenor, and collection, of various sources suffice for the recognition of executive powers. All of these are fuzzy, as none can show a pure pedigree derived directly from the constitution; therefore, their contours are even less decipherable than constitution-based constructs. Doctrines (1) and (4), political reality and 'historical gloss', were discussed in detail in Chapter 3 and are only briefly mentioned here. Completion of the analysis in this chapter bears proof of the richness of the ways legal systems have striven to embed non-statutory powers in their public law, above and beyond their recognized constitutional structures.

a. Political reality

Justifications drawing on political reality were discussed above and were linked to some commonly cited presidential speeches that based their action in war and peace on exigencies and political roles.[57]

In the UK, the late twentieth century emergence of the discussion of a 'third source' of powers—powers that are not prerogatives in the historical sense but have no statutory basis—represents a broader reading of political reality, under which the British government has always acted non-statutorily in fields that have not, and

[56] I set aside theories that accept flexibility both in the amendment and interpretation processes of a constitutional text, under constructs such as 'constitutional moments' and 'living constitutions', briefly discussed in ch 1.

[57] See eg the declarations of Presidents Lincoln and Roosevelt, ch 3.

should not, be recognized as prerogatives powers. Such identified non-prerogative powers included the creation and operation of ex-gratia payment schemes,[58] the issue of governmental pamphlets,[59] government policy-making by contract,[60] and, potentially, guidance published by ministries.[61]

The term, coined by BV Harris, was originally linked with personification, an additional doctrine discussed separately below, which offers a legal explanation for the legitimacy of such powers based on the capacity of the executive (or the state—fuzziness in the original) to act like any other legal person.[62] It should however have a life of its own, as some commentators have recognized.[63]

b. Sovereignty and nationhood

Under this doctrine, state sovereignty as a predecessor of the formal constitution has served as a basis for the recognition of unilateral powers invoked in the context of foreign relations. The source and mainstay has been Justice Sutherland's opinion in *Curtiss-Wright* (1936). Concerned with the indictment of military aircraft producers, who were charged with selling arms contrary to a Joint Resolution that banned export to warring entities, the main argument brought forth and decided upon was the companies' claim that that act was an unconstitutional delegation of law-making power to the president. Delegation, it was argued, was found in the grant of power to the president to order such embargos by proclamations. In deciding the case for the appellants (the US), Justice Sutherland offered a three-pronged argument that supported the president's power to act unilaterally in the field of foreign affairs. Two of these, concerned with the views of John Marshall on the matter and a reading of the constitution are, for our purposes, set aside. Under the third count, sole presidential power derived from the nature of the United

[58] For example, the Criminal Injuries Compensation Scheme, decided upon in *Lain* (n 9), and the government's scheme to award extra-statutory ex-gratia payments to some widowers, recognized as such but not expanded to all widowers, in *R (Hooper) v Secretary of State for Work and Pensions* [2005] 1 WLR 1681.

[59] *Jenkins* (n 12).

[60] Discussed in Daintith (n 11); Freedland (n 11) 291–95. Neither are wedded to the idea that such powers are exercises of the Royal prerogative.

[61] *New London College v Secretary of State for the Home Department* [2012] EWCA Civ 51.

[62] BV Harris, 'The "Third Source" of Authority for Government Action' (1992) 108 LQR 626 (Harris (1992)). For personification see section C.2.c below.

[63] See Max Harris, *Showcase—New Directions in Administrative Law Theory: The Prerogative, the Third Source, and Administrative Law Theory* (2019) Int'l J Const L Blog < http://www.iconnectblog.com/2019/09/showcase-new-directions-in-administrative-law-theory-the-prerogative-the-third-source-and-administrative-law-theory/>. See also my comments below. Others have rejected the notion that any non-statutory powers beyond prerogatives should exist, a stance that either calls for the obliteration of all true non-statutory powers or for the expansion of the history-based prerogative and its transformation. For an earlier assertion that rejected the second option, dissecting the powers recognized at the time that were not to be considered, in his view, to be pure prerogatives; HWR Wade, *Constitutional Fundamentals* (Rev ed, Stevens 1989). For Wade, some of these should be removed from the discussion, as they create no enforceable rights; this notion still does not offer an explanatory account of their continuous life, and the fact that they are relied upon both by the government and by affected individuals.

States 'as a member of the family of nations', which had received sovereignty on independence; since 'the Union existed before the Constitution', and the states were not granted power in this field, these powers 'did not depend upon the affirmative grants of the Constitution': thus, the constitution's text was set aside.[64]

Extensive debates over this doctrine ensued. Criticism on the correctness of all three prongs[65] has been supplemented by diverging views over the precedential nature of this reasoning: under the central reading, it was no more than a lengthy dictum, but other opinions exist.[66] In any case, consequent reliance by governments and courts have contributed to the retention of the sole-organ doctrine,[67] despite the retraction from sovereignty-nationhood thesis in *Zivotowsky* (2015), which reaffirmed the sole power of the president in recognizing foreign states, this time by reliance on the constitution and history.[68]

c. Personification

The third doctrine has not found purchase in the United States, but is central to the current debate on the legality of unilateral executive power in the United Kingdom.

Initially, the pairing of 'non-statutory' powers with 'prerogative' powers may have been intuitive, since the prerogative, indeed, does not derive from statute. The prerogative, nevertheless, is really something else, as it is deeply embedded in the historical unwritten basis of the English constitution.[69]

Personification preceded the recognition of third source powers, discussed above. In *Malone* (1979), arguments for the unlawfulness of police telephone-tapping in the absence of statutory authorization were curtly rejected in court by equalizing the individual's freedom to act unless prohibited by law with the

[64] *US v Curtiss-Wright*, 299 US 304 (1936) 317–18. See, in the same vein, *US v Belmont*, 301 US 324 (1923); *US v Pink*, 315 US 203, 223–24 (1942). This source is discussed as an 'extra-textual power' in Saikrishna Bangalore Prakash, 'A Taxonomy of Presidential Powers' (2008) BU L Rev 327, 333.

[65] See eg Louis Fisher, 'The Staying Power of Erroneous Dicta: From *Curtiss-Wright* to *Zivotofsky*' (2016) 31 Con Commentary 149, and the literature review, ibid 186–99.

[66] See eg ibid; but compare with Charles A Lofgren, '*United States v Curtiss-Wright Export Corporation*: An Historical Reassessment' (1973) 83 Yale LJ 1 (assessing that part as more than mere dicta).

[67] See Fisher's account of such reliance (n 65) 175–85, 201–06.

[68] *Zivotowsky v Kerry*, 135 S Ct 2076 (2015). Here, the Supreme Court affirmed the president's exclusive power to recognize foreign nations, finding sufficient authority in the Constitution. The challenged statute, The Foreign Relations Authorizations Act, Fiscal Year 2003 (116 Stat 1350), inter alia enabled the passport registration of US citizens born in Jerusalem to note 'Israel' as their place of birth, a provision that contradicted US policy at the time. Signed by President Bush, the Act was accompanied by a signing statement that declared, inter alia, that this provision 'impermissibly interferes with the President's constitutional authority to conduct the Nation's foreign affairs and to supervise the unitary executive branch' and that other provisions that 'purport to direct or burden the conduct of negotiations by the executive branch with foreign governments, international organizations, or other entities abroad or which purport to direct executive branch officials to use the US voice and vote in international organizations to achieve specified foreign policy objectives' were only advisory. For the signing statement see <https://www.presidency.ucsb.edu/documents/statement-signing-the-foreign-relations-authorization-act-fiscal-year-2003>. On signing statements see ch 5.

[69] See Margit Cohn, 'Medieval Chains, Invisible Inks: On Non-Statutory Powers of the Executive' (2005) 97 OJLS 97, 108.

government's power. In the words of Sir Robert Megarry VC, responding to the contention of illegality,

> [t]he underlying assumption of this contention, of course, is that nothing is lawful that is not positively authorised by law. As I have indicated, England is not a country where everything is forbidden except what is expressly permitted. One possible illustration is smoking. I inquired what positive authority was given by the law to permit people to smoke . . .[70]

The fact that 'governments' as such cannot smoke was apparently immaterial in this line of reasoning and assisted the court's decision to uphold the practice. Recognizing that the practice 'cried out for legislation', the court ruled that in the absence of a recognized right to privacy at the time, telephone-tapping could be carried out without breach of the law both by individuals and public bodies, and was thus safely within the scope of government action.[71] Although this practice was subsequently found unlawful in the European Court of Human Rights, and was later regulated by statute, the route to recognition of such a source of power had opened, and is still available.

If initial literature on 'new prerogatives' and similar powers only hinted at personification,[72] this doctrine was substantially boosted by BV Harris' work on the 'third source' of authority for executive action, discussed above.[73] Harris was adamant about distinguishing those powers from prerogative 'in the narrow sense',[74] and *Malone* provided an initial anchor.

In his first article of a series, Harris cited *Malone*, but with a possible twist that foresaw subsequent unclarity: for him, these powers derived from the 'freedom to do anything that is not prohibited by law'[75]—a concept discussed further below.

Fuelling the debate, the courts have offered inconsistent analyses. In *ex parte C* (2000), the Court of Appeal ruled that the Department of Health was empowered to maintain a list (index) of persons found unsuitable to work with children due to their past employment and behaviour. Rather than rely on *Malone* for the recognition of the power, the court reverted to a statement in *Halsbury's Laws* that '[a]t common law the Crown, as a corporation possessing legal personality, has

[70] *Malone v Metropolitan Police Commissioner* [1979] 1 Ch 344, 366.

[71] ibid 380–81.

[72] For earlier writing which hinted at that direction see Daintith (n 11) 42–3 (discussing the government's 'common law freedom' to choose parties to a contract, similarly to individuals, in the limited existence of public procurement laws at the time); George Winterton, 'The Prerogative in Novel Situations' (1983) 99 LQR 407, 409 (discussed, with some critique of the reliance on the analogy, leading to a call to constrain such powers only to cases when the government's action is identical to the individual's).

[73] Harris (1992) (n 62); see further BV Harris, 'The "Third Source" of Authority for Government Action Revisited' (2007) 123 LQR 225; BV Harris, 'Government "Third Source" Action and Common Law Constitutionalism' (2010) 126 LQR 373.

[74] See eg Harris (n 62) 626, 633, 650.

[75] ibid 633.

the capacities of a natural person and thus the same liberties as the individual'.[76] In *Hooper*, next in this series, mentioned above, the House of Lords found it sufficient to consider such powers as 'common law powers'.[77]

By that time, the government had unearthed a 1945 legal memorandum that, it is still argued, has provided a basis of power equivalent to those inhered in an individual or a body corporate. The memorandum, penned by First Parliamentary Counsel Sir Granville Ram, was disclosed in a Cabinet Office report only in 2002, and further debated in the House of Lords a year later.[78] The report traces three sources of executive power. In addition to express statute-based powers and implied powers incidental to the exercise of such statutory powers and implied powers, the report refers to the 'Ram Doctrine', under which 'a department can do anything that a natural person can, provided it is not forbidden from doing so'.[79] The content of the doctrine was disclosed in response to a series of parliamentary questions tabled by Lord Lester of Herne Hill, between January and April 2003.[80] Emphasis on corporatization of the Crown remained central in the government's reading of this memorandum, as presented in a written answer to Lord Lester's parliamentary questions in 2003, according to which 'the Ram doctrine reflects a well-established principle of constitutional law. Ministers and their departments have common law powers which derive from the Crown's status as a corporation sole'.[81] The Court of Appeal has relied on the memorandum at least once,[82] and its text is available on the Web.[83]

Responding to the criticism voiced against the Ram doctrine,[84] the courts became even more ambiguous about the force of personification and the nature of

[76] *R v Secretary of State for Health ex parte C* [2000] HRLR 400, 405.

[77] Hooper (n 58); for references to this appellation see n 91.

[78] Performance and Innovation Unit, Cabinet Office, Privacy and Data-Sharing: The Way Forward for Public Services, April 2002, 34; House of Lords debates referenced in Anthony Lester and Matthew Weait, 'The Use of Ministerial Powers without Parliamentary Authority: The Ram Doctrine' (2003) PL 415.

[79] Lester and Weait (n 78) at n 4 para 3.46.

[80] ibid.

[81] HL Debs vol 645, col WA 12 (25 February 2003).

[82] *Hooper* (n 58) [132].

[83] HL Debs vol 643, cols WA 98-9 (22 January 2003). The memorandum states that '[A] Minister of the Crown, even though there may have been a statute authorizing his appointment, is not a creature of statute and may, as an agent of the Crown, exercise any powers that the Crown has power to exercise, except so far as he is precluded from doing so by statute. In other words, in the case of a Government Department, one must look at the statutes to see what it may not do, not as in the case of a company to see what it may do ... the governing principle is that an express statutory provision is not necessary to enable a Minister to exercise functions'; for the text of the memorandum see <https://publications.parliament.uk/pa/jt200708/jtselect/jtstatin/47/4713.htm>.

[84] During hearings in the House of Lords' Select Committee on the Constitution held prior to the conclusion of the Committee's report on (see below), the Committee Acting Chairman, Lord Irvine of Lairg, claimed that the memorandum did not support the government's reading of it (it merely asserted the powers of ministers to do what the Crown was empowered to do); Professor Sir Jeffrey Jowell considered it 'a constitutional heresy' that would be overridden by the constitutional principle of the rule of law; Sir Stephen Sedley, the retired Justice of the Court of Appeal, maintained that although *Malone*, in its time, was neither 'right' or 'wrong', it could not stand in the post Human Rights Act era. See House of Lords, The Select Committee on the Constitution, 'Inquiry on Pre-emption of Parliament', Evidence

'third source' powers. Some criticism of references to analogies with the powers of natural person was voiced in *Shrewsbury and Atcham* (2008), but the challenged action (the introduction of reform of local government prior to legislation) was established as ancillary to the existing legislation; hence, the question, and the import of *ex parte C*, could be set aside.[85] In a more recent decision in this series, *New London College* (2013), heard and decided by the Supreme Court just after the publication of the House of Lords 2013 report, a non-statutory guidance that established a process for licensing academic institutions as sponsors for foreign students, was upheld, as in the prior decision, as an exercise of powers ancillary to the legislation; the exact juridical basis for 'third source' powers was considered 'controversial' and was not decided upon.[86]

For some commentators, the argument under 'freedom', first clearly voiced in Harris's first article, should be distinguished from the doctrine of personification. Perry identifies two 'accounts' of these powers, addressed as 'administrative powers': 'the residual freedom account', under which the Crown can act unless prohibited, and 'the common law account', which is explicitly linked with the equation of the Crown as a legal person.[87] Echoing, so it seems, Harris's views and the Ram doctrine respectively, I find this distinction unhelpful. The argument for freedom to act unless prohibited must rest on a personification analogy, as in *Malone*. Otherwise, it may rest on history and precedent, that is, past recognition that has nothing to do with personification—a direction missing from the debate and now to be discussed in conjunction with an entirely different version of a history-derived doctrine, developed in the US.

Session No 4, 27 February 2013, 27–30. <https://www.parliament.uk/documents/lords-committees/constitution/preemption/uc270213ev4.pdf>. In the report, published that year, the committee concluded its discussion of the doctrine by stating that '[t]he description of the common law powers of the Crown encapsulated by the phrase "the Ram doctrine" is inaccurate, and should no longer be used'. House of Lords Select Committee on the Constitution, 'The Pre-emption of Parliament' (2013) 13th Report of Session 2012–2013, HL Paper 165, 23; see also 4, 18. Other critiques include Lester and Weait (n 79); Cohn, 'Medieval Chains', (n 69), 109–11.

[85] *Shrewsbury and Atcham Borough Council v Secretary of State for Communities and Local Government* [2008] EWCA Civ 148.

[86] *New London College v Secretary of State for the Home Department* [2012] EWCA Civ 51. The decision spurred further comments on the nature of these powers, including Mark Elliott, 'Muddled Thinking in the Supreme Court on the "Third Source" of Governmental Authority', *Public Law for Everyone*, 23 July 2013 <https://publiclawforeveryone.com/2013/07/23/muddled-thinking-in-the-supreme-court-on-the-third-source-of-governmental-authority/; Paul Daly, 'I contract, therefore I am: the Third Source Powers of Government Entities: Part One', *Administrative Law Matters*, 31 July 2013 <https://www.administrativelawmatters.com/blog/2013/07/31/i-contract-therefore-i-am-the-third-source-powers-of-government-entities-part-one/>; Paul Daly, 'I contract, therefore I am: the Third Source Powers of Government Entities: Part Two', *Administrative Law Matters*, 31 July 2013 <https://www.administrativelawmatters.com/blog/2013/07/31/i-contract-therefore-i-am-the-third-source-powers-of-government-entities-part-two/>.

[87] Adam Perry, 'The Crown's Administrative Powers' (2015) 131 LQR 652.

d. 'Historical gloss'

Mentioned in Chapter 3, the United States' 'historical gloss' doctrine has supported rulings that past practice in the absence of Congressional objection, that is, the existence of positive inter-branch interaction over time, has served as an alternative theory of the legitimacy of non-statutory powers. Decades before *Youngstown*, the Supreme Court found that longstanding practices, supported by judicially recognized congressional acquiescence evident in oblique references to the said practice, appropriation of funds for its continuation, or simple inaction, were sufficient to justify the upholding of unilateral presidential action. In *Midwest Oil*, the court upheld the decision to temporarily deny access to and use of oil-rich public lands due to a shortage of natural sources, contrary to a statute that enabled free use of land. The court relied on decades of practice, never challenged by Congress, to uphold this one example of a decades-long pattern of interaction.[88] Upholding an action that contradicted statute, this decision, then, does not conform to the residuality principle.

The doctrine was well-expressed in Justice Frankfurter's oft-cited dictum in *Youngstown*:

> ... a systematic, unbroken, executive practice, long pursued to the knowledge of the Congress and never before questioned, engaged in by Presidents who have also sworn to uphold the Constitution, making as it were such exercise of power part of the structure of our government, may be treated as a gloss on 'executive power' vested in the President by S.1 of Art. II.[89]

The UK provides a second type of reliance on history, beyond the obvious historical basis of the royal prerogative: the loose use of the term 'common law powers'. As a concept, the term 'the common law' may connote a system in which much of its rules are judge-made, but history remains a crucial element to the understanding of this concept.[90] Cited by the House of Lords in *Hooper* (2005) in its decision on the legality of a scheme of ex-gratia benefits to all widowers that was not to be linked to the prerogative, no explanation as to the nature of these powers as 'common law' ones can be found in the decision.[91] Further confusion emerges in the literature, which, in some cases, links the 'common law account' of

[88] *Midwest Oil* (n 1).

[89] *Youngstown Sheet & Tube v Sawyer*, 343 US 579, 610–11 (1952). For subsequent decisions in this vein see *Massachusetts v Laird* 400 US 886 (1970) (the waging of prolonged hostilities was shared by both government branches, and the executive had acted 'not only in the absence of any Congressional conflicting claim of authority but with steady Congressional support'); *Dames & Moore* (n 1) (concerned with presidential signing of executive agreements and other compacts made between governments; all upheld despite arguments for unconstitutionality for breach of the treaty-making clause, with references to 'practice' and 'acquiescence').

[90] For a general description see eg Andrew DE Lewis and others, 'Common Law', Encyclopaedia Britannica online <https://www.britannica.com/topic/common-law>.

[91] *Hooper* (n 58), eg [81] (per Lord Hope), [96] (per Lord Scott), [103] (per Lord Brown).

such powers to those available under the common law to natural persons, that is, to personification.[92]

In my view, reliance on the 'common law' as a separate source of authority must draw on the nature of common law as based on history and precedent. The tectonic move of the debate towards personification, discussed above, has marginalized arguments akin to those heard in the context of the history-backed prerogative and the US 'historical gloss'. Still, history, as embodied in the reliance on 'the common law', remains a central element of the discussion.

e. Aggregation of powers

The fifth and last construct draws on the concept of 'aggregated' powers, referring to a collection of sources which, combined, may uphold powers that are not easily traceable to any single source of power. The main judicial endorsement of the idea is found in Chief Justice Vinson's dissenting opinion in *Youngstown*. Upholding President Truman's order to seize steel mills on strike during the Korean War, Chief Justice Vinson's dissenting opinion recognized the longstanding practice of presidential action during emergencies, discussed separately above, but he also cited a statement written by the Attorney General at that time, Robert Jackson, who was one of the Justices on the *Youngstown* bench. Read before the Senate in May 1943, that statement supported President Roosevelt's seizure of an aviation plant in California due to a strike. In that statement, Jackson opined inter alia that '[t]he Presidential proclamation rests upon the aggregate of the Presidential powers derived from the Constitution itself and from statutes enacted by Congress'.[93] Some of the aggregated sources cited in Justice Jackson's speech were the take-care clause and the commander in chief clause, but these did not exclude all other sources.[94]

Although this alternative source of action has not attracted much attention since, it has been well-internalized by all presidents. One clear example is found in virtually all recitals of executive orders issued by presidents since the mid-twentieth century. Executive Order 10340, which authorized the seizure of the steel mills in this case, contained the following recital:

> ... by virtue of the authority vested in me by the Constitution and laws of the United States, and as President of the United States and Commander in Chief of the armed forces of the United States, it is hereby ordered as follows ...[95]

[92] See eg Perry (n 87) 659–70.

[93] 89 Cong Reg 3992 (1943), 5 May 1943. Cited in *Youngstown* (n 89) 695–96.

[94] In the further words of Attorney General Jackson, 'For the faithful execution of such laws the President has back of him [sic] not only each general law-enforcement power conferred by the various acts of Congress but the aggregated of all such laws plus that wide discretion as to method vested in him by the Constitution for the purpose of executing the law.' ibid.

[95] Executive Order 10340, *Directing the Secretary of Commerce to Take Possession of and Operate the Plants and Facilities of Certain Steel Companies*, 8 April 1943, 17 FR 3139.

This formula, sometimes supplemented by references to statutes that may, or may not, offer additional sources of power, has become the standard in the penmanship of executive orders, and its fuzziness is more than evident: it allows presidents to legitimate their action without linking it with any specific authority.[96]

D. Legal Constraints on Unilateral Non-Statutory Powers

In this section, I consider the two central legal constraints that may be applied to limit unilateral, constitutional-derived executive powers: their subjection to statute, under the doctrine of residuality, and their subjection to judicial review. I show that acceptance of these constraints in the UK and the US varies, and that even when such a constraint is recognized and embraced, its impact can be diluted, by use of legal tactics that considerably weaken its force.

1. The Residuality Doctrine

The British rule of residuality is the archetype of the first legal constraint.[97] The classic version of this rule—prerogative cannot be exercised when a statute regulates the same field of action—has nevertheless been amenable to dilution in several ways.

The doctrine has deep historical roots. Justice Coke's decision in *The Case of Proclamations* (1611), in which he declared that 'the King hath no prerogative, but that which the law of the land allows him', is considered a harbinger for the final assertion of the supremacy of statute law by 1689, although the tension between parliamentary and Crown legislation continued to escalate before its resolution; prior to the constitutional settlement at the end of that century, the courts moved towards a more lenient attitude, upholding the setting of taxes and other coercive action.[98] The reassertion of the rule in *De Keyser* (1920)[99] was reinforced in later decisions, such as the *Laker Airways* case. Here, applicants challenged a decision to revoke a license to operate a flight service between London and New York, adding

[96] On the practice of multi-source citation see ch 3; see further analysis in ch 5.

[97] Above, text to n 99.

[98] *Case of Proclamations* 77 ER 1352 (1611), 1354. Other decisions of that period that declared the supremacy of the Common Law—not statute—over the royal prerogative include *Prohibitions del Roy*, 12 77 ER 1342 (1607) (the King had no power to prohibit building in London or prevent the production of starch); *Commissions of Enquiry*, 77 ER 1312 (1608) (hearing of offences by special commissions); *Chancey's Case*, 77 ER 1360 (1610) (jailing without trial). Cases upholding Royal power include *Case of Impositions (Bate's Case)* 2 St Tr 371 (1606); *The King's Prerogative in Saltpetre*, 12 Co Rep 1295 (1607); *Darnel's Case (The Five Knights' Case)*, 3 St Tr 1 (1627); *Case of Ship Money (Hampden's Case)*, 3 St Tr 825 (1637).

[99] *De Keyser Royal Hotel* (n 31).

to the existing one operated by a state-owned airline, following a treaty signed between the US and the UK to limit long-haul flight routes to a single airline. The government argued inter alia that its policy decision was made under the prerogative of foreign affairs and could therefore be effected without reversion to the Civil Aviation Act. Citing *de Keyser*, the court relied upon three features of the Civil Aviation Act, which effectively removed the power to revoke a licence outside of its framework.[100]

Embedded as the central constraint on the prerogative, the true extent and force of the residuality rule is continuously debated. Three issues arise: the 'coverage' question, the subsequent life of a prerogative power ostensibly removed by statute, and the force of a prerogative explicitly preserved in a statute concerned with a similar field of action.

First, then, is the question whether the residuality doctrine is at all applicable. Under the doctrine, when an issue is sufficiently 'covered' by statute, reliance on prerogative is indeed removed, but this result depends on the interpretation of the statute alleged to have covered the field. This interpretive feat was achieved in the case of *de Keyser*. The court relied on existing legislation concerning the requisitioning of property in wartime that gave right to compensation; hence, requisition without compensation, ostensibly done under the prerogative, could no longer be upheld. Still, in other cases, interpreters may discover minimal or no overlap, leading to the upholding of the prerogative.[101]

The second issue, discussed but not resolved by the court, concerns the subsequent life of a prerogative power ostensibly removed, in the case of the repeal of the statute that replaced it.[102]

Finally, some prerogatives have been explicitly preserved in a statute. In such a case, the residuality doctrine itself, not the prerogative, seems to have been abrogated.[103]

[100] *Laker Airways v Department of Trade* [1977] QB 643. The court held that the Act, regulating the civil aviation field, contained a detailed provision concerning revocation of licences, and authorized the Crown to delegate to the Civil Aviation Authority the performance of various of the Crown's functions under aviation treaties, a road not taken by the government.

[101] See analysis below, text to n 109.

[102] For a relatively clear preference of prerogative re-emergence see *Burmah Oil v Lord Advocate* [1965] AC 75, 148; for more oblique discussions see eg see *De Keyser* (n 31) 539–40; *R v Secretary of State for Foreign Affairs, Ex p Rees-Mogg* [1994] QB 552, 567. Under a variant of this position, the prerogative will not re-emerge if the repealing statute clearly indicates that the prerogative was not intended to be revived. The opposite position could be supported by dicta such as 'a prerogative power however well-established may be curtailed or abrogated by statute', if 'abrogation' receives its full meaning (see the use of these terms by Lord Neuberger for the majority in *Miller* (n 30) [48]). On this question see Robert Craig, 'Casting Aside Clanking Medieval Chains: Prerogative, Statute and Article 50 after the EU Referendum' (2016) 79 MLR 1041.

[103] See for example section 33(5) of the Immigration Act 1971, which stipulates that '[t]his Act shall not be taken to supersede or impair any power exercisable by Her Majesty in relation to aliens by virtue of Her prerogative'. In such a case, application of any type of a residuality rule would require an acrobatic interpretative exercise that is most likely to fail.

Moving to the US, *Youngstown* seems, if only skimmed through, to offer a reinforcement of the residuality doctrine. The plurality in the Supreme Court found that the challenged presidential seizure of steel mills during the Korean War, motivated by a threat of a strike, was unlawful, since statutes in force regulated the management of industrial action. Rejecting arguments that relied on 'the aggregate of the [president's] powers under the Constitution', that is, the vesting clause, the take-care, and the commander-in-chief clauses, Justice Black also ruled that the president could not seize steel mills in order to prevent an industrial action, since an impressive body of statute-law offered channels of action, a clear expression of the residuality rule.[104] However, the complex web of opinions in *Youngstown* conveys much more.

The most memorable and frequently used part of the decision is contained in Justice Jackson's concurring opinion, in its offering of three 'practical situations', or categories of interaction between statute and executive action. First, Justice Jackson reminds his readers that executives often act under statute, a truism that at this point is excluded from our analysis. The next two categories are relevant to the understanding of residuality in a system that offers the president powers under a written constitution. Under the second category, the president's own independent powers under the constitution are supplemented by powers emerging from 'a zone of twilight in which he and Congress may have concurrent authority, or in which its distribution is uncertain', a fuzzy enough reference, not only to text, but to other forms of implied authorization—and to the recognition that those 'concurrent' powers may be seized by the president alongside Congress.[105]

The third category seems to reiterate the residuality principle, but with a triple twist. Jackson's focus here is on action that is 'incompatible with the expressed or implied will of Congress', yet, in his words, when such contradiction occurs, the president's power is 'at its lowest ebb': he may act in ways that are incompatible to statute, but only as far as his powers derive directly under the constitution. This neat formula befits a polity that offers direct executive powers in its constitution, but, considering the fuzziness of the US constitution, discussed above, it offers potential for future manipulation: this parallel source of authority provides a rich repository of power.[106]

Further whittling down the force of the principle of residuality, the US Supreme Court upheld a presidential executive order issued as part of the resolution of a prior freeze of Iranian assets in 1979. In *Dames & Moore v Regan*, the court found a statutory basis for nullifying previous attachments over Iranian assets; however,

[104] Opinion of the Court, *Youngstown* (n 89) 582–89. See also *Chamber of Commerce v Reich*, 74 F3d 1322 (DC Cir 1996) (executive order with no specific statutory base found contrary to legislation).

[105] *Youngstown* (n 89) 636–37. Justice Jackson's third category, action contrary to statute, is excluded from discussion here. For the dicta on 'historical gloss' see text to n 88.

[106] In Justice Jackson's words, 'he can rely only upon his own constitutional powers minus any constitutional powers of Congress over the matter'. ibid 637.

the suspension of claims filed in US courts against Iranians was not directly authorized by statute. Rather than finding the suspension to be *ultra vires* (through the interpretation of the statute concerned with international sanctions), Chief Justice Rehnquist followed the *Midwest Oil* reasoning, referring to statutes that, although they did not contain a specific authorization for the suspension, were 'highly relevant in the looser sense of indicating congressional acceptance of a broad scope for executive action in circumstances such as those presented in this case'. The court further addressed supporting precedent, which included a reading of *Youngstown* that emphasized Justice Jackson's three categories and the importance of flexible classification.[107]

Later Supreme Court decisions seem to have required clear statutory authority for presidential action that affects a constitutionally protected right, as in the case of *Hamdan*, in which the court found no statutory basis for the deprivation of habeas corpus. Deciding that the joint resolution authorizing the president to act against forces involved in the September 11 terrorist attacks did not authorize the setting of a military commission, which was also in violation of the Unitary Code of Military Justice, the ruling implies that no such action can be exercised unilaterally. However, this case involved the limitation of habeas corpus, enshrined in the Second Amendment of the US Constitution, a feature that explains the majority's stance.[108]

Even without reliance on the constitutional text or reversion to doctrines such as congressional acquiescence and 'historical gloss', courts can be, and have been, creative in upholding non-statutory action despite the existence of statute. In some cases, courts have found authority in statute, despite initial government reliance on anything but the statute, thereby denying the action's non-statutory nature. Secondly, courts have sometimes interpreted statute as not excluding supplementary extra-statutory action. Both paths are part of the reasoning in the British case of *Northumbria Police Authority*. Applicants argued that a provision in the Police Act that stated that local police authorities were to provide for the supply of equipment to their local forces. Challenged by the riots and disturbances of the early 1980s, the Home Office offered police forces access to their stores to be supplied with CS gas and plastic baton rounds. The applicants' argument, that the statutory provision concerning the provision of supply of equipment by (local) police authorities should be read as prohibiting other supply paths, was rejected in the Court of Appeal on two counts. It first found sufficient authority in another provision in the Police Act, generally authorizing the Home Secretary to provide services that

[107] *Dames & Moore* (n 1) 657, 668.

[108] *Hamdan* (n 1); *Boumediene v Bush*, 553 US 723 (2008). The expansive vision of the president's power can still be found in the dissenting opinions of these decisions (see eg *Hamdan* 679–80) and remains linked with earlier arguments that drew on 'the aggregate' of presidential powers under the constitution, an aspect dealt with above (text to n 93).

he considers to be 'necessary or expedient for promoting the efficiency of the police'. The court then upheld the Divisional Court's ruling that allowed such action, under a (newly) discovered prerogative to keep the peace of the realm.[109]

A similar judicial practice is evident in the US. US courts have sometimes found sufficient statutory basis for presidential action, even when no specific statute was originally cited, thereby fully legitimizing the challenged action and extracting it from the realm of the unilateral.[110]

A third possible path for upholding non-statutory powers despite the existence of statute is opened when courts interpret the action as belonging to an entirely different field of action. An example, in which that path was not taken, is the *Laker Airways* case. As discussed above, the government argued inter alia that its policy decision was made under the prerogative of foreign affairs; rejecting this argument, the court linked the decision to the field of civil aviation, hence effectively applying the residuality rule. Had the court been ready to accept that the government's action pertained to its foreign affairs powers, rather than part of its civil aviation policy, the case may have been decided differently.[111]

2. Subjection to Judicial Review

The second legal constraint on unilateral power, its amenity to judicial scrutiny, is again seemingly established in both systems, but has in fact had a mixed direct impact. The survey of the extent of judicial review in the UK and the US spans both constitutional- and administrative-type review. This distinction is based on the type of reasoning and grounds applied by courts overviewing non-statutory unilateral executive action. Constitutional-type review occurs when this action is measured against the text of a written constitution, or against various grounds that carry a constitutional nature, such as the residuality doctrine, personification, or sovereignty, all discussed above.[112] In administrative-type review, the legality of a challenged action may be decided by applying recognized grounds for review of administrative action.

Of course, in most, if not all, challenges of executive action, applicants tend to forward mixed arguments. Any challenge to the legality of a source of executive

[109] *R v Secretary of State for the Home Department ex parte Northumbria Police Authority* [1989] QB 26 (CA); The Police Act 1964, sections 4(1), 41.

[110] As in the case of the series of executive orders that subjected government contractors to non-discrimination and other social policies: see eg *Farmer* (n 1); *Farkas v Texas Instrument*, 375 F2d 629 (5th Cir 1967); *Contractors Association v Secretary of Labor*, 442 F2d 159 (3d Cir 1971); *AFLCIO v Kahn*, 618 F2d 784 (DC Cir 1979). For a more skeptical view see *Chrysler v Brown*, 441 US 281, 304–05 (1979) (origin of order obscure, no need to decide whether authorized by statutes). Compare to the British *Northumbria* case, text to n 109.

[111] *Laker* (n 100).

[112] See Section C. Residuality draws on the principle of the sovereignty of parliament, and the others rely on general principles of the system.

action is likely to include arguments from the constitutional sphere, and may further be based on administrative law grounds, when the exercise of the powers is challenged.[113] This distinction is however important for improving our understanding of the ways courts have addressed, and may address in the future, the legality of executive action. Application of the distinction also enables us to assess the relative importance that each system grants to the constitutional element as compared to the administrative level.

The most far-reaching judicial reform in the UK has been the evolvement of readiness to subject to review the exercise of the traditional prerogative, by recognizing action under the prerogative as equivalent to regular administrative action. This development on the constitutional level transformed earlier understandings. Initially, the courts intervened only when the challenged executive action should have been exercised under existing statute, as in the *De Keyser* case.[114] In addition to the application of this residuality rule, the courts were only ready to decide the question of whether the challenged executive action was indeed part of the prerogative. When it was so defined, that was the end of the matter: a general immunity from review derived from the remaining link between these powers and the Crown. The full subjection of the prerogative to run-of-the-mill judicial review was gradual. Initial judicial dicta, first expressed in the 1960s and 1970s,[115] were the harbingers of the House of Lords' groundbreaking declaration in the mid-1980s that prerogative powers, exercised under modern constitutional convention by the government rather than the Crown, were subject to the same review applied to statute-based power.[116] In *GCHQ*, the court was concerned with a delegated power under a prerogative-based order in council; the amenability of review of an order in council itself, the legal status of which remains unclear, was affirmed in *Bancoult 2* (HL) (2008).

[113] For example, the appeal decided by the House of Lords in *Bancoult 2* (HL) (n 6) decided upon a mix of arguments brought by the parties. Constitutional-type arguments included the government's claim that orders in council of the sort challenged here were not reviewable, both as prerogatives and under an 1865 Act that so precluded; on the side of the Chagossians, it was argued inter alia that the evacuation was contrary to fundamental common law principle, if not directly protected under the Human Rights Act. On the administrative, or 'public law' level, arguments were shaped around the grounds of legitimate expectations, irrationality, the existence of an improper purpose, and, generally, illegality and abuse of power. Likewise, in *Hoareau and Bancoult* (n 7), some of the arguments were constitutional in nature, referring to alleged breaches of Art 8 of the European Convention on Human Rights and a British statute setting an equality duty on the public service; grounds of review pertaining to administrative law involved, in addition to an argument that the results of a consultation process were not properly taken into account, a focus on the ground of irrationality (unreasonableness). On the courts' reasoning see below.

[114] *De Keyser* (n 31).

[115] *Chandler v DPP* [1964] AC 763, 810 (per Lord Devlin: courts will intervene to correct excess or abuse); *Lain* (n 9) 881 (review of quasi-judicial action); *Laker* (n 100), 705 (per Lord Denning: improper or mistaken discretion in the exercise of prerogative powers is examinable in courts).

[116] *Council of Civil Service Unions v Minister for the Civil Service* [1985] AC 374, 400, 407, 410, 417–18, 423–24 (1984) (GCHQ) (per Lord Fraser, Lord Scarman, Lord Diplock, Lord Roskill, and Lord Brightman, respectively).

In this decision, the House of Lords established that prerogative-based orders in council—not merely an order made under them, as reviewed in *GCHQ* (1985)—were not immune from judicial review (at the time, all primary legislation was fully immune from review).[117] The court conceded that the challenged order in council made in 2004, which established a new constitution to BIOT, was 'primary legislation in the sense that the legislative power of the Crown is original and not subordinate', and that such orders 'resemble Acts of Parliament', but found that such measures did not share all the characteristics of primary legislation, since they lack the imprimatur of Parliament and are executed by the executive alone. Hence, these orders were to be reviewable on par with other types of executive-made rules.[118]

The reasoning in both decisions was functional rather than historical. Consider Lord Hoffmann's opinion in the latter decision:

> It is true that a prerogative Order in Council is primary legislation in the sense that the legislative power of the Crown is original and not subordinate ... But ... [t]he principle of the sovereignty of Parliament, as it has been developed by the courts over the past 350 years, is founded upon the unique authority Parliament derives from its representative character. An exercise of the prerogative lacks this quality; although it may be legislative in character, it is still an exercise of power by the executive alone ... I see no reason why prerogative legislation should not be subject to review on ordinary principles of legality, rationality and procedural impropriety in the same way as any other executive action.[119]

Since *GCHQ*, review of the prerogative, now seemingly equal to statute-based powers in this context, 'depend(s) on the subject matter of the prerogative power which is exercised'.[120] Indeed, amenability in principle may not lead to de facto constraint, especially since many of the challenged unilateral actions pertain to sensitive areas of national security and foreign affairs. Indeed, one of the strongest bars from such intervention, the justiciability/political questions doctrine, was used both in *GCHQ* and *Bancoult 2* (HL), and led to the rejection of the applications.[121]

The early *Bancoult* decision offers another example. In the first challenge against the denial of abode, decided by the Queen's Bench in 2001, the court ruled that the order in council that constituted the constitution of BIOT at the time could

[117] *Bancoult 2* (HL) (n 6); *GCHQ* (n 116).

[118] *Bancoult 2* (HL) (n 6) [34]–[35]. For overviews of the stepping-stones that led to the subjection of prerogative-based orders to judicial review see eg Brigid Hadfield, 'Judicial Review and the Prerogative Powers of the Crown' in Maurice Sunkin, Sebastian Payne (eds), *The Nature of the Crown* (OUP 1999) 197; Richard Moules, 'Judicial Review of Prerogative Orders in Council: Recognising the Constitutional Reality of Executive Legislation' (2008) CLJ 12 (writing on *Bancoult 2*, decided by the Court of Appeals and later overruled); Cohn (2015) (n 8) 76–77.

[119] *Bancoult 2* (HL) (n 6) 969.

[120] *GCHQ* (n 116) 418.

[121] *GCHQ* (n 117); *Bancoult 2* (HL) (n 6).

not authorize the promulgation of an ordinance that denied abode in the territory, since the removal of its entire civilian population was not conducive to a territory's peace, order, and good government, ensured in the governing order in council.[122]

Most informative in this regard are the two *Miller* decisions, concerned with government reliance on the prerogative in the context of Brexit. Highly political, both challenges were not summarily dismissed—rather, the courts ruled in favour of the applicants.

In *Miller 1* (2017), the British Supreme Court ruled that withdrawal from the EU, required under Article 50 of the Lisbon Treaty to be made 'in accordance with [the member's] own constitutional requirements', could not be effected merely by reliance on the foreign relations prerogative. Under the rather complicated majority ruling, withdrawal would effectively remove rights embedded in domestic law and frustrate the application of statutes, most notably, the European Communities Act 1972.[123]

While *Miller 1* followed recognized doctrines such as the residuality doctrine and the principle of legality, under which a statutory basis is needed to remove existing rights,[124] *Miller 2* (2019) charted new paths. The prorogation of Parliament (the declaration of a temporary suspension that marks the closure of a parliamentary session) is a recognized prerogative, ordered by the Crown in Privy Council and, alike other prerogatives, directed by the Prime Minister. Applicants challenged the 2019 prorogation, which was to extend for about five weeks and end two weeks before the 31 October deadline for the UK's final decision to exit, an almost unprecedented lengthy period, designed to minimize debate in Parliament. Redefining the challenge as one concerned with the lawfulness of the Prime Minister's advice to the Queen (thereby reducing the sensitivity of this direct attack on the order signed by the Crown), the Supreme Court rejected arguments for non-justiciability, and relied on constitutional conventions and principles, notably parliamentary sovereignty and the accountability of the executive to parliament, to find the prorogation unlawful.[125]

122 *R (on the application of Bancoult) v Secretary of State for Foreign and Commonwealth Affairs* [2001] QB 1067 (*Bancoult 1*). On *Bancoult 2* (HL) (n 6) see n 113 and below.

123 *R (on the application of Miller) v Secretary of State for Exiting the European Union* [2017] UKSC 5 (*Miller 1*). For a few examples of the flood of commentaries see Paul P Craig, 'Structural Constitutional Review and the Limits of Prerogative Power' [2017] PL 48; Mark Elliott, 'The Supreme Court's Judgement in *Miller*: In Search of Constitutional Principle' (2017) 76 CLJ 257; Gavin Phillipson, 'Brexit, Prerogative and the Courts: Why Did Political Constitutionalists support the Government side in Miller?' (2017) 36 U Queensland LJ 211; Mark Elliott, Jack Williams, and Alison Y Young (eds), *The UK Constitution after Miller* (Hart 2018).

124 On the latter principle and its interpretation see *R v Secretary of State for the Home Department, Ex p Simms* [2000] 2 AC 115; *Miller 1* (n 123) [87], [108].

125 *R (Miller) v The Prime Minister and Cherry v Advocate General for Scotland* [2019] UKSC 41 (*Miller 2*). On the decision see Aileen McHarg, 'The Supreme Court's Prorogation Judgment: Guardian of the Constitution or Architect of the Constitution?' (2020) 24 Edinburgh L Rev 88.

This is not to say that courts have always found non-statutory powers constitutionally unsound. The pattern of divergence is not surprising; the issues brought before the courts differed in their contexts and features. First, some applications and appeals were rejected as non-justiciable, pertaining to the so-called 'excluded categories of review', the doctrine that hovers above both levels of review.[126] In other cases, constitutional-type arguments failed; for example, in *Bancoult 2* (HL), arguments that the eviction orders breached the Magna Carta, the Human Rights Act, fundamental common law principles, and international law, were all rejected by the majority in the House of Lords.[127] In general, recognized prerogative powers, such as the creation and operation of the passport regime, the regulation of the civil service before its full legislation, and decisions concerned with the conduct of foreign affairs,[128] were never successful on the basis of constitutional-type arguments; their fate was decided on the administrative law level, to which I now turn.

As for review on the administrative law level, the emerging pattern is as expected just as patchy, for here, too, cases differ in their features. Alongside some successful applications, in which issues of high policy such as national security or foreign affairs were not involved,[129] the better known are those that failed. In *GCHQ*, for example, the court considered the government's decision under the doctrine of legitimate expectations, but refused to intervene due to the subject matter; in *Bancoult 2* (HL), none of the grounds of review on the public law level was successful.[130]

In sum, British courts no longer award non-statutory powers, even those with the 'prerogative' imprimatur, special immunity from review, but such powers remain one of the governance tools available to the executive. When pertaining to non-justiciable fields of action, judicial review may still be barred, but this hurdle applies both to statute-based and non-statutory powers. Finally, although the distinction between constitutional and administrative law grounds of review is not part of the usual discussion of the matter, the caselaw shows judicial reliance on both, and a pattern of divergence in both spheres of review.

The pattern in the US is just as complex, if not more so, and is discussed here under the distinction between review of presidential action under the constitution/

[126] For this term of art see *GCHQ* (n 116) 418 (per Lord Roskill). Such decisions include *GCHQ* itself, *Chandler* (n 115); *R (Abbasi) v Secretary of State for Foreign and Commonwealth Affairs* [2002] EWCA Civ 1598.

[127] *Bancoult 2* (HL) (n 6), for example [33]–[51] (per Lord Hoffmann).

[128] See respectively, eg, *Everett* (n 10), *GCHQ* (n 116), *Chandler* (n 115).

[129] See eg *Rahman v Secretary of State for the Home Department* [2015] EWHC 1146 (Admin) (QB) (refusal to renew passport found irrational due to flaws in the decision process). *Bancoult 2*, decided in the Court of Appeals followed a similar path offers an additional example, but was overturned by the House of Lords (*Bancoult 2* (HL) (n 6)). (*R (Bancoult) v Secretary of State for Foreign and Commonwealth Affairs (No 2)*, [2008] QB 365 (CA), deciding that the government decision negated a fundamental right and frustrated legitimate expectations that rose from previous government representations.)

[130] *GCHQ* (n 116); *Bancoult 2* (HL) (n 6). Similarly, in *Hoareau and Bancoult* (n 7) the Divisional Court found that the main ground of review was irrationality, which was found unsuccessful.

constitutional constructs, and review of presidential/government action in the seemingly more mundane field of review of action under administrative law.

Review under the first category has the potential of being more intense. In this context, decisions have involved not only action that involves a breach of a protected right, such as in the case of *Hamdan*, in which no statutory basis was found for the de facto removal of the right for habeas corpus,[131] but also action found to be an undue incursion into the sphere of the other two branches, relying on the constitutional structure of the separation of powers. Several decisions found non-statutory presidential action unconstitutional or unlawful for the latter reason. An earlier context concerned the removal of high-level officers by the President, an area fraught with difficulties.[132] Recent decisions on President Trump's policies that involved unilateral action have sometimes been decided against him. Most of these were adjudged in Federal District and Appeals Courts, for example, decisions concerned with the President's immigration policy,[133] and with his order to transfer (or 'reprogram') funds from the Department of Defense to fund the US-Mexico wall project following his declaration of emergency.[134] In another context, the Supreme Court rejected the President's challenge against the institution of criminal process against him, and an order requiring the submission of his financial records. The President's argument for presidential immunity, and his argument that in the case of the president, a heightened standard of the need to issue subpoenas against a sitting president, both relied on a reading of the constitution that was judicially rejected.[135]

Youngstown, the most famous decision in this context, should be positioned slightly further towards the accommodation pole of this spectrum. Deciding for the applicant, the Supreme Court did hold that an executive order, issued under claims of necessity emerging in wartime, was unlawful—quite a feat in itself.

[131] *Hamdan* (n 1).

[132] For the invalidation of presidential power in this field see eg *Humphrey's Executor v United States*, 295 US 602 (1935) (invalidating the removal of a member of the Federal Trade Commission for a cause not listed in statute); *Wiener United States*, 357 US 349 (1958) (invalidating presidential removal at will of War Claims commissioners appointed by Congress, exercising an adjudicatory function). For the patchiness of the doctrine, and its contextual nature, hinging inter alia on the nature of the office and the body to which the removal power was granted, see eg Jonathan L Entin, 'The Removal Power and the Federal Deficit: Form, Substance and Administrative Independence' (1986) 75 Kentucky Law Journal 699. See also ch 1.

[133] See *Trump v Hawaii*, 138 S Ct 2392 (2018) (rejecting the argument that the ban on entry of citizens of designated Muslim countries, effected by a proclamation made under Executive Order 13769, contravened the Constitution's Establishment Clause; the court also found it to be authorized under statute).

[134] Note the decision of the Federal Appeal Courts for the 9th District (California) that the transfer of funds by the Department of Defense, designed to fund expenses incurred in building the wall between US and Mexico and ordered under the direction of President Trump, had no basis in the appropriations act and, important in our context, 'lacked independent constitutional authority'. *Sierra Club v Trump*, 26 June 2020 (9th Cir 2020). At the time of writing (July 2020), the issue has not been decided by the Supreme Court. For the 2019 decisions concerned with the grant of an injunction, decided on administrative law grounds, see below.

[135] *Trump v Vance*, WL 3848062 (9 July 2020).

However, the multiple opinions offered in this decision reflect a much more complex pattern. Justice Jackson's two categories of action beyond or alongside statute were mentioned above in the context of residuality;[136] other elements of the decision offer readings that support presidential aggrandizement. Five of the nine Justices did not rule out unilateral presidential action during 'true' emergencies.[137] The decision, then, cannot support the rejection of all emergency powers. To these, one must add the references to 'historical gloss' in this decision.[138] The overall meaning of this decision is, as many have noted, sufficiently open to accommodate differing applications.

Then there are cases in which courts decided not to decide, using non-justiciability doctrines (such as the political questions doctrine, lack of standing, mootness, and ripeness),[139] and by denying certiorari, which, inter alia, has enabled the Supreme Court to remove itself from the debate over the constitutionality of the Vietnam war and the US participation in other hostilities that were unilaterally initiated by the president.[140] In all of these cases, non-intervention in the decisions of lower courts effectively upheld the challenged measures and at least indirectly promote consecutive reliance on such modes of action. Other forms of non-interference are found in cases decided on the basis of non-reviewability due to the lack of 'force of law' of the challenged measures.[141]

Courts have not consistently accepted arguments against constitution-based exercise of presidential power. The 'historical gloss' decisions discussed above offer an example of reliance on constitution-type reasoning that upheld presidential action,[142] as did the reliance on sovereignty in *Curtiss-Wright*,[143] and in *Zivotofsky* (2015), which held that the president possessed the exclusive power to recognize foreign nations, hence denying Congressional intervention by statute that effectively contradicted foreign policy.[144]

[136] Above text to n 106.

[137] Alongside the three dissenting Justices and Justice Jackson's rather open-ended repository of presidential action, Justice Clark, in another concurring opinion, found that the Constitution does grant the President unilateral powers 'in times of grave and imperative emergency' (*Youngstown* (n 89) 662): in effect, he joined the dissenters in this matter.

[138] For analysis of this mode of accommodation see above, text to n 89.

[139] For reliance on the political question doctrine in challenges against the exercise of non-statutory unilateral executive powers see eg *Da Costa v Laird*, 471 F2d 1146 (2d Cir 1973) (operations in North Vietnam); *Crockett v Reagan*, 558 F Supp 893 (DDC 1982) (military aid to El Salvador). For denial for lack of standing see *Raines v Byrd*, 521 US 811 (1997); *Campbell v Clinton*, 203 F3d 19 (DC Cir 2000). See also *Conyers v Reagan*, 765 F2d 1124 (CADC 1985) (mootness); *Doe v Bush*, 323 F3d 133 (1st Cir 2003) (ripeness). But see *Massachusetts v Laird*, 451 F2d 26 (1971) (decision on the merits: steady Congressional support found sufficient).

[140] As in *Massachusetts v Laird*, 400 US 886 (1970) (lack of original jurisdiction); *DaCosta v Laird*, cert den 405 US 979 (1972); *Holtzman v Schlesinger*, cert den 416 US 936 (1974).

[141] See eg *Independent Meat Packers v Butz*, 526 F2d 228, 236 (8th Cir 1975) (Executive Order 1182 requiring agencies to conduct impact analysis prior to the making of regulations was primarily 'a managerial tool', not enforceable by private civil action).

[142] See text to n 88; *Midwest Oil* (n 1); *Dames & Moore* (n 1).

[143] *Curtiss-Wright* (n 64). See, in the same vein, *US v Belmont*, 301 US 324 (1923); *US v Pink*, 315 US 203, 223–24 (1942).

[144] Zivotofsky (n 68); see there for details.

As for review of administrative action under administrative law—in US parlance, essentially considered under the Administrative Procedure Act (APA)—it should be noted that executive action in the US is relatively insulated from review in all areas non-constitutional (that is, when public acts are challenged at the administrative law level), supported by a strong culture of judicial deference in this field.[145] Paradoxically, then, despite the fact that, from inception, the president as the head of state was not protected by the aura of monarchy, no move for equating direct presidential action to run-of-the-mill output of administrative agencies, traced above in the context of the UK, can be discerned. Moreover, and further limiting the impact of the administrative law level, cases involving presidential action have generally been decided on the constitutional level, which is much more developed in comparison with the UK. Decisions in this category will usually involve action formally made by an agency, rather than the president, who is not an 'agency' under the APA.[146]

Still, some cases can be identified. *DHS v Regents of the University of California* (2020) involved memoranda issued by the Department of Homeland Security, which rescinded policies regarding some residency rights of children born in the US and their families, under presidential direction. The Supreme Court found that these memoranda were made in breach of the requirements of the APA.[147] Another decision, overturned by the Supreme Court in 2019, was the decision of lower Federal Courts in California to grant a permanent injunction against the transfer of funds to finance the building of the US-Mexico border wall, decisions that were couched in administrative law doctrine.[148]

A more permissive stance, at least potentially, is found in the Supreme Court's 2019 decision to stay the injunction issued by a California District Court, upheld by the Appeals Court of the Ninth Circuit. Here, the majority of the Supreme Court stayed the injunction, ruling, in a laconic decision, that '[a]mong the reasons is that the Government has made a sufficient showing at this stage that the plaintiffs have no cause of action'.[149] Merely a decision concerned with an interim stage of the main challenge, some indication of the court's future attitude is found, and the majority found no need to commit further at that stage.

[145] See eg Peter L Strauss and others, *Gellhorn and Byse's Administrative Law: Cases and Comments* (12th edn, Foundation Press 2018). See also Antonin Scalia, 'Judicial Deference to Administrative Interpretations of Law' (1989) Duke LJ 511; Richard J Pierce Jr, 'What Do the Studies of Judicial Review of Agency Actions Mean?' (2011) 63 Admin L Rev 77; John C Reitz, 'Deference to the Administration in Judicial Review' (2018) 66 Am J Comp L 269;

[146] See *Franklin v Massachusetts*, 505 US 788 (1992).

[147] *Department of Homeland Security v Regents of the University of California*, 140 S Ct 1891 (2020). Although the memoranda were not issued by the President, President Trump's direct direction is recognized in the decision (as was President Obama, under whom these policies were instated).

[148] *Sierra Club v Trump*, 379 F Supp 3d 883 (ND Cal 2019); *Sierra Club v Trump*, 929 F 3d 670 (9th Cir 2019).

[149] *Trump v Sierra Club*, 140 SCt 1 (2019). For the lower courts' decisions see n 148.

E. Concluding Remarks

Unilateral action of the executive is an important element of state action. This chapter offered a survey of the sources of such powers and assessed the force of two legal constraints on their exercise. Despite the evident constitutional problem inhering to their existence, discussed in the introduction to this chapter, I have shown that non-statutory executive powers have long pedigrees and are well-embedded in the constitutional practice of at least two Western democracies. Indeed, the incompleteness of law, supplemented by the political expediency of reliance on non-statutory rules—especially when the executive is challenged by a relatively hostile legislature—virtually guarantees their invocation. Different constructs have contained such powers, using a variety of mechanisms, from pure history, as in the UK, through reliance on a variety of doctrines in addition to constitutional texts, as in the US.

The chapter also shows that the systems share two central constraints, the first removing non-statutory powers in the existence of statute under a residuality rule, the second subjecting them to judicial review. The power of both is not absolute. A general residuality principle is indeed central to British law, but exceptions and competing older rulings challenge its robustness. Residuality is much less emphasized in the US; despite its recognition, it has had a lesser impact. In both systems, such powers are potentially subject to judicial review, but the foci and the depth of review vary. Based on a rough distinction between review on the constitutional level and on the administrative, or public law level, I show that the feat of the UK courts, subjecting prerogative powers to review, has led to a rise of review on the administrative level, and that some decisions have indeed risen to the constitutional level. This readiness to review has made a difference—no longer are parts of government action immune from review—but the impact of this subjection relies on the force of justiciability doctrines and on the particulars of each case. In the US, unilateral presidential action has always been reviewed on the constitutional level, which is much more developed in comparison with the UK. Most of the review has been conducted on this level, mainly due to the existence of a written constitution and the emergence of parallel constitution-type doctrines. Review on the administrative level is negligible: both the general culture of deference in matters not linked with constitutional issues, and the exemption of the President from the requirements set under the APA, the central framework that inter alia advises review, have contributed to this marginalization.

Despite the obvious differences in relative emphasis on different levels of review, both systems show a mixed pattern. These constraints are at their lowest ebb in two contexts: when presidents/prime ministers are involved in the making of general social and economic policy, and when subject-matter sensitivity is likely to enjoin courts from intervention by using non-justiciability doctrines. Furthermore, in both systems, these constraints have been judicially diluted, either actively, by creating doctrines that uphold some of these powers, or passively, by refusing to review the decision-making process and the invocation of non-statutory powers.

The surprising degree of convergence in two systems under differing regimes that, at least formally, sustain opposing visions of the nature of the executive, merits further attention. Chapter 5 offers an in-depth comparative analysis of four main aspects of written unilateral executive action: a comparison of the forms, their claimed sources of power, their identified legal status, and their accessibility to the public.

5

The Nature and Use of Unilateral Executive Measures

A Comparative Analysis

A. Introduction 137
B. The Curious Case of Mixed-Authority Orders in Council, Executive Orders, and Others 139
1. The United Kingdom: Orders in Council and Proclamations 139
a. The forms 139
b. Fuzziness I: multiple and mixed authorities 141
c. Fuzziness II: the legal status of unilateral measures 145
d. Fuzziness III: access difficulties 146
e. Interim conclusion 149
2. The United States: Proclamations, Executive Orders, Memoranda, and Other Measures 149
a. The forms 150
b. Fuzziness I: multiple and mixed authorities 156
c. Fuzziness II: the legal status of unilateral measures 158
d. Fuzziness III: access difficulties 160
C. Comparative Analysis 161
D. Concluding Remarks 163

A. Introduction

As expounded in the previous chapter, constitutions and constitutional constructs offer executives a repository of fuzzy sources of power which enable unilateral action; that chapter was dedicated to the exposition of the different ways and forms used to ground this type of power in the realm of legality. This chapter continues by focusing on one of these forms: executive making of (semi)-formal unilateral measures. These orders and edicts have an important edge: on their face, they are 'lawlike', and seemingly carry the imprimatur of binding law, even when their legal status is fuzzy. I use comparative methodology in order to show the strong similarity between such measures as they emerged and continue to be applied in the two systems compared in this book. Orders in council, executive orders, and the like, such as the ones brought before the courts in *Bancoult* and *Youngstown*, have been at the focus of extensive study; yet to date, such measures, issued in both systems, have never been conjointly discussed. This chapter offers the first comparative analysis.

A Theory of the Executive Branch. Margit Cohn, Oxford University Press (2021). © Margit Cohn.
DOI: 10.1093/oso/9780198821984.003.0006

This novel comparative exercise leads to the discovery of a surprising convergence—surprising, if attention is focused on structural regime elements. The findings support two of the main themes advanced in this book: that the emergence and retention of fuzzy legality is an unavoidable feature of the state, despite the ingrained danger it poses to the proper functioning of democracies. A third theme, concerned with the need to constrain fuzziness by robust judicial oversight, is addressed in the last chapter of this book. This chapter reveals the convergence, thereby further fleshing out the nature and operation of constitution-derived fuzziness. It also offers new insights on the unclear distinction between constitutional- and statute-derived fuzziness, again, a feature shared by both systems.

The absence of recognized similarities between these two types of written manifestations of unilateral power is a central outcome of the dearth of comparative work on executive powers, noted in Chapter 1. The convergence, both in nature and function, is quite astounding. In both cases, two types of fuzziness emerge: pure constitutional and mixed authority non-statutory measures. Some of these measures seem to rely on the constitution and/or constitutional doctrine alone: indeed, under the usual understanding of these orders, they are unilaterally made by the executive. However, in both systems, some such measures, carrying identical titles, draw their authority also from statute and could thus be treated as equivalent to secondary legislation; yet, to further obfuscate the matter, a good number of such measures recognize, or cite, both the constitution *and* statute, rendering their legal status undiscernible, or at least extra-fuzzy. Considering the focus of this chapter, which is dedicated to unilateral, constitution-derived measures, the parts of this discussion pertaining to measures derived only from statute should have been set aside; statute-based measures have little to do with general constitutional-type sources of authority. However, the use of a single title to head both types of measures, and the practice of reliance on mixed authorities (constitutional *and* statutory), render useless the distinction between these two sources of power.

This fuzziness has contributed to the growth of a related difficulty: in both systems, the legal status of non-statutory measures is not entirely clear. Are measures made under the constitution equivalent, in any way, to run-of-the-mill administrative statutory-based rules? Alternatively, are they no more than indications of will, or perhaps equivalent in some way to legislation? And what is the status of mixed-authority measures? While some indications that support the first option are found in both systems, a definite placing of these measures is yet to be reached.

Finally, a third form of fuzziness emerges when those measures are not consistently published and are therefore difficult to access. Fuzziness emerges here too, not only due to the limited access, in itself a form of fuzziness due to the difficulty, if not inability, to plan ahead, but also since it is virtually certain that some of these measures are unavailable, and that no full list of unilaterally made rules can be compiled.

The chapter opens with overviews of these measures as developed in the UK and the US and concludes with a comparative discussion of the shared nature of this fuzzy form of executive rule-making.

B. The Curious Case of Mixed-Authority Orders in Council, Executive Orders, and Others

1. The United Kingdom: Orders in Council and Proclamations

a. The forms

The origin of all public lawmaking power in the United Kingdom traces back to the Monarch. The Royal power to make laws was sometimes expressed in legal form as Royal proclamations, and, later, in orders in council. Both are still made in the Privy Council sitting, that is, outside of Parliament, and are designed and applied by the government.[1]

According to Youngs's definition, a proclamation was

> a royal command, normally cast in a distinctive format, which was validated by the royal sign manual, issued under a special Chancery writ sealed with the Great Seal, and publicly proclaimed.[2]

An early compiler of proclamations has gone back to the thirteenth century,[3] but those measures gained importance during the Tudor and Stuart periods. Some set

[1] For the exit of the Crown (as person) from political decision-making see chs 3 and 4. For the nature and constitution of the Privy Council see eg Encyclopaedia Britannica, 'Privy Council' <https://www.britannica.com/topic/Privy-Council-United-Kingdom-government>; <https://privycouncil.independent.gov.uk/>; AW Bradley, KD Ewing, and CJS Knight, *Constitutional and Administrative Law* (18th edn, Pearson 2018) 253–55.

[2] Frederic A Youngs Jr, *The Proclamations of the Tudor Queens* (CUP 1976) at 9–10. Hughes and Larkin's tentative definition adds a reference to the prerogative (an early Tudor proclamation was 'a public ordinance issued by the King, in virtue of his royal prerogative with the advice of his council, under the Great Seal, and by royal writ'; Paul L Hughes and James F Larkin, *Tudor Royal Proclamations: The Early Tudors (1485–1553)*, Vol I (Yale University Press 1964) xxiii). For other compilations of Tudor and Stuart proclamations see Robert Steele, *A Bibliography of Royal Proclamations of the Tudor and Stuart Sovereigns, and Others Published under Authority, 1485–1714* (Clarendon Press 1910); Paul L Hughes and James F Larkin, *Tudor Royal Proclamations: The Later Tudors (1553–1587)*, Vol II (Yale University Press 1969); Paul L Hughes and James F Larkin, *Tudor Royal Proclamations: The Later Tudors (1588–1603)*, Vol III (Yale University Press 1969); James F Larkin and Paul L Hughes, *Stuart Royal Proclamations*, Vols I, II (Clarendon Press 1973, 1983); Youngs, ibid 253–68; RW Heinze, *The Proclamations of the Tudor Kings* (CUP 1976) 296–303. For studies of these measures see, in addition to the above, Heinze, ibid 1–295.

[3] Steele cites four proclamations made by King John (1204–16), the fourth being the Magna Carta ('Publishing the peace (MAGNA CARTA)'). Steele (n 2) Vol I, clvii.

penalties or ordered the arrest of specified persons or groups of offenders.[4] A large number were concerned with the enforcement of statutes, and some ordered the (usually temporary) suspension or so-called 'mitigation' of statutes.[5] Others were concerned with the exercise of powers, for example foreign affairs with foreign countries, military action, Royal pardons, and regulatory rules concerned with a variety of issues, inter alia commerce, public safety, monopolies, licensing, buildings, wages, and coinage.[6] Since its establishment in 1665, proclamations have been published in the London Gazette.[7]

The Statute of Proclamations, enacted by Henry VIII, could be read as a general statutory backing for the making of proclamations, subject to an important reservation. All legal rules before the establishment of parliamentary supremacy emanated from the Monarch, and anything close to a distinction between acts made in Parliament and Royal measures during that period was yet to emerge. Still, the act represented a clear political acceptance of the power and transformed the power to a statute-based one while setting some limits on the exercise of this power.

[4] See eg 'Ordering Punishment for Rumors of Further Coin Debasement', 24 July 1551 (5 Edward VI), Hughes and Larkin (n 2) Vol I, 528; 'Announcing Arrest of Earl of Essex', 9 February 1601 (43 Elizabeth I), Hughes and Larkin (n 2) Vol III, 230.

[5] See eg 'Enforcing Statute against Water Pollution', 6 June 1590 (32 Elizabeth I), Hughes and Larkin (n 2) Vol III, 57; 'Suspending Statute on Sale of Meat until 1 November 1541', 27 October 1540 (32 Henry VIII), Hughes and Larkin (n 2) Vol I, 291; 'Suspending Statute against Foreigners', 1 September 1540, Hughes and Larkin (n 2) Vol I, 291; 'Mitigating Statutes for Wool Cloth Manufacture', 13 March 1590 (32 Elizabeth I), Hughes and Larkin (n 2) Vol III, 52.

[6] See eg 'Announcing Peace Treaty with France', 12 December 1492 (8 Henry VII), Hughes and Larkin (n 2) Vol I, 31; 'Declaring War Against France', 2 August 1543 (35 Henry VIII), Hughes and Larkin (n 2) Vol I, 320; 'Ordering Soldiers to Report for Embarkation', 4 October 1588 (30 Elizabeth I), Hughes and Larkin (n 2) Vol III, 26; 'Pardoning Pilgrimage of Grace', 9 December 1536 (28 Henry VIII), Hughes and Larkin (n 2) Vol I, 246; 'Pricing Meats', 21 May 1544 (36 Henry VIII), Hughes and Larkin (n 2) Vol I, 331; 'Ordering Peace Kept on Scottish Borders', 13 August 1597 (39 Elizabeth I), Hughes and Larkin (n 2) Vol III, 181; 'Granting Monopoly for Saltpeter', 13 January 1590 (32 Elizabeth I), Hughes and Larkin (n 2) Vol III, 49 (the issue adjudged in *The Case of the King's Prerogative in Saltpetre*, 77 ER 1294 (1606)); 'Renewing Monopoly for Playing Cards', 13 June 1588 (30 Elizabeth I) Hughes and Larkin (n 2) Vol III, 8 (adjudged in *The Case of Monopolies* (*Darcy v Allein*, 77 ER 1260 (1603)); 'Prohibiting Export of Victual', 8 October 1548 (2 Edward VI), Hughes and Larkin (n 2) Vol I, 435; 'Prohibiting Further Building or Subdividing of Houses in London', 22 June 1601 (44 Elizabeth I), Hughes and Larkin (n 2) Vol III, 245 (the issue adjudged in *The Case of Proclamations*, 77 ER 1352 (1610)); 'Regulating London Wages', 23 July 1589 (31 Elizabeth I), Hughes and Larkin (n 2) Vol III, 40; 'Declaring All King's Pence Legal Tender', 23 March 1499 (14 Henry VII), Hughes and Larkin (n 2) Vol I, 48.

[7] At first, the Gazette published only notifications of their issuance (for the first published notification see The London Gazette No 227, 20 January 1667). See <https://www.thegazette.co.uk/London/issue/224/page/1>; <https://www.thegazette.co.uk/London/issue/224/page/2>; <https://www.thegazette.co.uk/London/issue/234/page/2>; <https://www.thegazette.co.uk/London/issue/234/page/1>. Searched through https://www.thegazette.co.uk/. See also eg Proclamation (regarding peace with Spain), 12 February 1667, London Gazette Issue 234, 1–13 February 1667 1. Starting in 1671, the texts themselves have been published. See eg two proclamations made on 23 and 25 March 1671, the first ordering Jesuit and other priests linked with Rome to depart from the country, the second concerned with the prizing of wine, London Gazette Issue 559, 23–27 March 1671. For a recent proclamation, see eg 'A Proclamation Determining the Specifications and Designs for a New Series of Fifty Pence Coins in Gold, Silver and Cupro-Nickel Celebrating the Literary Character Paddington Bear', London Gazette Issue 62614, 15 April 2019.

Following its repeal in 1547, consequent proclamations made by Tudor and subsequent kings were once again unilateral, unless authorized in statute.[8]

Proclamations have long lost their central role in Privy Council rulemaking; instead, the order in council is now central to so-called unilateral rule-making. Research on their history and contexts is limited; no collections similar to those on proclamations exist.[9] Similarly to proclamations, these orders are made in a formal meeting of the Privy Council. Some sources mention that they were first issued in the eighteenth century,[10] yet much earlier ones have been designated as such.[11] Possibly the best-known early orders in council are the orders in council made in November 1807, blocking trade and commerce during the Napoleonic wars.[12]

As mentioned below, proclamations and orders in council are either statute-based or derive from prerogative (or both). Under government practice, statutes opt for an authorization to make an order in council rather than regulations, 'where an SI made by a Minister would be inappropriate'; examples include the transference of ministerial functions, and legislation that extends beyond the territory of the UK.[13]

b. Fuzziness I: Multiple and mixed authorities

Textually, some of the sixteenth and seventeenth century proclamations were made independently of statute, that is, relying on the prerogative,[14] while others could be considered to be made under statutes that authorized the making of a proclamation;[15] however, as mentioned above, the distinction between constitution-based

[8] 31 Hen 8 c 8. On the statute and its repeal see Heinze (n 2) 153–77.

[9] For a short overview see Cyril ES Horsford, 'The Order in Council' (1987) 131(15) Solicitors Journal 462 (1987).

[10] 'Order in Council', *Encyclopaedia Britannica*, <https://www.britannica.com/topic/order-in-council>.

[11] The earliest measure so designated by the National Archives was in fact issued by a court ('Order in council for protection of those going to Wales and for the removal of the courts to Shrewsbury, Salop', National Archives, Kew, C/49/1/21). The first order with a political, executive context recognized as such by the British National Archives dates from 1308 ('Order in council for the issue of writs of Great and Privy Seal relating to the affairs of Scotland, 16 August 1308, National Archives, Kew, C 47/22/12/26).

[12] For information and links see Tom Holmberg, 'The Acts, Orders in Council, &c. of Great Britain [on Trade], 1793–1812' <http://www.napoleon-series.org/research/government/british/decrees/c_britdecrees1.html>.

[13] The National Archives, *Statutory Instrument Practice* (5th edn 2017) para 1.4.9.

[14] Including grants of monopolies, pardons of offenders, and rules regarding coinage, all of which are considered well-established prerogative powers (the latter was legislated centuries later), but also proclamations concerned with commerce and other regulatory issues. See eg 'Granting Monopoly for Saltpeter' and 'Renewing Monopoly for Playing Cards' (n 7); 'Pardoning Pilgrimage of Grace' (n 6); 'Prohibiting Export of Victual' (n 7).

[15] For early statutes that mentioned the making of proclamations see eg Nuisances in Towns Act 1388, 12 Ric II c 13, 2 Stats of the Realm 59 (proclamations may be made to tackle city pollution); the Sunday Fairs Act 1448, 27 Hen VI c 5, 2 Stats of the Realm 351 (prohibition of fairs and markets on Sundays and religious holidays, unless permitted by proclamation); Continuation of Acts etc Act 1603, 1 Jac I c 25 section III, 4(2) Stats of the Realm 1050–51 (exportation of corn may be prohibited by proclamation). Proclamations that contain exhortations to enforce statutes, common throughout those periods, can also be included in this category, since they refer to statutes and require those authorized to apply them to do so, but one could argue that the authority to make such enforcement orders may derive

and statute-based proclamations may not be helpful for the understanding of these early proclamations. Modern proclamations, on the other hand, could be classified under this formalist distinction. Proclamations concerning coinage offer a salient example. Before the nineteenth century, several statutes regulated some aspects of coinage, but the entire field was not regulated under statute, and coinage proclamations did not mention statutes.[16] Reforms in the nineteenth century culminated in the 1870 Coinage Act, designed to consolidate the regime of coinage; inter alia, it authorized the making of proclamations to regulate aspects of coinage.[17] Since then, coinage proclamations, bearing the same title, are made by reference to the statute in force.[18] Currently, in addition to coinage proclamations, bank holidays are also declared in the form of this measure, again made under statute.[19]

Alike proclamations, orders in council appear in two forms: purely non-statutory and those made under a statutory authorization.[20] Indeed, existing non-statutory orders in council pertain to the exercise of the remaining areas regulated under the prerogative.[21] The passport regime, still unlegislated, has not been

from the general authority of the Crown. For such proclamations see eg 'Enforcing Statute against Water Pollution' (n 5) (which expressly cites the Nuisances in Towns Act 1388 (n 15)); 'Enforcing Statutes against Export of Gold and Silver', 18 March 1600 (42 Elizabeth I), Hughes and Larkin (n 2) Vol III, 210 (citing several statutes).

[16] Early legislation includes An Act for Encouraging of Coynage 1666, 18 & 19 Car II c 5, 5 Stat of the Realm 598; An act for regulating and ascertaining the Weights to be made use of in weighing the Gold and Silver Coin of this Kingdom 1774, 14 Geo III c 92, Stats at Large Vol 13 807. For early coinage proclamations see eg 'Declaring All King's Pence Legal Tender' (n 7); 'A Proclamation for reforming sundry inconveniences touching the Coins of this Realm', 31 July 1619 (James I), Larkin and Hughes (n 2) Vol I, 436.

[17] Coinage Act 1870, 33 & 34 Vict c 10, section 11. The earlier 1816 Coinage Act, which established a new coinage regime ('Great Recoinage of 1816'), did not mention rule-making by proclamations, but subsequent proclamations issued referred to this act. See eg 'Proclamation', London Gazette No 17225 489; 'Proclamation', London Gazette No 17225 490 (both referring to the Act, the first declaring currency, the second prohibiting the use of old coins).

[18] For current proclamations see eg n 7. All such proclamations cite the Coinage Act 1971.

[19] Proclamations declaring bank holidays are made under the Banking and Financial Dealings Act 1971; see eg 'Proclamation Appointing Tuesday 1st January 2019 and Monday 6th May 2019 as Bank Holidays in England, Wales and Northern Ireland and Appointing Friday 12th July 2019 as Bank Holiday in Northern Ireland, 11 July 2018', London Gazette 62352, 16 July 2019. These are the only fields in which proclamations are issued under statute (conclusion derived from the perusal of the Privy Council meetings protocols for 2018 and 2019 available online at <https://privycouncil.independent.gov.uk/privy-council/orders/>(. The London Gazette classifies public appointments orders in council as 'proclamations' (see eg notice, 10 April 2019 <https://www.thegazette.co.uk/notice/3252341>). This, and similar measures, are discussed below as orders in council.

[20] See eg *Encyclopaedia Britannica* (n 10); Horsford (n 9); Richard Moules, 'Judicial Review of Prerogative Orders in Council: Recognising the Constitutional Reality of Executive Legislation' (2008) CLJ 12, 12–13

[21] See eg the British Indian Ocean Territory (Constitution) Order 2004, challenged in *R (on the application of Bancoult) v Secretary of State for Foreign and Commonwealth Affairs (No 2)* [2008] 3 WLR 955 (*Bancoult 2*) (made 'by virtue and in exercise of all the powers in Her Majesty vested'); the Requisitioning of Ships Order 1982, *Statutory Instruments* 1982 Part I 1693 (made during the Falkland War, mentioning that the order was done on the advice of the Privy Council with no other reference to authority).

formalized, to the best of anyone's knowledge, in any order in council (or other accessible format).[22] The best-known non-statutory orders in council are those challenged in court, as in the *GCHQ* and *Bancoult* affairs, representing two fields of action—the regulation of the civil service, legislated in 2010, and rule-making in British colonies and territories.[23]

As in the case of proclamations, legislation authorizing the making of orders in council is not uncommon, although these acts generally concern areas that were previously regulated under the prerogative, such as foreign affairs, war powers, the civil service, and the setting of territorial waters.[24] The Territorial Sea Act 1987 reasserted the force of pre-legislation orders in council, and other acts expressly preserve other powers held by the Crown.[25] In both cases, confusion may arise. In the first case, recognition of the status of a measure carrying the title 'order in council' requires knowledge of the law before and after legislation; an earlier order made before legislation, if in force, is essentially different in status from others made after legislation. Even assuming that the court is now ready to review prerogative-based

[22] No statute exists. The Immigration Act 2016, currently in force, authorizes the making of regulations concerning fees and mentions 'passports' in passing, but contains no authorization regarding their issuance; see also Passport (Fees) Regulations 2018, SI 2018/414 (made under this act). Judicial decisions on the matter repeatedly link the field with the prerogative, as in *R v Secretary of State for Foreign and Commonwealth Affairs Ex p Everett* [1989] QB 811; *R (XH) v Secretary of State for the Home Department* [2018] QB 355.

[23] The Civil Service Order in Council 1982; the British Indian Ocean Territory (Constitution) Order 2004 and the Indian Ocean Territory (Immigration) Order 2004 (for the accessibility of BIOT orders see below text to n 38), addressed, respectively, in *Council of Civil Service Unions v Minister for the Civil Service* [1985] AC 374 (1984) (GCHQ), and the series of cases commencing in *R (Bancoult) v Secretary of State for Foreign and Commonwealth Affairs* [2001] QB 1067 (*Bancoult 1*)).

[24] For early statutes see eg the Exportation Act, 1756, 29 Geo 2, *c* 16 (the King can prohibit the export of saltpetre 'by Proclamation or Order in Council, when he shall see cause'); Distillation Act, 1757, 30 Geo 2, c 15; Distemper Amongst Cattle Act, 1757, 30 Geo 2, c 20; Trade Act 1822 (the King may, by order in council, deny privileges to foreign shipping vessels granted in statute, and extend the territorial application of the Act beyond the ports mentioned in the Schedule); British North America Act, 1840 (the Queen can disallow, by order in council, Bills proposed by the Governor of Canada). More recent statutes include the United Nations Act 1946 (authorizing the making of orders in council for applying resolutions made by the United Nations Security Council with respect to setting sanctions on foreign entities); the European Communities Act 1972, eg s 2 (authorization to provide for the implementation or enablement of obligations under EU law and the designation of responsible departments of ministers; the European Union (Withdrawal Act) 2018, eg Sch 7 para 2(14) (revocation of certain regulations made jointly with a devolved authority, under certain conditions). As a final example, the Civil Aviation Act 1982 offers an example of extensive use of this measure: inter alia, it authorizes the making of orders in council in the extension of the act to overseas and other territories (eg s 41, s 108), the giving effect to international conventions (s 60, s 90), the application of related bodies of law such as the law of wrecks or salvage (eg s 87), the making of rules for mortgaging aircraft (s 86), and even the setting of civil jurisdiction in proceedings involving aircraft (s 91). This act, as others, also delegates to secretaries of state and ministers the more common power to make regulations.

[25] The Territorial Sea Act 1987 s 1(4) ('As from the coming into force of this section the Territorial Waters Order in Council 1964 and the Territorial Waters (Amendment) Order in Council 1979 shall have effect for all purposes as if they were Orders in Council made by virtue of subsection (1) (b) above ...'); retention of other powers, which expressly or impliedly include prerogative, is found eg in the Immigration Act 1971 s 33(5) ('This Act shall not be taken to supersede or impair any power exercisable by Her Majesty in relation to aliens by virtue of Her prerogative'); the Municipal Corporations Act 1882 s 259; the Crown Proceedings Act 1947 s 11; the Court-Martial (Appeals) Act 1968 s 54.

orders in council as equivalent to statute-based regulations, as is the case in the UK,[26] understanding the status of the order required legal professional knowledge; it also enables the government, the rule-maker, to go ahead with the making of a rule without fully recognizing its nature. The second practice of legislative design offers a direct path to the creation of parallel measures, a potential for 'patchwork legislation', a form of fuzziness discussed in Chapter 7: in such a case, the ability of those potentially impacted by a rule to foresee the type of rule to be applied, and hence to properly prepare for it, is potentially impaired.

In the context of maintaining clarity and foreseeability, the emergence of a third type of order in council is just as concerning. Orders that cite as their sources of authority a mix of statutes *and* a general reference to 'all other enabling powers' are not uncommon. This pattern has become the norm in certain areas, such as the setting of sanctions on foreign countries, either following a UN Security Council decision or made by the United Kingdom in pursuance of its foreign policy, when the power to set such sanctions is extended to overseas territories. Consider one example of the opening statement of such an order:

> Her Majesty, in exercise of the powers conferred on Her by section 1 of the United Nations Act 1946, section 112 of the Saint Helena Act 1833, the British Settlements Acts 1887 and 1945, and all of the other powers enabling Her to do so, is pleased, by and with the advice of Her Privy Council, to order as follows . . .[27]

A similar opening statement, minus the reliance on the United Nations Act, opens orders concerning sanctions that do not follow a UN resolution, again in the context of extension of the sanctions to overseas territories. With some exceptions, the dominant pattern is the inclusion of mixed authorities in opening statements.[28]

The British practice of reliance on mixed authorities is relatively limited in scope; as I show below, it is much more widespread in the US. Still, this type of fuzziness

[26] On the gradual subjection of prerogative-based executive measures see ch 4.

[27] The ISIL (Da'esh) and Al-Qaida (Sanctions) (Overseas Territories) Order 2016, SI 2016/1218. This formula appears in almost all orders in council made after 2006 that were concerned with the setting of sanctions following a resolution of the UN Security Council. Earlier, the introductory text of such orders cited only a single statutory basis, the United Nations Act 1946 (n 24) (see eg The Iraq (United Nations Sanctions) (Overseas Territories) Order 2000, SI 2000/3242). Current overseas sanctions orders not made following a UN resolution cite the other statutes cited above, as well as the general reference to authority.

[28] See eg The Venezuela (Sanctions) (Overseas Territories) Order 2018, SI 2018/179; the Chemical Weapons (Sanctions) (Overseas Territories) Order 2018, SI 2018/1361 (both citing 'the Saint Helena Act 1833, the British Settlements Acts 1887 and 1945, and all of the other powers enabling Her to do so'. For orders not citing this formula see eg The Antarctic Act 1994 (Overseas Territories) Order 1995, SI 1995/1030 (made under the authorization to make orders in council under the Antarctic Act 1994); The Export Control (Burma Sanctions) (No 2) Order 2018, SI 2018/894 (relying on the European Communities Act, implementing EU regulation, and the Export Control Act 2002). No direct explanation as to the absence of the general reference is readily available: both these examples, alike those that do offer mixed authorizations, pertain to foreign relations and to the application of measures in overseas territories.

requires attention even in the British context. How should an order in council opening with the statement of authority of the type cited above be considered? The British Settlements Acts, cited in the cited order, do authorize action in overseas territories by order in council, and the Saint Helena Act is relevant to the application in that territory; one may therefore argue that sufficient statutory authorization has rendered redundant the general reference to 'all of the other powers enabling [Her Majesty]'—an oblique reference to the prerogative. However, when such statutory authority is insufficient to authorize the rule, the vague general reference has indeed supported reliance on the prerogative, at least in the context of foreign affairs.[29] Thus, mixed-authority measures are extra fuzzy: they enable the government to make a rule without being required to commit to its source of legality, ensuring legality by using a vague reference to undefined powers.

c. Fuzziness II: The legal status of unilateral measures

The above survey of unilateral measures in the UK identifies the tendency of successive governments to cite mixed authorities as bases for many such measures, but even those that are 'purely' constitution-based fit uncomfortably within the classic distinction between primary and secondary legislation.

No clear direction as to the status of unilateral, prerogative-, or third-source based measures can be found in the British constitution or in legislation.[30] In the absence of a text-based definition, attention to judicial decisions is natural: after all, in common-law systems, courts are the qualified interpreters of law. Yet, as shown in the previous chapter, despite having decided many disputes in which a unilateral executive lawmaking power was involved, as far as resolving the issue of the exact nature of these commonly used measures, the judicial record is not too impressive: having decided that orders in council are to be reviewable on par with other types of executive-made rules, no decision regarding the formal status of such orders has emerged.[31] Furthermore, courts (as well as scholars) have not dwelt on the

[29] In the first of the *Bancoult* cases, decided in 2001, the Queen's Bench considered an ordinance made under the British Indian Territory Order 1965, an order in council that served as the first constitution of the territory (SI 1965/1920), a measure that cited mixed authorities ('by virtue and in exercise of the powers in that behalf by the Colonial Boundaries Act 1895(a), or otherwise in Her Majesty vested'). The court found that the statute had not authorized the order in council, and proceeded by considering the order to be made under royal prerogative. *Bancoult 1* (n 23) 1076.

[30] The Human Rights 1998 Act identifies orders in council made under prerogative as 'primary legislation', and those made under another authority as 'subordinate legislation' (Section 21 (1)). The Act does not address mixed-authority measures (nor does it address proclamations), and, in any case, is limited to the extent of its application. Orders in council made under statute are recognized, in tandem with minister-made orders under statute, as statutory instruments (subordinate legislation) (Statutory Instruments Act 1946 s 1(1)). See also House of Commons Information Office, Statutory Instruments, Factsheet L7 Legislative Series, rev May 2008 11. According to this factsheet, 'Orders in Council are issued "by and with the advice of Her Majesty's Privy Council", and are usually classified as secondary legislation (although some can be primary legislation), and are made under powers given in a parent Act'. This confusing definition, which seems to exclude prerogative-based measures, may be understood otherwise by the uninitiated. Mixed-source measures are entirely outside of any definitional exercise.

[31] See ch 4.

difficult question of the status of mixed-authority orders. Final rulings on the legal status of unilateral law-making has, then, not been part of the judicial exercise; decisions on equal treatment may have also rendered the question moot.

This state of affairs should not necessarily be viewed as a failing of the respective judicial branches: after all, courts should resolve actual disputes and not provide solutions to theoretical questions that are incidental to the actual dispute. The question of status might be material to the decision only if the case involved a direct challenge to the validity of the order. If no such challenge is involved—for example, when an applicant relies on an order and demands its application to his case—the question of status is unlikely to be material to the decision. But even when applicants challenge an order's validity, the decision does not necessarily require a clear ruling as to the exact legal status of the order. Courts may uphold or invalidate a measure without deciding on its exact status, for example, when they find no source of authority of any kind. A ruling on status would only be essential to the decision when the challenge to the order's validity was based on an argument that the order contradicted statute—a feat that only a statute could accomplish.

The outcome, then, is fuzziness. Orders in council of all types may be treated by courts as reviewable, but this does not necessarily imply that they do not carry some features of primary legislation, especially those that squarely rely on the royal prerogative. The definition of the latter measures as primary legislation in the context of the Human Rights Act has, in fact, only further obfuscated the issue.[32]

d. Fuzziness III: Access difficulties

Since the enactment of the Rules Publications Act 1893, measures made by Her Majesty in Council were to be formally published, but this act, and the 1946 Statutory Instruments Act that repealed it, apply only to statute-authorized measures.[33] This is the case in areas that were historically governed by prerogative and were then regulated under a new statute (such as coinage, foreign affairs, and territorial seas), and in areas in which a statute delegates new powers to promulgate orders entitled 'orders in council' (or 'proclamations'), covering

[32] See n 30.

[33] The Rules Publication Act 1893, 56 & 57 Vict c 66 applied to all 'rules, regulations, or byelaws' made in Council under statute, hence also proclamations: see indeed above citations of much earlier proclamations printed in the London Gazette. The Statutory Instruments Act 1946 retains this requirement for all measures made under statutes that were enacted before its entry into force, and refers only to orders in council made under post-1946 legislation to be published as 'statutory instruments'; proclamations, if authorized under such a newer statute, are exempt. Whether this was an error, or a reflection of the waning importance of proclamations remains an open question. Still, as shown above, the London Gazette does publish some proclamations made under post-1946 statutes; see eg proclamations cited in n 18, 19.

diverse fields such as air navigation, recognition of tax agreements, and the declaration of bank holidays.

No statute requires the publication of non-statute, prerogative-based measures, and some are still notoriously difficult to find. Since 1894, some non-statutory orders have been published in special appendices to the Statutory Rules and Orders/Statutory Instruments collection, but they are sporadic.[34] Others remain untraceable.

Consider one example that would have been somewhat entertaining had it not reflected a general pattern. In 1959, The Times of London published a letter to the editor sent by one 'Stanley de-Smith from the London School of Economics', later to become the renowned Downing Professor of the Laws of England in Cambridge and the author of the leading textbook on judicial review. In the letter, titled 'Orders in Council', the author, who had received his doctorate that year, lamented his inability to access two orders in council that constituted the constitutions of Malta and Basutoland, despite his heroic attempts which included contacting four agencies, finally receiving copies of these orders from the Privy Council Office, 'out of the small number held there'.[35] Five days later, a letter signed by Mr P McGrath, then Director of Publications at HMSO explained that '[r]equests from members of the public for copies of Orders in Council made under the royal prerogative are very rare, and for this reason it

[34] For example, the appendix to the 1894 Statutory Rules and Orders contained three orders in council, all concerned with the governance of colonies (amendments to the Malta and Mauritius constitution orders and an order regulating the currency of British Honduras); 'An Appendix of Certain Orders in Council Issued under the Royal Prerogative', Statutory Rules and Orders 1894 520–25. The appendix to the 1905 Statutory Rules and Orders contains thirteen measures, all pertaining to the governance of British colonies, one of them a constitution order; see 'Appendix of Prerogative Orders', Statutory Rules and Orders 1905 1439–95. None of them are proclamations. One of the appendices to the 1982 Statutory Instruments volume contains two coinage proclamations, four orders concerned with overseas territories and Commonwealth country laws (two assents to legislation passed in Australia, one of them an amendment to the Constitution Act and two Letters Patent), and, probably the best-known, an order in council enabling the requisitioning of ships, made during the Falkland War ('Appendix, Instruments Not Registered as Statutory Instruments', Statutory Instruments 1982, 1685–94). More recent volumes of SI include only statute-based proclamations in these appendices, as in 1999, 2000, 2001, and 2011, despite the continuing use of the title of the appendix as one that contains 'orders in council, letters patent, royal instructions, royal proclamations'. A selective publication policy may be applied: sensitive prerogative-based orders in council have not been formally published, as in the case of the measures challenged in *GCHQ* (n 23) and the *Bancoult* decisions, starting in *Bancoult 1* (n 23).

[35] In his letter, de Smith concedes that that these orders 'will ultimately be published in an appendix to the annual bound volumes of Statutory Instruments', a remark that may have been overly optimistic. He continues to inform his readers that after contacting no less than three offices, the Crown Agents for Oversea Governments and Administration [sic], the Colonial Office, and Commonwealth Relations Office, which kindly sent him a spare copy of the Basutoland order, before receiving both, as a matter of courtesy, from the Privy Council Office. Recognizing that '[a]ll the officials to whom I spoke where courteous and cooperative', de Smith ends the letter with a less than gentle criticism: 'it is surely absurd that members of the public should experience such difficulty in securing access to law-making instruments made by Her Majesty in Council. Is there any good reason why prerogative legislative instruments should not be published and put on sale by the Stationary Office as soon as they have been made?' SA de Smith, 'Orders in Council', *The Times*, Letters to the Editor, 4 December 1959 13.

has been considered that the expense of general publication would not be justified'.[36] The author of this letter did inform his readers that future orders in council affecting colonies and Commonwealth countries 'will be formally published and made available at the Government bookshops and through book-sellers', but this promise was not meticulously kept even in that defined field: the British Indian Ocean Territory Orders, including the 2004 Constitution Order challenged in *Bancoult*, were virtually protected from publication.[37]

This is not a unique case: other prerogative legislation is equally difficult to track down. For example, in addition to the absence of public access to the passport rules, the orders in council pertaining to the management of the civil service in England, prior to the legislation of the field, and amendments to the Civil Service Commissioners (Northern Ireland) Order 1999, were never easily accessible.[38]

[36] P McGrath, Director of Publications HMSO, 'Orders in Council', *The Times*, Letters to the Editor, 9 December 1959 13.

[37] A painstaking attempt to trace the orders in council and other legal measures relevant to the *Bancoult* affair (see ch 4), including the two orders in council creating the constitutions of the territory, found that these measures were virtually impossible to trace. Published only in the BIOT Gazette, of which only twenty copies were distributed, sixteen of them were sent to government bodies. Holdings in the few libraries that do hold some copies are incomplete, and no online access is available. See Ronan Cormacain, 'Prerogative Legislation as the Paradigm of Bad Law-Making: the Chagos Islands' (2013) 39 Commonwealth Law Bulletin 487, 503–05, 507–08. This was no oversight: the government's decision to opt for publication only in the BIOT Gazette was grounded in its virtual inaccessibility: in a government minute from 1971, it was mentioned that '[t]he ordinance would be published in the BIOT Gazette, which has only very limited circulation both here and overseas, after signature by the Commissioner. Publicity will therefore be minimal'. Cited in *Bancoult 1* (n 23), 1086; discussed in Cormacain, ibid 505. According to the government's undertaking, copies of these orders could be found in the library of Parliament, but this is possibly the outcome of the public outcry and the return of *Ilois*' plea to public attention. For this undertaking see Annex 1 to letter sent by the Foreign Secretary, Jack Straw, to the Chairman of the Select Committee on Foreign and Commonwealth Affairs, 15 June 2004. See <http://www.publications.parliament.uk/pa/cm200405/cmselect/cmfaff/115/115we05.htm>. A much better source for rules and orders made for BIOT is managed by the activist RP Dunne (mentioning inter alia the limited access to the BIOT Gazette, copies of which were to be sent to the British Library, but many were missing). See <https://sites.google.com/site/biotgovernment/biot-government-royal-prerogative-orders-in-council/laws-of-the-biot>.

[38] No reference to rules regarding passports can be found in the Passport Office website, <https://www.gov.uk/government/organisations/hm-passport-office>. The Immigration Act authorizes the making of regulations concerning fees and mentions 'passports' in passing, but contains no authorization regarding their issuance; see Immigration Act 2016 ss 86, 87; Passport (Fees) Regulations 2018, SI 2018/414, made under this act. Facing no success in accessing the general rules concerning the passport regime, and in an attempt to uncover them, the author submitted a Freedom of Information request July 2019 to the Passport Office, requesting information about the rules in force. A prompt reply by a member of the Freedom of Information Team (24 July 2019) noted that 'Section 21(1) of the FOIA exempts Her Majesty's Passport Office from having to provide you with this information, because it is already reasonably accessible to you', supported by a link to a written statement, submitted to the House of Commons on 25 April 2013 by the then Home Secretary Theresa May, which contains some general information about the grant, refusal, and withdrawal of passports—a far cry from any form of rule-book or guidance (for the link as supplied in this response see https://www.gov.uk/government/speeches/the-issuing-withdrawal-or-refusal-of-passports). The result of this exercise clearly shows the impact of this fuzziness: the government is able to deny access to its unilaterally made rules, if such do exist in this case.

The legislation of the prerogative to manage the Civil Service does not apply in the Northern Ireland branch (Constitutional Reform and Governance Act 2010 s 1(2)(d)). Hence, orders not based on

e. Interim conclusion

Under a theme of diminishing fields of Crown involvement, unilateral lawmaking of the Head of State remains part of the British constitutional structure. Both orders in council and proclamations have been retained, and both maintain their dual (or, rather, triple) nature: they may be statute-based, non-statutory, or they can rely, at least formally, on a mix of statutes and general references to 'other powers'. Finally, the actual power to initiate and design these measures is entirely in the hands of the executive.

Surprisingly, as seen in the next section, the same features appear in the US constitutional sphere, notwithstanding the entirely different constitutional structure, and the avowed aim of the founding fathers to reject any relics of a monarchic or otherwise central government power.

2. The United States: Proclamations, Executive Orders, Memoranda, and Other Measures

The extent of use of semi-formalized non-statutory measures in the US is even more pervasive than in the UK; similarly, the volume of academic debates over their nature and use is continuously both broad and loud.[39] The interest is not

legislation continue to reign, and some of them are undisclosed, including amendments to the Civil Service Commissioners (Northern Ireland) Order 1999, itself made by the Secretary of State '[i]n exercise of the powers conferred on me by Letters Patent of Her Majesty dated 20 December 1973 and of all other powers enabling me in that behalf' (<https://www.nicscommissioners.org/wp-content/uploads/2011/06/CSCNI-Order-1999.pdf>); see Cormacain (n 37) 505.

[39] For some of the studies from the past two decades see Kenneth Mayer, *With the Stroke of a Pen* (Princeton University Press 2002); Phillip J Cooper, *By Order of the President: The Use and Abuse of Executive Direct Action* (2nd rev ed, University Press of Kansas 2014); Tara L Branum, 'President or King? The Use and Abuse of Executive Orders in Modern-Day America' (2002) 28 J Legislation 1; William G Howell, *Power without Persuasion: The Politics of Direct Presidential Action* (Princeton University Press 2003); Kevin M Stack, 'The Statutory President' (2005) 90 Iowa L Rev 539; Harold C Relyea, *Presidential Directives: Background and Overview*, Library of Congress, Congressional Research Service 98-611 GOV (updated 26 November 2008), available at <https://fas.org/sgp/crs/misc/98-611.pdf> (2005). Several journals have devoted special issues to unilateral powers (see eg the Presidential Studies Quarterly Vol 35(3) (2005)); Michelle Belco and Brandon Rottinghouse, *The Dual Executive: Unilateral Orders in a Separated and Shared Power System* (Stanford University Press 2017). For a general overview and a list of additional publications see William G Howell, 'Unilateral Powers: A Brief Overview' (2005) 35 Pres Stud Q 417. Earlier important contributions include W D Neighbors, 'Presidential Legislation by Executive Order' (1964) 37 U Col L Rev 105; J L Fleishman and A H Aufses, 'Law and Orders: The Problem of Presidential Legislation' (1976) 40(3) L and Contemp Prob 1; Peter Strauss, 'Presidential Rulemaking' (1997) 72 Chi-Kent L Rev 965. Citation of the rich literature concerned with specific executive orders is unnecessary.

Earlier studies, compilations and indices of executive orders and proclamations include Clifford L Lord, *List and Index of Presidential Executive Orders, Unnumbered Series*, New Jersey Historical Records Survey Project, Newark, NJ (Historical Records Survey 1943); Clifford L Lord, *Presidential Executive Orders* (WPA Historical Records Survey, Archives Publishing 1944); Committee on Government Operations, House of Representatives, *Executive Orders and Proclamations: A Study of a Use of Presidential Powers*, 85th Congress, 1st Session, Committee Print 89166, (Government Printing

limited to academia: any student of presidential powers, indeed any follower of the daily press, must be aware of presidential use of executive orders, the measure that usually attracts public attention. Photos of President Trump flourishing his pen and signing such orders, the first twelve made during his first week in office, reflect a centuries-long presidential practice.[40] A closer focus on these—and other similar written measures deemed to be unilaterally made by presidents asserting and implementing their policy agendas—reveals a complex pattern. These measures feature some surprising similarities to the British ones discussed above, minus the pomp of the prerogative and the sitting of the Privy Council; here, too, these measures may be constitution-derived, statute-derived, or, most confusingly, both—or neither.

a. The forms

As Samuel Huntington noted in 1968,

> The American Revolution removed the English Crown from the American scene [and] made history by establishing the people as the constituent power ... (but) its political institutions did not undergo revolutionary changes ... the English colonist took ... late medieval and Tudor political ideas, practices and institutions across the Atlantic with them.[41]

Indeed, echoing English history, the first formalized edicts made by US presidents were entitled 'proclamations'; President Washington's order, *Defining the Boundaries of the District of Columbia*, is generally considered Proclamation 1, although earlier proclamations were issued.[42] Some of those early measures were no

Office 1957 (1957 Committee Report); Hugh C Keenan, 'Executive Orders: A Brief History of Their Use and the President's Power to Issue Them', in Senate Special Committee on National Emergencies and Delegated Legislation, 93rd Congress, 2nd Session, *Summary of Executive Orders in Times of War and National Emergency* 20 (1974); *CIS Index to Presidential Executive Orders and Proclamations* (Congressional Information Service 1988). For quantitative studies see Gary King and Lyn Ragsdale, *The Elusive Executive: Discovering Statistical Patterns in the Presidency* (CQ Press 1988) esp chs 3, 4; literature cited in Terry M Moe and William G Howell, 'The Presidential Power of Unilateral Action' (1999) 15 JLEO 132, 134 (1999).

[40] During his two first weeks in office (20 January–2 February 2017), President Trump signed seven executive orders, eight memoranda, and two proclamations (on these forms see below); measures uploaded onto the White House website <https://www.whitehouse.gov/presidential-actions>. In comparison, President Obama's first two weeks produced nine executive orders, eight memoranda, and one proclamation. Search, American Presidency Project (APP) website, which collects an impressively large number of presidential measures; <https://www.presidency.ucsb.edu/documents>. Signing statements are available on the latter website; none were made during these periods. On the nature of the latter measures see below.

[41] Samuel P Huntington, *Political Order in Changing Societies* (Yale University Press 1968), 93, 96–97, citing Charles Howard McIlwain, *The High Court of Parliament and Its Supremacy* (Yale University Press 1910) 386.

[42] Issued 24 January 1791. See Jack D Warren, Jr (ed), *The Papers of George Washington, Presidential Series* (University Press of Virginia 1998) Vol 7, 278–80. Recognized as 'Proclamation 1' by <https://www.presidency.ucsb.edu/documents/proclamation-1-defining-the-boundaries-the-district-columbia>.

more than a written endorsement of a written proposal, or a letter sent to a government official or envoy requiring specific action—for example, George Washington's declaration of neutrality of 1793, which gave rise to the first dispute over the extent of presidential powers; this, as others, is usually considered a proclamation.[43] All presidents since then have issued proclamations, usually to mark days of remembrance, but they have been used for other policy purposes, for example President Trump's 2019 recognition of the Golan Heights as part of the State of Israel.[44]

As in the UK, proclamations are now less central to presidential rulemaking. Distinctly, a range of other unilateral measures have emerged and continue to be used: alongside the main measure, the executive order, presidents have issued memoranda, signing statements, differently named directives in the national security field, in addition to unilateral signing of so-called executive agreements in the transnational sphere.

The title 'executive order' became a common designation in the mid-nineteenth century. There are conflicting views on the identity of the first executive order, but the consensus seems be that it was made by President Lincoln in 1862 in the context of the military occupation of Louisiana.[45] The contexts in which such orders are made vary, and cover most aspects of governance: the National Archives subject classification of executive orders made by president ranges alphabetically from Banking to Terrorism for Donald Trump, and from Abortion to Yemen for Barack Obama.[46] Notable executive orders ordered the requisitioning of lands for a variety

For an example of an earlier proclamation see George Washington's proclamation of 3 October 1789, *Day of National Thanksgiving*, in Dorothy Twohig (ed), *The Papers of George Washington, Presidential Series* (University Press of Virginia 1993) Vol 4, 131–32.

[43] The message declares the neutrality of the United States in the war between France and Great Britain, indicates the absence of support United States citizens were to receive when involved, and threatens to prosecute citizens violating the law of nations. *A Proclamation*, 22 April 1793, in James R Richardson (ed), *A Compilation of Messages and Papers of the President 1789–1897* (Government Printing Office 1896–99) Vol I, 156–57. 'Numbered 4 in the Presidency Project website, the research and archive website managed at UC Santa Barbara; see < https://www.presidency.ucsb.edu/documents/app-categories/written-presidential-orders/presidential/proclamations?field_docs_start_date_time_value%5Bvalue%5D%5Bdate%5D=1793>.'

[44] Examples from 2019 include the proclamation of the Armed Forces Day and the World Trade Week, limiting the import of steel for national security reasons, and recognizing the Golan Heights, annexed by Israel (Proclamation 9892, *Armed Force Day*, 17 May 2019, 84 FR 23701; Proclamation 9891, *World Trade Week*, 17 May 2019, 84 FR 23699; Proclamation 9894, *Adjusting Imports of Steel into the United States*, 19 May 2019, 84 FR 23987; Proclamation 9852, *Recognizing the Golan Heights as Part of the State of Israel*, 28 March 2019, 84 FR 11875). On these measures see Cooper (n 39) 171–205.

[45] Lord's 1944 study of executive orders numbers as No 1 an order issued on 20 October 1862 that established a Provisional Court to function during the military occupation of Louisiana, opening a practice of numbering most executive orders (some have escaped the list); Lord, *Presidential Executive Orders* (1944) 1. For the text see <https://www.presidency.ucsb.edu/documents/executive-order-establishing-provisional-court-louisiana>. Earlier measures are identified as 'executive orders' or 'orders', the earliest being President Adams's order on the death of Thomas Jefferson, made on 11 July 1826, yet it is unclear whether the title was an editorial decision made in an era where executive orders were well established. See <https://www.presidency.ucsb.edu/documents/executive-order-the-death-thomas-jefferson>.

[46] See <https://www.archives.gov/federal-register/executive-orders/trump-subjects> and <https://www.archives.gov/federal-register/executive-orders/obama-subjects.html>, respectively.

of purposes, inter alia: to establish military reservations and to temporarily ban entry to mineral-rich land;[47] to be used as an initial measure to order the interning of Americans of Japanese ancestry during World War II;[48] to subject government contractors to anti-discrimination policies after efforts to apply them at the national level failed;[49] to regulate agencies in ways that impact on their activity, hence on those regulated by them;[50] and to set sanctions over foreign states, economies, and exceptionally, on persons associated with international bodies.[51]

Serial numbering of executive orders was introduced in 1907. The numbering reaches back to 1862, but according to estimates, the number of non-serial unnumbered orders ranges from 15,000 to 50,000.[52]

The third most commonly discussed measure, designated as 'memorandum', is usually a document directed to a secretary of state or another high-level officer in the administration. Some memoranda declare policies, are concerned with delegation of powers pursuant to statute, order the reorganization of government functions, or require bodies established by the measure, or agencies, to conduct studies or make reports on defined policy issues.[53] Note that the term 'memorandum' is commonly used in the US for opinions and other reports made by officials and experts. The infamous 'torture memo', signed in August 2002 by Assistant Attorney General Jay S Bybee, at the Office of Legal Counsel of the US Department of Justice, which recognized the use of 'enhanced' methods of interrogation was directed

[47] See eg unnumbered executive order, 5–6 November 1850, concerning the reservation of certain lands in the Bay of San Francisco for military purposes, cited in Clifford L Lord (ed), *List and Index of Presidential Executive Orders, Unnumbered Series (1789–1941)* (Michael Glazier Inc 1979) 15 (upheld in *Grisar v McDowell*, 73 US 363 (1867); *US v Midwest Oil*, 236 US 459 (1915) (upholding an order temporarily banning entry and finding 252 executive orders made before 1910 that designated land for Indian reservations, military reservations, and bird reserves).

[48] Executive Order 9066, *Authorizing the Secretary of War to Prescribe Military Areas*, 19 February 1942, 7 FR 1407 (affirmed in *Korematsu v US*, 323 US 214 (1944), decided after the enactment of a statute enacted less than a month later, a 'lopsided' statute that reaffirmed action and set penalties for breach of the order and measures made under it; see ch 3). For the act see 56 Stat 173 (prior to its repeal in 2001, located at 18 USCA § 97a, as cited in *Korematsu*, ibid 216).

[49] See eg Executive Order 11246, *Equal Employment Opportunity*, 24 September 1965, 30 FR 12319.

[50] See eg Executive Order 13371, *Reducing Regulation and Controlling Regulatory Costs*, 30 January 2017, 82 FR 9339 (for analysis of these executive orders in the context of Presidential dominance over agencies see ch 1).

[51] See eg Executive Order 13846, *Reimposing Certain Sanctions with Respect to Iran*, 7 August 2018, 83 FR 38939; Executive Order 13928, *Blocking Property of Certain Persons Associated with the International Criminal Court*, 11 June 2020, 85 FR 36139.

[52] On the 1907 numbering project see Terrence Gough, 'Introductory Note to the 1979 Edition', Lord (n 47) v.

[53] For a few examples see President John F Kennedy's 1962 memorandum on the development of the DC region towards the year 2000, and President Trump's reporting requirements in the context of his policy of ending the 'catch and release' policy at the US border, implemented by executive order 13768. John F Kennedy, *Memorandum on the Year 2000 Plan for the National Capital Region*, 27 November 1962, 27 FR 11753, <https://www.presidency.ucsb.edu/documents/memorandum-the-year-2000-plan-for-the-national-capital-region>; Donald J Trump, *Memorandum on Ending 'Catch and Release' at the Border of the United States and Directing Other Enhancements to Immigration Enforcement*, 6 April 2018, 83 FR 16179, <https://www.presidency.ucsb.edu/documents/memorandum-ending-catch-and-release-the-border-the-united-states-and-directing-other>.

inter alia to President George W Bush's Attorney General, is hence formally not a direct unilateral measure;[54] they still can directly impact on the ways the executive branch exercises its powers. Setting these aside, many memoranda were issued by presidents rather than high-level officers. For example, President George W Bush's 2001 military order that set the anti-terrorism detention regime, adjudged in a series of decisions, is classified as a memorandum in at least one project.[55] Other examples include President Obama's memorandum to all heads of departments and agencies, establishing an inter-departmental working group concerned with considerations of climate change in the context of national security and requiring the addressees to ensure the consideration of climate change impact, President Trump's 2018 memorandum ending a policy of deferred departure of Liberian nationals who resided in the US, first established in 1991 and extended thereafter, and his memorandum requiring the Secretary of Homeland Security to enhance its action in the southern border of the US.[56] Although a large number of these memoranda are policy declarations and directions to the administration, the latter memoranda exemplify the potential weight of such measures.[57]

Signing statements may have received lesser public attention—orders concerning incarceration and immigration naturally receive more publicity—but the ways in which presidents have acted to constrain the implementation of duly enacted legislation when a presidential veto is politically unavailable have had just as strong an impact on the public sphere, if not stronger. The tenacity of presidents' intent to dominate national policy through shaping the implementation of statutes and the expenditure under them is reflected in several practices that emerged serially: after one of these practices was taken off the menu of available powers, another entered the arena. Unilateral impoundment of funds, a practice of under-expenditure exercised since the earliest presidencies, was prohibited by statute in 1974, after a marked rise in the practice, although, contrary to some understandings, has not exited the scene.[58] Next, the line-item veto, legislated by President

[54] Jay Bybee, 'Memorandum for Alberto R Gonzales, Counsel to the President', 1 August 2002, https://nsarchive2.gwu.edu/NSAEBB/NSAEBB127/02.08.01.pdf ('torture memo'). On this, and other memoranda made at the time and concerned with global terrorism see eg David Cole, *Torture Memos: Rationalizing the Unthinkable* (The New Press 2009).

[55] George W Bush, *Detention, Treatment, and Trial of Certain Non-Citizens in the War Against Terrorism*, 13 November 2001, 66 FR 57833 (published as a 'notice', classified as a memorandum in the APP website at <https://www.presidency.ucsb.edu/documents/military-order-detention-treatment-and-trial-certain-non-citizens-the-war-against>).

[56] Barack Obama, Memorandum on Climate Change and National Security, 21 September 2016; Donald J Trump, *Memorandum on Expiration of Deferred Enforced Departure for Liberians*, 27 March 2018; Donald J Trump, *Memorandum on Securing the Southern Border of the United States*, 4 April 2018. For these memoranda, uploaded onto the APP website, see <https://www.presidency.ucsb.edu/documents/memorandum-climate-change-and-national-security>; <https://www.presidency.ucsb.edu/documents/memorandum-expiration-deferred-enforced-departure-for-liberians>; <https://www.presidency.ucsb.edu/documents/memorandum-securing-the-southern-border-the-united-states>.

[57] For a detailed analysis of memoranda, addressing their content and attraction to presidents, see Cooper (n 39) 115–69.

[58] The Impoundment Control Act, Title X of the Congressional Budget and Impoundment Control Act 1974, passed by the Congress during President Nixon's last month in office, established a procedure

Clinton in 1996, enabled the president to cancel discretionary expenditure items or tax benefits contained in laws upon notification to Congress, which retained the authority to disapprove by passing a bill to the contrary. That attempt to move this power out of the unilateral sphere was found unconstitutional in the US Supreme Court two years later, for violating the procedure for the enactment of laws set in the presentment clause of the Constitution.[59] The signing statement, the next and current measure, seems to have successfully replaced the former practices. Essentially, these are statements made by presidents at the time of the signing of the bill into law. They carry their own history (the commonly cited first signing statements are President Monroe's two statements interpreting legislation, issued in 1819 and 1822), but they have become the common tool for expressing presidential dissatisfaction with a statute, and often contain more than a hint about presidential nonconformity with challenged provisions.[60] As such, signing statements are in fact a diluted type of line-item veto, declaring a critical, if not negative, attitude towards an authorized action, usually without openly declaring non-constitutionality, instead heavily hinting at the interference with his presidential powers. Others go further, by pinpointing the problematic nature of certain provisions of a signed statute, even directly declaring that the provisions will be considered to be merely 'advisory and non-binding'.[61]

Consider President Trump's statement of February 2019 on signing the Consolidated Appropriations Act 2019, ending the government shutdown of 2019.

that requires presidents initiating rescission or deferral of expenditure to send a message to Congress, and grants Congress the right to review and negate or approve such presidential initiatives (PL 93–344 §§, 2 USC §§681–88). Applied and interpreted in *Train v City of New York*, 420 US 35 (1975). See AJ Mikva and MF Hertz, 'Impoundment of Funds—The Courts, the Congress and the President: A Constitutional Triangle' (1974–1975) 69 Northwestern U L Rev 553. But see RE Brownell II, 'The Constitutional Status of the President's Impoundment of National Security Funds' (2001) 12 Seton Hall Constitutional LJ 1 (impoundment is still a feature of national security expenditure).

59 Line Item Veto Act, Public Law 104–30 (1996); *Clinton v City of New York*, 524 US 417 (1998).

60 These are two messages that provided President Monroe's interpretation of two acts, issued long after their enaction. See James D Richardson (ed), *James Monroe: A Compilation of The Messages And Papers Of The Presidents*, Vol 2 632, 698. The first cited statements made on the time of signature were made by President Tyler in 1830. On these, and on the measure in general, see Christopher N May, 'Presidential Defiance of "Unconstitutional" Laws: Reviving the Royal Prerogative' (1994) 21 Hastings Const LQ 865.

61 The term was used in President Trump's signing statement of 15 February 2019, issued on the date of presidential signature of the Consolidated Appropriations Act 2019 (see below), and refer to provisions that prohibit, under conditions and in certain contexts, the payment of salaries to 'personnel who prepare or submit appropriations language as part of the President's budget submission to the Congress for programs under the jurisdiction of the Appropriations Subcommittees on Agriculture, Rural Development, Food and Drug Administration, and Related Agencies' (Division B, section 715), and a provision that requires the Secretary of Homeland Security to provide the Committees on Appropriations of the Senate and the House of Representatives specific reductions in proposed discretionary budget commensurate to proposed funding reductions or assumptions of revenues (Division A, section 537). Donald Trump, 'Statement on Signing the Consolidated Appropriations Act, 2019', 15 February 2019. Text available at <https://www.whitehouse.gov/briefings-statements/statement-by-the-president-28/>.

This statement lists a good number of provisions found to be problematic. Some 'could, in certain circumstances, interfere with the exercise of the President's constitutional authorities to negotiate international agreements'; another, in the context of a provision that prohibited funding to transform water policy, 'significantly impedes the President's ability to supervise the executive branch or obtain the assistance of aides in this function [and] violates the separation of powers by undermining the President's ability to fulfill his constitutional responsibilities, including the responsibility to faithfully execute the laws of the United States'. Hence, in the latter context, the President declared that 'my Administration will, therefore, construe these restrictions . . . consistent with these Presidential duties'.[62]

Presidential executive agreements, made by presidents in the transnational sphere, have almost completely replaced the Constitution's arrangement that requires Senate approval of treaties. Commentators identify several types of arrangements with foreign countries that do not follow the constitutional framework. The most common are the product of congressional-executive participatory processes, and are of lesser interest here, although these too are likely to be made under presidential initiative. Two other types of agreements seem truly unilateral: the 'sole' executive agreement, made by presidents on the basis of their reliance on the Constitution, and the more recently recognized agreement, dubbed by some the 'executive agreement+'—an agreement that is 'consistent' with existing law, or 'complementing' domestic measures, that is, supported, but not specifically authorized, by congressional action.[63] Quantitative studies show that most

[62] See ibid. For another well-known example see President George W Bush's signing statement to the Detainee Treatment Act (2005), in which the President stated that the statutory prohibition of 'cruel, inhuman or degrading treatment or punishment' (Public Law 109–48, §1003) was to be construed 'in a manner consistent with the constitutional authority of the President to supervise the unitary executive branch and as Commander in Chief and consistent with the constitutional limitations on the judicial power, which will assist in achieving the shared objective of the Congress and the President, evidenced in Title X, of protecting the American people from further terrorist attacks' (George W Bush, 'Statement on Signing the Department of Defense, Emergency Supplemental Appropriations to Address Hurricanes in the Gulf of Mexico, and Pandemic Influenza Act, 2006', text available at <https://www.presidency.ucsb.edu/documents/statement-signing-the-department-defense-emergency-supplemental-appropriations-address>). On signing statements see Cooper (n 39) 323–84; May (n 60); Curtis A Bradley and Eric A Posner, 'Presidential Signing Statements and Executive Power' (2006) Const Commentary 307; Ian Ostrander and Joel Sievert, 'The Logics of Presidential Signing Statements' (2019) 66 Political Res Q 141.

[63] The literature dubs the two participatory types of agreements 'ex-ante' and 'ex-post' congressional-executive agreements: the first is made under statutory authorization, the second approved by statute after presidential signature. 'Sole' executive agreements are unilaterally made; the fourth type, as Bodansky and Spiro argue, differs by its reference (explicitly made by presidents or impliedly so) to its compatibility with law. General analyses include Congressional Research Service, 106th Congress, *Treaties and Other International Agreements: The Role of the United States Senate* (US Government Printing Office 2001) (presenting a detailed history accompanied by a quantitative study); Curtis A Bradley and Jack Goldsmith, 'Presidential Control over International Law' (2018) 131 Harv L Rev 1201; Stephen Mulligan, *International Law and Agreements: Their Effect upon US Law*, Congressional Research Service 7-7500, RL32628 (updated 2018), available at <https://crsreports.congress.gov/product/pdf/RL/RL32528>; Cooper (n 39) 277–321. For focus on congressional-executive agreements see eg Anne Hathaway, 'Treaties' End: The Past, Present and Future of International Lawmaking in the United States' (2008) Yale LJ 1236. On 'executive agreements+' see Daniel Bodansky and Peter

agreements are congressional-executive, but 'sole' agreements are still part of the presidential menu of unilateral measures.[64]

The title 'presidential directive' is sometimes used to identify several types of written measures that instruct government agencies to provide information to the president or convey policy determinations, most notably in the field of national security. The government considers them akin to executive orders.[65]

b. Fuzziness I: Multiple and mixed authorities

In a manner identical to the UK case, presidential measures are classically presented as either statute-based or generally based on the constitution. Indeed, some measures rely purely on statute, and others cite only the constitution.[66] However, most of them, especially those issued in the past several decades, are both.

Consider, as one example, President Trump's 2018 order that reimposed sanctions on Iran, which commences as follows:

> By the authority vested in me as President by the Constitution and the laws of the United States of America, including the International Emergency Economic

Spiro, 'Executive Agreements+' (2016) 49 Vand J Transnational L 885 (drawing on arguments made by Professor Harold Koh as the legal adviser to Obama Administration's State Department); see also Harold Hongju Koh, 'Triptych's End: A Better Framework to Evaluate 21st Century International Lawmaking' (2017) 126 Yale LJ Forum 338; for critique on the soundness of this category as distinct see David A Wirth, 'Executive Agreements Relying on Implied Statutory Authority: A Response to Bodansky and Spiro' (2017) Vanderbilt J Transnational L 741.

Examples of 'pure' sole agreements include President Obama's joining the Iran Nuclear Agreement and his signature to the Paris Agreement on Climate Change (2015 and 2016, respectively; on these, see eg Bradley and Goldsmith (n 63) 1203–04), although the proponents of the 'executive agreement+' category identify both as examples of that category, identifying both as compatible with extant law (Bodansky and Spiro, ibid 916, 914 n 157). President Obama's signature of the Minamata Convention on Mercury in 2013, accompanied by a press release that declared that '[t]he Minamata Convention complements domestic measures by addressing the transnational nature of the problem' can be considered an example of an 'executive agreement+' for those who identify this category (see US Department of State Media Note, 'United States Joins the Minamata Convention on Mercury', 6 November 2013 https://2009-2017.state.gov/r/pa/prs/ps/2013/11/217295.htm); Bradley and Goldsmith, ibid 1216.

[64] See Hathaway (n 63) 1252–71; Bradley and Goldsmith (n 63) 1213 (about 80–85% of executive agreements are ex ante congressional-executive agreements). The authors of both studies note the difficulty of tracing all agreements, but their findings show an overwhelming distinct majority of presidential-executive treaties.

[65] For general analyses of the variety of measures see Cooper (n 39); Harold C Relyea (n 39). On 'national security directives', Cooper 207–75; Patrick A Thornson, 'Toward Comprehensive Reform of America's Emergency Law Regime' (2013) U Michigan J L Reform 737, 741–42. Studies have identified others, such as announcements, reorganization plans, and interpretations (see eg Relyea, ibid). My concern here is with those measures that authorize action. For the government's position on the nature of presidential directives see Randolph D Moss, *Legal Effectiveness of a Presidential Directive, as Compared to an Executive Order*, Memorandum Opinion for the Counsel for the President (29 January 2000) available at <https://www.justice.gov/olc/opinion/legal-effectiveness-presidential-directive-compared-executive-order>.

[66] For an example of the first see Proclamation No 1, defining the boundaries of the District of Columbia (n 42); for an oft-discussed example of the second type see Executive Order 10340 (1952), challenged in *Youngstown Sheet & Tube v Sawyer*, 343 US 579 (1952).

> Powers Act (50 U.S.C. 1701 et seq.) (IEEPA), the National Emergencies Act (50 U.S.C. 1601 et seq.) (NEA), the Iran Sanctions Act of 1996 (Public Law 104–172) (50 U.S.C. 1701 note), as amended (ISA), the Comprehensive Iran Sanctions, Accountability, and Divestment Act of 2010 (Public Law 111–195) (22 U.S.C. 8501 et seq.), as amended (CISADA), the Iran Threat Reduction and Syria Human Rights Act of 2012 (Public Law 112–158) (TRA), the Iran Freedom and Counter-Proliferation Act of 2012 (subtitle D of title XII of Public Law 112–239) (22 U.S.C. 8801 et seq.) (IFCA), section 212(f) of the Immigration and Nationality Act of 1952 (8 U.S.C. 1182(f)), and section 301 of title 3, United States Code, in order to take additional steps with respect to the national emergency declared in Executive Order 12957 of March 15, 1995 ...[67]

Reliance on this formula, often in addition to the citation of statutes, has become the governing pattern.

In the mid-twentieth century, purely statute-based executive orders comprised a large portion of the orders: a study spanning 1,013 executive orders issued between 1945 and 1956 found that 48% of them were purely statute-based. All other orders, but three, cited different forms of general authority, usually the now well-established formula 'the constitution and laws of the United States'. A third of all these orders (35%) cited mixed authorities, that is, relied on the general formula a well as one or several legislative provisions.[68]

The pattern has materially changed since then. For several decades now, only a marginal number of executive orders or other presidential measures are purely statute-based. No less than 93% of the measures that contain rules, issued during the financial year 2019–20, cite the formula, either with or without a reference to a statutory authority. This pattern also appears in memoranda and other measures that are plain delegations of power under a cited statute.[69]

[67] Executive Order 13846 (n 51).

[68] Committee on Government Operators, *Executive Orders and Proclamations: A Study of a Use of Presidential Powers* (Government Printing Office 1957) 39–40. Three of these measures cited no basis of authority.

[69] Out of 119 executive orders, proclamations and memoranda issued between 1 April 2019 and 31 March 2020, found on the White House website under 'Presidential Action', seventy-six (63.87%) cite both the general formula and at least one statutory provision. Thirty-five (29.41%) relied solely on this general formula. Only two measures refrained from using it and cited a statute (the remaining six either cited no authority, contained a general reference to constitutional powers, or referred to previous executive orders). Excluded in this quantitative exercise were proclamations declaring remembrance and national periods, notifications concerning appointments, and veto messages. The inclusion of the formula in no less than 83% of these measures sufficiently reflects the ongoing use of this formula. Search, 4 May 2020 (measures found <https://www.whitehouse.gov/presidential-actions/>). These results reinforce earlier ones. See ch 3 (search of 2018 executive orders); Adam L Warber, *Executive Orders and the Modern Presidency: Legislating from the Oval Office* (Lynne Rienner 2006) 89–105 (showing a gradual rise of citations of vague sources of authority); a separate search of executive orders issued in 2011–12 (all fifty-eight executive orders made during this period relied on 'the Constitution and laws'; in fifty-four of them, it was the only source cited. Search, 13 February 2013, of orders then available on the White House website).

The same questions asked in the British context are relevant here, if not more so, due to the complete victory of mixed, general sources in presidential rulemaking. How should this order, and scores of similar ones, be treated? As above, such orders offer the possibility of non-commitment to any clear source of authority; their very legality, or at least, their legal status, is unclear.

c. Fuzziness II: The legal status of unilateral measures

As in the case of the UK, there is no clear judicial ruling as to the exact legal status of unilateral measures, and some of this unclarity derives from the neglect of the distinction between measures made under statutes and those that may be made under the constitution. For some, such as the American Bar Association's account,

> Both executive orders and proclamations have the force of law, much like regulations issued by federal agencies ... Executive orders are not legislation; they require no approval from Congress, and Congress cannot simply overturn them. Congress may pass legislation that might make it difficult, or even impossible, to carry out the order, such as removing funding. Only a sitting U.S. President may overturn an existing executive order by issuing another executive order to that effect.[70]

What is the exact meaning of this paragraph? Does the first cited sentence signify that all unilateral power should be considered akin to regulations made under a statutory authorization? How should the term 'force of law' be construed? And can the claim that Congress cannot repeal such measures be sustained, either with regards to statute-derived measures, constitution-based ones, or both?

The limited jurisprudence of federal courts on the matter has not dispelled this confusion, which, similarly to the UK, is not usually required to be decided, due to the rarity of cases in which the validity of such an order is challenged. Retracing the sources of the recognition that such measures have 'the force of law' is straightforward enough, but these sources do not offer definitive answers to the above questions.

Jenkins v Collard (1892) was one of the series of decisions in which the Supreme Court was required to decide on the impact of the post-Civil War Presidential pardon issued by proclamation in 1868 on the rights of heirs of original owners of property from whom property was seized under statute.[71] During the war, two

[70] American Bar Association website, 'What is an Executive Order?' 27 November 2018 <https://www.americanbar.org/groups/public_education/publications/teaching-legal-docs/what-is-an-executive-order-/>.

[71] *Jenkins v Collard*, S Ct Rep 868 (1892); Proclamation 179, *Granting Full Pardon and Amnesty for the Offense of Treason Against the United States During the Late Civil War*, 25 December 1868. Text at <https://www.presidency.ucsb.edu/documents/proclamation-179-granting-full-pardon-and-amnesty-for-the-offense-treason-against-the>.

statutes authorized, inter alia, the seizure of land belonging to Confederate supporters. The second, a joint resolution, clarified that such seizure was to be in effect during the life of the offender.[72] The land and property in question, seized during the war, was sold to a third party, and the heirs of the original owner sued for their rights. In deciding for the heirs, the court found that the purchaser's omission of challenging the proclamation did not change the state of affairs, as 'the pardon and amnesty were made by a public proclamation of the president, which has the force of public law, and of which all courts and officers must take notice, whether especially called to their attention or not'.[73] This iteration of the doctrine of judicial notice had little to do with the question of the legal status of the proclamation, or whether this proclamation was a pure equivalent of statute, nor should such a jurisprudential inquiry have been made.

A series of District Court and Federal Appeals court decisions should have been read as relevant only to measures that relied on statute, with little to say about pure constitution-based measures such as the amnesty and pardon proclamation discussed above. Some of these decisions were concerned with executive orders that ordered the inclusion of non-discrimination clauses in government contractors. Executive Order 10925, the first of these measures discussed by Federal courts in the 1960s, cited 'the authority vested in me as President of the United States by the Constitution and statutes of the United States'. In *Farmer* (1964), the Court of Appeals for the Third Circuit found these orders were authorized by statutes, and proceeded to address the order as equivalent to rules and regulations promulgated under statutes, all having 'the force and effect of law', a formula often used in the rulings on statute-based regulations and guidance rules.[74] Three years later, a different District Court followed this dicta, but one of the keynotes preceding the decision stated that 'Executive order of the President is to be accorded the force and effect given to a statute enacted by Congress'.[75] This possible misrepresentation, which could be interpreted as a ruling that equates *all* executive orders with Federal legislation, was adopted in subsequent decisions. For example, in 1980, the DC District Court ruled that 'an Executive Order, if issued pursuant to legitimate Presidential authority, would be accorded the force and effect given to a statute enacted by Congress'.[76]

[72] For these facts see *Jenkins v Collard* (n 71) 870–71.

[73] ibid 873.

[74] Executive Order 10925, *Establishing the President's Committee on Equal Employment Opportunity*, 6 March 1961, 26 FR 1977; *Farmer v Philadelphia Electric Company*, 329 F 2d 3, 7 (3rd Cir 1964). For the use of the formula in the consideration of regulations see eg *Maryland Casualty v US*, 251 US 342, 349, 473 (1920); *Chrysler Corp v Brown*, 441 US 281, 294 (1979).

[75] *Farkas v Texas Instrument*, 375 F3d 629, 630 (5th Cir 1967).

[76] *AFL-CIO v Freeman*, 498 F Supp 651, 658 (1980) (no executive order issued). See also *Association for Women in Science v Califano*, 566 F 2d 339, 344 (DC Ct of Appeals) (executive order citing a statute as well as a general reference to 'the President of the United States'); *City of Albuquerque v United States Department of Interior*, 379 F 3d 901, 913, 915 (10th Cir 2004) (executive order relying solely on statute). Early decisions that identified the 'executive' nature of statute-based executive orders include *Jones v*

All of these dicta were not concerned with unilateral measures that had no link with statute.

The question regarding the status of unilaterally made orders remains open, and is more acute due to the almost universal reliance on the constitution in measures issued in the past decades, discussed above.

In sum, apart from a small number of dicta on the nature of unilaterally made measures that should be criticized as misunderstandings of precedents, the courts have not contributed to the understanding of the legal status of pure constitutional proclamations and executive orders. The only distinct and consistent feature of the case-law is the scant attention granted to the recitals as determinants of the source of authority: in some cases, orders based on unilateral or mixed general sources (such as 'the constitution and the laws') were linked to statutory bases, in others, such cited bases were found lacking, leading the courts to continue to address the measure as non-statutory.[77] No clear conclusion on the nature of these orders can be gleaned from this source.

d. Fuzziness III: Access difficulties

Under the Federal Register Act 1935, proclamations, executive orders, and 'documents or classes of documents that the President may determine from time to time have general applicability and legal effect' are to be published in the Federal Register, unless they do not have 'general applicability and legal effect or effective only against Federal agencies or persons in their capacity as officers, agents, or employees thereof', a clause that may leave out all measures formally addressed to government officers, including all memoranda and some proclamations.[78] Some memoranda are indeed published in the Federal Register, although this is discretionary; for example, the 'torture memos' were not published, as were other measures concerned with the fight against terrorism.[79] Signing statements, as such, are not published. Additional exemptions from publication for national security reasons derive from the Freedom of Information Act.[80]

US, 137 US 202, 217 (1890); *US v Gilbertson*, 111 F 2d 978 (7th Cir 1940); *Hampton v US*, 276 US 394, 410–11 (1927).

[77] Cases in the first group include *Farmer* (n 74) and *City of Albuquerque* (n 76). In the second group see also *Dames & Moore v Regan*, 453 US 654 (1981).

[78] PL 74-220 §5(a), 44 USC §1505. The Federal Register Office at the National Archives offers online lists of orders from 1933 to 2017 at <http://www.archives.gov/federal-register/executive-orders/disposition.html>, and links to the text and details of orders since 1994 at <https://www.federalregister.gov/presidential-documents/executive-orders>.

[79] For a list of, and links to other anti-terrorism memos see <https://web.archive.org/web/20090130084952/http:/www.propublica.org/special/missing-memos>. Of the seven examples of memoranda cited above, some chosen by notoriety, others as random examples (nn 53–56), four were formally published (including President Bush's military order, published in the 'notice' section (see n 55).

[80] PL 89–554, 5 USC §552(b), as amended, lists several exceptions from the duty to publish in the Federal Register, including matters that are 'specifically authorized under criteria established by an Executive order to be kept secret in the interest of national defense or foreign policy and (B) are in

Beyond formal publication in the Federal Reporter, a codification of proclamations and executive orders issued between 1945 and 1989 (and some earlier ones), not only classifies the measures but also collates amendments and changes, was prepared by the Office of the Federal Register and is available online, but it has not been updated: its utility is therefore limited.[81] Other online sources are available, but none commit to providing a full repository of these measures, nor do they offer workable search engines.[82] The outcome, then, is that measures may escape detection, especially those not published in the Federal Register. This state of affairs is better than the parallel situation in the UK, where publication of orders in council, especially those that do not derive from a specified statute, is the exception and not the norm. However, in a system that publishes most unilateral measures, those that escape publication, under the prescribed exceptions and beyond them, in ways that do not accord with the publication requirements, may be less accessible: belief that the Federal Register, the White House website, and other websites contain all executive orders lowers the credibility of the existence of errant unilateral measures. Hence, such measures may escape attention.

C. Comparative Analysis

On its independence, the political structure of the United States of America was designed as an antithesis to the former British regime. Initially a loose federation with a limited-power central government, the reform established by the constitution

fact properly classified pursuant to such Executive order'. The current executive order, Executive Order 13526, *Classified National Security Information* (29 December 2009) 75 FR 718, prescribes, in its words, 'a uniform system for classifying, safeguarding, and declassifying national security information, including information relating to defense against transnational terrorism', and is set out in a note under 50 USC §3161. Note that this provision, applicable to agencies, broadly defines the term as including the Executive Office of the President (5 USC §522(f)(1)).

[81] See <http://www.archives.gov/federal-register/codification/numeric.html>.

[82] The White House website has offered repositories of such measures. Prior to President Trump's administration, measures were classified by type (separating between executive orders, proclamations, etc), and access to previous administrations was directly available on the White House website (author's experience). Since 2017, only the current President's measures are available, and they are contained in one list, 'presidential actions'; although a search by type is possible, it is not offered through easily viewed links, and trawling through all those considered as such, including appointments and delegations, is therefore required (<https://www.whitehouse.gov/presidential-actions/>). The current setup has weakened the utility of reliance on this source. A better repository is found in the APP website, which continues to offer access to measures, classified by type and available for all presidencies, although the search engine is limited (<https://www.presidency.ucsb.edu/documents>). Paid-for databases, such as Heinonline, offer access to the FR, but currently has no database dedicated to these measures, although its 'presidential papers' library is a welcome addition. For overviews on searching presidential measures see eg Wellesley College's web manual on presidential directives, which provides explanation and links to several available sources, at <http://libguides.wellesley.edu/govdocs/directives>. See also Rick McKinney, 'A Research Guide to the Federal Register and the Code of Federal Regulations' (2002) 46(1) Law Lib Lights 10.

that entered into force in 1789 was still a written document which shared virtually nothing with its British counterpart. Even the designs of those whose vision leaned towards the establishment of extensive executive powers if not quasi-monarchism, like Alexander Hamilton, did not support their vision on the history of the English constitution. Despite Hamilton's declaration during the Philadelphia Convention debate that 'the British Government was the best in the world',[83] this, and other such utterances, should be set against Hamilton's general vision and, more importantly, the emerging structure had little affinity to the unwritten understandings, ie the constitution, still evolving across the Atlantic Ocean.

History is but one element of this comparative exercise. The subsequent evolution of these distinct regimes, election systems, legal cultures, and, just as importantly, visions of the nature of the executive, have all contributed to the distancing process. However, the theme of functional convergence, central to the analysis of the dominance of both heads of these executive branches expounded in earlier chapters, has only been further vindicated in this chapter.

Indeed, the starting point couldn't have been more functionally different: powers pertaining to the Crown and retained through centuries of constitutional strife had little to do with powers deduced from the written constitution and from other evolving constructs. However, even in the historical respect, some similarity emerged when early presidents used the title 'proclamation', clearly imported from England, in some of their first edicts.

Beyond historical origins, this and the previous chapter have shown a parallel growth of a second measure, which, in both systems, overshadowed the proclamation. Whether executive orders, which emerged in the US in the mid-nineteenth century, emulated British orders in council, extensively issued in England, is an open question. Surely, the respective process of their promulgation has little in common: a solemn sitting in the Privy Council, based on a longstanding tradition under which the Crown (under advice, if not diktat of the government) issues its rules, is far removed from presidential pen-flourishing, avidly photographed these days, to symbolize the president's role as the leader of the country.

Yet another difference may be identified in the growth in the US of other semi-formal measures that have become staples of the presidential menu: memoranda, signing statements, and other such measures have no equivalents in the UK. Still, the similarity of several central features of the use of unilateral measures in both systems is no less than astounding and has never been recognized before.

As far as their legal status, both systems feature a confusing mix between three types of such measures, best found in the above analysis of orders in council and executive orders, the prominent current measures used by the respective executives. I show that some of these measures derive only from the constitution—be it

[83] See Max Farrand (ed), *The Records of the Federal Convention of 1787* (Yale University Press 1966) Vol I, 288.

the written US Constitution and accompanying doctrines such as gloss and sovereignty, or the Royal prerogative as exercised by the British government. In both systems, some of these measures are grounded in statute, rendering them another form of pure secondary regulation. But mostly, and almost universally in the case of the US, these measures are at least formally cited as deriving their authority from both sources—a feature that not only reflects the governments' strong interest in retaining all possible sources of authority, including the imprimatur of high importance by the mention of the constitution or related constructs. This mixed-authority citing practice renders the status of such measures unclear and may impact on the types of judicial review available to those who opposed their introduction.

Yet even pure constitution-derived orders have not been granted a definitive recognition. The question of whether they should be considered as pure secondary legislation or as edicts akin to legislation has generated attention in both systems. The contribution of the courts to the understanding of the legal nature of these measures has only led to further confusion.

Finally, I noted that in both systems, access difficulties contribute to the fuzziness of these measures, albeit in two different ways. Publication of such measures is not the norm in the UK, unless a measure is considered to have been made under statute; in the US, formal requirements to publish the central measures issued by the US presidents may reduce the degree of fuzziness that is the result of inaccessibility, but, as discussed above, not all measures are subject to this requirement and, in such a regime, the remaining unpublished measures may be doubly difficult to unearth, first due to the assumption of full publication that leads to the conclusion that no such measures exist, secondly due to the need to conduct archival searches in fields less conducive to openness. The existence of compilations in web sources is likewise both a blessing and a possible problem: measures remaining classified may well escape attention exactly due to the relative richness of available sources in which most are noted and cited.

D. Concluding Remarks

This chapter and the preceding one were dedicated to an analysis of a central form of constitution-derived fuzziness: executive unilateral making of semi-formal measures that rely on the constitution or on constitutional constructs. Chapter 4 presented this form of fuzziness and identified the variety of sources and justifications to their continued emergence and use. This chapter moved forward in two directions. The comparative analysis of the main features of such measures, which led to the recognition of a surprising similarity despite the distinct features of the two compared regimes, also unearthed the existence of mixed-authority based measures. Therefore, this chapter has moved beyond mere attention to the constitution as generator of fuzziness, but also to the fuzziness that is the result of mixing two seemingly distinct sources of power.

Finally, neither system has relied on its sister's experience as justification for the rise and continuing dual nature of unilateral lawmaking. This convergence is not only based on an early American adoption of these governance tools as features of Tudor England; more importantly, it points at the shared politics of executive power.

These observations lead to a call for further focus on the ways politics operate as an explanatory factor to the emergence of fuzziness, further discussed in Chapter 9.

PART III

LEGISLATION AND EXECUTIVE-GENERATED FUZZY LAW

6

Case Studies

Emergency and Air Pollution, Overviews

A. **Introduction** 167
B. **Emergency Law** 169
  1. General 169
  2. Emergency Law in the UK 171
    a. General 171
    b. Layers of law pertaining to emergencies 173
      (1) Customary international law 173
      (2) Constitutional law 175
      (3) International treaty law and UN measures 176
      (4) EU law 177
      (5) Domestic primary legislation 179
  3. Emergency Law in the US 180
    a. General 180
    b. Layers of law pertaining to emergencies 181
      (1) Constitutional law 181
      (2) Customary international law 182
      (3) International treaty law and UN measures 184
      (4) Federal primary legislation 185
C. **Air Pollution Law** 186
  1. General 186
  2. Air Pollution Law in England 188
    a. General 188
    b. Layers of law pertaining to air pollution 189
      (1) International law 189
      (2) EU law 190
      (3) Domestic primary legislation 192
  3. Air Pollution Law in the US 194
    a. General 194
    b. Layers of law pertaining to air pollution 194
      (1) Constitutional law 194
      (2) International and transnational law 195
      (3) Federal primary legislation 196
D. **Concluding Remarks** 197

A. Introduction

The main task of this chapter is to offer a general introduction to the legal ordering of two fields, national emergency and air pollution, chosen as the case-studies discussed in the next two chapters. In addition to providing general backgrounds for those analyses, these introductions present initial accounts on the complexity of both bodies of law in two legal systems, thereby offering four glimpses of the ways fuzziness can, and does, develop and flourish in law. These overviews may be also be useful to those who study these fields.

The choice of maintaining a focus on two fields of government action, national emergency and air pollution, requires that those who wish to better grasp the

A Theory of the Executive Branch. Margit Cohn, Oxford University Press (2021). © Margit Cohn.
DOI: 10.1093/oso/9780198821984.003.0007

nature and impact of these examples of fuzzy forms of law had best have some preliminary knowledge of these areas of action. Any form of fuzzy law, indeed, any form of social ordering, legal or other, can only be understood and assessed against the background that includes all other such forms of ordering. Hence the importance of this chapter, which can however be skipped by those who are less concerned with the value of examples.

Commentaries on specified areas of law often tend to direct their attention to a small number of measures—those that could be considered *the* 'legislative mandates' under the ideal-type vision of regulation—but, true to one of the themes of this book, attention should also be cast elsewhere. Attempt has been made to include as many provisions as possible in the following two overviews, which serve as the basis for the next chapters. However, these surveys should not be considered as fully conclusive, even at the date of their compilation, more so in the future.

The overviews presented here span the legal rules directly targeting the regulation of two fields of government action: emergency and air pollution. They do not include provisions inserted in arrangements that are concerned with a specific aspect covered by public law; thus, the overview of emergency law does not include provisions in sector-specific bodies of rules that authorize public bodies to act during contingencies designated as emergencies in that specific context, and tailored to promote the distinct purposes of such sector-specific arrangements. Nor do the overviews contain references to rules made in a variety of contexts that require authorized bodies to take into account considerations of national security or air quality, as in the cases of aviation or planning law: here, too, the impact on the fields chosen as case-studies is tangential and centrally uncontrolled. Delegated legislation, made under statute, is likewise absent. Unilateral measures, a typical form of fuzziness analysed in Chapters 4 and 5 are discussed in the context of the constitutional law of both systems, as they essentially rely on their constitutional framework. Finally, this chapter is dedicated to surveys of the rules in force; implementation is not considered here, and is partially discussed in Chapter 8.

Parts B and C, dedicated to separate overviews of the two fields of action, open with a general introduction to the field, and then scan the structure of the respective legal frameworks. These skeletal, snapshot descriptions of the legal measures in force at the time of writing, reflect the complexity of those bodies of law both in the UK and the US. Well beyond the complexity arising from the nature of these fields, which requires an impossible balancing between unforeseen exigencies and the retention of some form of legality, the politics of power contribute to the piecemeal emergence of overlapping, competing, and contradicting arrangements, addressed in this section. The essential transnational and international elements in these fields of action introduce additional layers of pressure and legal rules and further contribute to this inherent complexity.

B. Emergency Law

1. General

On 15 February 2019, US President Donald Trump issued a proclamation declaring a national emergency 'concerning the southern border of the United States'.[1] Relying on the National Emergencies Act, other legislation and the regularly used formula 'by the authority vested in me by the Constitution and the laws of the United States of America',[2] President Trump found that the emergency arose from the growth of illegal entry from Mexico, which, according to the proclamation, enabled the entry of 'criminals, gang members and illicit narcotics'. Under the declared emergency, the use of armed forces was authorized; the order also directed relevant government departments to 'take all appropriate actions, consistent with applicable law' to support the use of authorities invoked.

This was but one element of the constitutional maelstrom that raged around the refusal of Congress to appropriate funds for the building of the US-Mexico wall, one of the mainstays of President Trump's political agenda, which led, first, to the longest government shutdown in the country's history, then to the presidential declaration of emergency, issued in tandem with the 2019 Appropriations Act, to which the President attached a signing statement that denigrated some of its provisions.[3] To date, two attempts to override the declaration of emergency by joint resolutions did not receive the majority required to override a presidential veto; the President duly vetoed both.[4]

This affair represents several aspects of the nature and extent of reliance on, and creation of, emergency rules and action. Well before the unfolding of this crisis, much of the scholarship on executive powers, especially in the US, revolved around powers invoked during emergencies. President Lincoln's actions beyond law and his justifications of the invocation of power, discussed in Chapter 3, were the product of the exigencies of the Civil War, and presaged subsequent reliance on such powers. The penchant for research on emergency powers is explainable not only due to a general preference to consider extreme cases rather than down-to-earth ones, and thus address the furthest ends of power, but also due to the potential impact on human rights inhering in emergency action. Although the importance of the study of the ways executives tackle situations considered

[1] Proclamation 9844, *Declaring a National Emergency Concerning the Southern Border of the United States*, 15 February 2019, 84 FR 4949.

[2] On this formula and on mixed-authority unilateral measures see Chapter 5.

[3] On this signing statement, and signing statements in general, see ch 5.

[4] See eg Eric Beech, 'Trump vetoes measure to end his emergency declaration on border wall', Reuters, 19 October 2019 <https://www.reuters.com/article/us-usa-trump-congress-emergency/trump-vetoes-measure-to-end-his-emergency-declaration-on-border-wall-idUSKBN1WV06P>.

exceptionally dangerous to their societies is uncontested, my second case-study aims to balance this, by introducing elements of so-called humdrum policies administrative powers.

Most of the aspects concerning the notion of emergency are under dispute, starting with the debate over the contours of emergency. Rather than enter the discussion on what constitutes an 'emergency', suffice to note here that to qualify as an emergency, the main element would be the existence of a serious threat to a society, ranging from threats to national security, through threats to political or economic cohesion, to hazards deriving from natural disasters.[5] In this book, attention is limited to threats to national security, interpreted relatively broadly as including war and other armed conflict, with a special focus on anti-terrorism law. To ensure manageable comparison and analysis, economic crises and natural disasters are excluded from this case-study.

The literature concerned with emergency law identifies two models of emergency frameworks: the law of emergency is either contained in the system, usually under a constitutional provision and legislation made under it, or is extra-legal and extra-constitutional. Under an analytically possible variant of this extra-legal model, a system may have neither a constitutional provision nor legislation treating emergency conditions, but this variant of the model has no purchase in reality, more so in today's administrative state, which puts a premium on regulation by statute. These are mere archetypes: scholars have offered sophisticated versions of these models.[6] For the purposes of this book, the starting point is a simplified distinction that revolves around the existence or absence of a formal constitutional arrangement concerned with emergencies.

[5] See the influential definition of emergency in the Paris Minimum Standards adopted by the International Law Association: 'an exceptional situation of crisis or public danger, actual or imminent, which affects the whole population or the whole population of the area to which the declaration applies and constitutes a threat to the organized life of the community of which the state is composed'. For the text see Richard B Lillich, 'Current Developments: The Paris Minimum Standards of Human Rights Norms in a State of Emergency' (1985) 79 Am J Int'l L 1072. See also the meaning of 'public emergency' in Article 15 of the European Convention for the Protection of Human Rights, which largely follows the above definition.

[6] Lobel distinguishes between absolutist, relativist, and liberal models (under the first, only powers explicitly granted in the constitution serve to provide emergency authority; the second model supports flexible interpretation of the constitution to recognize such powers; under the third, liberal model, a dichotomy between ordinary and emergency powers is maintained in separate legal frameworks, with seepage towards empowerment). Jules Lobel, 'Emergency Power and the Decline of Liberalism' (1989) 98 Yale LJ 1385. Oren Gross's three models of emergency frameworks are based on a substantively similar distinction between negation ('the business as usual model'), recognition under the constitution or law (models of accommodation), and a third, 'extra-legal' model, under which action beyond and contrary to law is either condoned or condemned *ex post facto*; see Oren Gross, 'Chaos and Rules: Should Responses to Violent Crises Always Be Constitutional?' (2003) 112 Yale LJ 1011, further developed in Oren Gross and Fionnuala Ní Aoláin, *Law in Times of Crisis: Emergency Powers in Theory and Practice* (CUP 2006). See also David Dyzenhaus, 'States of Emergency', in Michel Rosenfeld and Andras Sajo (eds), *Oxford Handbook on Comparative Constitutional Law* (OUP 2012) 442; Karin Loevy, *Emergencies in Public Law: The Legal Politics of Containment* (CUP 2016).

Under the first model, the research has also identified two different modes of treatment by law. Under the traditional mode, legal treatment of an emergency is a two-step process, the first being a declaration, which authorizes subsequent action under a separate distinct regime. The second mode is more 'civilified': emergency provisions are embedded in the law, and the state of emergency becomes less of an anomaly, more of an unavoidable feature of modern life.

One may submit that emergency laws in both the US and the UK are made in the second mode, due to the similar absence of a clear constitutional framework. The written constitution of the US does not include a clause concerned with emergencies, although for some, its open-ended and malleable Article II clauses offer sufficient basis for authorization; in the UK, the prerogative of war powers, still part of the unwritten constitution, provide some authority to act. Indeed, the overviews of the law in force in both systems, presented here, provide more than plain proof for the fuzzy legal nature of emergency powers, but in both, legislation has gained an important position. Designed to trace the existing statutory arrangements, constitution-derived powers are only briefly mentioned here; they were discussed in Chapters 4 and 5.

All designers of statute law are required to address unforeseen conditions on the basis of past experience. This demanding task reaches high levels of difficulty in the context of emergency law. Not only are drafters unable to fully forecast the ways a future emergency will emerge and unfold; the exceptional dangers resulting from failure challenge politicians' futures, and, indeed, the future of the state itself. Either under a constitutional provision or without it, emergency law also represents the ultimate challenge to democratic liberal states. The general tension in public law between the need to grant power to face future exigencies and the importance of reining power and avoiding abuse, which stands at the basis of this book, is heightened in an area where exigencies and strong political pressure to act forcefully essentially endanger the very basis of a polity committed to democratic representation and the protection of rights and interests.

2. Emergency Law in the UK

a. General

The power to wage war under the prerogative continues to be recognized in the current constitutional structure,[7] although three important developments have transformed the role of the prerogative in this field. First, as will be seen in the US too, formal warfare, preceded by a declaration and followed by the deployment of armed forces, is only one form of modern belligerencies, and a marginal one at

[7] For the history of the war prerogative and its modern form (spanning 1600–2012), see Rosara Joseph, *The War Prerogative: History, Reform and Constitutional Design* (OUP 2013).

that. Secondly, alongside constitutionally based powers, an extremely rich body of legislation has been introduced since the early twentieth century, covering all aspects of the field; the legal terrain has thus been transformed into a statute-led field, albeit one that is highly fuzzy, inter alia due to the existence of multiple, often overlapping arrangements. Finally, and more recently, enhanced participation in parliament through the emerging constitutional convention that requires parliamentary approval prior to the launch of military operations has had some effect on the unilateral nature of this power, but has not substantially transformed the government's dominance, as discussed below. Emergency management clearly remains in the hands of the executive branch.

Setting aside economic and natural disasters, the British have experienced four periods of national security emergencies from the early twentieth-century onwards: the two world wars, the fight for Irish independence waged in Northern Ireland, and the current terrorism threat, globally waged under the banner 'the war on terror'. All have involved the introduction and operation of massive sets of emergency rules made both under the prerogative and legislation, with the evident rise of the latter.

The early paradigm of 'emergency law' was linked with the pre-twentieth century perception of the introduction of special states of emergency, that is, the carving out of special states of affairs that engender a distinct regime, with 'martial law' as their extreme version. In the UK, 'emergency' was the commonly used term in the First World War; in addition to initial introduction of measures under prerogative orders in council, subsequent statutory arrangements authorized the declaration of a special emergency period, during which emergency powers were set, generally in statute-based orders in council. Typically limited in time, such orders regulated diverse areas ranging from the seizure of enemy property and ships to the introduction of emergency economic powers.[8] A general statute enacted between the two world wars, the Emergency Powers Act 1920, followed this model without being prompted by a specific emergency, introducing a two-stage process that required a declaration of emergency prior to the enactment of emergency regulations (the statute however was used only in response to several nationwide strikes). The model applied in the First World War was followed during the Second World War, again under the assumption that the measures were to be temporary.[9] The second half of the twentieth century was marked by a central focus of emergency in and about Northern Ireland, again initially enacted as temporary legislation, then,

[8] See, for example, the first of a series of collections of measures issued during the First World War, made first under the prerogative, and subsequently under statute, mainly the Defence of the Realm Act 1914: Alexander Pulling (ed), *Manual of Emergency Legislation* (HM Stationary Office 1914).

[9] For an overview of emergency legislation during these three periods see eg Cornelius P Cotter, 'Constitutionalizing Emergency Powers: The British Experience' (1953) 5 Stanford L Rev 382.

towards the end of the decades-long practice, in several statutes carrying the title 'terrorism'.[10]

Currently, as a key-word, 'emergency' has all but been replaced by 'terrorism'. Nine statutes have carried the word 'terrorism' in their title: while some are collections of amendments to legislation in force, others, as shown below, are the product of separate initiatives, containing some overlapping grants of power.

b. Layers of law pertaining to emergencies

The British legal sources relevant to national security emergencies range from international law, through constitutional law, a small number of international conventions incorporated into domestic law, primary legislation, and some EU law, which, post-Brexit, is either introduced directly into domestic law or is bound to expire.

(1) Customary international law

In a dualist system such as the UK, treaties become part of domestic law only by incorporation in statute. Rules accepted as 'customary law' on the other hand, apply directly to the system, and should therefore be considered part of British domestic law.[11] The definition of 'customary' law is in itself fuzzy; under the usual understanding, two elements are required for the recognition of a rule as customary: consistent practice and *opinio juris*, that is, the existence of a general perception of the duty to comply.[12] Despite the emergence of codifications, commentaries, and analyses, the contours of customary law, both in its formation and application, remain under-defined; some have considered the process of their emergence as 'mysterious', regarding the question of the link between recognition and subsequent (non)implementation as unresolved.[13] This body of rules often sets limitations on

[10] For a snapshot of the law in the context of Northern Ireland from 1997, before 9/11 and the emergence of global terrorism, see AW Bradley and KD Ewing, *Constitutional and Administrative Law* (12th edn, Longman 1997) 681–84. The Terrorism Act 2000, still in force today, broadly defined to address all hazards to the security of the state, contained a special part, Part VII, concerned with Northern Ireland. Originally designed again to be in force for a year, extendable by the Secretary of State, the Part was extended by the Terrorism (Northern Ireland) Act 2006, which repealed some of the provisions of the 2000 Act. Despite that appeasement of events, several statutes are still in force, including the two mentioned above.

[11] For the distinction see Malcolm Shaw, *International Law* (8th edn, CUP 2017) 105–19. Reaffirmed in *R (on the application of Miller) v Secretary of State for Exiting the European Union* [2017] UKSC 5 [55]. The impact of incorporated treaties is discussed below, in the context of statute law.

[12] See Shaw (n 11) 53–66. Under the Statute of the International Court of Justice, two of the sources applied by the court are 'international custom, as evidence of a general practice accepted as law' and 'the general principles of law recognized by civilized nations' (article 38(1)(b), (c)). The first subsection is usually viewed as a reference to customary law. See eg decisions of the International Court of Justice (ICJ): *North Sea Continental Shelf Cases (FRG v the Netherlands)* [1969] ICJ Rep 3 [77]; *Continental Shelf (Libyan Arab Jamahiriyah v Malta)* [1985] ICJ Rep 29 [27].

[13] See eg Tullio Treves, 'Customary International Law', *Max Planck Encyclopedias of International Law* (OUP 2006) <https://opil.ouplaw.com/view/10.1093/law:epil/9780199231690/law-9780199231690-e1393?rskey=fLAHxM&result=5&prd=MPIL> 2.

state action, and is particularly relevant to emergencies. Indeed, the main foci of customary international law pertains to warfare and armed conflicts, and much of it has gained the status of 'customary', generally under the title 'international humanitarian law'.[14] The protection of human rights has likewise been recognized, thereby additionally implicating on emergency state action, since breaches of rights are often presented as justified due to emergency conditions. Inter alia, the rights recognized by the ICJ as customary in nature include the prohibition of slavery, genocide, and torture, although other, more expansive lists have been recognized, encompassing all key human rights, which are also protected in human rights treaties.[15]

Under a classic judicial formulation, customary international law should be treated by British courts as incorporated into domestic law.[16] Essentially rules that limit the use of power during war and war-like circumstances, the import of this body of rules remains despite the rising number of statutes. Still, the changing circumstances in which emergencies are legally and politically considered render some of these free from the impact of customary international law. In the context of the UK, all recent configurations considered as emergencies, since the

[14] See the codification of customary rules prepared by the International Committee of the Red Cross (ICRC), which classifies customary international humanitarian law, to be applied during wartime under 161 rules, concerning issues ranging from the principle of distinction between civilians and combatants to the definition of war crimes. Jean-Marie Henckaerts and Louise Doswald-Beck, *Customary International Humanitarian Law* (CUP rep 2009). Some of the rules are found in treaties, namely the Hague Conventions of 1899 and 1907 and the Geneva Conventions 1864, 1906, 1929, and 1949, including the Additional Protocols of 1977, but those treaties do not encompass the entirety of the rules.

[15] The UN Human Rights Committee, established in the International Covenant on Civil and Political Rights (ICCPR) recognized the following rights, which cannot be derogated from, due to their nature as 'represent[ing] customary law'. Accordingly, the CCPR has recognized that '[a] State may not reserve the right to engage in slavery, to torture, to subject persons to cruel, inhuman or degrading treatment or punishment, to arbitrarily deprive persons of their lives, to arbitrarily arrest and detain persons, to deny freedom of thought, conscience and religion, to presume a person guilty unless he proves his innocence, to execute pregnant women or children, to permit the advocacy of national, racial or religious hatred, to deny to persons of marriageable age the right to marry, or to deny to minorities the right to enjoy their own culture, profess their own religion, or use their own language. And while reservations to particular clauses of article 14 may be acceptable, a general reservation to the right to a fair trial would not be.' Office of the High Commissioner for Human Rights, CCPR General Comment No 24: *Issues Relating to Reservations Made upon Ratification or Accession to the Covenant or the Optional Protocols thereto, or in Relation to Declarations under Article 41 of the Covenant*, CCPR/C/21/Rev.1/Add.6 (1994) s 8.

For analyses that address these two types of customary law see eg René Provost, *International Human Rights and Humanitarian Law* (CUP 2002); David Weissbrodt and others, *International Human Rights: Law, Policy and Process* (4th edn, LexisNexis 2009); Philip Alston and Ryan Goodman, *International Human Rights* (OUP 2013) (the latter two textbooks discuss humanitarian law as well as human rights).

[16] *Chung Chi Cheung v The King* [1939] AC 160, 168. For analysis of the early acceptance of customary international law by British courts see eg JES Fawcett, 'Customary International Law in the Courts of the United Kingdom' (1968) 21 Revista Espanola de Derecho Internacional 459; Frederick Alexander Mann, *Foreign Affairs in English Courts* (OUP 1986) 121–23. For critical analyses of judicial avoidance see eg Patrick Capps, 'The Court as Gatekeeper: Customary International Law in English Courts' (2007) 70 MLR 458.

Second World War, have not amounted to war or belligerency to which this body of rules apply.

(2) Constitutional law

In the absence of a written constitution, the main source of a constitutional nature in the context of emergency power is the prerogative, as discussed above and, more generally, in Chapter 4. The analysis of statute-law below reflects the shrinking of the prerogative in this field. Under the Bill of Rights 1689, 'the raising or keeping a standing army within the kingdom in time of peace, unless it be with consent of Parliament, is against law'. The residuality doctrine, the main constraint on the retention of prerogative, was judicially embedded in the common law in *de Keyser Royal Hotel*, the post-World War I decision that prohibited the seizure of property during wartime without compensation, due to the existence of legislation which guaranteed this right.[17] Since then, the rise of statute law, promoted inter alia by the introduction of the Human Rights Act (HRA) and the recognition that action impacting on human rights must be backed by clear authorization in statute,[18] legislation has replaced some of the prerogatives. The Ponsonby rule, which requires that treaties are generally to be laid before Parliament prior to their ratification, was originally an unwritten constitutional convention, and is now statute-based, subjecting to parliamentary scrutiny yet another aspect that may relate to emergency aspects.[19]

The force of the constitutional convention regarding participation of parliament in the decisions to embark on war and other forms of military action is currently being debated due to recent practice. The convention was recognized in the Cabinet Manual of 2011, the document that incorporates the rules of government practice.[20] Referring to a government undertaking made that year, it states that 'a convention had developed in Parliament that before troops were committed the House of Commons should have an opportunity to debate the matter', and that the government 'proposed to observe that convention except when there was an emergency and such action would not be appropriate'.[21] Fikfak and Hooper's analysis of the de facto operation of the convention shows that the government has retained dominance throughout.[22]

17 *A-G v De Keyser Royal Hotel* [1920] AC 508. See ch 4 for a detailed analysis.

18 For this 'principle of legality' see *R v Secretary of State for the Home Department, ex parte Simms* [2002] 2 AC 115, 130–32; *HM Treasury v Ahmed* [2010] 2 AC 534, eg [111]–[117].

19 Effected in the Constitutional Reform and Governance Act 2010, Part 2.

20 Lacking a formal statutory backing, the Manual operates as the central guidance for all workings of government. See *The Cabinet Manual: A Guide to Laws, Conventions and Rules on the Operation of Government* (Cabinet Office 2011).

21 Cabinet Manual [5.38]. Citation of the government's undertaking leads to a statement made by the Leader of the House of Commons, Hansard HC col 1066 (10 March 2011).

22 In its heyday, a failure to pass a vote supporting the deploy of military forces into Syria, led to the government's retreat, but a patchier pattern is evident in subsequent cases. In the latest to date, the government's decision in 2018 to participate in air strikes in Syria was not subjected to this process; in response to political pressure, two post-event debates were held, with the government's position that the

(3) International treaty law and UN measures

As mentioned above, some provisions in written treaties have, by general understanding, attained the status of customary law. To apply domestically in the UK, other treaty provisions must be incorporated by statute.[23]

To the traditional body of conventions concerned with general emergencies threatening national security, the events of recent decades have led to the growth of a body of treaties designed to combat global terrorism, now recognized as a distinct field of action. In the context of the first group of treaties, the most distinct ones are human rights treaties that allow for special derogation in times considered to present a grave national threat, as in the case of the International Covenant on Civil and Political Rights 1966 (ICCPR), which enables derogation from most of its protected rights.[24]

The ICCPR and the Convention against Torture and Other Cruel, Inhuman, or Degrading Treatment or Punishment (UNTC), were ratified by the UK, but have not been incorporated into domestic law as such, nor have other UN human rights conventions.[25] As for UN anti-terrorism treaties, out of the nineteen conventions and protocols concerned with terrorism, listed online by the UN Office of Counter-Terrorism, thirteen were ratified by the UK, and eleven have been either incorporated by statutes or referred to in a statutory text.[26] They are thus to be considered in the category of statutes, discussed below.

decision was excepted from the convention. On the now-called 'war powers' convention see Veronika Fikfak and Hayley J Hooper, *Parliament's Secret War* (Hart Publishing 2018), esp Veronika Fikfak, 'The Convention as a Battlefield' ibid 67; Claire Mills, *Parliamentary Approval for Military Action*, House of Commons Briefing Paper CBP 7166, 8 May 2018. On the 2018 events and an analysis of the current state of the convention see Veronika Fikfak and Hailey J Hooper, 'Whither the War Powers Convention? What Next for Parliamentary Control of Armed Conflict after Syria?', UK Const L Blog (20 April 2018) <https://ukconstitutionallaw.org/2018/04/20/veronika-fikfak-and-hayley-j-hooper-whither-the-war-powers-convention-what-next-for-parliamentary-control-of-armed-conflict-after-syria/ >.

[23] See text to n 11. For a judicial perspective see Lord Mance, 'International Law in the UK Supreme Court', 13 February 2017 <https://www.supremecourt.uk/docs/speech-170213.pdf>.

[24] Article 4(1): 'In time of public emergency which threatens the life of the nation and the existence of which is officially proclaimed, the States Parties to the present Covenant may take measures derogating from their obligations under the present Covenant to the extent strictly required by the exigencies of the situation, provided that such measures are not inconsistent with their other obligations under international law and do not involve discrimination solely on the ground of race, colour, sex, language, religion or social origin.'

[25] Ratifications in 1988 and 1976, respectively, with several notifications and comments. See through UN depositary online, Chapter 4, via <https://treaties.un.org/pages/Treaties.aspx?id=4&subid=A&clang=_en>.

[26] For the list and further information on these treaties, made in contexts including civil aviation, maritime navigation, protection of nuclear and explosive materials, bombings, and financing, see <https://www.un.org/counterterrorism/international-legal-instruments>. Information on ratification is available through <https://treaties.un.org/Pages/ParticipationStatus.aspx?clang=_en>. For incorporating and applying legislation see the Hijacking Act 1971, the Internationally Protected Persons Act 1978, the Taking of Hostages Act 1982, the Nuclear Material Offences Act 1983, the Aviation and Maritime Security Act 1990, The Marking of Plastic Explosives for Detection Regulations 1996, and the Extradition (Terrorist Bombings) Order 2002. See also the EU measures, discussed below.

Another important source, resolutions of the United Nations Security Council (UNSC), is considered to legally bind all member states.[27] Thus, as far as a resolution requires members to take legal measures domestically, compliance is required. A large number of UNSC resolutions pertain to terrorism, and requires states to take steps against terrorist organizations, inter alia curbing the movement of their suspected members, their financing, and their links with organized crime.[28] The domestic application of these resolutions may require the introduction of a statute, but the requirements to legislate and otherwise act to combat aspects of terrorism are broadly penned; the UK's counterterrorism laws, discussed below, address these aspects. The issue of implementation is, again, set aside in this chapter.

Most of the provisions set by the UN have been implemented through EU measures, a source of law to be now considered.

(4) EU law

This section opens with two introductory comments: a short overview of the force of EU measures, and a comment on the impact of the exit of the UK from the European Union (commonly known as 'Brexit').

In the pre-Brexit era, several types of EU legal rules applied in the UK in accordance with their status in EU law. The European treaties, at the top of the EU pyramid of norms, do not contain specific, directly applicable rules for emergencies, and can thus be set aside despite their importance to EU governance. Most relevant are regulations, directly binding on member states, and directives, which set targets and general rules, allowing member states to design the detailed frameworks under their general duty to adopt (transpose, in EU lingo) them into domestic law. Other rules of import that are nevertheless not universally binding include decisions (issued by the European Council, the European Commission, and the European Court of Justice). Judicial decisions bind the states to which they are addressed on the EU level, without necessarily requiring introduction into domestic law. Finally, recommendations and opinions are unbinding but are intended to influence member action.[29]

More than three and a half years after the June 2016 referendum to leave the EU, Brexit was formally finalized in the European Union (Withdrawal Act) 2020. In preparation for this event, the European Union (Withdrawal) Act 2018 set a

[27] Article 25, Charter of the United Nations ('The Members of the United Nations agree to accept and carry out the decisions of the Security Council in accordance with the present Charter').

[28] See eg S/RES/2178 (2014), *Threats to international peace and security caused by terrorist acts*; S/RES/2195 (2014), *Threats to international peace and security*; S/RES/2482 (2019), *Threats to international peace and security*. For a link to all resolutions pertaining to terrorism (and to other resolutions and UNSCR measures) see <https://www.securitycouncilreport.org/un-documents/terrorism/>.

[29] See Article 288, Treaty on the Functioning of the European Union. See Paul Craig and Gráinne de Búrca, *EU Law: Text, Cases, and Materials* (6t edn, OUP 2015) 106–10. For an EU overview see European Commission, *Types of EU Law* <https://ec.europa.eu/info/law/law-making-process/types-eu-law_en>.

general rule for the preservation of European laws in force in the UK. Under this Act, as amended, 'exit day' was finally set to 31 January 2020. Repealing the European Communities Act 1972 (ECA), the laws establish the rules for some retention of EU measures. In accordance with the Withdrawal Agreement, a transition period (recognized in the British legislation as an 'implementation period') was introduced, to last until the end of 2020, unless further extended by agreement for up to two additional years.[30] During this interim period, EU law, and domestic legislation passed under the obligations set under the UK's membership in the EU ('EU-derived domestic legislation') will continue to be applicable, unless otherwise indicated.[31] The final exit from the EU will not only involve the cessation of the relevant law, but also the termination of UK membership in several programmes that share information and expedite reciprocal extradition and the serving of sentences, an aspect not discussed further here.[32] At the end of the implementation period, replacement of the measures discussed below may have been needed, although the extensive amendments introduced in the Counter-Terrorism and Border Security Act 2019, discussed below, may have been considered sufficient. Still, it is useful to briefly note the rules made by the EU in this context, as they will all apply to the interim post-Brexit era, which may be extended.

Most of the EU measures relevant to the context of emergencies were made after the rise of awareness to global terrorism.[33] The majority of these have largely followed or cited UN measures, most notably the resolutions of the UNSC.[34] The EU has also adopted its own conventions, as well as a strategy designed to tackle terrorism; all of these largely follow principles set out in the UNSC.[35] Their impact on

[30] *Agreement on the Withdrawal of the United Kingdom of Great Britain and Northern Ireland from the European Union and the European Atomic Energy Community*, OJ 29/7, 31 January 2020, Arts 126, 132 (Withdrawal Agreement). The Agreement contains a large number of specially tailored arrangements in specified areas, which are not discussed here.

[31] European Union (Withdrawal Act) 2018, ss 1A, 1B. Set in Withdrawal Agreement (n 30) Art 127.

[32] For concerned analysis, written before the completion of the withdrawal agreement, see Rumyana van Ark, *Post Brexit EU (In) Security*, International Centre for Counter Terrorism (The Hague 6 June 2019) <https://icct.nl/publication/post-brexit-eu-insecurity/>.

[33] For a few examples see Regulation 2580/2001 *On Specific Restrictive Measures Directed against Certain Persons and Entities with a View to Combating Terrorism*, 28 December 2001, OJ L 344–370; Regulation 596/2013 *Amending Regulation (EC) No 881/2002 Imposing Certain Specific Restrictive Measures Directed against Certain Persons and Entities associated with the Al-Qaida Network*, 24 June 2013, OJ L 172/1; Directive 2005/60/EC *On the prevention of the use of the financial system for the purpose of money laundering and terrorist financing*, OJ L 309/15; Council Decision 2016/1693 Concerning Restrictive Measures against ISIL (Da'esh) and Al-Qaeda and Persons, Groups, Undertakings and Entities Associated with Them and Repealing Common Position 2002/402/CFSP, 20 September 2016, OJ L 255/25; Council Decision 2019/1296 *In Support of Strengthening Biological Safety and Security in Ukraine in Line with the Implementation of United Nations Security Council Resolution 1540 (2004) on Non-Proliferation of Weapons of Mass Destruction and Their Means of Delivery*, OJ L 204/29.

[34] All the measures cited ibid at least refer to UN resolutions; all but one (Directive 2005/60) cite specific UNSC resolutions.

[35] See eg *Convention on the Prevention of Terrorism 2005* (Council of Europe Treaty Series No 196); Additional Protocol to the Council of Europe Convention on the Prevention of Terrorism (Council of Europe Treaty Series No 217) (both only signed by the UK; the Terrorism Act 2006 introduces offences 'parallel . . . to those offences mentioned in the Council of Europe Convention on the Prevention of Terrorism'; explanatory notes, s 11); Directive 2017/541 On Combating Terrorism and Replacing

UK law depends on their nature: regulations and decisions, as mentioned above, are directly part of the law of the land, and their future in the UK is subject to the post-IP completion day regime.

The European Convention of Human Rights, incorporated almost in full by the HRA 1998, contains a derogation clause similar to the one found in the ICCPR. This clause has not been incorporated in the HRA; the alternative derogations and reservations provisions introduced by the HRA are discussed in the next section.

(5) Domestic primary legislation

Alongside a general statute designed to apply in all emergency contingencies, the British system has amassed a large number of anti-terrorism statutes, described as a 'messy' collection of 'knee-jerk' reactions to contingencies.[36] This extreme example of piled-up patchworked anti-terrorism law is described in further detail in Chapter 7. Here, a short overview of these statues will suffice.

The Civil Contingencies Act 2004, which replaced the Emergency Powers Act 1920, is designed to enable domestic arrangements in the face of 'emergency', a situation that exists when a threat of 'serious damage' to human welfare, the environment, or the security of the state exists.[37] This regime is permanent, that is, powers are to be applied with no need for an initial declaration of emergency in events considered sufficient under the act. The two main parts of the Act require, first, that designated local and national public bodies ('responders') prepare for contingencies, by planning and advising. Part 2 empowers the Crown and ministers to promulgate emergency regulations if conditions so require; limited in time to a maximum of thirty days, they may still be re-promulgated; emergency regulations are to be scrutinized by parliament, which may pass a resolution repealing or amending a regulation.[38]

The HRA, which did not incorporate the derogation clause that is part of the ECHR, introduced its own mechanisms of 'designated derogations' and 'designated reservations'. These may be issued by Secretaries of State; no pre-instatement conditions are set.[39]

Council Framework Decision 2002/475/*JHA and Amending Council Decision 2005/671/JHA*, 15 March 2017, OJ L 88/6; *Council of Europe Counter-Terrorism Strategy (2018–2022)* < https://search.coe.int/cm/Pages/result_details.aspx?ObjectId=09000016808afc96>. See generally, Dan Keohane, *The EU and Counter-Terrorism* (Centre for European Reform Working Paper 2005); Fiona de Londras and Josephine Doody (eds), *The Impact, Legitimacy and Effectiveness of EU Counter-Terrorism* (Routledge 2015).

[36] David Anderson QC, *The Terrorism Acts in 2001: Report of the Independent Reviewer on the Operation of the Terrorism Act 2000 and Part 1 of the Terrorism Act 2006* (The Stationary Office 2012) 133; Andrew Neal, 'Terrorism, Lawmaking, and Democratic Politics: Legislators as Security Actors' (2012) 24 Terrorism and Polit Viol 358.

[37] Civil Contingencies Act 2004, s 1, which further contains highly detailed categories of states of affairs that may pass this test.

[38] As in the case of the other Acts discussed in this chapter, statutory instruments made are excluded from the discussion.

[39] HRA, ss 14, 15.

As for anti-terrorism law, no less than six statutes are concurrently in force. The Terrorism Act 2000, a mega-statute designed to consolidate emergency powers, was initially designed to deal with the Northern Ireland 'troubles', but has since been transformed to a central anti-terrorism tool. It does not stand alone. The Anti-Terrorism, Crime and Security Act 2001, part of which was repealed and replaced by the Prevention of Terrorism Act 2005 as a response to the House of Lords decision in the *Belmarsh* case[40] replaced once again in 2011, the Terrorism Act 2006, the Counter-Terrorism Act 2008, the Terrorist Asset-Freezing Act 2010, the Terrorism Prevention and Investigation Measures Act 2011, which repealed the 2005 Act, the Counter-Terrorism and Security Act 2015—all of these regulate a variety of aspects of British governments' anti-terrorism commitments. All of these statutes include amendments to former statutes, but no consolidation has been attempted. The most recent statute to date, the Counter-Terrorism and Border Security Act 2019, consists of amendments to a large number of statutes in force but also adds an independent arrangement concerned with border security, which provides, in a detailed schedule, powers to stop, search, and detain persons at ports or border locations.[41] This patchworked structure is discussed in detail in the next chapter.

3. Emergency Law in the US

a. General

The governance of the United States, it is often observed, has been coloured by a culture of constant crisis. 'There's no such thing as normal times anymore', declared Professor G Casper in 1973 in his testimony before a US Senate Special Committee on the Termination of the National Emergency.[42] Indeed, as Professor Jules Lobel claimed in 1989, '[t]he United States' new role as the world's superpower fed on an obsession with crisis... Every challenge to United States hegemony anywhere in the world began to be perceived as a threat to national security'.[43] Such perceptions have only been vindicated in the current age of global terrorism since the September 11 attacks and the following rise of nodes of Islamic terrorism.

In response to these forces, as in the British case, US anti-terrorism law has developed as a distinct sub-field. Still, and distinctly to the US, some of the

[40] *A v Secretary of State for the Home Department* [2004] UKHL 5.

[41] Counter-Terrorism and Border Security Act 2019.

[42] *Hearings before the Senate Special Committee on the Termination of the National Emergency*, 93r Cong, 1s Sess 83 (1973), cited in Lobel (n 6) 1400.

[43] Lobel (n 6) 1400. See also Arthur Schlesinger's analysis, which at the time focused on the force of the Communist threat as fuelling the 'hypnosis of crisis'. Arthur Schlesinger, *The Imperial Presidency* (Houghton Mifflin 1973) 163–64. See also Sanford V Levinson, 'Constitutional Norms in a State of Permanent Emergency' (2006) 40 Ga L Rev 699; Kim Lane Scheppele, 'Small Emergencies' (2006) 40 Ga L Rev 835 (both noting the perpetuity of emergencies, while reaching different conclusions).

measures presented as emergencies are still part of the state's role as an influential but sometimes covert player in the international sphere, as in its past action in Latin American and South-East Asia and current action in Iraq, Afghanistan, and elsewhere. The role of reliance on emergency law to promote and enforce foreign policy is not generally treated here.

A dominant player in the UN, both in and out of the Security Council, the US has influenced some aspects of international law, which are discussed below. Finally, the use of economic sanctions, ranging from embargoes to the freezing of private assets, features in both types of emergencies; as such, they are considered in the overview below only as much as they can be viewed as relating to emergencies and not to global politics.

b. Layers of law pertaining to emergencies

Here, too, the overview scans measures that range from the Constitution, through two levels of international law, to domestic legislation. State law is excluded from this overview. As above, the following overview of the law currently in force sets aside issues of compliance and enforcement, discussed in Chapter 7.

(1) Constitutional law

This source is discussed first, as there are different views regarding the subjection of the constitutional structure to norms that are generally accepted as customary international law, a debate I refer to in the next section.

The well-known absence of a direct provision concerned with governance during periods of emergency has been well-recorded and analysed. Apart from the grant of authority to Congress to suspend the habeas corpus 'when in cases of rebellion or invasion the public safety may require it', no direct reference to war or other emergency powers can be found in the text.[44] The discussion at the time of the framing and beyond focused on war (so-called small emergencies and other crises are relatively recent additions). Never reaching universal agreement on the matter, the text followed the principle that no direct authorization to the President to act during wars should be included in the Constitution, since, in James Madison's words, '[w]ar is in fact the true nurse of executive aggrandizement'.[45] Under the belief that the normal state of affairs would be peace, the waging of war was to be directed under statutes. Alternatively, presidents were to follow the model Jules Lobel called 'the absolutist model', and temporarily act beyond the law in order to preserve the nation.[46]

44 For clauses that have been interpreted as granting powers see below.

45 James Madison, 'Helvidius 4' in Alexander Hamilton and James Madison, *The Helvidius-Pacificus Debates of 1793–1794* (Morton J Frisch ed, Liberty Fund 2007) 84, 86.

46 See eg Thomas Jefferson, Letter to Governor William CC Claiborne, 3 February 1807, written at the time of the indictment of former Vice President Aaron Burr for treason ('[o]n great occasions every good officer must be ready to risk himself in going beyond the strict line of law, when the public preservation requires it'). *The Writing of Thomas Jefferson* (HA Washington ed, Derby and Jackson 1859)

Despite this absence, presidents have found constitutional authority to act during emergencies (true or perceived), relying on the Commander-in-Chief clause and other sources.[47] If in early times, legislation was not central, it would seem that the current proliferation of legislation, discussed below, should have removed reliance on the ambiguous text of the constitution, but the Commander-in-Chief clause and the spirit of the constitution have supported more recent arguments for presidential involvement, most notoriously in the 2002 'torture memos'.[48]

(2) *Customary international law*

As in the case of the UK, customary law which applies during emergencies is essentially of a constraining body of rules. In this system, too, customary international law is generally considered an intrinsic part of US domestic law, as expressed well before the *Paqueta Habana* Supreme Court decision of 1900, considered as the landmark decision confirming the subjection of the US to customary international law.[49] However, several elements have contributed to the complexity, if not fuzziness, of the issue. First are differing understandings of the existence of a body of '(general) federal common law', a term that for some, connotes a body of law that is equivalent to customary international law; in a similar vein, there are varied opinions regarding the status of customary international law as a source of federal law, and its subsequent ability to override state law.[50] Next is the linked question regarding the supremacy of international customary law over the constitution and over Federal statutes. The academic debate over the constitutionality of presidential avoidance and violation of customary international law[51] has been held against

Vol V 40. Lobel (n 6). For President Lincoln's unilateral action during the Civil War and his justification see ch 3.

[47] See ch 4.

[48] See chs 4 and 5.

[49] *The Paquete Habana*, 175 US 677, 700 (1900). For a celebratory account, which cites a large number of pre-1900 judicial decisions, see Jordan J Paust, *International Law as the Law of the United States* (Carolina Academic Press 1996) 6 and n 38. See also Shaw (n 11) 119–22; for a more cautionary view see Curtis A Bradley, *International Law in the US Legal System* (2nd edn, OUP 2015) 139–67. The tests for the recognition of rules as customary (see n 12) apply here too. The Restatement (Third) of Foreign Relations Law of the United States sets a similar set of conditions. Restatement, Third, Foreign Relations Law of the United States (1987) §102(2) ('Customary international law results from a general and consistent practice of states followed by them from a sense of legal obligation').

[50] Opinions on these matters range from rejection of customary international law as source of federal law (see Curtis A Bradley and Jack L Goldsmith, 'Customary International Law as Federal Common Law: A Critique of the Modern Position' (1997) Harv L Rev 815; Bradley (n 49) 145–58) to firm declarations that this body of law is 'federal', and therefore, determinations in federal courts bind state courts (see *Restatement (Third) of the Foreign Relations Law of the United States*, §111, reporters' notes 2, 3). See also Stephen P Mulligan, *International Law and Agreements: Their Effect upon US Law*, CRS RL32528 (Congressional Research Service 2018) 29–30.

[51] Cf Derek Jinks and David Sloss, 'Is the President Bound by the Geneva Conventions?' (2004) 90 Cornell L Rev 97 (generally answering in the affirmative) with Curtis A Bradley and Jack L Goldsmith, 'Presidential Control over International Law' (2018) 131 Harv L Rev 1201, 1233–35

the background of assertions by several presidents that they have power to do so.[52] Likewise, lower federal courts have held that federal statutes prevail over customary international law when these sources conflict: this rule can also be gleaned from *Paquete Habana* itself.[53]

This ambiguity can be also found in *Hamdan*, the seminal modern decision on the invocation of powers during emergencies, in which international humanitarian law was heavily, and rarely, featured. Relying on the references to the law of war in the Uniform Military Code of Military Justice (UCMJ), which inter alia authorizes the establishment of special military commissions and regulates their action, the plurality ruled that the applicant was to be guaranteed the right to be judged by courts that provide sufficient protection, as required in Common Article 3 of these conventions.[54] Under a common reading, 'the Court determined that the Geneva Conventions are incorporated by Article 21 of the Uniform Military Code of Military Justice',[55] but the term 'incorporated' can be misleading. Under this reading, the ruling seems to imply that the Geneva Conventions reign over domestic law, but the import of the ruling is much more limited. Setting aside the dissenting opinions and some academic criticism against the plurality's reasoning and the outcome,[56] the reasoning in *Hamdan* is inexorably linked with the provisions of the UJCM. Dicta such as Justice Stevens' 'compliance with the law of war is the condition upon which the authority set forth in Article 21 [the authority to court-martial] is granted', fall far short of a recognition that the laws of war as recognized in customary law are an integral part of US law. The decision only establishes that

(generally supporting presidential control of the entire field, under enhancement of some accountability processes).

52 Prior to *Hamdan*, briefly discussed below, President Bush maintained that he was not bound domestically by the Geneva Conventions due to his constitutional authority to protect national security. See Jinks and Sloss (n 51) 100–03. During his presidency campaign, President Trump was cited as considering the Geneva conventions 'a problem': see Kellan Howell, 'Donald Trump: Geneva Conventions is "the problem," makes U.S. soldiers "afraid to fight"', Wash Post 31 March 2016 <https://www.washingtontimes.com/news/2016/mar/31/donald-trump-geneva-conventions-problem-makes-sold/>.

53 The famously cited ruling that '[i]nternational law is part of our law, and must be ascertained and administered by the courts of justice of appropriate jurisdiction' is followed by the just as important dictum that 'where there is no treaty and no controlling executive or legislative act or judicial decision, resort must be had to the customs and usages of civilized nations . . .', both allowing opposing positions regarding the force of customary law when domestic rules *do* exist (*Paquete Habana* (n 49) 700). For discussions see also Bradley (n 49) 153–54 (citing a series of decisions of lower federal courts that asserted the violating power); Mulligan (n 50) 30.

54 *Hamdan v Rumsfeld*, 126 SCt 2749, 2794 (2006). Common Article 3, part of each of the four 1949 Geneva Conventions, is understood as providing 'minimum standards' for the treatment of persons in the case of an 'armed conflict not of an international character occurring in the territory of one of the High Contracting Parties'.

55 Fionnuala Ní Aoláin, '*Hamdan* and Common Article 3: Did the Supreme Court Get It Right?' (2007) 91 Minn L Rev 1525, 1526.

56 See the dissenting opinions in *Hamdan*, and eg Julian Ku and John Yoo, '*Hamdan v Rumsfeld*: The Functional Case for Foreign Affairs Deference to the Judicial Branch' (2006) Const Comm 179.

the UCMJ is the source of the recognition of Common Article 3, and for its own purposes only.[57]

In sum, the recognition of the supremacy of customary law over domestic US law may be only surface-deep. The question of the domestic status of customary law is, at least in the eyes of some commentators, one of the unsettled issues linked with the status of international law in the US.[58] Still, as far as the law of war is concerned, and despite presidential declarations concerning the retention of their power to violate its rules, the balance of this example of fuzziness seems to lean in favour of the inclusion of this element of international law, although the multiple statutes in force, discussed below, offer direct authorizations to act.

(3) International treaty law and UN measures

As a monist state under the US Constitution, for a treaty to become the law of the land, it should be ratified by the Senate by a majority of two-thirds. In such a case, no further incorporation in statute is required. This seemingly clear rule has however been broken down under the distinction between self-executing and non-self-executing treaties. A treaty considered not self-executing does not create a private right of action within the US judicial system unless legislated, and therefore cannot be relied upon by persons or bodies arguing that an obligation under the treaty was breached.[59] Furthermore, the dominance of other processes of entry into transnational agreements, most notably 'executive agreements' and so-called 'congressional-executive' agreements, discussed in Chapter 4, requires careful attention to the status of all treaties and conventions.

In the context of measures pertaining to or impacting on emergency, this section follows the structure of the analysis on British law presented above. Regarding human rights conventions, the ICCPR and the UNTC were ratified by the US in 1992 and 1994, respectively, yet the host of reservations, understandings, and declarations added to both conventions challenge the extent of their domestic application. Under the most notable declaration attached to both treaties, the material rights-protection provisions (including, in the context of the ICCPR, the possibility of derogation in emergencies), are to be regarded as 'not self-executing'; in the absence of domestic legislation, then, they are of little direct value.[60]

57 See Ní Aoláin's criticism on this point: 'the majority in *Hamdan* resists the opportunity to assert that the "law" (Common Article 3) that it is dealing with is universal. Instead the Court refers to Common Article 3 only in very specific contexts but never makes overall claims about the status of the article as customary international law'. Ní Aoláin (n 55) 1547.

58 See Bradley (n 49) 335.

59 The distinction in itself, as well as its application by courts, are obvious sources of fuzziness. On the distinction see eg Jordan J Paust, 'Self-Executing Treaties' (1988) 88 Am J Int'l L 760; *Medellín v Texas*, 552 US 491 (2008); Shaw (n 11) 124–25.

60 See Declaration (1), attached to the ICCPR ratification <https://treaties.un.org/Pages/ViewDetails.aspx?src=TREATY&mtdsg_no=IV-4&chapter=4&clang=_en>, and Declaration (1), attached to the UNTC ratification <https://treaties.un.org/Pages/ViewDetails.aspx?src=TREATY&mtdsg_no=IV-9&chapter=4&clang=_en>. See also David Sloss, 'The Domestication of International Human Rights: Non-Self-Executing Declarations and Human Rights Treaties' (1999) 24 Yale J Int'l L 129.

Fifteen of the nineteen conventions and protocols concerned with terrorism, published by the UN Office of Counter-Terrorism, were ratified by the US.[61] As in the case of the ICCPR and the UNTC, attention to the reservations and declarations attached on ratification is required to understand their force in domestic law—in addition to the often separate need to consider whether they are self-executing under US law. Further detail is beyond the remit of this chapter.

Finally, the US is a key player in the UNSC. As mentioned in the overview of British law, a large number of its recent resolutions pertain to terrorism. Considered binding on all member states, the requirements to legislate and otherwise act to combat aspects of terrorism are to be found in US counterterrorism laws, discussed below.[62]

(4) Federal primary legislation

The British example of a 'pile-up' of emergency statutes, presented above, is differently constructed in US law.[63] At first glance, the United States Code (USC) should offer a full picture: surely, the codification of federal law by subject enables tracing all laws pertaining to any subject. However, this organization of a multitude of statutes and measures into a single, mammoth code, further expanded in its annotated version, in itself separates statutes and places part of them in different Titles. Attention is usually directed to Title 50, which carries the title 'War and National Defense'. The best-known statutes, the War Powers Resolution of 1973, the National Emergencies Act 1976, and International Emergency Economic Powers Act 1977, are all coded in Title 50, yet, in addition to the other provisions included there, other Titles offer sources of authority to introduce anti-terrorism measures, and some measures have not been coded. Searches for the entire framework are thus required, even in a system that codes its Federal laws, and overlaps are not uncommon.[64]

Furthermore, despite the generally successful attempt to provide a full account of all Federal legislation, some statutory arrangements have escaped inclusion in the US code. One example, policy riders in appropriations acts, was briefly addressed in Chapter 1, as an example of a mode of intervention with agency independence, but more should be said of these tools of policymaking. Directing policy by prohibiting funding for defined purposes, or limiting it by setting conditions, they are generally not cited or referenced in the USC or the USCA. Further discussion of all of these measures is relegated to Chapter 7.

[61] See n 26.
[62] For general analysis see text to n 28.
[63] On the practice of 'piling-up' as a form of patchwork legislation see Chaps 3, 7.
[64] See further, ch 7.

C. Air Pollution Law

1. General

As a social construct, the idea of 'the environment' is relatively recent. Although some legal protection against smoke and other form of pollution can be found in the nineteenth century, the idea that the environment as such should be protected experienced a fast-paced development since the 1950s.[65] 'Environmental studies' today cover all cases in which the nature is perceived to be compromised by human action. Different ideologies placed along the spectrum between 'anthropocentrism' and 'ecocentrism' offer diverging emphases on the rationales, scope, and strategies best used to minimize damage.[66] Members of both camps, those who focus on the protection of humans and those whose concern expands to include non-human species and long-term global dangers, both direct attention to human-induced risks, to be resolved by human counter-action.

In current parlance, such counter-action falls under the rubric of 'regulation', a distinct term used in the context of a variety of government actions and studied under a distinct discipline that mixes insights from political science, public policy, law, history, and sociology.[67] The classical definition of regulation—'the sustained and focused control exercised by a public authority over activities valued by the community'[68]—is often linked with the idea of risk: when an activity is considered valuable but carries a risk to society, 'regulation' is perceived as the way to balance the utilities and the risks involved.[69]

Rather than discuss state-directed action against all risks to the environment, this case-study focuses on the sub-field of air pollution, directed, as in the case-study on emergency law, by a decision to limit its confines to a manageable size which enables comparison without falling into the trap of over-coverage. For the same reason, the case-study is limited to action in the core field of air pollution.

[65] For a recent important contribution to the study of the history of the idea of 'the environment' see Paul Warde, Libby Robin, and Svrker Sörlin, *The Environment: A History of the Idea* (Johns Hopkins University Press 2018). See also Jedediah Purdy, 'American Natures' (2012) 36 Harv Env L Rev 169, 173 (recognizing the emergence of the idea of 'progressive management' of the environment). For a historical view from the US see Christopher Sellers, 'Three Eras of Environmental Concern' (2018) 1 Mod American History 363, and, for the UK, see eg Stuart Bell and others, *Environmental Law* (9th edn, OUP 2017) 18–21.

[66] See Robyn Eckersley, *Environmentalism and Political Theory* (State University of New York Press 1992); Fisher, Lange, and Scotford (n 65) 47–48.

[67] For a general introduction to the field see eg Robert Baldwin, Martin Cave, and Martin Lodge, 'Introduction: Regulation – The Field and Developing Agenda', in Robert Baldwin, Martin Cave, and Martin Lodge (eds), *The Oxford Handbook of Regulation* (OUP 2012) 3, and the chapters of this collection.

[68] Philip Selznick, 'Focusing Organizational Research on Regulation' in Roger Q Noll (ed), *Regulatory Policy and the Social Sciences* (University of California Press 1985) 363.

[69] For the focus on 'risk' see eg Fiona Haines, 'Regulation and Risk', in Peter Drahos (ed), *Regulatory Theory: Foundations and Applications* (ANU Press 2017) 181.

Climate change, a rising second sub-field, is well-linked with air pollution, as much of the damage in the latter context has been effected by emissions to the atmosphere; climate change is however set aside, again for the benefit of presenting a well-defined and contained case-study.

It is by now uncontested that human action—agriculture, production, industry, land, and air transportation, all generated by a growing global population, has had a gradually escalating severe effect on air quality due to the emission of a large number of compounds into the air.[70] The need for regulation is thus unchallenged: since these types of risk-generating actions are considered valuable to the community, downright prohibition is ruled out in favour of the introduction of balanced framework designed to minimize negative effects without excessively curbing enterprise. Private law, mainly applied through the law of nuisances, is no longer deemed sufficient. This difficult task, to be undertaken through forms of systematic control and the setting of constraints on private and market action, required further law-based frameworks; state regulation was further backed by both economic and socio-moral arguments.[71] Law, and regulations, are thus crucial to the field.

Commentators note the complexity of law in this field; that complexity differs from the complexity of emergency law presented above, but is just as pervasive. Here, too, some forms of complexity, simply inherent to the field, can be set aside. The rules in all aspects of environmental law and regulation are necessarily intricate, as they are essentially the outcome of a mix of constantly transforming scientific, cultural, and political understandings. Moreover, this field is also beset by its innate transnational nature, as a source of pollution in one country may affect other countries, as in the case of air pollution. As in the case of the former case-study, this case-study is focused on the complexity introduced through legal design that offers the executive fuzzy modes of action.

Generally, three bodies of law are relevant to the regulation of air pollution. Historically, much of the field was directed under the laws of nuisance. The whittling-down of nodes of pollution through the implementation of tort and

[70] For a survey of the main compounds and substances directly affecting the atmosphere, addressed in the law, see eg Fisher, Lange, and Scotford, *Environmental Law* (n 65) 606–10.

[71] Under a neo-liberal ideology, pollution is often presented as a classic example of a market failure arising from the existence of negative externalities in a given sector; this market failure has also been recognized, in the context of the environment, under the title 'the tragedy of the commons'. For the seminal work in this context see Garrett Hardin, 'The Tragedy of the Commons' (1968) 162 Science 1243. As an alternative, the 'green' movement offers 'ecocentric' views, based on the centrality of nature and its future sustenance; although some participants have called for the minimization of regulation, to be replaced by internalized morals, this stream of thought is not averse to regulation. See Arne Næss, *Economy, Community and Lifestyle: Outline of an Ecosophy* (Trans David Rothenberg, CUP 1989); Herman E Daly and John B Cobb Jr, *For the Common Good: Redirecting the Economy Toward Community, the Environment, and a Sustainable Future* (2nd rev edn, Beacon Press 1994); Eckersley (n 66).

nuisance law remains in both systems; I set aside reliance on private law.[72] Moving to regulation via legislation, in the first group are laws and rules that are directly dedicated to this form of pollution, such as laws setting standards and ceilings for emission of dangerous substances and those requiring permits for the operation of potentially polluting installations. Other laws and rules that concern linked but distinct areas may impact on the regulation of air pollution, either directly or indirectly, for example rules concerned with planning permissions and those restricting the use of old vehicles. The latter are not discussed here.

The main techniques embedded in the regulation of air quality are, as is often the case in regulatory analysis, an array of command-and-control provisions that set standards and minimum requirements; licensing and permits requirements, set not only in environmental law but inter alia through planning law (and, in this context, the provision of a tradeable permit regime); and sets of sanctions for non-conformity with the rules.[73] In addition, the law may set duties on the regulators, for example requiring them to publish reports, prepare strategy documents, and decide upon short- and long-term policies. Two main tracks exists in many such frameworks. The first targets sources, considering their specific contribution to pollution; the second is concerned with the aggregation of pollution in defined areas, targeting 'ambient' emissions and other sources of air contamination.

2. Air Pollution Law in England[74]

a. General

English environmental law carries a historical background: its nascent forms emerged in the nineteenth century, both through legislation and through use of the common law.[75]

The law regulating this field was never ordered around single, clear legislative mandates separately governing each of its sub-fields. A report on the state of environmental law in 2011–12, published by the United Kingdom Environmental Law Association (UKELA) and King's College London, found the general legal arrangements lacking in many ways. This body of law, comprising a multitude of rules, was described as lacking coherence; its absence of integration or co-ordination

[72] For overviews of nuisance law in both systems see Bell and others (n 65) 356–92; Robert V Percival and others, *Environmental Regulation: Law, Science, and Policy* (8th edn, Wolters Kluwer 2018) 68–93.

[73] For a short overview of the main regulatory techniques, or 'strategies', see Robert Baldwin, Martin Cave, and Martin Lodge, *Understanding Regulation* (2nd edn, OUP 2012) 105–36.

[74] This section carries the title 'England' and not 'the UK', as Scotland and Northern Ireland have their own bodies of rules in addition to those originating from the UK and international/transnational sources. The overview and the discussions in the following chapters all focus on England and Wales.

[75] For a focus on the nineteenth-century measures concerned with air pollution see Noga Morag-Levine, *Chasing the Wind: Regulating Air Pollution in the Common Law State* (Princeton UP 2003) ch 6; for a condensed overview see Ben Christman, 'A Brief History of Environmental Law in the UK' (2013) 22(4) Environ Sci 4.

contributes to confusion and overlaps; and was far from transparent. While some of the complexity arose from the inherently technical aspects of the field and from the cross-border features that challenged consolidation, this state of affairs, it was reported, was also the result of idiosyncratically developed legislation and a general reluctance to bring the arrangements under a single roof.[76] The overview of air-pollution law in 2020, offered in this Part, demonstrates that this pattern has not changed.

b. Layers of Law Pertaining to Air Pollution

As in the case of emergency law, the overview of the measures relevant to air pollution moves from the transnational to the domestic levels setting aside, for now, issues of application and enforcement.

(1) International law

In comparison to emergency law, the role of customary law in this field is marginal.[77] Several principles recognized by the ICJ and by commentators establish, in a 'foggy' fashion, some rules of co-operation between states, and are less concerned with states' duties to individuals.[78] Treaties have a more significant role, as far as they are incorporated in domestic law and duly applied.

The decades-long concern of the UN with the environment has led to its introduction of eighteen international conventions.[79] Of these, the main international agreements concerned with air pollution, the 1979 Geneva Convention on Long-Range Transboundary Air Pollution (CLRTAP) and the Stockholm Convention on Persistent Organic Pollutants 2001, were ratified by the United Kingdom.[80] Other

[76] United Kingdom Environmental Law Association and King's College London, *The State of UK Environmental Legislation in 2011: Is There a Case for Reform?*, April 2012, summary at 6–7.

[77] For an introduction to the layers of international law see text at n 12.

[78] The usual principles cited are the duty to prevent significant harm, to exercise due diligence to avoid causing significant transboundary harm, to consult with neighbor states, and to conduct environmental impact assessments prior to a possibly hazardous act; only the latter sets a domestic duty. For an overview that emphasizes the 'slowly dissipating' fog effected by these nebulous rules see Pierre-Marie Dupuy, Ginevre Le Moli, and Jorge G Viñuales, *Customary International Law and the Environment*, C-EENRG Working Papers 2018–2 (Cambridge Centre for Environment, Energy and Natural Resource Governance 2018).

[79] Another applies to Latin America and the Caribbean. For links to all conventions, their protocols, and amendments, as well as their publication citations see *The United Nations Treaty Collection*, Chapter XXVII, at https://treaties.un.org/pages/Treaties.aspx?id=27&subid=A&clang=_en.

[80] By far the central convention, CLRTAP was ratified by the UK in 1982, and all its protocols that are currently in force were ratified between 1984 and 2012. The general commitment to 'endeavour to limit and, as far as possible, gradually reduce and prevent air pollution including long-range transboundary air pollution', set in the Geneva Convention, is supplemented by commitments concerned with information-exchange, consultation, and research; the convention further creates implementing bodies within the UN. Under the protocols to this convention, signatories commit to set national standards and reduce pollution in several contexts. Its protocols contain detailed information and guidelines concerning dangers, reduction strategies, processes, and even costs. Four set obligatory standards, limits, and/or timescales, either universal or country-specific, thereby creating measurable duties. The Stockholm Convention, ratified by the UK in 2005, regulates low- or non-degradable organic compounds such as those found in certain insecticides; it covers all types of pollution media, including air.

UN conventions that impact on national regulation of air pollution are concerned with the treatment of waste, the prevention of industrial accidents, and climate change.[81]

As mentioned above, as a dualist system, international measures ratified by the UK become part of its domestic law only upon incorporation by parliament.[82] British ratification has not led to direct incorporation.[83] To date, the UK has relied on EU law, further discussed below.

(2) EU law

Prior to Brexit, the central mode of domestic adoption of international law was effected through EU law, both through the automatic incorporation of EU regulations into domestic law and by British regulations made under the ECA 1972.[84] Following the introductory comments made above, the general pattern of government's reliance on EU law rather than on international law may be transformed after the UK's final exit from the European Union. Importantly, for the period starting on completion day, the Environment Bill 2019–21 was introduced in the House of Commons a day before exit day.[85] Described by the government as an initiative to fully address all aspects of the protection of the environment, in its form in July 2020, it contains some amendments to existing legislation, but does not replace other statutes through their repeal.

As in the case of the survey of EU impact on antiterrorism emergency law, offered above, the overview below focuses on the interim post-Brexit era, during which EU measures remain applicable, as the future regarding the possible extension of the interim period, as well as the fate of the Bill are unclear at the time of writing.

The EU has ratified or accessed the Geneva Convention and six of its seven active protocols, as well as the Stockholm Convention,[86] in addition to the making

[81] See the Basel Convention on the Control of Transboundary Movements of Hazardous Wastes and their Disposal, Basel 1989; Convention on the Control of Transboundary Effects of Industrial Accidents, Helsinki 1992; the Vienna Convention for the Protection of the Ozone Layer, Geneva 1985; and the United Nations Framework Convention on Climate Change, New York 1992.

[82] See (nn 11, 14, 15).

[83] CLRTAP is mentioned only once, in the Environmental Protection Act 1990, discussed below, and merely contains an authorization to grant financial assistance to aid the Convention, with the consent of the Treasury (s 153).

[84] See text to n 29.

[85] Environment Bill, Bill 9, 30 January 2020, House of Commons 58/1. For updates about its advancement, at this point in time, see https://services.parliament.uk/bills/2019-21/environment.html

[86] The only protocol that has been merely signed by the EU is the Geneva Protocol 1991 on volatile organic compounds emissions, which sets measurable duties on its members (Protocol to the 1979 Convention on Long-Range Transboundary Air Pollution Concerning the Control of Emissions of Volatile Organic Compounds or their Transboundary Fluxes, Geneva, 18 November 1991, United Nations Treaty Series, Vol 2001 p 187) ('Geneva Protocol 1991'). The UK has ratified it, but in the absence of incorporation, no direct formal internal duty to comply exists. Yet the EU has made a Directive concerned with the part of this issue, Directive 2004/42, which was followed by the promulgation of regulations (statutory instruments) in the UK (see n 91).

of its own rules on these matters. Indeed, these rules have been sometimes considered by the British government as EU implementation of the convention.[87]

Currently, two EU regulations directly impact on air pollution. The first regulates persistent organic pollutants emissions, prohibiting the production and use of defined substances, restricting the use of others, setting reporting framework and requiring member states to set penalties on infringements; the second regulates vehicle emissions.[88] The main bodies of rules are found in directives, which, as mentioned above, set targets and general rules to be transposed into domestic law by detailed national frameworks. Two central directives currently regulate ambient air quality and industrial emissions, respectively. A 2008 directive, designed to 'substantially revise' the field and replace existing directives on air quality with a single directive, inter alia sets limits of pollution levels of listed compounds, defines assessment criteria and rules regarding sampling points, and requires member states to set penalties and to transpose into its laws, by 2010, rules necessary for compliance with this Directive. The central rules regarding the regulation of industrial emissions under a permit regime are found in a directive made two years later.[89] A host of other Directives addresses various aspects of air pollution.[90]

[87] For example, the UK government has considered EU Directive 2016/2284 on the reduction of national emissions of certain atmospheric pollutants (mentioned below) as in effect an alternative 'transposition' into domestic law of the 1999 Gothenburg Protocol on national emissions. More accurately, DEFRA considers the ceilings set under this directive as ones that 'reflect the ceilings agreed internationally in the 1999 Gothenburg Protocol'. See Department of the Environment and Rural Affairs, *Air Pollution in the UK 2018*, September 2019, 6. <https://uk-air.defra.gov.uk/assets/documents/annualreport/air_pollution_uk_2018_issue_1.pdf.> On EU regulation concerned with persistent organic pollutants see below.

[88] Regulation 850/2004, *on persistent organic pollutants and amending Directive 79/117/EEC*, OJ L 158/7 (30 April 2004); Regulation 715/2007, *on type approval of motor vehicles with respect to emissions from light passenger and commercial vehicles (Euro 5 and Euro 6) and on access to vehicle repair and maintenance information*, OJ L 171/1 (29 June 2007).

[89] Directive 2008/50, *on ambient air quality and cleaner air for Europe*, OJ L 152/1 (11 June 2008), para (3) (sometimes titled the CAFÉ directive, the acronym for Clean Air for Europe, part of a broad programme addressing air quality. The directive regulates ambient (total) concentrations of six groups of substances, or 'six criteria', from sulphur dioxide to carbon monoxide, which are almost identical to those adopted in the US. For levels and objectives see Annexes I, II. The 2015 Thematic Strategy on Air Pollution (TSAP) supplements this programme, setting long-term objectives and strategies. On these programmes as presented by the EU see information and links at <http://ec.europa.eu/environment/archives/cafe/>; *Communication from the Commission to the Council and the European Parliament—Thematic Strategy on air pollution*, COM 92005) 446 <https://eur-lex.europa.eu/legal-content/EN/TXT/?uri=celex:52005DC0446>; Directive 2010/75 *On industrial emissions (integrated pollution prevention and control*, OJ L 334/17 (24 November 2010).

[90] See eg Directive 1994/63, *on the control of volatile organic compound (VOC) emissions resulting from the storage of petrol and its distribution from terminals to service stations*, OJ L 365/24 (31 December 1994); Directive 2004/107, *relating to arsenic, cadmium, mercury, nickel and polycyclic aromatic hydrocarbons in ambient air*, OJ L 23/3 (26 January 2005), and Directive 2016/2284, *on the reduction of national emissions of certain atmospheric pollutants, amending Directive 2003/35/EC and repealing Directive 2001/81/EC*, OJ L 344/1 (17 December 2016) (in addition to requirements to limit certain emissions according to set national emissions ceilings, the Directive contains requirements to draw up and implement programmes designed to achieve the required limits). For links provided by the EU see < https://eur-lex.europa.eu/summary/chapter/environment/2005.html?root=2005>; for general

Only one of these sets of rules was incorporated into English domestic law by primary legislation, discussed below. Most of the applicable EU measures were introduced by regulations that were either under ECA, or, more recently, under the Brexit legislation.[91] The future of all these measures is regulated under the 2018 and 2020 Withdrawal Acts, discussed above.[92]

(3) Domestic primary legislation

The internalization of EU-generated rules, discussed above, should not detract attention from the four British statutes currently in force in the UK that apply to the regulation of air pollution. As in any review of a regulatory regime, it is best to differentiate between three main aspects, rule-making powers, permit regimes and enforcement regimes, although overlap is not uncommon.

The Environmental Protection Act 1990 (EPA 1990) is concerned with various aspects of pollution.[93] Part I of this act, concerned with integrated regulation of pollution generated in all media (land, air, and water), which followed EC rules on the matter, was formally repealed in the Pollution Prevention and Control Act 1999: however, a commencement order was required for the coming into force of this repeal, and such an order was never made as far as its application to England and Wales.[94] The chapter, and the authorization requirement it contains is thus still formally in force, despite some representations that it has been 'replaced'.[95]

reviews of EU law from a British perspective see Bell and others (n 65); 568–74, Fisher, Lange and Scotford (n 65) 622–33.

[91] For the former type see the Air Quality Standards Regulations 2010 (implementing directives 2008/50 and 2004/107); the Volatile Organic Compounds in Paints, Varnishes and Vehicle Refinishing Products Regulations 2012 (implementing Directive 2004/42); and the National Emission Ceilings Regulations 2018 (implementing directive 2016/2284, in itself an implementation of CLRTAP and the 1999 Gothenburg Protocol). For regulations made under Brexit legislation or under both sources see the Air Quality (Amendment of Domestic Regulations) (EU Exit) Regulations 2019; the Persistent Organic Pollutants (Amendment) (EU Exit) 2019; the Pollution Prevention and Control (Designation of Directives) (England and Wales) Order 2019 (the latter designates 26 EU Directives that can be considered by a Secretary of State in the regulation of polluting activity).

[92] See text at n 30.

[93] Part I introduces a requirement that 'processes' (activities capable of causing pollution) and substances, prescribed by the Secretary of State, require an authorization granted by an 'enforcing authority' (the Environment Agency, created in the Environment Act 1995, or local authorities). Further, a statutory nuisance framework set in the Act subjects certain defined activities that endanger health or are considered a nuisance to summary proceedings under which sanctions ranging from prohibition and abatement orders to fines may be set. The Act grants extensive discretion in its authorizations to prescribe and define regulated activities. EPA 1990, esp Parts I and III.

[94] Pollution Prevention and Control Act 1999, Ch 24, Schedule 3. The Pollution Prevention and Control Act 1999 (Commencement No 1) (England and Wales) Order 2000 (SI 2000/800) brought into force amendments specified in Schedule 2 of the Act. Schedule 3, concerning repeals, was commenced in Scotland by the Pollution Prevention and Control Act 1999 (Commencement No 3) (Scotland) Order 2015 (SSI 2015/74), signed by the Scottish Minister for Environment, Climate Change, and Land Reform.

[95] See ch 8 for this example of 'pastiche law'.

Moving now to the statute that could have been considered the main locus of air pollution law, at least according to its title—the Clean Air Act 1993. Its first three parts are concerned with the regulation of 'dark smoke' and other emissions from chimneys, furnaces, and the like, all echoing historical regulatory frameworks.[96] Provisions were inserted to set the relation between these chapters and the 1990 and 1999 Acts, essentially ruling for non-application of the former in certain defined aspects regulated under the more recent statute—a rare case of a formal minimization of overlap.[97] Part IV is seemingly broader; concerned with 'air pollution'—a term that is not defined—its provisions concern powers to regulate the composition of fuel (used by motor vehicles, furnaces, and engines). The addition of regulation of some minor activities still retains the nature of the statute as targeted to specific aspects of pollution generation.[98]

The Environment Act 1995, the next chronologically listed statute, introduces an institutional framework by creating the Environment Agency (and its Scottish equivalent) and transfers to it certain powers from other bodies, only marginally concerned with air quality.[99] Finally, the most recent statute currently in force dedicated to pollution, the 1999 Pollution Prevention and Control Act, is explicitly defined as the implementation of the EU directive on integrated pollution prevention and control; it provides an extensive basis for the regulation of pollution at large, including air pollution.[100] The Act includes a lengthy and detailed Schedule that lists 'purposes', the achievement of which is to be effected under regulations made by the Secretary of State, and all aspects of such regulations including permit and enforcement regimes.

[96] Here, the Secretary of State is authorized to make rules and regulations on these aspects of activity, while local authorities may designate orders declaring areas to be 'smoke-controlled', with additional powers to the Secretary of State in cases where intervention is required.

[97] Clean Air Act 1993, Ch 11, sec 41, 41A. On overlap as a form of patchwork legislation see Chaps 3 and 7.

[98] The application of the dark smoke prohibition to colliery spoilbanks (coal and shale mines), railway engines, and water vessels (ss 42–44) only emphasizes the historical flavour of this statute.

[99] Environment Act 1995, Ch 25. Essentially considered an 'enforcement agency', the Environment Agency is inter alia granted powers of entry and removal of imminent danger, and is empowered to give directions in case of local authority failure. Part IV of the act, and Schedule 11, concerned with air quality, mainly address powers granted to the Secretary of State and to local authorities Sec 38 authorizes delegation of power from the Minister to the Agency by bilateral agreements. The statute also requires ministerial publication of a national air quality strategy, to which the agency should adhere in its actions; local authorities are required, inter alia, to conduct reviews of air quality and designate problem areas and implement special regimes ('action plans') in such areas, while the Secretary of State retains her reserve powers; the agency may also give directions to failing local authorities; regulations, guidance rules, and offences are to be made by the Secretary of State.

[100] Pollution Prevention and Control Act 1999 (n 94) (under its preamble, which cites a since-replaced directive, the Act operates 'for otherwise preventing and controlling pollution … and for connected purposes'). The currently in force Directive 2010/75, cited in sec 1(1)(a) of the Act, required 'transposition' of its provisions into domestic law by laws regulations, and administrative provisions (n 89, Article 80). The Act is thus designed to incorporate the rules contained in this directive.

3. Air Pollution Law in the US

a. General

For any new student of the regulation of air pollution in the US, a single source seems to encompass the whole field, and a single regulator seems to be fully charged with the regulation of air pollution throughout the country. This understanding does not reflect reality, neither the black-letter arrangement nor the politics of regulation in the field. The Clean Air Act (CAA), in its different forms since 1970, is indeed the prominent body of legislation, the seemingly single legislative mandate, codified in Title 42 of the USC, and this statute did establish the Environmental Protection Agency (EPA), the Federal body entrusted with regulation of this field. Yet complexity lurks behind this seemingly simple layout; although federal law is relatively recognizable and contained, state-law, which is not discussed in detail, provides additional important sources of power. Federal legislation contains some provisions that are not part of the CAA, granting power to bodies beyond the EPA, and a few provisions are not codified nor mentioned in the USC. Hence, here, too, the very idea of codification of this field enables some sources of authority to escape attention.

The structure of the survey of US law follows the survey of English law. As a Federal state, and one that is not a member of a binding transnational arrangement similar to the EU, emphases differ, as does the nature of the complexity.

b. Layers of Law Pertaining to Air Pollution

(1) Constitutional law

Being a modern aspect of governance, no reference to the environment can be found in the US Constitution. Potentially, presidents could ground their action in the field in the take-care clause, expansively read,[101] but as seen below, the legislation in the field is vast, and not all presidents have set the environment high on their political agenda.

The other possible reliance on the constitution can be found in the ongoing use of the formula 'the constitution and the laws', contained, for several decades, in almost all executive orders and other unilateral measures.[102] In the field of air pollution, such measures either apply generally to all administrative agencies, thereby applying to the Environmental Protection Agency (EPA) and all other bodies involved in the regulation of air pollution, or contain rules concerned with air quality. A recent example of the former type, the 'two for one' Executive Order 13771, requires all agencies to repeal at least two regulations for each introduced, and naturally impacts on the activity of the EPA and of all other bodies regulating

[101] On the interpretation of the take-care clause see ch 3 and 4.
[102] For analysis of this practice see ch 5.

air quality.[103] Moving to specific measures, President Trump's memorandum of 12 April 2018, which directs the EPA to reduce 'unnecessary impediments to new manufacturing and business expansion essential for a growing economy' is but one example.[104] Some unilateral measures in this field only rely on this formula, but most append the formula to a statutory authority.[105] Still, as mentioned above, the formula need not only be a declaratory adornment to a statute-based measure. In addition to the re-emphasis on the role of the Constitution at the apex of the system, reliance on the constitution functions to insure the legality of the measure in case the statutory authority or authorities are found wanting.[106]

(2) International and transnational law

The United States' partial commitment to the international law of air pollution is evident even on the formal level. The US was one of the signatories of CLRTAP, the main UN multilateral agreement concerned with air quality.[107] Signed and accepted (considered by the UN to have entered into force by the US), only four of its protocols share the same status, and most of those were accepted with reservations.[108] The EPA, to be soon discussed, does provide references and links to these sources, but does not offer direct access to the reservations appended to them.[109] The second central UN convention directly concerned with air pollution, the 2001 Stockholm Convention on Persistent Organic Pollutants, was signed by the US but was never accepted (or ratified). In addition, the US maintains bilateral frameworks

[103] Executive Order 13771, *Reducing Regulation and Controlling Regulatory Costs*, 30 January 2017, 82 FR 9339. For EPA information about its action after the issue of the order see <https://www.epa.gov/laws-regulations/executive-order-13771-reducing-regulation-and-controlling-regulatory-costs>. See also, eg, Executive Order 12088, *Federal compliance with pollution control standards*, 2 November 2010, 43 FR 47707; Executive Order 13432, *Cooperation Among Agencies in Protecting the Environment With Respect to Greenhouse Gas Emissions From Motor Vehicles, Nonroad Vehicles, and Nonroad Engines*, 14 May 2007, 72 FR 27717. For a discussion of orders submitting agencies to rules made by the President see ch 1.

[104] Memorandum, *Promoting Domestic Manufacturing and Job Creation—Policies and Procedures Relating to Implementation of Air Quality Standards*, 83 FR 16671 (12 April 2018). See further, ch 1. See also, eg Memorandum, *Implementation of Revised Air Quality Standards for Ozone and Particulate Matter*, 62 FR 38421 (6 July 1997) (concerning EPA implementation of new standards 'approved' by the president).

[105] For an example of formula-only reliance see Executive Order 13432 (n 103). Other measures cited above (n 103) cite both sources.

[106] See analysis in ch 4.

[107] On the Convention see n 80.

[108] The first Geneva Protocol of 1984, concerned with the financing of a co-operative monitoring program; the 1988 Sofia Protocol, concerning nitrogen oxides emissions; the 1998 Aarhus protocol, concerned with heavy metals pollutants; the 1999 Gothenburg Protocol, addressing acidification and other processes; and the 2012 Geneva protocol, amending provisions of the main Convention. The latter three were accepted with declarations or reservations. For UN links, offering access to declarations and reservations, see n 79.

[109] See https://www.epa.gov/international-cooperation/selected-multilateral-environmental-instruments-force-us#unfccc. See also <https://findit.state.gov/search?utf8=%E2%9C%93&affiliate=dos_stategov&query=Convention+on+Long-Range+Transboundary+Air+Pollution

with its two land-connected neighbours, Canada and Mexico. International law in this context has thus been limited.[110]

(3) Federal primary legislation

The Clean Air Act, the mammoth statute that dominates the field, is justifiably the first Federal statute to be reckoned with. The powers granted to the EPA span all aspects of regulatory governance. Based on a concept of shared Federal-state responsibility, it is the EPA that has the final say. Regulation applies to all aspects of pollution. In the context of the regulation of ambient air quality, the EPA is authorized to establish national ambient air quality standards (NAAQs); these established standards for six of the most common air pollutants, known as the 'six criteria'. It is then for states to establish their implementation plan (SIP), submitted to the EPA for approval.[111] A separate, Federal implementation plan (FIP) is sometimes added, as aids to states or tribes that are considered to require help, either generally or in specific contexts. Areas that fail to achieve regulatory goals can be designated as nonattainment areas; continued failure may lead to sanctions, including the limiting of federal financial assistance. Attainment areas, that conform with, or exceed, the standards, are regulated separately.[112] Supplementing this detailed regulatory framework, a parallel, just as comprehensive, part of the statue regulates the operation of polluting sources, both stationary and mobile (ranging from industry to vehicles), existing, and new ones. The regime includes licensing, standard setting and limitations on use and operation.[113] Both strata of regulation are enforced through a mix of penal and civil sanctions.[114]

[110] Relations with Canada are regulated under a 1991 bilateral agreement. Border 2020, the fourth version of the 1983 La Paz agreement between US and Mexico signed in 2012, identifies the reduction of air pollution as the first of its six goals, and sets arrangements for its achievement. For program documents see <https://www.epa.gov/border2020>. Climate control is not discussed here; it would however be in place to note that the US is almost alone in its non-ratification of the Kyoto Protocol to the 1992 United Nations Framework Convention on Climate Change (UNFCCC), a convention it did sign in 1998 (a second Western signatory, Canada, withdrew in 2012). For information on signatories to the protocol see <https://treaties.un.org/Pages/ViewDetails.aspx?src=TREATY&mtdsg_no=XXVII-7-a&chapter=27&clang=_en>).

[111] Powers are also granted to Tribal Nations, an aspect that is set aside.

[112] Clean Air Act (42 USC 7661 et seq). For textbook analyses of the Clean Air Act see Steven Ferrey, *Environmental Law* (7th edn, Wolters Kluwer 2016) 183–248; Robert V Percival and others, *Environmental Regulation: Law, Science, and Policy* (8th edn, Wolters Kluwer 2018) 524–655. For some of the information offered by the EPA in this context see <https://www.epa.gov/laws-regulations/summary-clean-air-act> (CAA summary); <https://www.epa.gov/criteria-air-pollutants> (criteria pollutants); <https://www.epa.gov/air-quality-implementation-plans> (types of implementation plans, including SIPs); <https://www.epa.gov/air-quality-implementation-plans/basic-information-about-air-quality-fips> (FIPs); <https://www3.epa.gov/airquality/greenbook/ancl.html> (list of nonattainment areas); https://www.epa.gov/nsr/prevention-significant-deterioration-basic-information> (Significant Deterioration Program, applied to either attainment or unclassified areas).

[113] For EPA information on this regulatory regime see <https://www.epa.gov/enforcement/air-enforcement>.

[114] See <https://www.epa.gov/enforcement/basic-information-enforcement>.

As in the case of emergency law, sole reliance on the CAA as codified at Chapter 85 of Title 42 USC may be understandable, but is problematic. This is yet another case of piling-up by dispersion, further discussed in Chapter 7.

D. Concluding Remarks

This chapter provided an introductory overview to the following two chapters, concerned with forms of fuzziness generated by legislators and executives. The two fields of action chosen as examples in this book, emergency and air pollution, are both important to the operation of a well-functioning society. The above surveys show that both fields are regulated by a mix of rules that have emerged in both the international and domestic levels. The place of EU-generated rules in the UK is likely to be marginalized after completion date; this transformation will strengthen the importance of the other two levels. The federal structure of the US has some impact in the so-called 'mundane' area of air quality; states are still subject to federal overview, although in other contexts, not discussed in this book, the local may overshadow the national. Yet even on such local levels, fuzziness will be part of the legal arrangement: my argument addresses fuzziness as a universal feature, part of state (and local) governance just as much as it features on the national level.

A main aspect in all of these overviews, then, is the number of arrangements introduced and applied in all studied fields. Multiple rules cause fuzziness, which are further discussed in Chapter 7. Moving to executive-generated fuzziness, Chapter 8 delves into two aspects of the application and implementation of these rules.

7
Legislation-Generated Fuzziness
Patchwork Legislation

A. **Introduction**	198
B. **Piling-up**	199
1. General	199
2. Examples	200
a. UK anti-terrorism law	200
b. UK Brexit legislation	203
C. **Dispersion**	204
1. General	204
2. Examples	205
a. US air pollution	205
b. US emergency law	208
D. **The Fuzzy Consequences of Patchworking**	212
1. Redundancy/Complexity	212
2. Contradiction	216
3. Under-Funding/Denial of Funding	218
E. **Concluding Remarks**	222

A. Introduction

Legislation can be fuzzy in at least six ways, as discussed in Chapter 3. In this chapter I dedicate further attention to one of these, patchwork legislation, a state of affairs under which multiple statutes are layered onto each other or side-by-side, to produce a virtually indecipherable framework.

As noted previously, under classic accounts, a single, overarching, and all-inclusive legislative mandate or organic statute grants executive agencies the authority to act in a specified field of action, and delineates the contours of their action by setting limits and conditions. However, as any practitioner can attest, the legislative mandate, when it exists, is never the sole source of executive authority. It is always supported by other legal rules. I set aside secondary legislation and other executive rules made under the legislative mandate; these are obvious forms of potential fuzziness-by-dispersion, but they, at least, rely on the parent statute and can be easily traced. There will usually be other legal rules that have no direct link to the legislative mandate, when it exists: other statutes, executive orders, and other unilateral measures, and, in a Federal system, state law, when and as far as it pertains to any aspect of a Federal arrangement (or vice versa).

Under both patterns of patchwork legislation, piling-up and dispersion, the existence of multiple rules fuzzies-up the law. Under the first pattern, multiple frameworks may overlap; under the second, rules are dispersed across multiple

A Theory of the Executive Branch. Margit Cohn, Oxford University Press (2021). © Margit Cohn.
DOI: 10.1093/oso/9780198821984.003.0008

frameworks. Although these patterns often exist concurrently, this chapter considers them separately and offers examples of both, to promote the understanding of these two sub-types of fuzziness. The chapter ends with an analysis that contrasts the unavoidable nature of these patterns of executive action with the costs incurred by those who wish to rely on the law.

Most of the examples discussed in this chapter concern the two fields of action reviewed in the previous chapter, emergency law and air pollution regulation. Varying in intensity and form, patchwork law is a common feature of these four examples of domestic authorizations to act under, and beyond, formal law.

B. Piling-Up

1. General

In her comparative study of emergency laws, which drew inter alia on reports submitted by twenty-four states, Nicole Questiaux identified a recurring practice, under which legal regimes introduce, over time,

> [a] great number of parallel or simultaneous emergency rules whose complexity is increased by the 'piling up' of provisions designed to 'regularize' the immediately preceding situation and therefore embodying retroactive rules and transitional regimes.[1]

Questiaux focused on legislators recovering from an emergency and found that they tend to supplement existing powers with new ones, relying on the recent experience as inspiration. Since a subsequent emergency would not necessarily follow the contours of its predecessor, new requirements would lead to the introduction of yet another legal measure after the resolution of the emergency, once again looking backwards rather than ahead to (uncertain) futures. Further, new legislation can be introduced *during* an emergency, to answer pressing needs; and incentives to legislate anew are many, as Gross comments:

> ... it is often easier to pass new legislation than to examine why it is that the existing legislation ... was not sufficient. This allows government to demonstrate that it is doing something against the dangers facing the nation rather than sitting idly.[2]

[1] Nicole Questiaux, *Study of the Implications for Human Rights of Recent Developments Concerning Situations Known as States of Siege or Emergency*, UN ESCOR, 35th Sess, Agenda Item 10, UN Doc E/CN.4/Sub.2/1982/15 (1982) 29.

[2] Oren Gross, 'Chaos and Rules: Should Responses to Violent Crises Always be Constitutional?' (2003) 112 Yale L J 1014, 1032.

According to this literature, one of the main problems inhering in this practice is the danger of the creation of an excessively severe emergency regime, which also tends to extend beyond the actual emergency. But fuzziness exists even when a new arrangement is *not* stricter than its precursors, since the executive retains the ability to choose from the existing menu of power sources.

Attention to this legislative practice has focused on emergency law, but again, is much more commonplace, as the examples provided in the following section amply show.

2. Examples

a. UK anti-terrorism law

I begin with an overview of British law in this context. This is a stark example of piling up, which is not backed by a guiding rule concerning the ordering of these statutes.

Analyses of British anti-terrorism laws consider them to be 'all too often rushed, reactive, and repetitious', 'knee-jerk legislation … the inevitable response to terrorist attacks',[3] with initial legislation added onto by 'two hastily enacted and poorly deliberated pieces of legislation'.[4] In itself, rushed legislation as such does not necessarily contribute to piling-up, but the introduction of a new statute, which does not require careful consideration of existing arrangements, contributes to speedy legislative process. Indeed, anti-terrorism law has been describe as 'bitty, messy and hard for even its practitioners to comprehend as a whole'.[5]

The latter observation of this body of law as 'messy' was made in 2012; since then, the messiness has grown, as the chronological analysis below shows. Since 2000, eight statutes dedicated to the 'war on terror' were enacted, and six of them are currently in force.[6] Only one of them, designed as a temporary measure and replaced the same year, may be excluded from this extensive collection of piled-up patchwork legislation.[7] Despite the existence of cohesive reports of the legislative arrangements in the field, ordered by topic and context rather than by their formal

[3] Andrew Neal, 'Terrorism, Lawmaking, and Democratic Politics: Legislators as Security Actors' (2012) 24 Terror and Pol Violen 358.

[4] Keith Syrett, 'The United Kingdom' in Kent Roach (ed), *Comparative Counter-Terrorism Law* (CUP 2015) 167, 199.

[5] David Anderson, *The Terrorism Acts in 2001: Report of the Independent Reviewer on the Operation of the Terrorism Act 2000 and Part 1 of the Terrorism Act 2006* (The Stationary Office 2012) 133.

[6] Two of these, the Prevention of Terrorism Act 2005 and the Terrorist Asset-Freezing (Temporary Provisions) Act 2010, were replaced by subsequent legislation.

[7] The Terrorist Asset-Freezing (Temporary Provisions) Act 2010, which came into force in February 2010, was designed to validate and grant the force of law to a series of orders in council that incorporated United Nations measures. The Terrorist Asset-Freezing Act 2010, enacted in December that year, two weeks before the expiration of the former Act, introduced a detailed framework for the implementation of those measures.

sources and submitted annually to Parliament by the Independent Reviewer of Terrorism Legislation, who acts mainly under law,[8] the existence of multiple sources, which can at any time be supplemented by new ones, does not offer much in the way of clarity.

When enacted in 2000, the Terrorism Act was designed to consolidate emergency powers, at least those concerned with terrorism.[9] In its pre-9/11 version, acts of terrorism were mainly linked with the 'troubles' in Northern Ireland; extensively amended since, it remains the starting point of any discussion of current emergency law. Designed as a permanent, rather than a temporary measure, its eight parts and eighteen schedules (two were added to the original sixteen) provide government bodies with a broad array of powers. Under a definition of 'terrorism', which emphasizes the existence of an ideological agenda and the seriousness of threats or risks incurred by such action, organizations may be 'proscribed', either under the original statute, or by ministerial addition to the list set in Schedule 2.[10] A detailed list of terrorist-related offences, ranging from participation to non-disclosure of information, is followed by parts that enhance the powers of security and police forces, including the powers to search, seize, detain, and arrest. The special Part on Northern Ireland (Part VII) only serves to emphasize the universal extent of this Act.[11] This highly detailed statute, then, amended since to include a large number of foreign groups considered a threat to the nation's security, could have continued to operate as the single legislative mandate, with changes deemed necessary introduced into its framework. This has not been followed; instead, a series of statutes concerned with terrorism has been added on, in response to events and crises.

Next in this sequence, the Anti-Terrorism, Crime and Security Act 2001, remains the source of some anti-terrorism powers, although the indefinite detention regime of foreign suspected terrorists introduced in Part IV, backed by a derogation order made under Art 15 of the European Convention of Human Rights, were found unlawful in the *Belmarsh* decision (*A v Secretary of State*), and replaced in 2005.[12] Its provisions include the authorization to freeze, forfeit, and seize terrorist property, the addition of new offences, inter alia concerning the use of 'weapons of mass destruction', nuclear weapons, and toxins, the enhancement of police powers, and detailed provisions about the application of

[8] For the most recent annual report to date see Jonathan Hall, *The Terrorism Acts in 2018: Report of the Independent Reviewer of Terrorism Legislation on the Operation of the Terrorism Acts 2000 and 2006* (Crown Copyright 2020).

[9] See Council of Europe, Committee of Experts on Terrorism (CODEXTER), *Profiles on Counter-Terrorism Capacity: United Kingdom* (April 2007) 1; Alexander Horne, 'Reviewing Counter-Terrorism Legislation' in Adam Mellows-Facer (ed), *Key Issues for the New Parliament 2010* (House of Commons Library Research 2010) 90.

[10] As of July 2020, more than eighty such organizations are such proscribed in Schedule 2, most of them foreign.

[11] For overviews of the act see eg Clive Walker, 'Briefing on the Terrorism Act 2000' (2000) 12 Terror and Pol Violen 1; CODEXTER report (n 9) 1–6.

[12] *A v Secretary of State for the Home Department* [2004] UKHL 5.

the EU's 'third pillar', concerned with police and judicial co-operation in criminal matters.

Three years later, the Civil Contingencies Act, designed to address various forms of emergency, still defines one of the three types of emergency conditions, 'war, or terrorism, which threatens serious damage to the security of the United Kingdom'.[13]

Next, the Prevention of Terrorism Act 2005 was the source of authority for the issuing of control orders, a measure that replaced the detention regime removed from the 2001 Act, until its repeal in 2011.

The next anti-terrorism act, the Terrorism Act 2006, was enacted as a reaction to the July 2005 London bombings, and augmented the existing measures by adding offences of encouragement of terrorism, dissemination of terrorist publications and media, training and preparations of acts, among other constraining authorizations. Some amendments to the Terrorism Act are included, but most of the Act offers additional and parallel powers.[14]

The Counter-Terrorism Act 2008, not triggered by any specific event, enhanced police powers, extended the periods of criminal sentences, alleviated procedures and rules of evidence, established a registry of persons convicted for terrorism offences (the 'notification' mechanism inter alia required financial information) and authorized the issuing of directions to financial institutions to monitor and report suspected terrorist financing and money laundering.

Two years later, the Terrorist Asset-Freezing Act 2010 introduced further measures regarding the freezing of assets of designated persons involved or linked with terrorist activity, once again, despite the existence of previous legislation, especially the 2000 Act, originally designed to be the conclusive framework in this field. The Terrorism Prevention and Investigation Measures Act 2011 replaced the 2005 Act, introducing a 'lighter' version of control order.[15]

This series of anti-terrorism legislation did not end there. In 2015, in response to the violence of ISIL, or the Islamic State movement, in Syria and Iraq, the Counter-Terrorism and Security Act was designed to address the threat incurred by foreign terrorist fighters and supporters from within. Here, too, amendments of existing legislation were supplemented by the introduction of new frameworks of action, including the setting of restrictions of travel in and out of the UK of those found to be connected with terrorism-related activity, and the requirement that a host of institutions, including schools, universities,

13 Civil Contingencies Act 2004, s 1(1)(c), 19(1)(c).

14 On the act see eg Ellen Parker, 'Implementation of the UK Terrorism Act 2006—The Relationship between Counterterrorism Law, Free Speech, and the Muslim Community in the United Kingdom versus the United States' (2007) 21 Emory Int'l L Rev 711.

15 On both Acts see Alexander Horne and Clive Walker, 'Lessons Learned from Political Constitutionalism? Comparing the Enactment of Control Orders and Terrorism Prevention and Investigation Measures by the UK Parliament' (2014) PL 267.

health and prison institutions operate, under guidance, to 'have due regard to the need to prevent people from being drawn into terrorism'.[16]

The last statute to date dedicated to terrorism, the Counter-Terrorism and Border Security Act 2019, consists only of amendments to statutes in force. Furthermore, in addition to this large number of statutes, others contain arrangements concerned with combatting terrorism, especially in the context of maintaining public order, further contributing to the complexity of the statutory terrain in this field.[17] All these statutes, mainly concerned with global terrorism, do not neglect the possible aspects of a renewed flare-up of 'troubles' in Northern Ireland,[18] but the emphasis is clear.

This striking example of 'piling up' clearly fits within Questiaux's and Gross' general analyses. Most of these statutes were enacted in response to specific global terrorist events, under a climate of urgency that pervaded the polity at their enaction.[19] The addition of a new statute that is distinct from former ones serves a political aim: it emphasizes the readiness of the government to act swiftly and powerfully in the face of crisis, by introducing a 'new' arrangement.[20]

b. UK Brexit legislation

A single example of the series of statutes and other measures made in this context will suffice. The European Union (Withdrawal Act) 2018 was designed to provide the general framework for future exit from the European Union.[21] Originally 101

[16] The Counter-Terrorism and Security Act 2015, Parts 1, 4, and 5. On the Act see Jessie Blackbourn and Clive Walker, 'Interdiction and Indoctrination: The Counter-Terrorism and Security Act 2015' (2016) 79 MLR 840.

[17] To name but two, see the Criminal Justice Act 1993 (inter alia, a 'terrorism offence' is one of the offences specified as a 'dangerous offence', for which a stringent regime of detention and sentencing exists; Chapter 5 of Part 12); the Sanctions and Anti-Money Laundering Act 2018 (the first two items in a list of domestic purposes the attainment of which supports a Minister's promulgation of regulations are '(a) further the prevention of terrorism, in the United Kingdom or elsewhere, (b) be in the interests of national security'; section 1).

[18] The Justice and Security (Northern Ireland Act) 2007, and the dedicated Part VII in the Terrorism Act 2000 provide sufficient evidence.

[19] The 2001 Bill rushed through the House of Commons with minimum debate; some amendments submitted in the House of Lords were uncontested. See Helen Fenwick, 'The Anti-Terrorism, Crime and Security Act 2001: A Proportionate Response to 11 September?' (2002) 65 MLR 724, 727–30. An attempt to employ a rushed legislative process was partially thwarted by parliamentary irritation that led to the production of several studies, consultation papers, and impact assessments, but the political atmosphere at the time was clearly marked by sentiments of crisis. Blackbourn and Walker (n 16) 843.

[20] See for example Theresa May's speech in September 2014, prior to the enaction of the 2014 Act. Delivered in her capacity as Home Secretary, the speech offers a discussion of the rising threats and the measures taken by that and the previous government, and culminates with a declaration that 'the Government will on Wednesday introduce a new Counter-Terrorism and Security Bill', seeking to 'build on our existing counter-terrorism strategy' by providing 'new powers'—words that convey more than merely an undertaking to amend current laws, thereby projecting a high commitment to a newly redesigned body of laws. See *Home Secretary Theresa May on Counter-Terrorism*, delivered on 24 November 2014, transcript at <https://www.gov.uk/government/speeches/home-secretary-theresa-may-on-counter-terrorism>.

[21] According to Explanatory Note 10 of the Bill, as introduced in the House of Commons in 2017, '[t]he principal purpose of the Act is to provide a functioning statute book on the day the UK leaves the

pages long, with twenty-five sections and nine detailed schedules, the European Union (Withdrawal Agreement) 2020 contains substantial amendments to the 2018 Act. Yet, the 2020 Act also provides a small, but not insubstantial set of provisions concerned with the post-Brexit regime. These independent provisions contain, for example, authorizations to ministers to make regulations designed to apply important provisions in the EU-UK agreements, concerning inter alia, rights of residence of European citizens and their equal treatment and non-discrimination. These are to enter into force by regulation made by a Minister.[22] Regulations to be made in the future will thus be made under the 2020 Act. Other provisions of that act establish an Independent Monitoring Authority, in charge of implementing these rights; define the financial source for paying expenses to the EU; and (re) establish the principle of parliamentary sovereignty.[23] Other financial sources, mainly concerned with domestic expenditures, are provided in the 2018 Act. This, then, is not only a case of dispersion, but also a potential case of overlap.

C. Dispersion

1. General

The second form of patchworking is so common that it is rarely considered a fuzzy legislative practice. Here, redundancy is replaced by dispersion: fields of law are rarely, if ever, regulated by a single legislative mandate.

All cases of 'piling up' over time create dispersion, but this common form is not linked with emerging exigencies or political preferences, as in the case of the accumulation of emergency rules over time. Only super-meticulous rule-drafters could manage to avoid dispersion; this is a highly unlikely situation, not only due to time and resource constraints on all rule-makers, but also due to the plurality of rule makers and the intersection between different aspects of life. Parliaments have little incentive to research the produce of former parliaments, and the several government ministries and agencies that may have authority or a linked authority to act, are likewise more eager to issue rules that are close, or closer, to their core authority, than to weave their own initiatives into the existing regulatory fabric. The unavoidable result is the existence of several arrangements, and the creation of overlaps and contradictions. All such cases share the problem evident in the piling

EU'. See https://services.parliament.uk/Bills/2017-19/europeanunionwithdrawal/documents.html. On the legal arrangements regarding Brexit see ch 6.

22 European Union (Withdrawal Act) 2020 §§7, 42(7).

23 ibid §§15, 20, 39.

up of legislation: a search for all sources of authority is likely to be unsuccessful, rendering the law fuzzy.

Optimists, including the designers of the US Code, may attempt to counter this difficulty by coding all legislation under a themed structure. As in the case of piling up, the very existence of codification leads to the assumption that what is included consists of the entire body of relevant rules and deflects attention from those provisions that are not coded; examples are provided below.

2. Examples

a. US air pollution

Setting aside regulations and other forms of secondary legislation, as well as state laws, none of which are discussed here, air pollution rules are dispersed in four directions: statutes coded in Title 42 of the USC, concerned with public health and welfare, in its chapters dedicated to the environment; statutes that directly or indirectly affect the field, located in other Titles of the USC; statutory provisions that have escaped inclusion in the USC; and executive orders and other unilateral measures that impact, directly or indirectly, on the regulatory framework.

The Clean Air Act (CAA) is indeed the central Act concerned with air pollution. This agency-state framework of collaboration, codified as Chapter 85 of Title 42 USC, grants the EPA the central place in the regulation of air quality nationwide.[24]

Yet reliance only on the CAA does not offer a full grasp of the law in this field. First, other statutes coded in different chapters of Title 42 are relevant to the regulation of air pollution by the EPA. The Pollution Prevention Act 1990 directs the EPA to conduct a separate program to prevent or reduce pollution at the source; the Comprehensive Environmental Response, Compensation, and Liability Act, 1980 (CERCLA), creates and operates a fund ('superfund') under which taxes originally set on users of petroleum and other substances, and now funded out of general revenues, supports the funding of removals and clean-ups of contaminated sites, setting liability on identifiable polluters; and the Resource Conservation and Recovery Act empowers the EPA to regulate hazardous waste, which can potentially cause harm by emissions.[25]

Beyond powers granted to the EPA, the Department of Energy operates a large number of funding and loan programs, aimed at supporting technology that reduces hazardous emissions or otherwise develop cleaner energy sources. Those include the Clean Air Coal Program, the grant of incentives for natural

[24] Clean Air Act, coded as 42 USC Chapter 85. See ch 5. For a short overview see ch 6. For textbook analyses of the Clean Air Act see Steven Ferrey, *Environmental Law* (7th edn, Wolters Kluwer 2016) 183–248; Robert V Percival and others, *Environmental Regulation: Law, Science, and Policy* (8th edn, Wolters Kluwer 2018) 524–655.

[25] Coded in 42 USC Chapters 133, 103, and 82, respectively.

gas production from the Gulf of Mexico and other various clean power projects, and a variety of programmes aimed at supporting research and development of alternative energy processes and vehicle technology, all found in Title 42.[26]

Several additional relevant statutory provisions, concerned inter alia with dangerous substances, the improvement of vehicle emissions, and energy generation, are codified in other USC Titles.[27] Tracing Federal legislation in this field requires, then, more than reliance on Chapter 42.

In addition to all of those, some statutes apply across the administration, most importantly the National Environmental Policy Act 1969 (NEPA), which applies to all federal agencies. Alongside the creation of the Council on Environmental Quality (CEQ), an agency authorized to perform several planning, advising, and funding functions, the most direct impact of this statute is the requirement that all federal agencies prepare environmental impact assessments in their proposals of legislation and 'other major Federal actions' that may significantly affect human environment. While not focused on air pollution as such, this arrangement clearly applies in the field of air pollution, and to the EPA, which is also the body that reviews the environmental impact statements of other federal agencies and recognizes and offers a repository of such statements.[28]

Some statutory provisions are not codified (or mentioned) in the USC, rendering them exceptionally fuzzy. The difficulty, first, is in the awareness that they exist at all; even when known, tracing them is no easy task. Riders in annual appropriations acts serve as prime examples. Recall that such riders are usually the outcome of Congressional opposition to the President's budgetary agenda, or the result of interest groups pressures that succeed in overtaking both branches.[29] Prohibiting expenditure in defined fields of action, such riders, strewn in their hundreds in annual appropriations acts, shape all regulatory terrains. Very few are cited or referenced in the USC; they are thus virtually inaccessible to the general public.[30] One such rider, discussed in Chapter 1, has

[26] Enacted as part of the Energy Policy Act 1992, coded as 42 USC Chapter 134, §§13571–74; Energy Policy Act 2005, coded as 42 USC Chapter 149, §§15904, 15971–72; Energy Independence and Security Act 2007, coded as 42 USC Chapter 152, §§17151–724, 17013. I set aside provisions coded in the same Title which require agencies and departments to take into account aspects of environmental air protection, or as in the case of the National Environmental Policy Act 1969 (NEPA), which requires all agencies (in US parlance, all bodies granted a regulatory authority, including government departments) to undertake an assessment of the environmental effects of their proposed actions.

[27] See eg the Toxic Substances Control Act 1976, codified as Title 15, Chapter 53 USC (§§2601–97); the Federal Insecticide, Fungicide, and Rodenticide Act, 7 USC 136–136y; the 'retrofit' program, concerned with devices to be installed in vehicles to improve their fuel economy (49 USC §32918, part of the Title on transportation; retrofit requirements for buses are coded in 42 USC §7554(d)); and provisions concerned with the generation of power, coded in 16 USC Chapter 12 (titled 'Federal Regulation and Development of Power').

[28] In doing so, the EPA relies on §309 of the CAA (42 USC §7609). For an overview see <https://www.epa.gov/nepa>.

[29] See ch 1.

[30] On this feature see eg Sandra Beth Zellmer, 'Sacrificing Legislative Integrity at the Altar of Appropriations Riders: A Constitutional Crisis' (1997) 21 Harv Envtl L Rev 457; Zachary S Price, 'Funding Restrictions and Separation of Powers' (2018) 71 Vanderbilt L Rev 357. For a stronger

consistently appeared in appropriation acts since 2010, and effectively constrain the promulgation or implementation of any regulation requiring the issuance of permits under title V of the Clean Air Act.[31]

The next layer of rules, executive orders, proclamations and other unilateral presidential measures, are not absent in this context, but most of these measures apply generally to all administrative bodies, hence also to those authorized to act in the field of air pollution. For example, Executive Order 12866 sets reporting and review duties on all agencies, and the 'two for one' Executive Order 13771 requires all agencies to repeal at least two regulations for each introduced. Both naturally impact on the activity of the EPA and of all other bodies regulating air quality.[32] Other executive orders that specifically address the environment likewise target the administration and agencies at large.[33] Measures addressing the EPA have been issued in memoranda, for example President Trump's memorandum of 12 April 2018, which directs the EPA to reduce 'unnecessary impediments to new manufacturing and business expansion essential for a growing economy' is but one example.[34] Some relevant executive orders are cited in the USC, but they are usually unavailable at that source.[35] Their impact, however, cannot be denied.

emphasis on the implications for Congress see eg Jack M Beermann, 'Congressional Administration' (2006) 43 San Diego L Rev 61; Richard J Lazarus, 'Congressional Descent: The Demise of Deliberative Democracy in Environmental Law' (2006) 94 Geo LJ 61; James Wallner, 'How to Spot Policy Riders in Appropriations Bills', 22 August 2018 <https://www.legbranch.org/2018-8-22-how-to-spot-policy-riders-in-appropriations-bills>. A search of the USCA on Westlaw found eighty-six citations of such riders (search term 'none of the funds made available', search of all USC titles, conducted 14 April 2020). For discussion and examples see ch 1 and below.

[31] Under this rider, '[n]otwithstanding any other provision of law, none of the funds made available in this Act or any other Act may be used to promulgate or implement any regulation requiring the issuance of permits under title V of the Clean Air Act (42 USC 7661 et seq) for carbon dioxide, nitrous oxide, water vapor, or methane emissions resulting from biological processes associated with livestock production'. For its inclusion in the 2020 Appropriations Act see Further Consolidated Appropriations Act 2020 §437.

[32] Executive Order 12866, *Regulatory Planning and Review*, 30 September 1993, 58 FR 51735 (see chs 1 and 4); Executive Order 13771, *Reducing Regulation and Controlling Regulatory Costs*, 30 January 2017, 82 FR 9339. For EPA information of its action in accordance with these orders see <https://www.epa.gov/laws-regulations/summary-executive-order-12866-regulatory-planning-and-review>; <https://www.epa.gov/laws-regulations/executive-order-13771-reducing-regulation-and-controlling-regulatory-costs>.

[33] See eg Executive Order 12088, *Federal Compliance with Pollution Control Standards*, 2 November 2010, 43 FR 47707; Executive Order 13432, *Cooperation Among Agencies in Protecting the Environm ent With Respect to Greenhouse Gas Emissions From Motor Vehicles, Nonroad Vehicles, and Nonroad Engines*, 14 May 2007, 72 FR 27717; Executive Order 13783, *Promoting Energy Independence and Economic Growth*, 28 March 2017, 82 FR 16093.

[34] Memorandum, *Promoting Domestic Manufacturing and Job Creation—Policies and Procedures Relating to Implementation of Air Quality Standards*, 83 FR 16,671 (12 April 2018) (see further ch 1). See also Memorandum, *Implementation of Revised Air Quality Standards for Ozone and Particulate Matter*, 62 FR 38421 (6 July 1997) (concerning EPA implementation of new standards 'approved' by the president).

[35] Measures directed at all agencies do not appear in each and every USC Title, hence not necessarily in Title 42 and other titles that contain air pollution provisions. Executive Order 12866 is mentioned or cited fourteen times across the USCA; cited in full once as a note to 5 USC §601 (definition of 'agency'),

b. US emergency law

Rules concerned with emergencies in general and with antiterrorism action are strewn across the system, in a manner similar to air-pollution law, but with the important addition of constitution-derived reliance.

Despite the absence of an explicit reference to emergencies in the Constitution, the constitution and constitutional doctrines play a much more central role in this context. Famous early examples, the 1793 neutrality proclamation and Executive Order No 1 of 1862 that established a Provisional Court functioning during the military occupation of Louisiana, did not cite any source of authority: neither the constitution nor any statute were mentioned.[36] A more direct link to the constitution is found in President Lincoln's famous justification for his suspension of the habeas corpus during the Civil War, and other acts made contrary to statute, in which he relied on his 'oath to preserve the constitution'.[37]

Since then, the Commander-in-Chief clause and the spirit of the constitution have supported arguments for presidential involvement, as in the case of the 'torture memo' of 1 August 2002. Signed by Jay Bybee, the Acting Assistant Attorney General at the Office of Legal Counsel, the memo, which supported and reflected the political *zeitgeist* at the time, contains a detailed analysis of the Commander-in-Chief clause as the source of the President's constitutional power to wage war, and inter alia to conduct extreme interrogation methods.[38]

other appearances are either mentioned in an executive order appended to sections, or mentioned in a research reference added by the editors. Executive Order 13771 is mentioned seven times, once in full in the same provision as above. Both memoranda cited above (n 34) are found in the USC, cited as full notes to 42 USC §7401 and §7407m respectively (searches via Westlaw, 14 April 2020).

[36] George Washington, *A Proclamation,* 22 April 1793, in James R Richardson (ed), *A Compilation of Messages and Papers of the President 1789–1897* (Government Printing Office 1896–99) Vol I, 156–57; Abraham Lincoln, *Establishing a Provisional Court in Louisiana,* 20 October 1862. Texts at <https://www.presidency.ucsb.edu/documents/proclamation-4-neutrality-the-united-states-the-war-involving-austria-prussia-sardinia<; <https://www.presidency.ucsb.edu/documents/executive-order-establishing-provisional-court-louisiana>. For further analysis see ch 4.

[37] Abraham Lincoln, Letter to Albert G Hodges, 4 April 1864 in Roy P Basler (ed), *Abraham Lincoln, The Collected Works* (Abraham Lincoln Association 1953–55) Vol VII 280.

[38] Memorandum for Alberto R Gonzales, Counsel to the President, Re: Standards of Conduct for Interrogation under 18 USC §§ 2340–2340A, 1 August 2002 <http://www.justice.gov/sites/default/files/olc/legacy/2010/08/05/memo-gonzales-aug2002.pdf>. Jay Bybee's memorandum cited several war-time judicial decisions and previous memos, finding the powers embedded in 'the text, structure and history of the Constitution ... the Commander-in-Chief power and the President's obligation to protect the nation imply the ancillary powers necessary to their successful exercise' (Part V, 37, 38). For an example of a similar, earlier memorandum which found support for action in Vietnam (written by William H Rehnquist, then Assistant Attorney General see *The President and War Power: South Vietnam and the Cambodian Sanctuaries*, Memorandum opinion for the Special Counsel to the President, 22 May 1970 <https://www.justice.gov/file/20826/download>. The 2004 memorandum that rescinded the torture memo refrained from commenting on the constitutional basis of action, noting that '[b]ecause the discussion in that memorandum concerning the President's Commander in Chief power and the potential defenses to liability was—and remains—unnecessary, it has been eliminated from the analysis that follows. Consideration of the bounds of any such authority would be inconsistent with the President's unequivocal directive that United States personnel not engage in torture'. *Definition of Torture Under 18 USC §§2340–2340A*, Memorandum opinion for the Deputy Attorney General, 30 December 2004, 28 Opinions of the Office of Legal Counsel 297, 298. See via <https://www.justice.

The ubiquitous pattern of reliance on the formula 'the Constitution and the laws of the United States' in executive orders and other unilateral presidential measures, discussed in Chapter 5, points to an equal proliferation of reliance on the constitution, if only as a token to ensure both the legality and the significance and weight of these measures.

In that chapter, I rejected the assumption that unilateral measures are either constitution-derived or made under statute: in fact, most carry a double provenance. According to an analysis of measures issued during the fiscal year 2019–2020, no less than 93% of the measures that contained rules or orders relied on this formula.[39] Executive Order 12333, a lengthy order issued in 1981 concerned with all organization and operational aspects of security intelligence, relies on an earlier version of the formula, and, as common, on a reference to a statute, and so have many others concerned with anti-terrorism measures and national security at large.[40]

The citation of 'the Constitution and the laws of the United States' in the recitals of almost all executive orders issued in past decades, even when made under statute, reflects the executive's reliance on a constitution that offers more than mere textual support. The identity of the Constitution as the centrepiece of the state, so central to US political culture, is not absent here.

As for statutes, the National Emergencies Act 1976 (NEA), together with the War Powers Resolution of 1973, were introduced to end the plurality of statutes that existed earlier. Yet complexity has re-emerged. A report analysing a compendium of emergency laws collected in 2013 found that there were no less than '123 statutory powers that may become available to the president when he declares a national emergency', and that '[a]n additional 13 statutory powers become available when a national emergency is declared by Congress'.[41]

gov/file/18791/download#:~:text=9%20Section%202340(1)%20defines,his%20custody%20or%20physical%20control>.

39 See ch 5.

40 *United States Intelligence Activities*, 4 December 1981, 46 FR 59941 (relying on 'the authority vested in me by the Constitution and the statutes of the United State of America, including the National Security Act of 1947'). See also eg Proclamation 9844, *Declaring a National Emergency Concerning the Southern Border of the United States*, 15 February 2019, 84 FR 4949 (President Trump's declaration of emergency, discussed in ch 5); Executive Order 12947, *Prohibiting Transactions With Terrorists Who Threaten To Disrupt the Middle East Peace Process*, 23 January 1995, 60 FR 5079; Executive Order 13886, *Modernizing Sanctions To Combat Terrorism*, 9 September 2019, 84 FR 48041.

41 Brennan Center of Justice, *A Guide to Emergency Powers and Their Use* (NYU School of Law, 5 December 2018) <https://www.brennancenter.org/analysis/emergency-powers>. See also Patrick Thronson, 'Compendium of Emergency Powers Statutes' <https://prospectusmjlr.files.wordpress.com/2013/10/national_emergency_powers.pdf>; See analysis in Jules Lobel, 'Emergency Power and the Decline of Liberalism' (1989) 98 Yale LJ 1385, 1412–21; Elizabeth Goitein, 'What the President Could Do If He Declares a State of Emergency', *The Atlantic*, January/February 2019 Issue, at https://www.theatlantic.com/magazine/archive/2019/01/presidential-emergency-powers/576418/ (noting that under a recent overview, 'thirty states of emergency are in effect today—several times more than when the [National Emergencies] act was passed'.

Still, attention is usually directed to Title 50, which carries the title 'War and National Defense'. Chapters 33, 34, 35 contain, inter alia, the War Powers Resolution, often cited as the formal source for the declaration of war; the NEA, designed to apply in situations that do not involve the deployment of military forces or the declaration of war; the extensively-used International Emergency Economic Powers Act (IEECPA); and several other statutes concerned with anti-terrorism measures.[42] These however are not the only relevant chapters contained in this Title.[43]

The next natural source to consider is part of Title 18 (coding criminal law and procedure); its Chapter 113B, entitled 'Terrorism' contains the Antiterrorism Act 1990 and its amendments, the best-known of which is the 2001 Uniting and Strengthening America by Providing Appropriate Tools Required to Intercept and Obstruct Terrorism (PATRIOT act). The chapter offers anti-terrorism measures ranging from the setting of criminal offences on action, support, and financial assistance to the prohibition of use of 'weapons of mass destruction', nuclear weapons, and missiles.[44] Title 10, concerned with the nation's armed forces, should not be sidestepped, and is further discussed below; other measures are strewn across various other Titles.[45] Searches for the entire framework are thus required even in a system that codes its Federal laws, and overlaps are not uncommon.[46]

Proof of this complexity can be found in recitals of executive orders. For example, Executive Order 13645 (2013), one in a series of executive orders setting sanctions on Iran, which lists no less than six statutory sources, in addition to the general formula of authorization:

> By the authority vested in me as President by the Constitution and the laws of the United States of America, including the International Emergency Economic Powers Act (50 U.S.C. 1701 et seq.) (IEEPA), the National Emergencies Act (50 U.S.C. 1601 et seq.), the Comprehensive Iran Sanctions, Accountability, and Divestment Act of 2010 (Public Law 111-195) (22 U.S.C. 8501 et seq.) (CISADA), the Iran Freedom and Counter Proliferation Act of 2012 (subtitle D of title VII

[42] See, respectively, 50 USC §§1543–45, §§1601–51, §§1701–708.

[43] See chs 44–47, concerned with various aspects of intelligence operations.

[44] 50 USC §§ 2331–39D.

[45] See inter alia Title 6, dedicated to domestic security. The International Money Laundering Abatement and Financial Anti-Terrorism Act of 2001, part of the PATRIOT act, is slotted into Title 31, Money and Finance (31 USC §§ 5311–32). Some statutes are inserted as a note to a coded statute, as in the case of the originally named Iran and Libya Sanctions Act 1996 (50 USC §1701 note).

[46] For example, almost all executive orders that applied the NEA involved the setting of economic sanctions and relied on both the NEA and the IEECPA; and the Iran and Libya Sanctions Act 1996, noted above, operates parallel to the IEEPCA (renamed in 2006 as the Iran Sanctions Act, the 1996 Act includes a sunset clause, last extended in 2016 for ten years). On one example of an overlap see Andru E Wall, 'Demystifying the Title 10-Title 50 Debate: Distinguishing Military Operations, Intelligence Activities & Covert Action' (2011) 3 Harv Nat'l Sec J 85.

> of Public Law 112-239) (22 U.S.C. 8801 et seq.) (IFCA), section 212(f) of the Immigration and Nationality Act of 1952 (8 U.S.C. 1182(f)), and section 301 of title 3, United States Code . . .[47]

As in the context of air pollution, some measures find no reference in the USC, and thus contribute to the fuzziness. Setting aside riders in appropriations acts that direct policy, which are just as common in this context, I turn to signing statements, again, an uncoded measure that may impact on the design and implementation of policy.[48]

In 1991, during the presidency of George Bush and under a strong Democratic majority, Congress enacted the Intelligence Authorization Act, an act designed not only to appropriate funds to intelligence activities of defined bodies, but also to reform several aspects of employment, reimbursement, types of action, and, in a special title, to transform and tighten Congress oversight of intelligence activities. The latter issue, further discussed below, was deemed central to the tension between the executive and legislative branches, in light of the extent of government reliance on covert, undisclosed activities outside of the US. The amended legislation, in a title headed 'Oversight of Intelligence Activities', contained a definition of the term 'covert action', which was supplemented not only by a list of actions to be excluded, but also with a prohibition of the use of covert activities intended to influence domestic politics, opinion, or media.[49] Most of this was not to the taste of the serving President. Signing the act into force, the President issued a signing statement, which, alongside some positive comments about Congress's readiness to change some features of the law, expressed concerns regarding two of its elements, the overly-broad requirements of disclosure and the definition of 'covert action'. Regarding the first element, the President stated that

> [t]hese provisions cannot be construed to detract from the President's constitutional authority to withhold information the disclosure of which could significantly impair foreign relations, the national security, the deliberative processes of the Executive, or the performance of the Executive's constitutional duties'.

47 For reliance on multiple sources of power as a form of executive-generated fuzziness see ch 5.

48 On signing statements see ch 4.

49 The Intelligence Authorization Act, Fiscal Year 1991, PL 102–88, 105 Stat 429. Inter alia, §601 amended the National Security Act 1947, by the addition of a new §503. In that section, §503(e) defined 'covert action', as used in that title, as 'an activity or activities of the United States Government to influence political, economic, or military conditions abroad, where it is intended that the role of the United States Government will not be apparent or acknowledged publicly'; to this, §503(f) prescribes that '[n]o covert action may be conducted which is intended to influence United States political processes, public opinion, policies or media'. Currently coded as 50 USC §3093(e), this provision has not been amended since its introduction.

As for the second element, the President further declared:

> I believe that the Act's definition of "covert action" is unnecessary. In determining whether particular military activities constitute covert actions, I shall continue to bear in mind the historic missions of the Armed Forces to protect the United States and its interests, influence foreign capabilities and intentions, and conduct activities preparatory to the execution of operations.[50]

This signing statement, as others, has not been appended to the USC, nor can it be found in an official publication.[51] Indeed, their legal force is dubious; still, such declarations of intent carry the potential for subsequent forms of creative compliance, if not downright non-implementation.

D. The Fuzzy Consequences of Patchworking

A plurality of rules that rely on several distinct sources contributes to fuzziness under three patterns: redundancy/complexity, contradiction, and under-funding/denial of funding.

1. Redundancy/Complexity

Multiple rules need not directly contradict each other to render the arrangement fuzzy. When two arrangements, different in their content or in their grantee of powers, potentially apply, choice of the law is open to the holders of authority. Three examples suffice to represent this common state of affairs.

In her examination of the 'piled up' Turkish emergency legislation, Questiaux noted that 'because of the growing complexity of this overlapping legislation, it has been extremely difficult in practice to contest the legality or constitutionality, as may be the case, of the state of emergency'.[52] Indeed, the existence of several sources of action renders an arrangement difficult to grasp and necessitates trawling through the entire legal system. Even reliance on experts who may be able

[50] George Bush, *Statement on Signing the Intelligence Authorization Act, Fiscal Year 1991*, 14 August 1991, <https://www.presidency.ucsb.edu/documents/statement-signing-the-intelligence-authorization-act-fiscal-year-1991>.

[51] Signing statements can be found online on the White House website, but currently, only measures issued by President Trump are easily accessible. Others are located online in presidential library archives managed by the White House. For this signing statement see <https://bush41library.tamu.edu/archives/public-papers/3302>. In addition to collections of presidential papers, the best source for tracing signing statements is the series of publications collecting presidential papers and the American Presidency Project website, the research and archive website managed at UC Santa Barbara. See link at n 50.

[52] Questiaux (n 1) 29.

to decipher the arrangement cannot fully dispel the fuzziness, as, using patchwork mechanisms, legislators may always add another source of power to their quiver, enhancing the complexity of an arrangement.

Moving to US national security and anti-terrorism law, the oft-called 'Title 10-Title 50 debate' in the US is concerned with the sometimes overlapping powers of the military and the CIA to initiate covert action. Title 10, dedicated to the military, organizes the military under the direction of the Secretary of Defense, and inter alia authorizes the department to collect intelligence and operate on its basis. Parts of Title 50 regulate the intelligence community, notably the CIA, independently established by statute and further regulated under a series of executive orders. In this context, debates have arisen about the possible overlap, if not possible clash, between the action of the two bodies. Most of the literature has observed that at least since 9/11, co-operation and co-ordination have coloured most of these operations.[53] Even if this is so (some operations may have remained truly covert), the potential of such conflicts remains.

Beyond the question of the roles of each of these two security organizations, another aspect of the same affair remains unresolved: that of congressional oversight. For some, the central reason for the legislation of some of these rules was the absence of presidential involvement of Congress during the conduct of some operations, such as interventions in Chile and Angola and the Iran-Contra Scandal.[54] The legislation sets notification and reporting requirements to Congressional Committees, setting distinct notification standards and processes which vary across type of action. Under the current set-up, military activity requires no prior notification to Congress, while intelligence community action requires such notice; oversight of intelligence activities is granted to the House Permanent Select Committee on Intelligence and to the United States Senate Select Committee on Intelligence, while military activity is within the remit of the Armed Services Committees of the House of Representatives and the Senate.[55] Even under the assumption that absolute accord between security bodies exists, and that the turf wars within both Houses of Congress are the main reason for the existence of the debate, such conflicts themselves represent the difficulties arising from the existence of parallel and overlapping arrangements. Accountability and oversight processes are likely to be weakened under such complex structures.

The second example represents a structural element evident in both US and UK air pollution regulation. Both regulatory systems are based on a high level of

[53] See Andru E Wall, 'Demystifying the Title 10-Title 50 Debate: Distinguishing Military Operations, Intelligence Activities & Covert Action' (2011) 3 Harv Nat'l Sec J 85; Robert Chesney, 'Military-Intelligence Convergence and the Law of the Title 10/Title 50 Debate' (2012) 5 J Nat'l Security L and Policy 539.

[54] See William J Daugherty, 'Approval and Review of Covert Action Programs Since Reagan' (2004) 17 Int'l J Intelligence and Counter Intelligence 62; Wall (n 53).

[55] Wall (n 53) 101–106. See also Michael E De Vine, *Covert Action and Clandestine Activities of the Intelligence Community: Framework for Congressional Oversight In Brief*, CRS Report R45196 (updated 9 August 2019, with references to two additional reports on the matter).

involvement of local authorities (states in the US, local authorities in the UK) in rulemaking and, more so, in implementation and enforcement. The regionalization of the field may be a welcome feature, as locations differ in their degrees of pollution-inducing activity, population size, geography, and climate, all of which necessarily shape local needs and problems. Still, divergence not only leads to the existence of multiple, possibly conflicting sets of rules, an especially problematic outcome in a field marked by cross-border flow; it offers more potential for local interest groups who may capture the rule-makers and influence local implementation to effectively thwart the efforts to rein pollution; and its success also depends on the funds each locality allocates to this field.

In the US, the sharing of responsibilities between Federal and state authorities, discussed in Chapter 6, is one of the basic elements of many regulatory structures. The eternal tension between state and federal powers is played here, and is coloured by special characteristics, ranging from the interstate element of air-flow, diverging conditions, cultures and attitudes, and sheer politics. Hence, the clean air sector is a perfect example for the relegation of some powers to the states.

It would however be more instructive to consider this element in the UK, which is smaller in size and population, less diverse although not homogenous, and is a unitary rather than a federal system. Setting history aside and focusing on the current framework, the system is a web of authorities that fuzzily links both layers of government, the national and the local, in a web of dispersed, sometimes overlapping frameworks. Suffice here to consider the web created by the four central statutes concerned with the regulation of air pollution.[56]

First, the Environmental Protection Act 1990 regulates the grant of authorizations to operate designate processes and grants enforcement powers. Beyond the powers to issue regulations in both fields of action, granted to the Secretary of State, the title of Part I, 'Integrated Pollution Control and Air Pollution Control by Local Authorities', reflects the mix of powers and the complex set-up of operations in the field. Under the designation of substances and processes to be regulated, made by the Secretary of State, local authorities seem to have been granted the primary authority to implement the rules applying to such designated activities, although the Secretary of State may transfer this power to the Environment Agency; all regulatory bodies, national and local, are required to give effect to issued regulations and directions; authorizations (permits) to perform such designated processes can be given by both national and local authorities, as are the serving of enforcement and prohibition notices, although the Secretary of State may issue directions to other bodies issuing such notices; and the Secretary of State is granted supervisory powers, through her power to require information from all involved bodies.[57]

[56] This overview focuses on the powers and responsibilities of local authorities; arrangements designed for Greater London and regional councils (both county councils and district councils) are excluded.

[57] Environmental Protection Act 1990 Part I, §§2, 4, 6, 13, 14, 19.

Thus, almost all powers under this Part are granted both to national and local 'enforcement agencies', as defined in the Act.[58] Part III, which introduces a detailed regime of statutory nuisances that explicitly include the discharge of smoke and other emissions, authorizes local authorities to serve abatement notices requiring the abatement of the nuisance; failure to remove the nuisance, which is a criminal offence, may lead to the institutions of summary proceedings against the person responsible for the nuisance.[59] In this context, the formal involvement of the government department is minimal, limited only to a requirement for the consent of the Secretary of State before the institution of proceedings concerned with certain nuisances, including smoke emitted from premises.[60]

Under the Clean Air Act 1993, mainly concerned with smoke emissions, local authorities may declare an area a 'smoke control area'; orders thus issued may limit or prohibit emissions. The process of pre-publication and public hearing does not include a requirement to consult or otherwise liaise with the central government. The Secretary of State is granted supervisory powers that can lead to the instatement of an order when the local authority fails to submit a satisfactory proposal and is found to be in default. In another part of this Act, local authorities are authorized to investigate air pollution and to collect local information, as prescribed by regulations made by the Secretary of State, which may direct local authorities to install required devices and to forward it to the government department.[61]

Next, the Environment Act 1995 established the Environment Agency (and its Scottish sibling agency), to which a long list of functions was transferred; the Secretary of State retains the power to make high policy, including, in the context of air pollution, a National Air Quality Strategy that is to direct the agencies in their control of that form of pollution. As in the earlier legislation, powers granted to local authorities are not absent. They are required to conduct reviews, designate air quality management areas, and issue orders requiring the making of assessments of air quality and detailed plans to remedy the situation.[62] However, in comparison to the earlier discussed statutes, their subjection to the national framework is tighter. Local authorities are required to consult with a large number of agencies and bodies, headed by the Secretary of State, prior to any action; in addition to her powers to make regulations, the Secretary of State may conduct independent reviews and give directions to local authorities considered to be failing in their achievements, and to issue general guidance to local authorities.[63]

The last full statute relevant to air pollution, the Pollution Prevention and Control Act 1999, was intended to implement the EU Council Directive carrying

58 ibid §1(7). For the repeal of Part I that has not entered into force see below and ch 7.
59 ibid §§79–83.
60 ibid §79(10).
61 Clean Air Act 1993, §18 and Schedule 1; §19; Part V, respectively.
62 The Environment Act 1995, §§82, 83, 84.
63 ibid §§ 87, 85, 88, respectively.

the same title, and contains no authorization to local bodies. Its main impact in this context was the repeal of Part I of the Environmental Protection Act 1990, which has not entered into force. Thus, the provisions in Part I, discussed above, remain in force, at least for the time being, a state of affairs that further obfuscates the structure of interaction between national and local authorities.[64]

As above, the adoption of localized regulation may be justified by geographic divergence. Whether this was the main motive for such an adoption—at least one commentator has identified this tendency as a case of 'passing the buck' of responsibility to the local level—or a true reflection of the understanding of the 'local nature of the problem', as stated in a recent Air Quality Plan, is a matter for further debate.[65] The formal structure, as depicted here, is nevertheless a mix of overlapping provisions and responsibilities that is extremely difficult to decipher. And this, of course, is merely the formal set of provisions; some aspects of the operation of these rules and their implementation are discussed in Chapter 8.

2. Contradiction

Contradiction between two provisions can also lead to a situation in which a regulated entity is unable to follow both. This is not a rare occurrence.[66] In the field of air pollution, consider the following contradiction between powers granted to the US Secretary of Energy and to the EPA, a case of conflicting laws that, when applied, essentially resulted in power plants' violation of one of these laws.

Under the Federal Power Act (FPA), the Secretary of Energy is authorized to issue special orders to power plants during emergencies, defined and applied broadly to include events of shortage of supply.[67] This provision was applied several times during crises resulting from natural disasters or other circumstances deemed suitable. In such cases, power plants were ordered to connect to other suppliers

64 See ch 8.

65 See Katie Nield, 'Clean Air: Our Right But Whose Responsibility?' (2018) J Planning & Environmental L 40; Department for Environment, Food, and Rural Affairs, Department of Transportation, 'UK Plan for Tackling Roadside Nitrogen Dioxide Concentrations: An Overview', 7 July 2017.

66 For an analysis in the general context of environmental law see Mary Jane Angelo, 'Discordant Environmental Laws: Using Statutory Flexibility and Multi-Objective Optimization to Reconcile Conflicting Laws' (2019) Stan Environmental LJ 165.

67 Federal Power Act 1920 §202(c), 16 USC §824a(c), as amended in 1953 (49 Stat 848). Under this provision, '[d]uring the continuance of any war in which the United States is engaged, or whenever the Commission determines that an emergency exists by reason of a sudden increase in the demand for electric energy, or a shortage of electric energy or of facilities for the generation or transmission of electric energy, or of fuel or water for generating facilities, or other causes, the Commission shall have authority . . . to require by order such temporary connections of facilities and such generation, delivery, interchange, or transmission of electric energy as in its judgment will best meet the emergency and serve the public interest . . .'. This power was transferred from the Federal Power Commission to the Secretary of Energy and DOE by the Department of Energy Organization Act 1977 §301(b), coded as 42 USC §7151(b).

of power, or to continue their operation or to operate units to answer reliability needs.[68]

Concurrently, the EPA and state agencies are broadly empowered to regulate power plants, by setting national standards of air quality (NAAQS), and setting sanctions when the state standards that follow them and are approved by the EPA are not met.[69] A situation in which a DOE emergency requirement to operate a station that was ordered to shut its premises due to non-attainment of clean air rules is not only a possibility. Two such reported cases involved the expenditure of sums by the operator that faced conflicting rules; in one of them, the station, which continued to operate under a DOE order, payed a fine set by the state air quality agency for exceeding the limit of emissions.[70]

This particular conflict was resolved by a statutory amendment that granted ascendancy to the DOE order. An amendment to the provision authorizing the DOE to act during emergencies was inserted in the Fixing America's Surface Transportation Act 2015, an omnibus statute providing funding for transportation infrastructure projects, supplemented by a large number of statutory amendments and reforms, many of which were directly linked with transportation issues. Setting the rules applying in cases of irresolvable conflict, the provision now stipulates that in cases of irresolvable conflict, any action that leads to noncompliance with other environmental rules will not be considered a violation, or subject the noncompliant to a civil or other suit. To date, the DOE has reported two instances of issuance of such an emergency order, both in 2017, one of them extended to 2019.[71]

Of course, contradictions and conflicts are part of any complex set of rules. Indeed, contradictions can be found within a single statute.[72] However, the larger the number of parallel or overlapping statutes, the higher the risk of such conflicts.

[68] For lists of events in which this power was used see *DOE's Use of Federal Power Act Emergency Authority* <https://www.energy.gov/oe/services/electricity-policy-coordination-and-implementation/other-regulatory-efforts/does-use>.

[69] See text to n 24 and 42 USC §7409.

[70] On this 2007 affair, involving the operation of the Potomac River Generating Station, and on the conflict between these two frameworks, see Michael Gergen and others, 'Walking the Line Between the Clean Air Act and the Federal Power Act: Balancing Emission Reductions and Bulk Power Reliability' (2012) 25(1) Elec Journal 16, 20–21. In the second affair, the result of a clash between a DOE order to answer the California energy crisis of 2000 and permit violations, FERC issued a clarification that reminded generators that they could seek a court declaratory order that allowed such infraction, after one generator settled (at a significant cost) a citizen suit filed against it. See ibid 21.

[71] Fixing America's Surface Transportation Act 2015 (PL 114–194) §61002 (16 USC §824a(c)). Under the amendment, in cases of irresolvable conflict, any action that leads to noncompliance with other environmental rules will not be considered a violation, or subject the noncompliant to 'any requirement, civil of criminal liability, or a citizen suit under such environmental law or regulation'. The force of such an order is limited to ninety days, but it can be reissued. See *DOE's Use of Federal Power Act Emergency Authority* (n 68).

[72] One extreme example was the result of the insertion of two opposing amendments to the CAA in 1990, an error that occurred when each House of Congress proposed a different version to the amended §111(d) of the Act concerned with the regulation of new stationary sources. Under a simple interpretation of both, the House's version, coded into the USC as 42 USC §7411(d), pollution generated by hazardous pollutants not listed under the concurrently amended §112 (42 USC §7412) could not be EPA

3. Under-Funding/Denial of Funding

Changes in government funding in a regulatory field can have an important impact on regulatory performance. Some decisions to under-fund or to remove funding are made by executives in their decisions to allocate existing funds; here, attention is directed to under-funding effected by statute.

In the context of the two case-studies discussed in the book, the risk of under-funding of emergency law is less of a concern when compared to the state of affairs in the field of air pollution, although some programs designed to address certain emergency concerns, even terrorism, may suffer from the same malaise.[73]

Several US acts contain funding provisions that list annual expenditures for several years;[74] following the termination of the stated periods, continued funding relies on the general funds available to the department or agency, or in specific appropriations specifying the activity to be funded. In other statutes, expenditure required to properly implement a statute is dependent on general funds since inceptions. In both cases, annual appropriations acts remain, then, the central source of funding, adding, as mentioned above, another layer to the patchwork of rules.

The most ubiquitous statutory form of under-funding or downright prohibition of action is only marginally discussed. Any assessment of patchworked legislation must include riders. Riders in appropriations acts which open with the words 'none of the funds made available in this Act', sometimes followed by an expansion by reference to 'any other act', discussed above and in previous chapters, effectively remove the possibility of the use of funds aimed at achieving the policy goal addressed by the rider. These riders have traditionally shaped government policies,

regulated, while the Senate's version seemingly allowed such regulation. The EPA changed its attitude towards this initially proclaimed ambiguity, arguing it should be interpreted as allowing regulation. The contradiction featured, inter alia, in the political and legal debate over the constitutionality of President Obama's Clean Power Plan, aimed at curbing climate change. Challenged in court, the challenge was rendered moot after the APA repeal of the Plan in 2019, following President Trump's policy reversal. On the affair see eg Lesley S Cruikshank, 'The "Drafting Error" That Could Derail the Clean Power Plan' (2016) 67 Alabama L Rev 887.

[73] In today's climate, evidence for cuts in this field is sparse. While not usually discussed in such a context, see eg reports on the funding cuts of the Department of Homeland Security (DHS) which, it is argued, have negatively impacted on action against 'domestic terrorism'. See Laura Strickler, Julia Ainsley, and Ken Dilanian, '"We Have a Problem": Federal Agencies Scramble to Fight Domestic Terror with Limited Resources', NBC News, 6 August 2019 <https://www.nbcnews.com/politics/national-security/we-have-problem-federal-agencies-scramble-fight-domestic-terror-limited-n1039441> (domestic terrorism is largely defined by the government as 'acts motivated not by foreign ideologies, like Islamic extremism, but US-based ideologies, like white supremacy' (ibid). This case of under-funding is therefore concerned with serious domestic crime rather than terrorism as such).

[74] See eg, the Clean Air Act, 42 USC §7626 (under the current text, authorization 'to carry out this chapter such sums as may be necessary' was granted for seven fiscal years commencing in November 1990); Energy Policy Act (n 26) §13574(c) (clean air coal program, awards to fund plants that inter alia deploy advanced air pollution control equipment and processes under §13572(a)(2), appropriations for years 2007–11); Energy Independence and Security Act (n 26) §17011(i) (ATVM program, appropriations for years 2008–12).

despite Senate Rule XVI, which constrains the use of riders in appropriations bills to transform legislation or its application.[75] Inserted in annual appropriations acts, it would seem that the force of appropriations acts' riders is limited to the fiscal year they are linked with. Some of these riders do also refer to future legislation that may follow the same pattern,[76] but more troubling are serial riders, introduced and reintroduced for years or decades. Such riders effectively allow the adoption of a continuing policy that is not backed by a general statute.

Consider but a few examples. One of the hundreds of provisions constituting the Consolidated Appropriations Act of 2020, repeats a provision included in previous Appropriations Acts at least since 2000. Under the title 'Prohibition on Assistance to Governments Supporting International Terrorism', the impact of the following provision extends well beyond the authorization of expenditure:

> None of the funds appropriated or otherwise made available under titles III through VI of this Act may be made available to any foreign government which provides lethal military equipment to a country the government of which the Secretary of State has determined supports international terrorism for purposes of section 6(j) of the Export Administration Act of 1979 as continued in effect pursuant to the International Emergency Economic Powers Act.[77]

As one example of an order applying directly to the EPA, consider the following provision, part of most appropriation acts since 2010:

[75] Senate Rule XIV, paragraph 2, stipulates: 'The Committee on Appropriations shall not report an appropriation bill containing amendments to such bill proposing new or general legislation or any restriction on the expenditure of the funds appropriated which proposes a limitation not authorized by law if such restriction is to take effect or cease to be effective upon the happening of a contingency, and if an appropriation bill is reported to the Senate containing amendments to such bill proposing new or general legislation or any such restriction, a point of order may be made against the bill, and if the point is sustained, the bill shall be recommitted to the Committee on Appropriations', via <https://www.rules.senate.gov/rules-of-the-senate>.

[76] See, for example, riders concerned with the Chemical and Biological Warfare Program, prohibiting funds for the transportation of lethal agents and for their production without Presidential certification. Parts of appropriations acts (Armed Forces Appropriations Authorization Act 1970, PL 91–121, §409(b), 409(c); Department of Defense Appropriation Authorization Act 1976, PL 94–106 §818; Department of Defense Authorization Act 1984, PL 98–94 §618) contain a clause such as 'none of the funds authorized to be appropriated under this Act or any other Act'. The reference to 'any other act' essentially introduces an authority to continue adopting the same policy, albeit in future legislation.

[77] Further Consolidated Appropriations Act, 2020 §7021(a)(1). The provision maintains a detailed arrangement that prohibits such assistance, including an authorization to furnish such assistance if the President 'determines that to do so is important to the national interest of the United States'. Its similes can be found in all accessible appropriation acts at least since 2000. For just a few of these, see the Consolidated Appropriations Acts of 2014 to 2019, sharing the identical text and numbering (§7021). A slightly different version appears in appropriations acts enacted during the first decade of the twentieth century. Designed to render this prohibition permanent, the provision was part of the Department of State, Foreign Operations, and Related Programs Permanent General Provisions Bill, 2019, §9, which did not reach fruition. Introduced and passed in the Senate in 2019, and referred to the Committee on Foreign Relations, its future is dubious; its appearance in the 2020 Further Consolidated Appropriations Act, enacted five months later, may have already signalled its demise.

> [n]otwithstanding any other provision of law, none of the funds made available in this Act or any other Act may be used to promulgate or implement any regulation requiring the issuance of permits under title V of the Clean Air Act (42 U.S.C. 7661 et seq) for carbon dioxide, nitrous oxide, water vapor, or methane emissions resulting from biological processes associated with livestock production.[78]

Some of these riders explicitly state that the action curbed is not to be applied, de facto repealing a rule promulgated by an agency, as in this rider, which is part of the appropriations acts for the fiscal years 2018, 2019, and 2020:

> None of the funds made available in this Act may be used to implement or enforce the regulation issued on March 21, 2011 at 40 CFR part 60 subparts CCCC and DDDD with respect to units in the State of Alaska that are defined as 'small, remote incinerator' units in those regulations and, until a subsequent regulation is issued, the Administrator shall implement the law and regulations in effect prior to such date.[79]

Other riders are not concerned with the action of a single agency, and apply across the administration. Consider the case of the following rider, found in all Appropriations Acts since 2012:

> None of the funds made available under this Act may be used to enter into a contract, memorandum of understanding, or cooperative agreement with, make a grant to, or provide a loan or loan guarantee to any corporation that was convicted (or had an officer or agent of such corporation acting on behalf of the corporation convicted) of a felony criminal violation under any Federal law within the preceding 24 months, where the awarding agency is aware of the conviction, unless a Federal agency has considered suspension or debarment of the corporation and has made a determination that this further action is not necessary to protect the interests of the Government.[80]

[78] See eg Further Consolidated Appropriations Act 2020 §437, serially included in previous appropriations acts. For a 2010 report on the first insertion of this rider see Robin Bravender, 'House and Senate Prevent "Cow Tax"', Scientific American, 28 October 2009 <https://www.scientificamerican.com/article/cow-tax-epa-clean-air-policy-methane-emissions/>.

[79] See eg Further Consolidated Appropriations Act 2020 §441. The most recent version of these regulations, included in 40 CFR Part 60, is *Standards of Performance for New Stationary Sources and Emission Guidelines for Existing Sources: Commercial and Industrial Solid Waste Incineration Units; Technical Amendments*, 84 FR 15846.

[80] Financial Services and General Government Appropriations Act 2020, in Consolidated Appropriations Act 2020, Division C §745. For 2012 see Consolidated Appropriations Act 2012 §8125.

This rider sets a substantive limitation on the operation of all the loan and support programs in all fields, including air pollution, either under the Energy Independence and Security Act 2007 or otherwise.[81]

Choosing the insertion of riders into appropriations acts to eject a certain activity rather than initiating an amendment of the statute may be the outcome of a conscious decision to 'test' such a removal for the duration of the relatively short period of a single fiscal year. However, the common reliance on serial riders challenges the force of this motive. In Chapter 9, I analyse the political economy of fuzziness, or the utilities of choosing fuzziness over clarity. This context is more than a typical example. Policy decisions that practically exempt livestock emissions and small Alaskan incinerators from regulatory oversight and enforcement were the outcome of sectorial political pressure;[82] inserting them in an appropriations act enabled their passage with limited public attention, and has virtually ensured that they would escape the attention of opposing politicians, interest groups, and market competitors in the political flurry of the passage of an annual appropriations act.

Generally unpublished and undisclosed, an exception can be found in the EPA's notification that it does not implement regulations concerned with mandatory reporting of manure management, a source of greenhouse gases, 'using funds provided in its appropriations due to Congressional restriction prohibiting the expenditure of funds for this purpose'—a reference to another rider that prohibits funding of programs setting mandatory reporting of greenhouse gas emissions from manure management systems.[83]

[81] For the 2007 Act see n 26.

[82] The political clout of the meat-producers' lobbies is a well-known feature of US politics: see eg Steve Johnson, 'The Politics of Meat' (undated) <https://www.pbs.org/wgbh/pages/frontline/shows/meat/politics/>; Debra L Donahue, 'Livestock Production, Climate Change, and Human Health: Closing the Awareness Gap' (2015) 45 Environmental L Reporter 11112. In the context of the small Alaskan incinerators, protected from regulation since 2018, the Alaska Gas and Oil Association and the Alaska Miners Association, as well as Alaskan Senator Lisa Murkowski, serving as Senator since 2002, were among those which launched a campaign at the time of the proposed EPA rule concerned with waste removal incinerators, arguing inter alia that no sufficient data support the application of the rule, and that the criterion of road distance, which determined inclusion, was unsuitable in a state in which many of these incinerators were not accessible by road. On the publication of the final rule, Senator Murkowski, chair of the Senate Committee on Energy and Natural Resources and of the Senate Interior Appropriations Committee, publicly expressed 'extreme disappointment'. Ultimate success of this campaign is now part of at least three appropriations acts. For some of the correspondence and public announcements see Alaska Oil and Gas Association, Alaska Miners Association, *Comments on EPA Proposed Rule; Reconsideration of Final Rule—Commercial and Industrial Solid Waste Incineration Units: Reconsideration and Proposed Amendments; Non-Hazardous Secondary Materials That Are Solid Waste—Docket ID No EPA-HQ-OAR-2003-0119*, a petition for consideration sent to the EPA, 12 October 2012 <https://www.aoga.org/sites/default/files/news/10-12-12-aoga-ama-comments-on-ciswi-sri-final.pdf>; Press Release, *New EPA Rule Dismantles Waste Disposal in Remote Areas of Alaska*, 16 December 2016, <https://www.murkowski.senate.gov/press/release/new-epa-rule-dismantles-waste-disposal-in-remote-areas-of-alaska_->.

[83] For examples of this serial rider see Appropriations Act 2010 §425, Further Appropriations Act 2020 §438. For the EPA information see <https://www.epa.gov/ghgreporting/subpart-jj-manure-management>. Although the reporting program is up and running, the EPA has never operated its

Most riders are virtually inaccessible to the general public. A search of the USCA found eighty-six citations of such riders. None of the riders cited above were found.[84]

E. Concluding Remarks

This chapter has traced the extremely elaborate patchworked structure of both fields studied in this book. The two patterns of patchworking—piling-up and dispersion—feature prominently in both the UK and the US. Despite some attempts at streamlining the law, notably in the case of the introduction of the War Ppowers Resolution discussed above, patchworking remains the governing pattern, even in that case. More generally, overlap is not uncommon, and even in the US, in which Federal law is coded in the USC, no single title contains the entirety of the law in a defined field of government action.

Both forms of patchwork legislation are generally unavoidable. Patchworking offers legislators the expediency of passing laws without recourse to the costly process of the careful re-organization of the law. This practice enables governments, intent on acting under law, to retain a choice between multiple options. Yet in such cases, no easy access to the law is available, and the ability to plan ahead is severely impaired. Patchworking, then, enhances the executive's freedom to act within formal legality while lessening the hold of accessibility—essential features of the rule of law, compromised by this form of fuzziness.

A full analysis of the impact of patchworking requires evidence of real-life reliance on the fragmented and complex available frameworks that have contributed to the emergence of results which are inconsistent, bordering on the illegal, or otherwise problematic to the proper running of government. Some hints for such reliance can be found in the chapter. However, this chapter was mainly targeted at finding the various ways in which patchworking is found in public law. The next chapter, concerned with implementation, offers further attention to this aspect; in the interests of economy, that is, length, further impact analysis is relegated to future study.

manure reporting program (confirmed by email to author, EPA Greenhouse Gas Reporting Program Help Desk, 1 May 2019). On the EPA admission that it no longer applies the arrangement see ch 8.

[84] Search of the USCA on Westlaw (search term: 'none of the funds made available') conducted 14 April 2020.

8

Executive-Generated Fuzziness

On the Spectrum of (Non)-Implementation

A. **Introduction** 223
B. **From Informal Enforcement to Creative Compliance** 225
  1. Informal Enforcement 226
    a. General 226
    b. Example: EPA's Supplemental Environmental Projects (SEPs) 228
  2. Creative Compliance 232
    a. General 232
    b. Examples 233
      (1) EPA's first two decades 233
      (2) Funding the US-Mexico wall 235
C. **'Pastiche' Law** 239
  1. General 239
  2. Examples 240
    a. Under- or never-implemented statutes 240
    b. 'Floating' statutes 242
    c. Under-funded law 247
D. **Fuzzy Implementation: The Prices Paid** 249
E. **Concluding Remarks** 251

A. Introduction

The previous chapters have shown that various forms of law, generated by the constitution and the legislature, open a menu of possibilities that can be picked up by executives, enabling them to act within law but without being subjected to its constraining elements. This chapter is dedicated to analyses of examples of executive-generated fuzziness in the context of implementation. I offer examples of the ways executives can *create* further nodes of fuzziness, by crafting the implementation of the law, be it fuzzy or relatively clear, in ways that further fuzzy-up the law.

As in the previous chapter, this chapter is designed to offer an analysis of examples selected from the list of fuzzy nodes briefly discussed in Chapter 3. Practices generated by the executive which do not feature in this chapter include patchworking that emerges from government addition of schemes and frameworks which operate parallel to existing legislation, relying, rather, on statute, on constitutional sources such as the British prerogative, or the US Constitution. Another form of executive-generated fuzziness, the making of regulations and other types of secondary legislation that formally rely on multiple sources, is similarly set aside in this Chapter. Likewise, only some of the aspects of enforcement are discussed

A Theory of the Executive Branch. Margit Cohn, Oxford University Press (2021). © Margit Cohn.
DOI: 10.1093/oso/9780198821984.003.0009

here; those not considered are however mentioned in the following general overview of enforcement.[1]

Under the classical vision of executive action, already sufficiently battered in this book, implementation and enforcement are straightforward processes, easily apprehended processes that follow the legislative mandate and are applied by authorized regulators. The well-developed body of research on the gap between law-on-the-books and law-in-action overviewed in this chapter more than challenges this vision. Either as proof of government failure, or, conversely, as an indication of well-thought-out responsive action aimed to achieve optimal results, all action located in this gap is fuzzy. Linked with this rich body of research, I discuss three practices that challenge the classical understanding of the nature of implementation. The focus here is, then, on the behaviour of the executive and the ways it applies a power granted to it in ways that frustrate the law without moving into the sphere of illegality.

First, it should be noted that I set aside the discussion of selective enforcement, as far as this practice is inextricably linked with improper motives such as discrimination.[2] Such a practice is but one case of a broader mode of enforcement, which is essentially partly applied.[3] Partial, incomplete enforcement is addressed here only when it contributes to or represents the three types this chapter is concerned with.

The first of these types of fuzziness is found when enforcers employ informal modes of interaction with violators, chosen as first steps in an escalating scale of enforcement. Sometimes considered as 'responsive', or at least enforcement policies that are intentionally aimed at the maximization of outcomes, when these practices are not sanctioned by law, fuzziness emerges.[4]

Under the second practice, labelled 'creative compliance', an executive body charged with implementation manipulates the legal framework. This state of affairs may occur when regulators are faced by an over-harsh legislative framework, introduced by an over-zealous legislature that wishes to convey a political message and is less concerned with actual implementation, or in cases in which the regulators oppose the introduced legislation. In such cases, regulators may interpret the framework in ways that do not conform with the letter of the law, but can be accommodated as not illegal.

[1] On these constitution-derived powers see ch 4; for a discussion of patchworking see ch 7. All are briefly surveyed in ch 3.

[2] This link is often considered as an essential element of this type of agency behavior. Michal Tamir defines 'selective enforcement' as a case in which 'a law that seems fair and impartial is applied, administered, or enforced by public authorities in a discriminatory manner'. Michal Tamir, 'Public Law as a Whole and Normative Duality: Reclaiming Administrative Insights in Enforcement Review' (2006) 12 Tex J Civ Lib and Civ Rts 43, 76–77. See also eg Karl S Coplan, 'Rethinking Selective Enforcement in the First Amendment Context' (1984) 84 Colum L Rev 144;

[3] For the definition of selective enforcement as a specific kind of partial enforcement see Tamir (n 2) 77. Others have used the terms in this more expansive mode and are discussed below.

[4] Rather than regain an outdated vision of the law as highly coercive, such measures could be incorporated into law and thereby lose some of their fuzziness. For this argument see below text to n 106.

The third type of fuzzy implementation emerges when an arrangement is under-applied to the point of its virtual expiration. Executive bodies may refrain from implementation as a result of lack of resources, when, under the ordering of their priorities, the prescribed action is low on the agenda list, but it can also occur due to the agency's opposition to the framework or the impossibility of implementation to the letter. Motives aside, an unimplemented rule may turn into 'pastiche', that is, it may exist in the rulebooks but have no effect in the public sphere. Three sub-types of this latter type of fuzzy implementation are considered: frameworks which have never been implemented; frameworks that had never formally entered into force by the very executive authorized to formally order its commencement; and those which virtually expire due to the lack of funding (in effect, usually a legislature-generated fuzziness, this form of pastiche law is discussed here to offer a complete analysis of this type of fuzziness).

Much of the groundbreaking studies of selective, responsive enforcement (pastiche law set aside) have emphasized the positive aspects of these types of flexibility, as the chapter shows. However, the fuzziness of practices which are materially different from accessible, formal rules creates accessibility and accountability problems. This fuzziness may be dispelled if proper information about actual forms of enforcement is offered, but some of these practices, especially selective enforcement, are based on that very fuzziness: proponents of this type of flexibility argue that maximum compliance of those regulated is ensured with minimum effort and expense when regulatees have limited knowledge about the likelihood of being sanctioned.

This state of affairs is not to be celebrated. Still, following the theme of this book, I do not preach here for absolute, one-to-one enforcement. More on this, and on the insights gleaned from the above admission, in the concluding remarks appearing at the end of the chapter.

B. From Informal Enforcement to Creative Compliance

The first two nodes of fuzziness in enforcement draw on the literature that has identified the principal-agent problem arising from the interaction between the legislature (or, in the US, the triangle of Senate, House of Representatives, and the President) and the executive body granted the task of implementing the frameworks manufactured by the former. This principal-agent problem may arise when the agent (the regulator, or the executive body) fails to deliver the framework introduced by the principal (the legislator, or the politicians).[5] Much of this literature is

[5] On this principal-agent problem see eg Barry Mitnick, 'The Theory of Agency: The Policing "Paradox" and Regulatory Behavior' (1975) Pub Choice 27; Barry R Weingast, 'The Congressional-Bureaucratic System: A Principal-Agent Problem' (1984) 44 Pub Choice 147; Mathew D McCubbins,

concerned with the procedural ways legislatures may overcome some of this recalcitrant response to legislation.[6] My attention lies elsewhere: I wish first to identify two of these 'gaps' between the statute and its implementation, and to highlight the prices paid by the existence of such forms of fuzziness, which are unlikely to be eliminated by even the most cunning legislator.

1. Informal Enforcement

a. General

Enforcement is never fully applied, and compliance is never fully achieved; these truisms are firmly embedded in all studies in this field. I am less concerned here with different forms of selective enforcement, a universal practice under which not all detected infractions lead to prosecution.[7] Our focus is on one offshoot of this strand of study, which identifies regulators' use of an escalating menu of sanctions, most of them informal.

Professor Keith Hawkins's seminal *Environment and Enforcement* was the product of two years of participant observation of water pollution regulators. Hawkins found that the enforcement of a statute that set strict liability offences in an area less tainted with moral turpitude, in which constant interaction was at the core of the regulatory process, followed a pattern of escalating responses. Regulators employed varied strategies before reaching prosecution. Negotiations toward settlement and the issuance of warnings were the usual fare; prosecution was reserved for blatant cases of pervasive pollution, often also considered socially blameworthy. None of these gentler tactics were illegal or prohibited: after all, the regulatory craft, including enforcement, is a matter for discretion. Legal sanctions and other statutory powers were used as a 'last resort', preceded, and usually replaced by gentler practices.[8]

Roger G Noll, and Barry R Weingast, 'Administrative Procedures as Instruments of Political Control' (1987) 111 J L Econ and Org 243.

[6] See eg McCubbins, Noll, and Weingast (n 5) Terry M Moe, 'Delegation, Control, and Study of Public Bureaucracy' (2012) 10 The Forum, Issue 2 Article 4.

[7] An initial focus on policing (for an early example concerned with the discretion of police commissioners due to limited means see *Gowan v Smith*, 122 NW 286, 299 (Mich 1909)) has led to general observations regarding the ubiquity of discretion in the implementation and enforcement of the law. Professor Davis famously opined that in the US 'selective enforcement may account for about half of all the discretionary power that is exercised in individual cases in our entire legal system, and I think it is likely to be more than half than less than half'. Kenneth Culp Davis, *Discretionary Justice: A Preliminary Enquiry* (LSU Press 1969) 166.

[8] See Keith Hawkins, *Environment and Enforcement* (Clarendon Press 1984) esp ch 10. See also Keith Hawkins, *Law as Last Resort* (OUP 2002) (expanding the analysis to other areas of regulation and inter alia further emphasizing prosecution as a symbolic act directed at audiences ranging from the regulatees to the general public).

Using the image of the 'enforcement pyramid', Ian Ayres and John Braithwaite's work on enforcement similarly drew an escalating series of tactics, under which a statute, with its formal sanctions which include fines and, at the top of the pyramid, licence revocation, usually operates as a 'benign big gun'. Under this framework, the legislative mandate is used as a persuasive threat that nudges the regulatees towards compliance. For Ayres and Braithwaite, compliance was best achieved when regulators carry such 'big sticks', enabling them to 'speak softly' most of the time and achieve the required compliance, often through persuasion. Some use of the harsher measures is still required to maintain the agency's image of invincibility, that is, its punitive powers; general inaction even in extreme, socially unacceptable cases of infraction, would cause the toppling of the pyramid and reversion to regulatory failure.[9]

A similar insight, this time in the context of environmental law, is found in Daniel Farber's treatment of 'slippages', situations in which regulatory (or other) bodies act in ways that do not conform with the letter of the law. Under the terms 'noncompliance and creative compliance', Farber distinguishes between 'negative' and 'affirmative'/'positive' slippage. The former occurs when regulators ignore the duties set upon them in the legislative mandate, inter alia by missing deadlines or refraining from action; 'positive' slippage, for Farber, occurs when regulators attempts to work around the text in order to achieve a regulatory outcome.[10] This distinction, while useful, requires fine- tuning. The adoption and application of informal measures, discussed in this part, should be distinguished from two other practices, which align, but do not conform, with Farber's distinctions, and are analysed in the next parts of the chapter.[11]

Alike Farber, but originating from political and organizational studies, an impressive body of research has built on the 'gap' between the primary rule makers—in the US, Congress, and the President—and the agencies awarded the power of implementation by making secondary formal rules and enforcing the whole regulatory package. Many have found that the gap has led to the emergence of informal rules, in this case, not necessarily sorted on an escalatory scale but ones that may flesh out the formal rules or replace them. Such informal rules include agency directives, guidance documents, and policy memoranda, in the words of Hamilton

[9] Ian Ayres and John Braithwaite, *Responsive Regulation: Transcending the Deregulation Debate* (OUP 1992) 19–53. See also Eugene Bardach and Robert A Kagan, *Going by the Book: The Problem of Regulatory Unreasonableness* (Transaction Publishers 2002).

[10] Daniel Farber, 'Taking Slippage Seriously: Noncompliance and Creative Compliance in Environmental Law' (1999) 23 Harv Envtl L Rev 297, 305–11.

[11] The term 'creative compliance', used by Farber in his title, is applied in the next section in the fashion of regulation scholars, to imply practices in which regulators work around a statute that they are opposed to; it is thus not dedicated to the use of informal measures; cases of inaction that slip into the defacto annulation of law as an organizer of a regulatory scheme are discussed in part C as an example of 'pastiche law'. On both see below. For another analysis which discusses various forms of slippage or 'adaptive implementation', without distinguishing them by their nature or motives see Richard Stewart, 'A New Generation of Environmental Regulation?' (2001) Capital ULR 21, 54–56.

and Schroeder, 'rules that are issued outside of the traditional APA paradigm of Federal Register notice-and-comment procedure'.[12] These are entirely different informal measures, tied, if admittedly loosely, to the formal measures found in the legislative mandate, as in the case of the introduction of guidelines and directives. I am less concerned with these types of rules: more important for our endeavour are those measures that are not directed at clarification, but open up alternative avenues of action. In this section, thus, I am concerned with truly informal enforcement tactics that have no direct link to any authorization in statute.

Another aspect of this literature is its link with questions of Congressional control of agencies that attempt to carve out their set of processes with minimal regard of congressional intent—an aspect partially addressed in the next section.

b. Example: EPA's Supplemental Environmental Projects (SEPs)

Some informal modes of enforcement are introduced and applied inconsistently: in other cases, the informal becomes a mainstay of a regulator's enforcement policy, despite its unclear provenance and fuzzy legal status. The use of SEPs by the Environmental Protection Agency (EPA) is an excellent example of the latter.

Typical of many legislative mandates, the US Clean Air Act (CAA) contains an authorization subjecting violators to civil penalties for certain infractions. Several provisions of the Act provide regulators, in setting civil penalties, the discretion to 'compromise, modify, or remit, with or without conditions, any administrative penalty which may be imposed under this section'.[13] These details are essential for an understanding of the longstanding practice of the EPA (and, in fact, of other regulatory bodies): reaching a settlement with violators, under which violators are required, in addition to the payment of a penalty, to allocate large amounts to fund projects which promote the protection of the environment. This well-established practice is not formally sanctioned in the CAA; despite doubts over its legality, the practice has early roots and remains central to the work of the agency.

In the words of the EPA, '[a]s part of a settlement, an alleged violator may propose to undertake a project to provide tangible environmental or public health benefits to the affected community or environment, that is closely related to the violation being resolved, but goes beyond what is required under federal, state or local laws. The voluntary agreement to perform a Supplemental Environmental Project (SEP) is one factor that is considered in determining an appropriate settlement penalty, and may be the basis for a reduction in the final penalty'.[14] Some

[12] James T Hamilton and Christopher H Schroeder, 'Strategic Regulators and the Choice of Rulemaking Procedures: The Selection of Formal vs Informal Rules in Regulating Hazardous Waste' (1994) 57 L and Contemp Probs 111, 127, 147.

[13] For example, CAA §113(d)(2)(B) (42 USC 7413(d)(2)(B)) authorizes the EPA Administrator to 'compromise, modify, or remit, with or without conditions, any administrative penalty which may be imposed under this section'. See also CAA §205(c)(1) (42 USC §7524(c)(1)); CAA §211 (42 USC §7545).

[14] *Supplementary Environmental Projects (SEPs)*, EPA website <https://www.epa.gov/enforcement/supplemental-environmental-projects-seps>. For a model SEP agreement see https://www.epa.gov/

of these arrangements are settled as a conclusion of a civil suit brought against the violator, but others are designed and finalized by and in the administration. Defined above as 'voluntary'—a rendition that may have been introduced to allay some issues of the legality of SEPs—the negotiations over the details of a SEP are clearly conducted in the shadow of the 'big sticks' that can be brandished against non-co-operating parties.

The use of SEPs was mentioned as an EPA practice in 1980, initially in pre-trial negotiations.[15] Their continued presence, further discussed in this section, has however been subject to criticism for illegality. Such questions were raised in the late 1980s and early 1990s, first in a hearing held in a subcommittee of the House of Representatives, in which an associate deputy attorney voiced his concerns, then in two reports of the Comptroller General, made in conjunction with the publication of a written policy in 1991.[16] The first of these reports opened with a presentation of EPA's position: for the agency, the policy was sufficiently authorized in the CAA regarding the legality of the program. The Comptroller General strongly disagreed, following the tenor of the concerns of the associate deputy attorney at the House Hearing. In this, and the following report of 1993, three points were made: the question of authority, the potential absence of nexus, or link, between some of the settlement projects and the violation (an aspect I set aside), and the issue of circumvention of a statutory provision prohibiting augmentation of appropriations and requiring agencies to deposit all monies received from any source into the Treasury.

In its initial response to allegations regarding insufficient authority to act, EPA relied on the clause 'compromise, or remit, with or without conditions, any administrative penalty' as a central basis for the adoption of SEPs in CAA §103; other clauses were found supportive enough to enable the policy; finally, Congress had ratified the practice in its 1990 amendments to the CAA.[17]

sites/production/files/documents/sepmodcafo-rpt.pdf>. For a mention of SEPs as an example of a creative enforcement measure see Farber (n 10) 309–11.

[15] See *EPA, Civil Penalty Policy—Clean Water Violators and Stationary Source Violators of the Clean Water Act*, 8 July 1980, cited in Kenneth T Kristl, 'Making a Good Idea Even Better: Rethinking the Limits on Supplemental Environmental Projects' (2007) 31 Vt L Rev 217, 222 n 19; on the policy decision see Kristl 223–24.

[16] For the records and opinions see *Environmental Credit Projects Under Clean Water Act: Hearing before the Subcommittee on Fisheries and Wildlife and the Environment and the Subcommittee on Oceanography of the Committee on Merchant Marine and Fisheries*, 100t Congress, First Session, on HR 3411, 4 November 1987, Serial No 100–36 (US Government Printing Office 1988); Comptroller General, Report B-247155 to Hon John D Dingell, 7 July 1992 (1992 GAO report) <https://www.gao.gov/products/402023#mt=e-report>; Comptroller General, Report B-247155.2, 1 March 1993, (1993 GAO report), < https://www.gao.gov/assets/200/195921.pdf>. For a general overview of these developments see eg Leslie J Kaschak, 'Supplemental Environmental Projects: Evolution of a Policy' (1995) 2 Env Lawyer 465, 467–69, 471–73; Kristle (n 15) 225–26, 230–33, 236–41.

[17] EPA further relied on section 103(a)(5), which required EPA to 'conduct and promote the coordination and acceleration of training relating to the causes, effects, extent, prevention, and control of air pollution' (42 USC §7403(a)(1)), and on the requirement that the Administrator seeks 'to improve

As for the augmentation problem, the Comptroller General raised the concern that SEPs circumvent the general rule against augmentation of appropriations. This argument was succinctly explained in one of the studies of SEPs, as follows:

> By requiring a Supplemental Environmental Project as part of a settlement agreement with an environmental defendant, the EPA (and the Department of Justice acting as counsel on behalf of the EPA), reduces the amount of fines or penalties that might be paid by the violator in exchange for the agreement to undertake the SEP. Such fines or penalties would otherwise be paid into the general treasury account pursuant to the Miscellaneous Receipts Act where they would be available for congressional appropriation. Such a policy arguably evades the requirements of the Miscellaneous Receipts Act and almost certainly raises the possibility of the agency augmenting its appropriations by requiring an environmental defendant to perform projects that might be within the scope of the EPA's duties, thereby leaving more funds available to the EPA for other purposes.[18]

In the midst of these events, the EPA continued its use of SEPs. The 1991 policy was amended in 1995, 1998, and 2015.[19] Meetings and negotiations held between interested parties in the 1990s led to a reformulation of the augmentation issue, under which care should be taken to avoid this pitfall.[20] First set in the 1998 policy, the current policy document of 2015, which provides a full framework for the application of all stages of the SEP process, offers the following solution: the current policy requires all parties to a SEP make 'a reasonable, but not heroic' inquiry to ensure the proposed SEP does not include a Federal augmentation, and one of its two appendices is concerned with this issue.[21] Formally, this seems to have allayed concerns regarding the possibility of a direct conflict with the appropriations augmentation prohibition, although the reference to 'a reasonable, but not heroic' inquiry raises some suspicion.

knowledge of the short- and long-terms effects of air pollutants on welfare' (former section 103(f)(1)(B), introduced in the Clean Air Amendments of 1970).

[18] Todd David Peterson, 'Protecting the Appropriations Power: Why Congress Should Care about Settlements at the Department of Justice' (2009) 2009 Brig Young U L Rev 327, 352. See 1992 GAO report (n 16), referring to 31 USC §3302(b).

[19] *Interim Revised Supplemental Environmental Projects Policy*, 10 May 1995, 60 FR 24856; Supplemental Environmental Projects Policy, 5 May 1998, 5 May 1998, 63 FR 24796; and the current 2015 policy, *US Environmental Protection Agency Supplemental Environmental Projects Policy 2015 Update* (2015 SEP Policy), which supersedes the above-cited policy and incorporates by reference several memoranda and guidance documents issued by the EPA since 1998 and listed in the same document. Available at <https://www.epa.gov/enforcement/2015-update-1998-us-epa-supplemental-environmental-projects-policy>.

[20] For an overview see eg Peterson (n 18) 354–58 (authored before the policy replacement of 2015, which further emphasized some of the relevant conditions).

[21] On appropriations augmentations in the 2015 policy see ibid 10–12, 39–47 (Appendix A, which provides directions and a checklist for the use of defendants). Citation at 41.

A study of the use of SEPs in all areas of EPA responsibility between 1992 and 2006 identifies a decline in the use of Federal SEPs in settlements, and links this tendency, inter alia, with the introduction of a stronger nexus requirement.[22] Whether this is indeed the case, the EPA continues to use this mechanism in its administrative settlements of air pollution. For example, in 2019, one of two final orders concerning a settlement consensually reached between the EPA and the Saint Paul Park Refining Co, a corporation operating an oil refinery in the vicinity of the Mississippi river, set a penalty of $725,000 and a SEP in the sum of $1,033,400 to settle infractions of CAA §§110, 111, and 502. Replacing a former settlement that was found inapplicable, the project to be funded was 'the replacement of a diesel-fired motive power on a commercial cruise boat operated near the St Paul, Minnesota area'.[23]

Finally, returning to the issue of legality, the 2015 policy declares that the source of its power is its 'broad discretion to settle cases, including the discretion to include SEPs as an appropriate part of a settlement'.[24] These, and other broadly penned clauses previously cited by the EPA, and some references to Congress recognition and acquiescence, still do not amount to an explicit statutory authorization.[25] The fuzziness here, then, lies in the relative informality of the arrangement. The policy document contains the following declaration:

> The EPA reserves the right to change this Policy at any time, without prior notice, or to act at variance with this Policy. This Policy does not create any rights, duties, or obligations, implied or otherwise, in any third parties.[26]

Indeed, in addition to unclarity as to its legality, inconsistent, undisclosed application remains an option, foreseeability is limited, and challenges to the application of the policy are unlikely to succeed. Unlike its two predecessors, the 2015 policy was not published in the Federal Reporter. It is available online, a source that would be open to most regulatees and concerned persons, but still does not carry the same imprimatur of an official publication. The retention of this arrangement,

22 Kristle (n 15) 244–45.

23 Final order issued 25 April 2019. Information via EPA website <https://echo.epa.gov/enforcement-case-report?id=05-2018-5025>. In another settlement reached in 2019, Equistar Chemicals, a large manufacturer of petrochemicals and polymers, agreed to pay a penalty of $25,000 and replace a component used in its Texas-based facility, to reduce the amount of gas flared, for the sum of $800,000. See < https://echo.epa.gov/enforcement-case-report?id=05-2019-5037>.

24 2015 SEP Policy (n 19) 7.

25 One possible misconception can arise by tracing the authority to CAA §707 (42 USC §7604), concerned with citizen suits. Under its subsection (g), penalties received in such an action will be deposited in a penalty fund, 'for use by the Administrator to finance air compliance and enforcement activities'; alternatively, the court may order that such civil penalties 'be used in beneficial mitigation projects which are consistent with this chapter and enhance the public health or the environment'. This provision has nothing to do with administrative out-of-courts settlements.

26 2015 SEP Policy (n 19) 3.

applied at least since 1980, as an exercise of discretionary power, voluntarily agreed to by violators, rather than its introduction in the CAA, is at least likely to be supported by the flexibility of this relatively fuzzy arrangement.

2. Creative Compliance

a. General

This term was originally used in the context of taxation. Noting that individuals and companies find ways to avoid the law through 'perfectly legal' measures, Doreen McBarnett and Andrew Whelan discussed such practices as ones that 'us[e] the law to escape legal control without actually violating legal rules'. This '*post hoc* manipulation of law … turn[s] it—no matter what the intentions of legislators or enforcers—to the service of [regulatees'] own interests and to avoid unwanted control'.[27]

The term has been imported to the discussion of regulators' response to statutes they are uncomfortable with. In such cases, informal measures are introduced by the regulators not as tools to improve regulatory outcomes, but to covertly express antagonism to the spirit of the law or exasperation with its de facto feasibility. While not illegal, the measures applied on the ground do not tally with the legislators' motives.

As in the case of informal measures, some of the literature has employed this term expansively. Farber gathers under the term all informal measure introduced beyond the law, with no special regard to the motives that lead to the adoption of such informal measures.[28] Others have identified motives which are of less interest here: as mentioned above, for Hamilton and Schroeder, agencies keen to escape the onerous notice-and-comment process required under the APA may opt for the adoption of informal rules.[29] My focus follows the central theme in the regulatory literature, which points at a specific set of motives: opposition to the introduced legislative mandate.

Such opposition may arise due to legislative introduction of a framework that the bodies granted the task of their implementation consider overly harsh or impossible to implement. Arrangements can be introduced by an over-zealous legislature, possibly keen to convey a political message regarding its commitment to the resolution of an issue that has gained social support. In such cases, the legislator

[27] Doreen McBarnet and Christopher Whelan, 'The Elusive Spirit of the Law: Formalism and the Struggle for Legal Control' (1991) 54 MLR 848, 848. See also Doreen McBarnet and Christopher Whelan, 'Challenging the Regulators: Strategies for Resisting Control' in Christopher McCrudden (ed), *Regulation and Deregulation: Policy and Practice in the Utilities and Financial Services Industries* (Clarendon Press 1998) 67; John Braithwaite, 'Large Business and the Compliance Model' in Valerie Braithwaite (ed), *Taxing Democracy: Understanding Tax Avoidance and Evasion* (Ashgate 2003) 177.

[28] Farber (n 10).

[29] Hamilton and Schroeder (n 12).

may be less concerned with actual implementation, or feel free to lay the responsibility of non-achievement on the regulator. As a way out of the resulting conundrum, regulators may act like any taxpayer who seeks loopholes that may benefit him without branding him a law-breaker; they may reinterpret the framework creatively, in ways that do not conform with the letter of the law, but can be accommodated as not illegal.

In their analysis of the possible processual limits which legislators may introduce to ensure agency compliance, McCubbin, Noll, and Weingast identified several tactics employed by agencies: they may revert to 'shirking by undersupplying policy outcomes; pursuing policy objectives that are inconsistent with the preferences of elected political officials; or creating new, organized political interests'.[30] In the face of legislative attempts to overcome such practices, agencies may sometimes retaliate by invoking additional noncompliance tactics. Thus, a cyclic process of creating congressional rules → agency noncompliance → creating additional rules, and so on, may emerge. Without acting illegally, then, the game resulting from legislative-executive tension can lead to the emergence of fuzziness.

Another possible tactic, not discussed in the above-cited literature, may be employed through the interpretation of an authorizing or limiting statutory rule in ways that seem to depart from the meaning of the text or the intent of its creators, in order to find a legal basis for a contentious action the legislator seems to have opposed. The assessment of the 'creativity' of the interpretation requires adopting an understanding of the zone of proper interpretation. As texts are open enough to enable several interpretations, the issue here is whether the interpretation of the agency is so remote from the text and its intent, that it is to be deemed an unreasonable or perhaps even arbitrary/capricious application of the law. Still, as long as presented as a legally backed argument, which is not rejected by a reviewing body, such an interpretation can continue to creatively support executive action.

b. Examples

(1) EPA's first two decades

The regulation of emission of hazardous air pollutants under an originally stringent legislative framework, which led to EPA's exercise of a variety of under-implementation tactics, offers an excellent example of the gap between the law in the books and its enforcement. A lengthy analysis of the decades of struggles over the implementation of the Clean Air Act, influenced by political conflicts between presidents, Houses of Congress, parties, strong interests groups, the media, and public opinion, all of them of both colours, is well beyond the scope of this chapter.[31] Suffice to focus on the ways the newly established EPA acted out its requirements to implement the Clean Air Act in the 1970s and 1980s

[30] McCubbins and others (n 5) 273.

[31] For the history see Michael E Kraft, 'US Environmental Policy and Politics: From the 1960s to the 1990s' in Otis L Graham (ed), *Environmental Politics and Policy, 1960s–1990s* (Pennsylvania State UP

The Clean Air Amendments 1970 Act was enacted under an exceptional set of circumstances that powerfully pushed towards the adoption of strict rules curbing emissions of air pollutants. The competition for the title of protector of the environment between President Nixon and his opponent, Senator Edmund Muskie, was crucial to the advancement of the Act. This race to the top was fuelled by the rise of public environmental concern, and led to the adoption of this highly stringent framework.[32] Under a structure of rulemaking and enforcement shared between the EPA and the states, the EPA was required, inter alia, to publish a list of hazardous air pollutants within ninety days from enactment; within 180 days from the inclusion of an air pollutant in the list, the EPA was required to publish proposed legislation, conduct a public hearing within thirty days, and set an emission standard. The criterion to be considered in CAA §112 was simple: the standard was to be set at the level which 'in [the Administrator's] judgment provides an ample margin of safety to protect the public health from such hazardous air pollutant'.[33] Economic costs or technological considerations were not mentioned; sufficient data reflects an intention to exclude such considerations.[34] Another example of the strictness of the framework was the requirement to prescribe by regulations standards regarding vehicle emissions of carbon monoxide and hydrocarbons for vehicles manufactured from 1975, which were to be reduced by ninety per cent in comparison with the standards applicable in 1970—effectively a duty to reduce emissions by ninety per cent over a period of five years.[35]

The act, considered 'symbolic' in John Dwyer's analysis, was never followed fully. The tightly designed deadlines were not met, possibly a case of direct infraction. Reflecting borderline infraction/creative compliance tactics, the EPA developed a reinterpretation of §112 by factoring economic and technological considerations into their rules—an example of the creative interpretation tactics employed by the agency,[36] as well as their development of standards based on 'best available

2000) 17, 21–35; for the official online version see *The Origins of EPA* < https://www.epa.gov/history/origins-epa>.

[32] Clean Air Amendments of 1970 Act, PL 91–604, 84 Stat 1676.

[33] Clean Air Amendments of 1970 Act, ibid, replacing the former §112(b). For a detailed account of the politics of the 1970 enactment see John P Dwyer, 'The Pathology of Symbolic Legislation' (1990) 17 Ecology L Q 233, 242–50; Alfred A Marcus, *Promise and Performance: Choosing and Implementing an Environment Policy* (Greenwood Press 1980); John D Graham, 'The Failure of Agency-Forcing: The Regulation of Airborne Carcinogens under Section 112 of the Clean Air Act' (1985) 1985 Duke L J 100, 105–107.

[34] Dwyer (n 33) 239–42.

[35] Clean Air Amendments of 1970 Act §6, replacing CAA §202 (classified at the time as 42 USC §1587f-1). The provision further offered manufacturers to request suspensions of the requirement 'for one year only' (§202(5)), more of an additional restriction than a substantive opening for the loosening of the requirement. This arrangement was materially changed in subsequent amendments; the current §202, as amended in the Clean Air Amendments Act 1990 (currently in 42 USC §7521) offers an entirely different, detailed structure, largely based on discretion.

[36] Dwyer (n 33) 251–53; Graham (n 33) 132–37.

technology', a well-established benchmark condition under which regulatees are to apply the best technology available on the market.[37] Squarely within the realm of creative compliance, very few substances were listed, and, at least partially due to the onerous process of rulemaking, very few standards passed the lengthy and elaborate processes of deliberation and design. Some of the responsibility lay with the EPA: for example, according to one commentator, the agency 'developed an extensive internal review process that delayed, and indeed, almost eliminated the adoption of emission standards'.[38] Some of the moves finally made were the result of court orders, including one contempt citation against the EPA issued in 1984.[39] One of the overviews of the life of the Act concludes that '[b]y the end of 1984, nearly fourteen years after the enactment of section 112, EPA had adopted emission standards for only seven hazardous air pollutants'.[40]

The adoption of such creative compliance tactics may have initially been the result of the harshness of the arrangement, perceived by the regulator as impossible to apply; still, it would be incorrect to view this period as one in which the regulator acted in defiance of the law, which continued to be backed politically. The lesser interest in the field during President Ford's administration, the gradual weakening of President Carter's commitment to environmental reform, budget shortages, and, markedly, the transformed political climate during President Reagan's terms, and ensuing appointments of like-minded officers, offered a supportive backdrop for EPA's limited performance during these periods. Yet, until 1990, the statute was not materially transformed, and much of the gap between the law and life was played out without excessive slippage into the realm of illegality.[41]

(2) Funding the US-Mexico wall

The war between President Trump and Congress over the funding of one of this president's central policies has been discussed and analysed from a variety of viewpoints. Here, I consider the President's responses to the funding limits set by Congress, which involved the interpretation of fund constraints set in the 2019 and 2020 appropriations acts as a possible example of creative compliance by interpretation.

[37] Dwyer (n 33) 254–57; Graham (n 33) 138–40.

[38] Dwyer (n 33) 258 and 259–60. On the deadlines and extended periods of rulemaking see also Graham (n 33) 123–25, 148.

[39] Dwyer (n 33) 261–62. For the latter see *Sierra Club v Ruckelshaus* 602 F Supp 892 (ND Cal 1984).

[40] Dwyer (n 33) 261–62. See also Graham (n 33) 148. Not all analyses follow this thesis; for a much more positive overview of EPA attempts to apply the CAA while brokering between Congress and the President, written from the vantage point of 1980, see Alfred A Marcus, *Promise and Performance: Choosing and Implementing an Environmental Policy* (Greenwood Press 1980). For other such examples, indiscriminately listed, see Stewart (n 11) 55–56.

[41] Evidence of such 'slippage' is of course also available after 1990, as it occurs in other fields of executive responsibility. For some attention to this aspect see Farber (n 10). Further analysis is relegated to separate research.

Aimed at curbing illegal entrance into the US, the first, 14 mile-long portion of a wall between Mexico and the US was completed in 1993. The gradual extension of the wall, backed by two statutes, the aggrandizement of agency powers, and presidential support[42] were not considered sufficient in the eyes of Donald Trump. In his campaign for presidency, Trump repeatedly declared that he would build a wall that would separate the entire land border and that Mexico would be charged for the cost.[43] Five days after his inauguration, President Trump signed Executive Order 13767. Declaring the policy of the executive branch to 'secure the southern border of the United States through the immediate construction of a physical wall in the southern border', the purposes cited for this exercise pointed at curbing illegal immigration, the infiltration of crime, and the smuggling of narcotics into the US. The order directed the Department for Homeland Security (DHS) to take all appropriate steps to immediately plan, design, and construct the wall, '[i]n accordance with existing law', the issue of funding this mammoth project was not, and could not have been authorized by the executive order alone.[44] Yet Congress was not compliant: full funding was not forthcoming.[45]

All of these events were challenged in courts, and are still discussed; here, I focus on one aspect—the transfer of funds beyond the sums specifically allocated for the construction of the wall.[46]

Initially, failure to secure the funding requested by the President led to the longest government shutdown in history, following Trump's declaration that he would veto the 2019 appropriations act if it didn't offer sufficient funding. On 15 February 2019, the President finally signed the Consolidated Appropriations Act 2019 into law. That Act contained provisions which limited funds for the construction of pedestrian fences and restricted their location, an authorization that far

[42] For an overview written in 2009 see Chad C Haddal, Yule Kim, and Michael John Garcia, *Border Security: Barriers Along the U.S. International Border*, CRS Report No RL33659 (2009).

[43] See eg Aaron Rupar, https://www.vox.com/2020/1/6/21051550/trump-iran-tweets-soleimani-war-powers- VOX (6 January 2020).

[44] Executive order 13767, *Border Security and Immigration Enforcement Improvements* (25 January 2017) 82 FR 8793. Citations from Sec 2(a), 4(a). Sources cited as authority included, in addition to several statutes, also the famous and pervasive formula 'the Constitution and the laws of the United States', discussed in ch 4 of this book.

[45] For an overview of the funds appropriated for 2017 and 2018 see *El Paso v Trump*, 408 F Supp 3d 840, 844 (WD Tex 2019) (*El Paso v Trump*).

[46] To date (August 2020), the latest decisions in this series are the June 2020 decision of the Court of Appeal for the 9th Circuit which ruled that the transfer of funds, discussed below, was unauthorized by the 2019 Appropriations Act, and the Supreme Court's July 2020 denial of a motion to lift the stay of an injunction set in an earlier decision. See also President Trump's petition to the Supreme Court, filed on 7 August 2020, challenging the first of this trio. See *California et al v Trump*, 963 F3d 926 (26 June 2020) (CA 9th Cir); *Trump v Sierra Club*, 591 US ____ (31 July 2020); *Trump v Sierra Club*, filed 7 August 2020 <https://www.supremecourt.gov/DocketPDF/20/20-138/149698/20200807161246572_Sierra%20Club%20-%20Section%208005%20-%20final.pdf> (Trump petition 2020). More applications and decisions are expected; the outcome can only be guessed. For some of the decisions delivered since July 2019 see *Sierra Club v Trump*, 929 F3d 670 (CA 9th Cir 2019); *Trump v Sierra Club*, 588 US ___ (2019); *El Paso v Trump* (n 45); *El Paso County v Trump*, 407 F Supp 3d 655 (WD Texas 2019); *California v Trump*, 407 F Supp 3d 869 (ND Calif 2019); *State of Washington v Trump*, 441 F Supp 3d 1101 (WD Washington 2020); *Sierra Club v Trump*, 963 F3d 874 (CA 9th Cir 2020).

from answered the President's needs.[47] On signing this appropriations act, Trump issued a declaration of emergency by proclamation, made under the National Emergencies Act and 'the authority vested in [him] by the Constitution and the laws of the United States of America'. Describing the state of the security of the border as an emergency, the proclamation authorized the reliance on statute to continue construction by the military.[48] A separate presidential address issued that day directed secretaries of state to divert some of their funds to the construction project.[49] A joint resolution terminating the President's declaration of emergency was vetoed by the President; the majority required to override the veto was not achieved.[50] Under a similar climate, the 2020 appropriations act granted the President 1.375 billion dollars for continuing construction.[51] Once again, the funds were considered insufficient.

Important in the context of this section, the President made several steps intended to overpass Congressional restraint of expenditure. The main tactic employed in 2019 and 2020 was the diversion of funds allocated for other purposes. Just before Trump's declaration of emergency, a 'senior administration official' stated publicly that beyond the 1.375 billion dollars allocated in the appropriations act of 2019, an additional 6.7 billion would be collected from three sources: the Treasury Department's drug forfeiture fund, the Department of Defense's drug interdiction programs, and its military construction account.[52] A year later, one of the many reports confirmed that the Pentagon had diverted 6 billion dollars of its budget to build barriers in California, Arizona, and New Mexico.[53] According to early 2020 reports, 7.2 billion dollars were to be diverted for this purpose in 2020.[54]

The exorbitant sums spent on this project—according to one report, the cost is likely to amount to 20 million dollars per mile[55]—may of course be of great

[47] §230 allocated some funds for the construction of fencing in a specified area only; §231 prohibited funding for construction in other border areas; and under §739, no further change in funding may be effected without amendment in an appropriations act.

[48] Proclamation 9844, *Presidential Proclamation on Declaring a National Emergency Concerning the Southern Border of the United* States, 15 February 2019, 84 FR 4949. On the nature of proclamations and the use of the formula 'the Constitution and laws of the United States' see chs 4, 5.

[49] 'President Donald J Trump's Border Security Victory', White House Fact Sheet <https://www.whitehouse.gov/briefings-statements/president-donald-j-trumps-border-security-victory/>.

[50] See details in *Sierra Club v Trump*, 379 F Supp 3d 883, 895 (ND Cal 2019).

[51] Consolidated Appropriations Act 2020, § 209(1).

[52] Amanda Macias and John W Schoen, 'Here's where the money for Trump's wall will come from', CNBC, 15 February 2019 <https://www.cnbc.com/2019/02/15/heres-where-the-money-for-trumps-border-wall-will-come-from.html>.

[53] Meghann Myers, 'Here's how much border wall has been built with the military's money', Military Times, 16 January 2020 <'https://www.militarytimes.com/news/your-military/2020/01/16/heres-how-much-border-wall-has-been-built-with-the-militarys-money/>.

[54] See eg Justine Coleman, 'Trump plans to divert $7.2 billion from Pentagon for border wall construction: report', 13 January 2020, The Hill <https://thehill.com/policy/defense/budget-appropriations/478102-trump-plans-to-divert-72-billion-from-pentagon-for>.

[55] John Burnett, '$11 billion and counting: Trump's border wall would be the world's most costly', 19 January 2020, npr <https://www.npr.org/2020/01/19/797319968/-11-billion-and-counting-trumps-border-wall-would-be-the-world-s-most-costly>.

concern. Here, though, the diversion of funds, the legality of which is still to be finally decided in courts, offers an example of the ways executives creatively work around prohibitions they do not wish to implement. In his August 2020 petition against the Circuit Court, which ruled that 2.5 billion dollars were diverted illegally, the President argued that nothing untoward has been done, relying on provisions in the relevant Appropriations Acts that have, in his view, sufficiently granted the challenged power.

Indeed, both appropriations acts authorize transfer of additional funds, albeit under set conditions. §8005 of both Appropriations Acts, authorizes the Secretary of Defense, '[u]pon determination by the Secretary of Defense that such action is necessary in the national interest', to transfer, under the approval of the OMB and subject to several additional conditions, sums not to exceed $4,000,000,000 of working capital funds of the Department of Defense or funds made available in this Act to the Department of Defense for military functions (except military construction) between such appropriations or funds or any subdivision thereof, to be merged with and to be available for the same purposes, and for the same time period, as the appropriation or fund to which transferred'.[56]

However, under one condition for the transfer of such funds, 'such authority to transfer may not be used unless for higher priority items, based on unforeseen military requirements, than those for which originally appropriated and in no case where the item for which funds are requested has been denied by the Congress',[57] a provision that was understandably central to the decision of the Ninth Circuit court which found the challenged transfer unlawful.

In his brief, Trump does not rely on his general powers under the constitution: under the Appropriations Clause of the US Constitution, '[n]o Money shall be drawn from the Treasury, but in Consequence of Appropriations made by Law'.[58] His is an argument based on a loose interpretation of that clause, supported by a legal opinion originating from the Government Accountability Office (GAO).[59] In a nutshell, it is argued, the Court of Appeal majority's holding that the transfers violated §8005 was 'inconsistent with the statutory text, history, and purpose of the proviso'. In some detail, and in line with the GAO opinion, it is argued that the building of the wall is of high priority; the term 'unforeseen' in the clause 'unforeseen military requirement' refers to the need to provide further funds, not known at the time of the Department of Defence's earlier budget requests; and that

[56] §8005 of the Consolidated Appropriations Act, 2020, supplemented by §9002, which authorizes the transfer of up to $2,000,000,000. Similar provisions are found in the 2019 HR 6157 (citing $4,250,000,000 in §8005 and $2,250,000,000 in §9002).

[57] Department of Defense Appropriations Act 2019, §8005; Consolidated Appropriations Act 2020 §8005.

[58] US Const Art I, § 9, Cl 7.

[59] Self-defined as an 'independent, nonpartisan agency that works for Congress', the GAO's role as an audit body, includes the issuing of opinions in response to questions tabled by members of Congress. See <https://www.gao.gov/about/>. For the opinion see <https://www.gao.gov/assets/710/701176.pdf>,

nowhere in the appropriations act can one find a denial of funding (the explicit sums directly allocated are not to be construed, under this interpretation, as a denial of the allocation of additional funds).[60]

Although this example seems to revolve around the interpretation of a statute, this case can also be considered a type of creative compliance, which may arise in cases of reliance on unlikely interpretation of a statute. Whether Trump's manoeuvre will succeed in court (or will not be decided against) is, at the time of writing, a matter for speculation. At this point, an interpretation that seems creative enough, and a series of court decisions that are not discussed here in detail, have enabled the President to continue the project.

C. 'Pastiche' Law

1. General

The third form of executive-generated fuzziness discussed in this chapter emerges when a statute is never, or virtually never, applied, despite their existence on the books. Pastiche law was briefly addressed in Chapter 3. Some statutes, such as Texas' sodomy law prior to *Lawrence v Texas* (2003),[61] were generally not enforced, considered as having lost touch with current reality and social norms, but remained on the books due to various considerations such as the social and political costs of their removal. Such a statute may be considered by academics as an exercise of the desuetude doctrine;[62] in any case, its continuing formal force challenges the ability to grasp the rules that govern a field of government action.

Pastiche law can also be unimplemented or rarely applied from inception. A statute may be introduced due to political pressure in the absence of true executive or agency support; in other cases, statutes may simply be set aside by the executive due to their onerous content. One of the best-known examples of this type of fuzzy statute, the War Powers Resolution, is discussed below.

Sometimes, the unimplemented law never enters into force. A statute may contain a provision regarding its commencement, either by an order to be issued by a Minister or other executive body, or by setting a date of commencement that can be extended by an order. In certain cases, commencement orders may not be forthcoming, or postponement orders are serially issued. In both cases, the statute is rendered a mere ghost, or pastiche law, found in the law-books but de facto no more than a text with a possible future. The common pattern of British statutes, in

60 Trump petition 2020 (n 46) 30 onwards.

61 539 US 558 (2003).

62 Cass R Sunstein, 'What Did *Lawrence* Hold? Of Autonomy, Desuetude, Sexuality, and Marriage' (2003) 55 Sup Ct Rev 27, 30. On this doctrine in the US and its relevance to prosecutorial discretion, see Note, 'Desuetude' (2006) 102 Harv L Rev 2209, esp 2222–25.

which provisions, sometimes entire chapters, or an entire Act, enter into force only after the promulgation of an order by a Secretary of State, colours the system as one that is rife with pastiche law of this type.

Another case of pastiche provision may arise when an agency decides to underfund or stop funding a certain function it has discretion to regulate. This practice echoes the type of statutory-generated fuzziness discussed in Chapter 7. Blanket non-implementation can emerge when one statutory provision effectively disables government action, as in the case of riders in appropriation laws that prohibit expenditure on an activity the legislature finds unattractive. However, regulators may effectively shut down certain functions due to budgetary cuts that leave the regulators the discretion to decide on how to allocate the shrunk funds available to them. When a certain activity is considered to be of lesser importance, agencies may effectively annul the application of a statutory provision, transforming this provision to be no more than pastiche. Several examples of executive-generated pastiche law now follow.

2. Examples

a. Under- or never-implemented statutes

A prime example of an act that set a process which was never implemented, the War Powers Resolution was enacted by the two houses of Congress, overriding President Nixon's veto.[63] Politically motivated by the rising dissent against the Vietnam War, and by the unpopular unilateral action of the President, the statute introduced an arrangement that was far from fuzzy. The inclusion of a 'purpose and policy' clause firmly embedded the statute as a reaffirmation of the framers' intent to share powers of Congress and the President in this field of action. This clause also explicitly enabled the President to despatch armed forces into hostilities only when one of three alternative conditions be met: a prior declaration of war, a specific statutory authorization, or the existence of 'a national emergency created by attack upon the United States, its territories of possession, or its armed forces'; no exceptions to these were allowed, and the text itself could only be narrowly interpreted.[64] In addition to the setting of consultation with Congress, the Act requires that in the absence of a declaration of war, the introduction of armed forces in specified factual cases, the President should submit reports to the speakers of

[63] War Powers Resolution (WPR), PL 93-148, 50 USC 1541–48. On the act, with some emphasis on its history, see Eugene V Rostow, '"Once More unto the Breach": The War Powers Resolution Revisited' (1986) 21 Valparaiso L Rev 1; John Hart Ely, *War and Responsibility: Constitutional Lessons of Vietnam and its Aftermath* (Princeton UP 1993).

[64] Section 2(a) opens as follows: 'it is the purpose of this joint resolution to fulfill the intent of the framers of the Constitution of the United States and insure the collective judgment of both the Congress and the President will apply to the introduction of United States Armed Forces into hostilities'. For the conditions see Section 2(c).

both houses and continue to report periodically. In the absence of congressional approval within sixty days, the President is required under the Act to terminate the use of armed forces, and to remove the forces if Congress so directs by concurrent resolution.[65] The Act further limited the interpretation of other statutes as legitimizing presidential action, unless specifically so authorizing.[66]

From inception, presidents have challenged the statute as an unconstitutional interference with their powers. According to a 2008 report, '[e]very President since Ford has questioned the constitutionality of the War Powers Resolution and submitted reports that are "consistent with", but not "pursuant to" the statute'.[67] Even if this is not entirely correct,[68] presidential action in contravention of the act has been the norm since its entry into force, and well after the publication of that report. All post-2008 presidents—George W Bush, Barack Obama, and Donald Trump—have followed a similar pattern: reports are submitted, most of them avowing to be 'consistent' with the Act, some of them not mentioning the source.[69] In addition, and in clear contradiction with the statute's requirements, almost all 'reports' were submitted after the deed had been done.[70] Some instances which involved the deployment of armed forces in potentially hostile situations were not reported at all. These include the shooting down of Libyan jets in 1981 and 1989 and Operation Desert Fox in Iraq in 1998.[71] President Trump has taken a different direction that has little to do with the tradition of legality: in January 2019, he used Twitter 'as notification to the United States Congress that should Iran strike any US person of target the United States will quickly & fully strike back', adding that '[s]uch legal notice is not required, but is given nevertheless!'[72]

[65] WPR Section 5. An exception allowing the presidential extension of the period for up to ninety days, is tightly worded: this option applies only under presidential written certification that 'unavoidable military necessity respecting the safety of the United States Armed Forces' so requires.

[66] WPR Section 8(a).

[67] National War Powers Commission, National War Powers Commission Report (Miller Center for Public Affairs, University of Virginia 2008), 24.

[68] See eg Michael J Glennon, 'The War Power Resolution, Once Again' (2009) 103 Am J Int'l L 75, 78 (mentioning that President Ford challenged the constitutionality of the sixty days requirement only after leaving office).

[69] A list of 168 events, reported under the WPR between 1975 and 2016, annexed in a Congressional Research Service report, shows that the vast majority of them were made after the events reported. Matthew C Weed, *The War Powers Resolution: Concepts and Practice*, Report R42699 (Congressional Research Service updated 8 March 2019), summary page and Appendix A (CRS Report R42699, updating former reports). The reporter found that out of the 168 reports submitted by presidents, only one cited section 4 of the WPR; as mentioned, at best, presidents asserted their action, noting that it was 'consistent' with the Act, rather than made under its provisions.

[70] ibid Appendix A.

[71] ibid Appendix B.

[72] Cited and graphically presented in Amber Phillips, 'What is the War Powers Act and what can Congress do to enforce it with Trump on Iran?' The Washington Post, 8 January 2019 < *https://www.washingtonpost.com/politics/2020/01/07/war-powers-act-explained/*>. For the tweet see <https://twitter.com/realdonaldtrump/status/1213919480574812160>.

b. 'Floating' statutes

British statutes often contain commencement provisions under which the statute, or parts of it, enter into force on a future date. Sometimes the future date is set; for example, the commencement section may designate its entry into force at an exact date or on the expiration of a designated period.[73] In other cases, commencement is effected by a minister's order: in such a case, the entry into force, and all its implications regarding power and enforcement, remains entirely at the discretion of the executive.

Such commencement orders may be a complex set of directions. For example, the commencement provision of the Counter-Terrorism and Border Security Act 2019, a substantial collection of amendments to no less than twenty-five statutes applicable to England which also introduced a new arrangement of border control,[74] presents all possible permutations:

> 27 Commencement
>
> (1) The following provisions come into force on the day on which this Act is passed—
> (a) section 21;
> (b) section 23(2) to (7);
> (c) section 26;
> (d) this section;
> (e) section 28;
> (f) paragraph 19 of Schedule 4 and section 23(1) so far as relating to that paragraph;
> (g) any other provision of this Act so far as necessary for enabling the exercise on or after the day on which this Act is passed of any power under Schedule 3 to make regulations or to issue codes of practice.
>
> (2) The following provisions come into force on such day or days as the Secretary of State may by regulations appoint—
> (a) sections 16, 17 and 18;
> (b) section 19 and Schedule 2;
> (c) section 22 and Schedule 3 (so far as not brought into force by subsection (1)(g) of this section);
> (d) paragraphs 17 and 18, 20 to 26 and 28 to 33 of Schedule 4 and section 23(1)so far as relating to those paragraphs.
>
> (3) The other provisions of this Act come into force at the end of the period of two months beginning with the day on which this Act is passed.

[73] See eg s 27(3) of the Counter-Terrorism and Border Security Act 2019, cited below.

[74] Counter-Terrorism and Border Security Act 2019. Ten of these twenty-five statutes were substantially amended; the others are considered to have undergone 'minor and consequential' changes.

(4) The Secretary of State may by regulations make transitional or saving provision in connection with the coming into force of any provision of this Act.
(5) Regulations under this section are to be made by statutory instrument.

The open-ended text of some provisions, which requires interpretation, is in itself a source of fuzziness. Consider subsection (1)(g): a provision that orders the immediate coming into force of 'any other provision of this Act so far as necessary for enabling the exercise on or after the day on which this Act is passed of any power under Schedule 3 to make regulations or to issue codes of practice' is far from easily understandable. In itself, this provision is a form of fuzziness generated by statute, under which entry into force is not dependent only on the understanding of what is 'necessary' for enabling powers under one of the Act's Schedules on the date of passing and beyond. Yet this form of fuzziness, emerging from the difficult task of interpretation, almost recedes into the background when compared to subsection (2).

Here, a host of meticulously selected provisions enter into force only after a minister so appoints. The entry into force, thus dependent on executive discretion, or goodwill may not be forthcoming—some of the examples below show a worrying pattern—the chimera that is a statute can mislead those who rely on the law in the books: the statute merely 'floats' above the legal system, at best offering some guidance as regards the original intent of the legislature at the time of legislation.

Such 'floating' statutes are not uncommon. For example, nine out of the thirty-one Public General Acts passed in 2019 contain provisions that are yet to be entered into force.[75] Only two have since been fully entered into force: eight still contain chapters or sections that have not yet moved from a shadowy semi-existence to full force.

As of 31 May 2020, substantial parts of the Counter-Terrorism and Border Security Act 2019 were yet to be entered into force. Those that are indicated as 'prospective' include, inter alia, amendments to the Terrorism Act 2000, including the addition of the right of a person detained under provisions of that act to be informed of his right to inform a person that he is being detained, and to consult a solicitor,[76] and a detailed framework regarding the retention of biometric data.[77]

[75] Search via legislation.gov.uk, conducted 16 August 2020. Most of these nine statutes contain substantial portions that are (still) floating. In addition to the Counter-Terrorism and Border Security Act 2019, those include The Offensive Weapons Act 2019 and the Mental Capacity Act. Two of the statutes enacted that year were concerned with budgetary issues, and contained no commencement provision (the usual pattern is to note the entry into force on the date of enactment), and two, concerned with the EU withdrawal, were repealed; hence, effectively, almost a third of the statutes enacted in 2019 enable the existence of a floating statutory arrangement, in average, more than one year after their enactment.

[76] The Counter-Terrorism and Border Security Act 2019, s 17, amending inter alia paras 6 and 7 of Schedule 8 of the Terrorism Act 2000. Under the law in force, a detained person may make a request to contact such persons, but there is no duty to inform the detainee of these rights.

[77] The Counter-Terrorism and Border Security Act 2019, s 17 and Schedule 2 (amending several statutes).

A commencement order issued on 22 July 2020, more than a year since its enactment in February 2019,[78] offers a mixed remedy:

2. Commencement

The following provisions of the Counter-Terrorism and Border Security Act 2019 come into force on the twenty-second day after the day on which these Regulations are made—

(a) section 16 (evidence obtained under port and border control powers);
(b) section 17 (persons detained under port and border control powers);
(c) section 18 (detention of terrorist suspects: hospital treatment);
(d) section 19 (retention of biometric data for counter-terrorism purposes etc) so far as relating to the provisions brought into force by paragraph (e);
(e) paragraphs 1 to 4 and 6 to 17 of Schedule 2 (retention of biometric data for counterterrorism purposes etc);
(f) section 22 (port and border controls) so far as relating to the provisions brought into force by paragraph (g);
(g) Schedule 3 (port and border controls) to the extent it is not already in force, except for paragraphs 44 and 45 in relation to Northern Ireland;
(h) section 23(1) (minor and consequential amendments) so far as relating to the provisions brought into force by paragraph (i);
 (i) the following paragraphs of Schedule 4 (minor and consequential amendments)—
 (i) 17 and 18;
 (ii) 20(2) to (8) and paragraph 20(1) so far as it relates to those sub-paragraphs;
 (iii) 21 to 26;
 (iv) 28 to 33.

For those still curious, as of August 2020, certain parts of the 2019 Act have not (yet?) entered into force.[79]

Similarly, to a lesser extent but still notably fuzzy, the Finance Act 2019, concerning taxation and linked issues, inter alia introduced a carbon emissions tax and a detailed framework for its administration; to date, again, the arrangement

[78] The Counter-Terrorism and Border Security Act 2019 (Commencement No 1) Regulations 2020, SI 2020/792.

[79] The remaining floating provisions concern three sections concerned with border control action, the full Schedule 2 on the retention of biometric data for counter-terrorism purposes, and five assorted amendments to statutes and regulations.

has yet to be entered into force.[80] This time, the floated status of this part is linked with the uncertainty of the post-Brexit era; the government maintains the tax will be set in case no agreement with the EU is achieved, in particular the continued participation of the UK in the EU Emissions Trading System.[81]

One may argue that postponement of entry into force for a short period, even a year or two, may be excusable, as sometimes elaborate arrangements are needed before commencement. More so when provisions are contingent on external forthcoming conditions, as in the case of the carbon emissions tax. However, some statutes or portions thereof have remained floating for much longer periods, or, considering the time lag, may be declared as provisions that have never entered into force and are unlikely to change their status.

The latter case is most worrying: unrepealed, statutes enacted at one point that are unlikely to be entered into force remain on the statute book, an evident case of non-dispelled fuzziness. Two examples in the areas studied in this book suffice.

The 2008 terrorism act contains a sub-chapter authorizing the removal of documents for examination. Part of the original act, this sub-chapter has been amended since, but has never entered into force.[82] After more than a decade, this sub-chapter may have entered into a state of permanent flotation.

The second example concerns an arrangement which repealed parts of a statute, but has never entered into force, creating a case of double arrangement or patchworking. Part I of the Environmental Protection Act 1990, which was the original locale of application of EU rules on integrated pollution control (a term of art originating from the EU, referring to the maintaining of regimes that address all environmental media (air, water, and land) to be applied in all EU member states). The Pollution and Prevention Act 1999, designed to implement a Directive on the matter, which came into force in 1996, inter alia repealed this Part 1.[83] However, under the 1999 Act, a commencement order was required for the coming into force of this repeal, and such an order has not been made as far as its application to England and Wales.[84] Part I, including the authorization requirement it contains,

[80] The Finance Act 2019, Part 3. This part, alike other parts and provisions of this statute, has a dedicated commencement provision, here, authorizing the Commissioners for Her Majesty's Revenue and Customs to appoint entry into force by regulations (s 79).

[81] On the most recent government communication on the matter see HM Revenue & Customs, *Changes for Tax Provisions for Carbon Emissions Tax*, Policy Paper (11 March 2020) <https://www.gov.uk/government/publications/changes-to-tax-provisions-for-carbon-emissions-tax/changes-to-tax-provisions-for-carbon-emissions-tax>.

[82] Counter-Terrorism Act 2008, sections 1–18. Since the legislation of the act, six of this part's provisions have been fully repealed, and five sections have been added. Information about the prospective nature of legislation is provided through <legislation.gov.uk> and can be accessed in some databases.

[83] Pollution Prevention and Control Act 1999, Ch 24, Schedule 3.

[84] Section 7(3). The Pollution Prevention and Control Act 1999 (Commencement No 1) (England and Wales) Order 2000, SI 2000/800 brought into force amendments specified in Schedule 2 of the Act, concerned with amendments to several acts. Schedule 3, concerning repeals, was commenced in Scotland by the Pollution Prevention and Control Act 1999 (Commencement No 3) (Scotland) Order 2015, SSI 2015/74, signed by the Scottish Minister for Environment, Climate Change, and Land Reform. To date, no other relevant commencement orders have been made.

is thus still formally in force, alongside the arrangements enacted by the 1999 Act, and despite some representation that the arrangement had been 'replaced'.[85] Nothing of this can be clear to the uninitiated.

Some of the obvious fuzziness surrounding such floating provisions has been dispelled by information provided in legal databases. Most accessible, the UK government legislation website likewise offers up-to-date versions of legislation in force: this website provided almost all the information relied upon in this section.[86] Still, the existence of provisions included in the statute books but not formally in force is, if not an anomaly, a concern: those who do not access updated sources of information may be misguided in the understanding of the law. Again, accessibility, the ability to plan ahead, as well as accountability, are all compromised.

Another problem linked with this form of legislation is that while floating, the executive may apply alternative, possibly entirely different, non-statutory arrangements, thereby piling one fuzzy node upon another. In the UK, the House of Lords set a limit on the extent of discretion allowed in such cases. The *Fire Brigades Union* case considered a floating 1988 statute, which legislated the central provisions of an existing *ex gratia* victim compensation scheme. The original scheme, instated in 1964 in the absence of a statute, was defined by the government as an exercise of prerogative.[87] Under the common pattern discussed here, the legislative scheme was to enter into force by an order made by a Secretary of State. Rather than give effect to the statute, the non-statutory scheme continued to operate. In 1994, the government introduced a new, less generous programme, and instated it alongside the floating statute. Applicants claimed that the abstention of the Secretary of State from making a commencement order was unlawful.

The court rejected this argument, but some relief was granted: the majority held that the discretion of the authorities in the design of an alternative framework was limited in two ways: first, the Secretary of State was required to periodically consider the commencement of the statute, a requirement not met as the new *ex gratia* scheme was understood to have been 'brought into operation on the footing that [it] ... will never come into operation'.[88] Secondly, being inconsistent with the statutory scheme, the continuation of the non-statutory arrangement effectively cancelled the Secretary of State's duty to keep the exercise of the commencement

[85] See Cobweb Information, *A Guide to the Environmental Protection Act 1990*, Business Information Factsheet BIF060. March 2016 (claiming that Part I of the Act, among other Parts, has been 'replaced by later legislation'—a term that does not necessarily connote repeal). According to a more accurate representation found on the Welsh government website, 'Part I is repealed by the Pollution Prevention and Control Act 1999 (although the repealing provisions have not yet been brought into force)'. See <https://law.gov.wales/environment/waste/environmental-protection-act-1990?lang=en#/environment/waste/environmental-protection-act-1990?tab=overview&lang=en>.

[86] Access via <http://www.legislation.gov.uk/>.

[87] *R v Secretary Of State For The Home Department, Ex Parte Fire Brigades Union* [1995] 2 AC 513. For the link with prerogative see *Criminal Injuries Compensation Board ex parte Lain* [1967] 2 QB 864 and ch 4.

[88] *Fire Brigades* (n 87) 578.

day power under review. In effect, then, the government's discretion to introduce an alternative non-statutory arrangement was limited only to arrangements that did not substantively differ from the floating one.[89] This decision expressed two powerful messages: first, a practice of non-commencement could only continue if periodically considered, and second, no substantively different alternative could be introduced. However, nowhere did the court brand such longstanding non-commencement periods as an improper case of executive discretion, nor did it rule that, at least in some cases, alternative non-statutory measures cannot be introduced. Moreover, even the limited outcome here, if a similar case occurred in the US, would not have been reached in US courts, notoriously constrained in matters of policy.[90]

In sum, as far as the UK is concerned, its Parliament is not limited in its insertion of commencement provisions that rely on future government goodwill, nor is the government obligated to exercise its discretion beyond the requirement to periodically consider the possibility of commencement. Only actions that practically negate the possibility of future commencement by introducing a long-term arrangement which would effectively cancel out that possibility may be found unlawful. The retention of such 'floating' fuzzy legislation for long periods, as the few examples discussed above show, offer sufficient evidence of the continuing force of this form of fuzziness.

c. Under-funded law

In some cases, statutory provisions turn pastiche due to intentional denial of funds for their implementation. Under-funding and denial of funding may be generated either by the executive or by the legislature; this section is mainly concerned with executive under-funding.

Usually, heads of government departments and agencies carry sufficient discretion to set their own funding preferences; set, itemized budgets still offer those authorized to spend to follow some of their preferences. In such cases, policy decisions to refrain from funding certain actions may emanate on the ministerial or the agency level, transforming the authorization to act into no more than a potential promise in case of its resurrection. Underfunding may also be directed by the central executive. Consider, for example, President Trump's 'Two for One' executive order 13771, issued during his first month in office.

[89] At the close of the decision, Lord Nicholls ruled that '[t]he inescapable conclusion is that the Home Secretary has effectually "written off" the statutory scheme and that once the tariff scheme has been introduced, there would be no realistic prospect of him being able to keep the exercise of the commencement day power under review. By setting up the tariff scheme the minister has set his face in a different direction. He has struck out down a different route and thereby disabled himself from properly discharging his statutory duty in the way Parliament intended. For this reason the new scheme is outside the powers presently vested in him'. ibid 578.

[90] On judicial review of administrative discretion in the US see ch 10.

Under this executive order, in order to reduce regulation and control regulatory costs, all agencies are required to eliminate two regulations for every new regulation issued. In addition, the order stipulates that

> [f]or fiscal year 2017, which is in progress, the heads of all agencies are directed that the total incremental cost of all new regulations, including repealed regulations, to be finalized this year shall be no greater than zero, unless otherwise required by law or consistent with advice provided in writing by the Director of the Office of Management and Budget (Director).[91]

Agencies intent on complying with this order would thus be required to prioritize their projects, and possibly decide that certain projects be effectively strapped in order to ensure the operation of other projects.[92]

Still, the emergence of most pastiche frameworks due to underfunding occurs due to budget reductions or funding prohibitions generated by statute. Such cases are still discussed in this chapter, dedicated to executive-generated fuzziness, in order to offer a complete overview of the ways operating rules transform into pastiche, dead-letter law. Consider, for example, the rider that has appeared in most appropriation acts since 2010, which serially prohibited the introduction of a permit regime concerning 'emission of gases from biological processes associated with livestock production',[93] or the rider that bars the funding of 'mandatory reporting of greenhouse gas emissions from manure management systems', both discussed earlier in this book.[94] As mentioned in Chapters 1 and 7, the EPA has openly admitted its inability to act in light of the first rider. In its webpage dedicated to the manure management reporting arrangement, under its Greenhouse Gas Reporting Program, it is noted that

> EPA is not implementing subpart JJ of 40 CFR Part 98 using funds provided in its appropriations due to a Congressional restriction prohibiting the expenditure of funds for this purpose.[95]

[91] Executive Order 13771, *Reducing Regulation and Controlling Regulatory Costs,* 82 FR 9339, §2(b).

[92] A study of the effect of this order is beyond the scope of this chapter, dedicated to a general overview of possible executive-generated fuzziness. On executive order 13771 and its application, the first highly critical, the second more supportive, see Holly L Weaver, 'One for the Price of Two: The Hidden Costs of Regulatory Reform under Executive Order 13771' (2018) 70 Admin L Rev 491; Bridget CE Dooling, Mark Febrizio, and Daniel R Pérez, *Accounting for Regulatory Reform under Executive Order 13771: Explainer and Recommendations to Improve Accuracy and Accountability* (Brookings 2019).

[93] For the text of this rider and further information, see ch 7.

[94] The full text of this rider, '[n]otwithstanding any other provision of law, none of the funds made available in this or any other Act may be used to implement any provision in a rule, if that provision requires mandatory reporting of greenhouse gas emissions from manure management systems', appeared, like the previously cited rider, in Appropriations Acts since 2010 (see eg Appropriations Act 2010 §425; Further Appropriations Act 2020 §438). In this case, the EPA has admitted that although its general reporting program is up and running,

[95] Greenhouse Gas Reporting Program (GHGRP) Subpart JJ—Manure Management, Rule Information, <https://www.epa.gov/ghgreporting/subpart-jj-manure-management>. This program

This example of agency capitulation may still raise questions. Have agencies faced with such riders reacted creatively, by making policy decisions that enabled parallel funding and continued action? If so, this response could be added as an additional case of creative compliance of the type discussed above. Although a study of agency responses to prohibitory riders in the field of air pollution is relegated to further study, the example in the case of congressional limitation of funding of the Mexico-US border wall, discussed above, may be illuminating, adding additional dimensions to the discussion of creative compliance. The de facto elimination of frameworks of executive action through under-funding, however, required further attention.

D. Fuzzy Implementation: The Prices Paid

Some fuzzy forms of implementation—those effected by informal measures and creative compliance—have been welcomed as beneficial supplements to law in the books. Within the regulation discipline, Hawkins notes that employing sanctions and other statutory powers selectively was viewed, at least by the regulators, as promoting the efficiency of regulatory action as well as its social legitimacy by better conforming with social conceptions of justice.[96] For him, this reliance on law as last resort could be an optimal 'messaging' tactic if it followed several conditions, namely commensurability with the moral fault involved in the infraction; consistency in application; expression of responsiveness and accountability; and the retention of the appearance of fairness, active involvement, and credibility, all with a move to prosecution in a 'big case'.[97] Bardach and Kagan's 'good inspector' employs responsive and flexible methods instead of tough 'legalistic' ones.[98] Ayres and Braithwaite present their enforcement pyramid not only as a reflection of regulatory reality, but also as one example of better, more responsive regulation that can 'transcend the intellectual stalemate between those who favor strong state regulation of business and those who advocate deregulation', by offering regulatory frameworks that are better attuned to the ultimate aims to be achieved while factoring-in both the needs and the potential of industry power to contribute to the design of working regulation.[99]

has never been applied in the context of livestock emissions (confirmed by email to author, EPA Greenhouse Gas Reporting Program Help Desk, 1 May 2019). On this congressional restriction see Michelle Nowlin and Emily Spiegel, 'Much Ado About Methane: Intensive Livestock Agriculture and Greenhouse Gas Emissions' in Mary Jane Angelo and Anél du Plessis, *Research Handbook on Climate Change and Agricultural Law* (Edward Elgar 2017) 228, 261–62.

96 Hawkins (n 8) ch 19.
97 Hawkins (n 8) esp ch 7.
98 Bardach and Kagan (n 9) 123–51.
99 Ayres and Braithwaite (n 9) 3 and passim.

Some of the participants in the debate over creative forms of application created and applied by the EPA and other regulators offer limited normative elements, but positive assessment is not absent: in the words of Richard Stewart, '[s]ometimes, the agency will effectively recast a program in order to make it more readily implementable and therefore more effective'.[100] Furthermore, discussing regulation by agreements, Stewart opines that

> In many cases, such agreements explicitly modify the regulatory requirements that would apply in the absence of such an agreement (the default requirements), thereby allowing for greater flexibility and responsiveness to the specific conditions of regulated industries, firms and facilities, and achieving more rapid environmental improvement than the standard regime.[101]

Despite these arguments, Stewart's message is also critical. He notes that the various forms of slippage or 'adaptive implementation' 'present important questions of the compatibility of such arrangements with democratic values of transparency, accountability, and the rule of law'.[102]

Sharing this criticism, Daniel Farber's study of noncompliance and creative compliance that addresses regulators' 'morphing' of standards, renegotiating/reinterpreting regulations, and introducing arrangements such as the SEPs discussed above,[103] expresses concerns regarding the transparency of these measures and their amenability to accountability processes. Farber notes that 'slippage raises substantial problems: regulatory inaction, negotiation practices, and all other forms of slippage' (as mentioned above, Farber does not distinguish between informal enforcement and creative compliance; indeed, both forms have shared features) 'take place in the shadow of the law, not in the light of public deliberation'; furthermore, the reinvention/reinterpretation of regulation may provide 'fertile ground for negative slippage', that is, forms of inaction and regulatory infraction.[104]

Another problem is the provision of a possibility of further slippage. This is a sophisticated slippery-slope argument, concerned with the addition of one slippage onto another:

> ... we must wonder how much additional slippage might occur between the reinvented regulatory regime and actual compliance. That is, will we have slippage (from the reinvented regulations to actual compliance) on top of slippage (from original standards to reinvented regulation)?[105]

100 Stewart (n 11) 54.
101 ibid 60.
102 ibid 57.
103 Farber (n 10) 305–11.
104 ibid 319.
105 ibid 318.

Indeed, those who recognize the distance between regulation as a harsh collection of command and control penal measures and the more nuanced reality, and preach for the beneficial contribution of adopting a pyramid model, may be commended, if indeed their informal tactics promote the common good. Yet, whatever the utilities of reversion to informal modes of action, relative agency freedom is ensured by this practice, while clarity and certainty are compromised; the dangers to proper administration by reliance on informal and creative compliance should not be overlooked.

A far better alternative exists. Moderation and escalatory tactics need not be the outcome of reversion to informality: the architecture of regulatory regimes could be transformed by embracing these tactics into the regulatory framework. All of the tactics located in Ayres and Braithwaite's pyramid, as well as Stewart's impressive list of measures that includes agreements of all types, negotiated arrangements (alongside other examples, SEPs are discussed in this context), negotiated rulemaking, and other participatory-induced frameworks could be incorporated in statute without losing their utility. A cautionary notice, or the imposition of a civil penalty, issued against the background of harsher penalties, would not lose their value when embedded in the statute; the opposite may be true.[106]

Of course, as argued throughout the book, fuzziness, here in the form of informality, has many attractions, and its eradication is a project that is unlikely to succeed. Still, recipes for improvement are essential and their adoption may whittle down some of the existing fuzzy practices.[107]

Pastiche law, the third type of fuzzy implementation discussed in this chapter, suffers from similar malaises, if not worse ones. The law in the books never fully reflects law in action, but an unimplemented law, or one that remains on the books but has not entered into force, challenges the very basics of the nature of law as accessible and decipherable. Much has been said in previous chapters on the prices paid by fuzziness, and a general discussion of this aspect is offered in the next chapter. Suffice, then, to end here.

E. Concluding Remarks

Contributing to the presence of fuzziness in the public sphere, executive bodies supplement the fuzziness offered by constitution and legislation by applying fuzzy implementation and enforcement practices. This chapter has identified three such

[106] Ayres and Braithwaite (n 9); Stewart (n 11). For an argument in this vein see Margit Cohn, 'Fuzzy Legality in Regulation: The Legislative Mandate Revisited' (2001) 23 L and Policy 469, 488–89.

[107] For analyses of both the politics of fuzziness and the contribution of review as an agent aimed at constraining it see chs 9 and 10.

practices located on this spectrum of implementation. First, as well-noted in both politics and in regulation studies, the regulatory mandate often operates as a background for the actual life of executive action. Within the sphere of legality, when the only option formally found in the framework is a harsh sanction, executive bodies pick from a diverse menu of options that are, as a matter of policy, considered as alternatives before choosing the last resort. The motivation may be laudable: rather than use the big guns, results may be achieved by 'speaking softly' most of the time, reaching arrangements that may be satisfactory without creating unnecessary conflict. Yet the only way, as the literature shows us, that such results can be achieved is the existence of the 'big stick', the severe measure that needs to be continuously brandished as a cautionary message to those who do not wish to comply with the requirement they are faced with. Whatever the utilities of this practice, the employment of measures organized under an 'enforcement pyramid', where full enforcement is 'selective', necessarily increases the degree of fuzziness in any regulated field of action. New or inexperienced regulatees, as well as other members of the public who may be affected by the action which the regulators seem to wish to curb, may not be aware of the law in action; accessibility to the life of the law and understanding its workings require expertise to a degree that does not comport with the values served by designing and applying a clear and universally applied framework. Moreover, the feature of selection, embedded in such a practice, at least offers the potential for abuse that would be difficult to identify and challenge. Strangely, little has been offered in the context of this literature by way of suggesting the formal introduction of carrots and smaller sticks to minimize the impact of informal enforcement.

By using creative compliance, the second practice discussed in this chapter, agencies introduce interpretations that are removed from original intent and even text. This may occur when rules are introduced as political solutions to a pressing public preference, with little attention granted to their feasibility, or when the executive body is in fundamental disagreement with the mandate it has been given. Acting within legality, but, once again, under a veil of inaccessibility, this practice challenges the same values mentioned above.

Finally, a set of rules that is merely pastiche, either from inception or due to the emergence of conditions that lead to its virtual expiration, is yet another form of departure from the ideal of law as organizer and should not be welcomed. This chapter addressed three such cases of pastiche law: statutes or rules that have never been implemented, rules that are not applied due to the removal of funding, and rules that have not entered into force. Easily traced in the rule-books, such rules have little to do with the reality of executive action. Once again, fuzziness emerges.

PART IV
ANALYSIS

9

Fuzzy Legality and the Challenge to Proper Governance

A. **Introduction** 255

B. **The Challenges of Fuzzy Legality to Proper Governance** 256

1. Introduction 256
2. Arguments from Democratic Theory 257
   a. The rule of law discourse 257
   b. Participatory/deliberative democratic theory 262
3. The Benefits of Fuzzy Legality? 265
4. Summary 268

C. **The Political Economy of Fuzzy Legality** 269

1. Introduction 269
2. The Rise and Retention of Fuzziness: Mapping the Explanatory Factors 271
3. Endogenous Reasons for Fuzziness 272
4. Exogenous Reasons for Fuzziness 278
   a. Power-accumulation and retention 279
   b. Disagreement 282
      (1) During the design stage 282
      (2) After introduction 284
   c. Pressure to act 285
   d. Marginalization 285

D. **Concluding Remarks** 286

A. Introduction

Opening the evaluative-normative part of this book, this chapter addresses two aspects of the propriety of reliance on fuzzy law as a central strategy for the retention of executive dominance over and under law. First, I collect the arguments put forward in the previous chapters, which touched upon the direct negative impact of fuzzy law on proper governance. These arguments are sorted around two nodes of democratic theory: 'the rule of law' and theories of participatory/deliberative democracy. Both offer good bases for embedding these arguments in the normative debate.

The second part of the chapter offers a hitherto untreated aspect: it traces the political economy of fuzziness. I trace the factors that enhance reliance on fuzzy modes of executive action, classified under a distinction between endogenous and exogenous factors. Beyond law's endemic fuzziness, I study a group of external factors that impact on the retention of fuzziness, ranging from power politics to the relative marginalization of the action exercised.

A Theory of the Executive Branch. Margit Cohn, Oxford University Press (2021). © Margit Cohn.
DOI: 10.1093/oso/9780198821984.003.0010

Combined, these analyses enrich the understanding of the ubiquity of fuzziness, while emphasizing the prices paid by continuous reversion to such practices.

B. The Challenges of Fuzzy Legality to Proper Governance

1. Introduction

Should 'is' imply 'ought', as some have suggested? If executive action under fuzzy law is inevitable, as the second part of this chapter further establishes, should it be embraced, or at least accepted as an unavoidable feature of governance?

The force of the interests that promote fuzziness, discussed below, is not a cause for alarm for some. Publishing during President Obama's presidency, Eric Posner and Adrian Vermeule argued that executive action unfettered by law is 'best in the thin sense that there is no feasible way to improve upon it, under the conditions of the administrative state'; as for black and grey holes, they claim that 'because their presence is inevitable, there is no point condemning them; to do so is quixotic'.[1] Clearly not a full-blown normative argument (curiously, the authors rely on the maxim 'Ought implies can'[2]), this seeming capitulation to politics squarely challenges the principles of justice and fairness that legitimate law's coercive nature.

This book rejects such directions, be they based on logic, politics, or normative grounds. Two sets of values from democratic theory justify scepticism towards fuzziness. The first is often addressed under the title 'the rule of law'. Fuzziness in law has been denigrated under both thin and thick varieties of this ideal (concurrently defined as formal and substantial),[3] all of them designed to ensure maximum individual liberty and welfare (again, in both their thin and thick varieties) under rules that are open and accessible. The ideal has been found under serious threat when states revert to reliance on emergency conditions.[4] This section further develops this argument by applying it to all political climates and to all forms of fuzzy law.

The second set of values derives from theories of participatory and deliberative democracy, which set a premium on active multi-player decision-making, and reject any notion of unilateral action, one of the forms of fuzziness.

At the outset, however, it should not be argued that fuzziness is an absolute wrong. Constitutions must generally be open-ended enough to secure their, and

[1] Eric A Posner and Adrian Vermeule, *The Executive Unbound: After the Madisonian Republic* (OUP 2011) 5, 92. Following an argument forcefully made in the context of the normative discussion of judicial review (Chap 10), here, too, it is to be hoped that their claims, couched as universal, were not informed by the politics of any single president.

[2] ibid 5.

[3] On the distinction between 'thin' and 'thick', or 'formal' and 'substantive' theories of the rule of law see below.

[4] David Dyzenhaus, *The Constitution of Law: Legality in a Time of Emergency* (CUP 2006).

their polities' stability; discretion, it is argued, is required for the maintenance of responsivity to the exigencies of political and social life and its governance, as are broad authorizations to delegate some decision-making powers; and life during a concrete, real emergency does not always enable governments to embed new required powers into the existing framework.

Still, the central utility arguably justifying the adoption of fuzzy law, efficiency/ease, poses a serious threat to the well-functioning democracy. Executive action in the absence of a clear authorization to act challenges the legitimacy of modern democratic government and carries a higher potential for unchecked abuse. Constitutions may grant the executive original, specific powers, but those are typically open-ended, hence fuzzy.[5] Setting aside such authorizations, the separation of powers principle in all its versions confers on the executive branch the role of executing statutes enacted by the legislature.[6] Representing the people through elections, rules made by legislators are the result of a potentially lengthy deliberative process, often enabling participation of actors in the public sphere. Both elements are compromised when the executive is the ultimate rule-maker.[7] And the higher the degree of fuzziness, the stronger the threat of abuse and misuse. Chapter 10 offers a counterbalance by arguing for vigorous participation as checks for unfettered powers, in courts and beyond, but for now, the focus is on the challenges.

2. Arguments from Democratic Theory

a. The rule of law discourse

Some of the debate over the propriety of reliance on similes of fuzzy law has been conducted under the title 'the rule of law', a concept that has been discussed and dissected by so many, and in so many ways, as to render the term well-nigh meaningless. Still, the concept does serve as an anchor for normative accounts that extend beyond the seemingly formalistic framework of the separation of powers.

Too often, claims that point out the dangers posed by indeterminate law to 'the rule of law' seem almost intuitive. A question such as '[i]s the rule of law optional for liberal democratic societies?'[8] which is not preceded by a robust discussion over the nature of 'the rule of law', seems to be based either on the assumption that all readers of that essay, indeed, all participants in the philosophical, political, and

[5] See Chap 1.

[6] MJC Vile, *Constitutionalism and the Separation of Powers* (Clarendon Press 1967).

[7] Of course, legislation is not necessarily a better governance tool. Vague statutes, broad delegations, and other forms of statute- and executive-generated practices may grant executive action a façade of legality while containing no substantive constraint. These types of 'fuzzy legality' are addressed in Chap 3 and Part II of this book. Despite this, statutes at least enjoy processual legitimacy, absent when executives act on their own initiative.

[8] Dyzenhaus (n 4) 1.

legal debates own sufficient knowledge of this multi-disciplinary discussion.[9] An overview of the nature and various forms of this ideal is in place.

The concept of 'the rule of law', often employed as one of the central elements of the liberal-democratic ethos, has notoriously varied meanings, ranging from a principle that focuses on minimal formal requirements to its equation of law as a morally laden agent. Recognizing that this broad array of meanings may have rendered the term 'meaningless', Judith Shklar still continued to analyse its pedigree and nature, as have countless philosophers of law, political scientists, and legal scholars.[10] Roots in early thought go back to Aristotle, with John Locke, Montesquieu, and the US Founding Fathers added to contribute to the lineage of this concept.[11] For our purposes, Dicey can be the earliest to be discussed.

The term as such was indeed coined, and introduced into general use by Dicey. One of the 'three leading characteristics in the current constitution of England' (together with the sovereignty of parliament and the conventions of the constitution),[12] Dicey presents the principle in *Introduction to the Study of the Law of the Constitution* as based on three conceptions, carrying three generally corresponding meanings. First is the supremacy of law and the rejection of arbitrariness; second is equality before the law, under which all persons are subject to law, regardless of rank or position; finally, Dicey focuses on the evolving nature of the English system under rules shaped by courts and parliament, which has led to the development of a constitution that derives from 'ordinary' law shaped by judicial treatment of claims concerned with the rights of the individual—presented as starkly different from countries that follow a code from which all arrangements are derived.[13]

Since Dicey, arguments about the nature of 'the rule of law' in fact constitute a discussion on the proper nature of law itself. As such, the debate is normative, directing attention to the ways law should be designed and applied. Justice cannot be done to the rich academic discussion, nor is it needed for our purposes. Suffice

[9] This is not to say that Dyzenhaus refrains from some definitional references, despite his concession that he 'will not at any point go into much detail about what [he claims] to be the content of the rule of law' (ibid 12), but he wishes to show the difficulties evident even under a conception 'that both links procedural constraints to substantive values and requires that all three branches of government regard themselves as participating in a common project of realizing those values' (ibid 14).

[10] Judith Shklar, 'Political Theory and the Rule of Law' in Allan C Hutchinson and Patrick Monahan (eds), *The Rule of Law: Ideal or Ideology* (Carswell 1987) 1. For just a few general analyses of the rich body of literature that generally addresses the principle see Brian Z Tamanaha, *On the Rule of Law: History, Politics, Theory* (CUP 2004); 'The Rule of Law', Stanford Encyclopaedia of Philosophy <https://plato.stanford.edu/entries/rule-of-law/>.

[11] Aristotle, *The Politics* (trans Ernest Barker, Clarendon Press 1946) §1287a (addressing the rule of a single king, '[t]he rule of law is therefore preferable ... to that of a single citizen ... He who commands that law should rule may thus be regarded as commanding that God and reason alone should rule' For an analysis of Locke, Montesquieu, and the Federalist Papers see Tamanaha (n 10) 47–59.

[12] AV Dicey, *Introduction to the Study of the Law of the Constitution* (8th edn, Macmillan 1915) xxxv.

[13] ibid 120–21. An earlier triad of conceptions found in the same chapter functionally equates the first meaning with the principle that no one may be punished or suffer in body or goods unless breaching a legal rule (effectively representing the maxim *nullum crimen sine lege*); the other two meanings are generally equivalent to the above. ibid 110–14.

to note the well-known distinction between two schools of inquiry, and rely on the 'thin' version.[14]

For some, perhaps the largest school, 'the rule of law' connotes a set of principles concerning the proper forms and processes which law should adopt and follow—a seemingly 'formal', or 'thin' version.[15] Towards the other pole on the continuum between 'formal' and 'substantive' versions of the ideal, are accounts that attach substantive values such as justice, fairness, the protection of human rights broadly penned, and other moral commitments to the requirement that a system follows 'the rule of law', reaching versions that equate the ideal with the full collection of values that support a vision of democracy laden with moral content.[16] Yet most of those who preach a relatively 'thin', formal/processual version that is not purely positivist, recognize the role of substantive values in the system without falling into the expansionist camp. The requirements proffered by Fuller and Raz are set to achieve an 'inner morality', in Fuller's words, or to maintain, under balancing, the ideals of liberty and/or dignity, the latter endorsed in Raz's account.[17] Other scholars who do not locate themselves in Dworkin's camp recognize some substantive values that are protected by the system, ranging from John Hart Ely's 'process writ small' that should be viewed as a minimalist reiteration of the values of some rights, through Cass Sunstein's 'core' of minimal commitments underlying his 'substantive minimalism',[18] to David Dyzenhaus's 'rather bare' version, subsequently described as an ideal that 'links procedural constraints to substantive values'.[19] For some, such discussions may be placed as 'middle-ground' theories;[20] in any case,

[14] For the distinction see Joseph Raz, 'The Rule of Law and Its Virtue' in Joseph Raz, *The Authority of Law* (Clarendon Press 1979) 211; Paul P Craig, 'Formal and Substantive Conceptions of the Rule of Law: An Analytical Framework' [1997] PL 467; Tamanaha (n 10) Chaps 7, 8.

[15] On the 'formal' pole of the continuum between formal and substantive understandings, Hayek recognized the ideal as requiring rules that are fixed, preordained, and enable those subject to the rules to fairly foresee the use of the powers and to plan ahead accordingly. Friedrich A Hayek, *The Road to Serfdom* (University of Chicago Press 1944) 54. See also Robert S Summers, 'A Formal Theory of the Rule of Law' (1993) 6(2) Ratio Juris 127. Still close to this pole are Lon Fuller and Joseph Raz, *The Morality of Law* (Yale University Press 1964); Raz (n 14). The formal/processual criteria differ.

[16] For central contributions see Ronald Dworkin, *A Matter of Principle* (Harvard University Press 1985) 11–13 (identifying a 'rights' conception of the rule of law alongside the 'rule-book conception'); Tom Bingham, *The Rule of Law* (Penguin 2010). The most expansive version usually cited was introduced in 1959 by the International Congress of Jurists; under this version, '[t]he function of the legislature in a free society under the Rule of Law is to create and maintain the conditions which will uphold the dignity of man as an individual. This dignity requires not only the recognition of his civil and political rights but also the establishment of the social, economic, educational and cultural conditions which are essential to the full development of his personality'. International Commission of Jurists, *The Rule of Law in a Free Society* (International Congress of Jurists 1959) 4, Clause 1.

[17] This is evident both in Fuller (n 15) and Raz (n 14) 220–21.

[18] John Hart Ely, *Democracy and Distrust* (Harvard University Press 1980); Cass R Sunstein, *One Case at a Time: Judicial Minimalism on the Supreme Court* (Harvard University Press 1999) 63–68.

[19] Dyzenhaus (n 4) 12–14; see also David Dyzenhaus, 'The Rule of Law Project' (2016) 129 Harv L Rev Forum 268, 269;

[20] See Craig (n 14) 484 (reviewing both camps and focusing inter alia on Raz's later work as one example of 'middle ground' theory).

the argument for the separation between form/process and substance is evident, especially in Raz's argument that substance had best be discussed separately.[21]

Without entering the debate between these two camps, or considering the option of a middle ground, it would suffice for our purposes to rely on Lon Fuller's eight principles, which for him comprise the 'inner morality of the law'. Fuller does not present this work as an explication of 'the rule of law' as such—the term is generally absent in his work—but his set of principles, or requirements of proper law, has become central to the discussion of this concept. For Fuller, laws should be general, public, prospective, and clear; they should contain no contradictions, require action that is within the powers of those affected by the rule, be relatively stable, and be generally applied in congruence with its edicts.[22] Despite the use of the term 'moral', as in the discussion of these principles as comprising 'the inner morality of law', these requirements are formal-processual. In their entirety, they deliver a vision of law that applies fairly and consistently, a form of 'thin' morality, without reaching to the content of rules. The values promoted here, then, are the ability of citizens, and others subject to a system's rules, to understand in advance the rules they are subjected to, and to plan their action accordingly.[23]

Fuller argues that a system which does not meet these requirements not only fails in producing a 'bad system'; in fact, 'it results in something that is not properly called a legal system at all'.[24] For our purposes, we can set aside the weighty question of the nature of law, reflected here. Arguments regarding the potential damage to society resulting from these 'failures' are sufficient for our discussion. Such potential damage is evident when fuzzy law organizes action, as discussed in previous chapters and further below.

Most of Fuller's principles resonate fuzziness; they are likely to be especially threatened when the law is fuzzy, although the link between the type of fuzziness and the potential of their breach varies. A breach of the first principle, requiring law to be generally applicable, may be introduced by statutes that seem to be penned broadly but in fact were intended to apply to a single case, through the crafting of conditions that can be met only once. This type of fuzziness is less pervasive when compared to the absence of publication. This second failure is found in the context of British orders in council made solely under the prerogative. As shown in Chapter 5, some of these orders were never published. Recall Professor De-Smith's difficulties in accessing orders in council, documented in his 1959 letter to the editor published in the Times of London, and discussed in that chapter.[25]

[21] See eg Raz (n 14) 226–29.

[22] Fuller (n 15) 39, 46–94. Cf Raz's list of requirements, adding requirements concerned with judicial process. Raz (n 14) 214–19.

[23] Other values, such as participation in rule-making, accountability, and review/checking mechanisms, are discussed in Chap 10 as part of the values promoted by deliberative democracy.

[24] Fuller (n 15) 39.

[25] Chapter 5. On this point see Ronan Cormacain, 'Prerogative Legislation as the Paradigm of Bad Law-Making: the Chagos Islands' (2013) 39 Common Law Bull 487, 503–505, 507–508.

The sporadic publication practices, discussed there, reflect a selective publication policy. Sensitive prerogative-based orders in council have not been formally published, as in the case of the measures challenged in *GCHQ*, *Bancoult 1*, and *Bancoult 2*.[26] In the absence of formal access to a rule, only those holding special access privileges will be able to assess their situation: even an academic who had just received his doctorate at LSE found access difficult.

Retroactive legislation, the third type of failure, is not unheard of, but is much less prevalent in fuzzy law: as long as the date of entry into force is clearly set, the act may be problematic, but the problem has little to do with fuzziness.[27] However, a second type of 'failure' pertaining to the temporal dimension and not recognized in Fuller's analysis, is the flip side of retrospective law. In the UK, at least, a statute may be enacted, but its entry into force may be dependent on the exercise of executive discretion. Several examples of the British legislative style of separating between the enactment of a law and its entry into force (often requiring an order made by a secretary of state or minister) were discussed in Chapter 8. These are no anomalies. In fact, a great number of British statutes do not enter into force on the day of their Royal signature. As a mere exercise, note that out of the eighteen statutes enacted during the first half of 2019, nine include prospective commencement provisions, requiring the promulgation of a commencement order in order to switch on parts of these statutes. Five of the remaining nine acts entered into force on their date of enactment, and four set a date for entry into force.[28] The period between enactment and entry into force varies, but in all such cases prospective legislation remains 'floating', despite its existence in the rule book; assisted search is required to grasp the force of any enactment.[29] No such pattern is evident in US federal law.[30]

The requirement for clarity directly links with fuzziness. In addition to the oft-recognized grants of open-ended and interpretable provisions, grants of discretion, and authorizations to delegate powers, discussed in Chapter 3, my detailed discussion of 'patchwork legislation' in Chapter 7 offered a different case

[26] *Council of Civil Service Unions v Minister for the Civil Service* [1985] AC 374 (1984) (GCHQ); *R (Bancoult) v Secretary of State for Foreign and Commonwealth Affairs* [2001] QB 1067 (*Bancoult 1*); *R (on the application of Bancoult) v Secretary of State for Foreign and Commonwealth Affairs* (*No 2*) [2008] 3 WLR 955 (*Bancoult 2*).

[27] Fuller is well aware of this: alongside the assessment of retrospectivity as a 'monstrosity' when taken in itself, he recognizes that sometimes such a rule functions to correct past injustice or to clear legal vacuums (with the exception of criminal law and, to a certain extent, tax law that operates as an alternative to the setting of a criminal offence). Fuller (n 15) 51–62. For a general study of this phenomenon see Charles CG Sampford, *Retrospectivity and the Rule of Law* (OUP 2006).

[28] Search through <legislation.gov.uk>, UK public general acts only. One of the nine statutes, the Stalking Protection Act 2019, is entirely prospective, that is, none of its provisions, except the commencement provision, came into force at the time of enactment.

[29] Such assistance is found online in the British repository of laws <legislation.gov.uk.>, administered by the National Archives. The Statutes at Large printed series does not, and cannot, follow post-enactment developments.

[30] None of the twenty-four Acts enacted during the same period (January–June 2019) included a commencement provision; all statutes thus entered into force on enactment.

of unclarity. In both case-studies, emergency law and air pollution regulation, a multitude of statutes rendered understanding the gist of the legal framework practically impossible. As mentioned there, when several sources of power are available, especially when they pile-up over time as in the case of emergency laws, executives can choose between them, while other players in the public sphere may need to second-guess the choice, or, in the case of patchworking by dispersion, scan the entire legal system to hopefully reach a conclusion. Even when reached, this conclusion can easily be merely temporary, due to the possible introduction of additional arrangements. In such cases, understanding the legal framework and planning ahead are seriously impaired.

Patchworking can also be conducive to contradiction, the next of Fuller's principles. Explicit contradiction, which occurs when two provisions cannot operate in tandem, is not a rare occurrence, but is most likely to appear when a single issue can be regulated under different arrangements. The most common type of non-congruence exists when two avenues of action exist, one of them more lenient, the other stricter. Consider, as an example, British anti-terrorism laws and the Civil Contingencies Act 2004. Designed to address various forms of emergency, the latter act defines one of the three types of emergency conditions as 'war, or terrorism, which threatens serious damage to the security of the United Kingdom'.[31] The measures available under these laws greatly differ.[32]

'Impossible laws', which require action that cannot be exercised, could also be considered under the term 'fuzzy legality', as would be rules that are constantly changed. More important is Fuller's last principle. One of the main examples of non-congruence between official action and the rule concerns implementation and enforcement, discussed in Chapters 3 and 8. In their most extreme case, a rule may be no more than an empty shell, 'pastiche law'. When laws are universally ignored or rarely applied, the gap between the rule in the books and law in action is unbridgeable. Once again, understanding law and planning ahead on its basis are severely impaired.

b. Participatory/deliberative democratic theory

The vision of democracy that drives the normative claim is based on a development of theories of participatory democracy and their offshoot, deliberative democracy. Few of the calls discussed below, that move from aggregation of public opinion via elections as a single mode of participation/deliberation, have ever been absolute. The emphasis on ongoing participation colours these variants of democratic theory, but theorists generally agree with Gerry Mackie's call for 'deliberation, but voting too'.[33]

[31] Civil Contingencies Act 2004 section 1(1)(c).

[32] See ch 6.

[33] Gerry Mackie, 'Deliberation, but Voting Too' in Robert J Cavalier (ed), *Approaching Deliberative Democracy: Theory and Practice* (Carnegie Mellon University Press 2011) 75.

Carole Pateman, one of the first advocates of the participatory democracy variant, challenged theories she called 'contemporary theories of democracy', under which elections were the ultimate form of the democratic process. Presented in Joseph Schumpeter's influential work as 'a competition for political leadership',[34] elections were considered the main, if not single, form of participation: the aggregation of preferences, expressed in periodically held nationwide election events, enables elected representatives to act on behalf of the people. Under these theories, limited intervention between elections is preferred: constant citizen input is not only unnecessary; in fact, 'bombarding [members of parliament] with letters and telegrams' is detrimental to proper governance as it challenges leadership.[35]

The elitist turn of such theories led Pateman and others to advance a mode of government focused on a more vigorous concept of participation.[36] Under participatory democracy, continuous involvement in the actual making of decisions is advocated not only as a proper form of democracy, but also as a method through which individuals develop their capacities. According to this theory, participation is not merely 'a protective device' that ensures proper operation of democratic institutions; it is in itself a value that benefits individual enhancement just as much as it holds the potential to prevent abuse of power by elected officers.[37]

In the footsteps of participatory democracy, political scientist Joseph Bessette coined the term 'deliberative democracy', but used it as a descriptive tool for a discussion of the US political structure, with 'deliberation' connoting, in Bessette's words, 'reasoning on the merits of public policy', that is, discussions held by legislatures and other political institutions.[38] Picked up by James Fishkin and others, the term became central to normative arguments on the proper modes of political decision-making. Here, too, the emphasis is on individual citizens' ongoing participation through communication.[39] Under these

[34] Joseph A Schumpeter, *Capitalism, Socialism, and Democracy* (3rd edn, Harper & Row 1950) 269.

[35] ibid 295. For Pateman's analysis of Schumpeter's and others' similar theories, see Carole Pateman, *Participation and Democratic Theory* (CUP 1970) 2–16.

[36] See Arnold S Kaufman, 'Human Nature and Participatory Politics' in William E Connolly (ed), *The Bias of Pluralism* (Atherton Press 1969) 178; Pateman (n 35); Jane J Mansbridge, *Beyond Adversary Democracy* (Basic Books 1980). For an overview of these and other contributions see Jeffrey D Hilmer, 'The State of *Participatory* Democratic Theory' (2010) 32 New Poli Sci 43, 45–49.

[37] According to a well-cited phrase, '[o]ne might characterise the participatory model as one where maximum input (participation) is required and where output includes not just policies (decisions) but also the development of the social and political capacities of each individual, so that there is "feedback" from output to input' (ibid 43). Pateman (n 35) 43: See also Pateman 14, 20.

[38] Joseph M Bessette, *The Mild Voice of Reason: Deliberative Democracy and American National Government* (University of Chicago Press 1994) eg 46.

[39] The rich literature on deliberative democracy is only selectively represented here. For some of the contributions see Amy Gutmann and Dennis Thompson, *Democracy and Disagreement* (Belknap Press 1996); Simone Chambers, 'Deliberative Democratic Theory' (2003) 6 Annu Rev Polit Sci 307; Amy Gutmann and Dennis F Thompson, *Why Deliberative Democracy?* (Princeton University Press 2004); and sources cited below.

theories, fora and modes of such participation vary, ranging from formally set alternative modes of decision-making to fluid forms of social interaction. As examples from the two opposite poles of this spectrum, consider James Fishkin's 'deliberative polls', and Jane Mansbridge's 'everyday talk'. Fishkin advancedopen events of deliberation by a 'representative microcosm', a relatively large representative group, that culminated in a poll concerning a specified issue.[40] Here, then, universal participation was marginalized in favour of a structured form of deliberation between a finite number of participants. Mansbridge sets her focus on the inclusion of largely informal deliberative processes held in all social fora, which potentially impact on society at large and on decision-making in particular.[41] In the middle of this spectrum are theories which broaden the more classic focus on the two-player interaction between the people and their direct representatives in parliaments to a multi-player game that is played in several arenas and under different sets of formal or informal rules. Such additional players include political parties, NGOs, and even schools, which should equip children with deliberation skills to ensure the continuance of robust deliberation.[42] Deliberative systems theory, the more recent turn in deliberative theory, emphasizes not only the importance of identifying multiple institutions and processes, both formal and informal, but also the constant interaction between them: interdependence and possible redundancy only serve to improve the overall functioning of a deliberative system.[43]

Key political philosophers around the globe hailed participation and deliberation beyond, and before, late twentieth-century theory in the US. Hannah Arendt rejected government-by-representation as a key feature of democracy. For her, a robust democracy relies on active human action. Human action is an essential characteristic of the political person; active participation promotes liberty and self-realization, even 'happiness'; societies organize and reorganize themselves through active citizen participation, both in times of regime change and as a political ideal; and the frustration of the faculty of action is likely to lead to disruptive social violence.[44]

[40] James S Fishkin, *Democracy and Deliberation* (Yale University Press 1991) 84 and passim.

[41] Jane Mansbridge, 'Everyday Talk in the Deliberative System' in Stephen Macedo (ed), *Deliberative Politics* (OUP 1999) 211.

[42] See eg Joshua Cohen, 'Deliberation and Democratic Legitimacy' in Alan Hamlin and Philip Pettit (eds), *The Good Polity: Normative Analysis of the State* (Basil Blackwell 1989) 17, 31–32 (emphasis on political parties); Gutmann and Thompson (n 39).

[43] Jane Mansbridge and others, 'A Systemic Approach to Deliberative Democracy' in Jane Mansbridge and John Parkinson, *Deliberative Systems: Deliberative Democracy at the Large Scale* (CUP 2012) 1. See also, eg, John S Dryzek, 'Deliberative Turns' in John S Dryzek, *Foundations and Frontiers of Deliberative Governance* (OUP 2010); J Kuyper, 'Democratic Deliberation in the Modern World: The Systemic Turn' (2015) 27(1) Crit Rev 49.

[44] See Hannah Arendt, *The Human Condition* (1958, 2nd edn, University of Chicago Press 1998); Hannah Arendt, *On Revolution* (Viking Press 1963, 1965) eg 221, 240, 277; Hannah Arendt, *On Violence* (Allen Lane 1970), eg 81–83.

The idea that active human discourse stands at the core of modern social life is also central to Jürgen Habermas's theories of rationality, social structures, and the life of the political sphere. Rationality-in-action requires the giving of reasons, which in its turn depends on active discourse between all members of society, each having an equal voice and a free opportunity to participate.[45] Thus, for Habermas, the legitimacy of all norms, including statutes, depends on the existence of that active discursive process.[46]

These calls for heightened involvement of multiple players in the public sphere were not directly concerned with executive powers, but their visions stand in complete contradiction to the legitimation of fuzzy executive powers, designed or applied with limited deliberation. Indeed, fuzziness in all its forms severely challenges the ideals of participation and deliberation: first and foremost, any unilateral rule-making or application cannot be accepted under these theories. Other modes of fuzziness are just as problematic. Participation requires knowledge. When it is nigh impossible to grasp the law as it is interpreted and applied in reality, little proper participation is to be expected. Open-ended provisions in written constitutions may empower citizens who wish to forward a position on the constitutionality of an executive act, but their arguments could be refuted by seemingly legitimate government interpretations to the contrary. The problem of interpretation is even more acute when the relevant constitutional-type arrangements are unwritten. Similar difficulties beset attempts at participation when statutes are open-ended, grant extensive discretion, or allow delegation to a degree that renders identification of the true wielder of power beyond the understanding of regular citizens, who should, under these theories, be granted the utmost power to contribute to the ways rules, primary and secondary, are designed and applied. Finally, executive action that further obfuscates the nature of the rules by creatively complying, adopting parallel extra-statutory arrangements, or ignoring the law, all suffer from the same malaise.[47]

3. The Benefits of Fuzzy Legality?

For some, the force of the interests which promote fuzziness is not a cause for excessive alarm. Two arguments are made in this context. The first concerns

45 See eg Jürgen Habermas, *The Theory of Communicative Action, Vol 1: Reason and the Rationalization of Society* (Thomas McCarthy trans, Beacon Press 1984) ch 1; Jürgen Habermas, *Between Facts and Norms: Contributions to a Discourse Theory of Law and Democracy* (William Rehg trans, MIT Press 1998) 104–11.

46 Habermas, *Between Facts and Norms* (n 45) 110.

47 For these, and other nodes of fuzziness, which carry the same implication for participation/deliberation see ch 3.

inevitability. As mentioned above, Posner and Vermeule posit that executive action unfettered by law is an unavoidable feature of politics and law.[48] Yet even those who accept this inevitability do not go as far as preaching full departure from law; they merely acquiesce with what they deem to be a sufficiently checked phenomenon, a claim I address as unfounded in the next chapter.

A second argument revolves around the so-called utilities of fuzzy law. The arguments are well-known, and have been repeatedly voiced in the context of the grant of discretion in the administrative state. In the context of the constitution, the open-endedness of text is considered a welcome feature: the elasticity of a constitution is designed to ensure longevity, hence sufficient stability. A similar argument for the elasticity of statutes and other rules authorizing the executive, draws on the familiar argument linked with the needs emerging in the modern administrative state. Under this argument, the evaluation of the law directing the government must be instructed by the two-way enlargement of state action. Over the past century, states have broadened and diversified the range of their involvement in the social and economic spheres: additional fields have been added to the repository of state responsibility, and the volume of action expected has amplified. Hence, power in the modern state necessarily requires constant retuning in order to accommodate rapid cultural and social changes as well as technological innovations and the growth of populations and their perceived needs.[49] Although diatribe against the growth of the administrative state does exist,[50] and mainstream political science research refrains from going normative, [51] the logical result of the argument for flexibility is acceptance of the inadequacy of detailed, closed rules as sole organizers of government action.

This argument has usually supported reliance on several forms of fuzziness: open-ended legislation, delegation, discretion, and unilateral executive

[48] See above text to n 1.

[49] The literature depicts a transformation from the Minimal State, through the Welfare State to the current Neo-Liberal State. Roughly, this corresponds to visions of the state as peace-keeper, through welfare-advancer, to regulator. See Karl Polanyi, *The Great Transformation* (Rinehart 1944); Giandomenico Majone, 'From the Positive to the Regulatory State: Causes and Consequences of Changes in the Mode of Governance' (1997) 17 J Pub Pol 139. In the context of law, see RB Stewart, 'The Reformation of American Administrative Law' (1975) 88 Harv L Rev 1667; K Culp Davis, *Discretionary Justice: A Preliminary Inquiry* (Louisiana State University Press 1969); DJ Galligan, *Discretionary Powers* (Clarendon Press 1986).

[50] Philip Hamburger, *Is Administrative Law Unlawful?* (University of Chicago Press 2014); Philip Hamburger, *The Administrative Threat* (Encounter Intelligence 2017).

[51] This is evident in public policy and some political science scholarship. See eg on delegation and discretion (David Epstein and Sharyn O'Halloran, *Delegating Powers: A Transaction Cost Politics Approach to Policy Making under Separate Powers* (CUP 1999); John D Huber and Charles R Shipan, *Deliberate Discretion? The Institutional Foundations of Bureaucratic Autonomy* (CUP 2002) and on enforcement (Eugene Bardach and Robert Kagan, *Going by the Book* (Temple University Press 1982); Keith Hawkins, *Environment and Enforcement: Regulation and the Social Definition of Pollution* (Clarendon Press 1984).

action.[52] However, the same reasoning could be extended to all forms of fuzziness. Under the same rationale, the existence of several potential holders of authority, the piling-up of arrangements, selective enforcement practices, and the introduction of parallel schemes that do not comport with statute, to name some other types of fuzzy law discussed in this book, are all tools that are used, it is argued, to combat the needs of the modern administrative state.

The fallacy of this argument as a normative claim is twofold. First, the argument assumes that under looser authorizations to act the outcome will necessarily be 'better'. Up to now, I have not discussed the important issue regarding the *content* of rules; the analysis has been mainly, and purposefully, structural. Moving to content, there is no causal link between fuzzy law and 'good' law. The only direct benefit of fuzziness is utility, reflected in ease in rule-making and flexibility in its application. However, content should be differentiated from structure: rules may be 'good' irrespective of their structure. Fuzzy nodes of law may serve as repositories of power employed for the public good just as much as they can be sources for abusive government action. Similarly, abusive power may be authorized by a detailed statute—after all, statutes can grant extensive power and refrain from setting limits on its exercise—as much as they can offer detailed and balanced frameworks of action. Once the link between form and content is severed, attention must return to the processual flaws endemic to the making and application of fuzzy rules, discussed above.

The second fallacy of the argument for efficiency/ease is concerned with the temporal element. Arguably, unexpected exigencies may justify some fuzzy rule-making. The typical examples, wars and emergency conditions, can be supplemented by economic crises, periods of political impasse that do not allow smooth operation of parliaments, and periods of political transition. During such periods, it is argued, fuzziness is indeed inevitable. Constitutions should prepare for loosely authorized action. Statutes should offer platforms for such periods, inter alia by granting discretion and authorizing executives to promulgate delegated legislation; provide authority to several, rather than single officers; and be less concerned with piling-up of arrangements. Likewise, and turning to executive action, systems should tolerate constrained and selective enforcement and the making of policy beyond statute; finally, delegated legislation with an uncertain pedigree had best cite all possible sources of potential authority.

This list of possibilities corresponds to all forms of fuzziness discussed in this book. The argument that such exceptional periods tend to produce rules and practices which are products of hyperactivity and are essentially disproportionate, over-extending in time, hence exploiting the so-called requirements emerging in

52 See eg the works cited ibid.

exceptional times, has been well-discussed.[53] Yet another point must be made. As amply shown in the previous chapters, the breadth of the development and reliance on fuzzy forms of law extends long beyond periods of special exigencies. If indeed the argument for efficiency/ease were valid, it would be expected that no fuzziness would emerge during 'normal' periods, and that each and every resort to fuzzy law would be corrected once the special period ended. However, the reality in both studies systems could not be more different.

Yet much of this book attests to the continuous use of fuzziness beyond exceptional times. Centuries of reliance on the prerogative and of rulemaking by orders in council in the UK, and the thousands of non-statute-based executive orders and other measures signed by all presidents since the independence of the US, provide sufficient evidence.

4. Summary

Under the central requirements of a formal/processual version of the rule of law ideal, the rules should be accessibility, intelligibility, and congruence. Participatory/deliberative theories all emphasize the importance of active citizen involvement in the design and implementation of the rules that apply in a polity. All of these values are seriously compromised when law turns fuzzy. During their design stage, fuzzy rules are more likely to suffer deficits in participation, deliberation, and representation; the multi-player interaction inherent to the legislative process is essentially replaced by single-player rule-making by bodies that lack the proper attributes of representation. Once embedded within the legal or semi-legal spheres, the opacity of fuzzy rules severely constrains citizens' reliance on them when planning ahead, and facilitates the inconsistent application of rules. Further, accountability and review processes, when available, are weakened: under conditions of lower accessibility and clarity, a properly detailed challenge to a fuzzy arrangement may be difficult, if not impossible. Fuzziness may also render reporting and other post-implementation review to be no more than a charade: when access to the data is largely limited to the government, the assessment of reports is just as difficult. Similar concerns over the proper operation of a democracy arises under theories that recognize the value of participation and multi-player deliberation. In sum, then, the lesser the detail set on the exercise of power, or, the stronger the ability of the executive to choose between options or to create new ones when expedient, the greater the danger of employing power in ways that escape processual systemic constraints designed to promote legitimacy.

[53] As in Dyzenhaus (n 4).

C. The Political Economy of Fuzzy Legality

1. Introduction

Is fuzziness unavoidable? Beyond the general recognition that law, in any and all fields, is essentially indeterminate due to the limits of language,[54] is the law that directs and instructs the executive particularly unavoidably fuzzy?

Words such as 'unavoidable' and 'inevitable' could emerge in situations that have little to do with choice and human design. Forces of nature are largely 'inevitable', as are rules of physics (setting aside modern science and philosophical questioning). This understanding is clearly not part of the argument made by those who argue for the 'inevitable' and 'unavoidable' nature of undefined executive powers. These arguments are used throughout the book, but are concerned with the emergence and retention of fuzziness. Some fuzziness is internal to the law, but it is mainly due to external political and social forces. .

The well-worn argument about the inevitable need for open-ended rules in the modern administrative state serves, again, as a good starting point. This argument has been employed in two main contexts: grants of discretion by open-ended rules and the delegation of rule-making powers to the executive.[55] The traditional justification for the emergence and retention of discretion and delegation, which could be extended to other forms of fuzziness, focuses on the argument that these features of law by the needs of the modern administrative state, which require the adoption and maintenance of flexible rules made by experts (that is, the executive rather than the legislature), and necessitate their constant and swift retuning by those experts. Tying this argument with the concept of 'grey holes', consider Posner and Vermeule's argument that '[g]rey holes arise because administrative law in any modern state cannot get by without adjustable parameters'.[56]

The excessive traditional focus on delegation and discretion deflects attention from other forms of fuzziness, a recurring theme in this book. Should the introduction of a 'lopsided' statute, the continuous patterns of excessive selective enforcement, or the transformation of a statute to a dead-letter law (some of the types of fuzziness discussed in this book) be likewise explained?

I do not reject this type of explanation: the needs of modern governance may well require open-endedness. In the constitutional sphere, gaps in the text, or 'gags' that exclude subsequent debates over an open issue, may be inserted into constitutions not only due to disagreement, a factor discussed below, but also as the best available option to maintain stability, under the assumption that highly sensitive

[54] See HLA Hart, *The Concept of Law* (2nd edn, Clarendon Press 1994) 124; Timothy Endicott, *Vagueness in Law* (OUP 2000).

[55] See Jack M Beermann, 'The Never-Ending Assault on the Administrative State' (2018) Notre Dame L Rev 1599, and ch 1.

[56] Posner and Vermeule (n 1) 105.

issues are better removed from the discourse.[57] And, extensively discussed, societies' needs to enable swift, flexible action in the modern administrative sphere may well be presented as justifying some open-endedness.[58] However, this book is concerned with *excessive* open-endedness. Grants of discretion that are sufficiently cabined by conveying a general understanding of the purpose of the grant of power and discretion, and outlining the contours of its limitation, are not considered to be fuzzy. When such grants provide holders of authority with virtually unlimited, or highly unrestricted, choice to decide upon their action, the legal framework will enter the realm of fuzziness. The arguments for expertise, flexibility, and the like fall short of fully explaining the need to go that far; such grants of discretion cannot be entirely credited to bona fide attempts to improve governance.

Hence, these justifications are set aside in order to award attention to other explanations for the reversion to fuzziness. In other words, I am interested in those cases in which the fuzziness found in law does not seem to emerge from the requirements of governance in the administrative state.

Offering a tentative analysis of the factors that contribute to fuzziness, this part opens with a distinction between endogenous and exogenous causes. In the first group are factors that draw on the nature of law as an organizing social construct, on a new-institutionalist theory that focuses on the historical stickiness of arrangements and cultures. Political preferences, which have little to do with a bona fide intent to ensure optimal governance, are classified as exogenous, and include interests concerning the amassing of relative power, disagreement over the content of a rule, the existence of political or transnational pressure to make a rule in the absence of a true commitment to its application, and the marginalization of the need to set a detailed arrangement due to its relative unimportance or the relative importance of other pressing issues. These exogenous factors are discussed in this chapter under four heads: power-accumulation, disagreement, political pressure to act, and marginalization.

The accumulation of these factors offers a general answer to the question that opened this introduction: fuzziness is likely to be unavoidable, due to the existence of an impressive collection of factors that push towards its creation and continuity. On the flip side, forces that drive towards the dissipation of fuzziness, and its related dangers to the proper operation of the public sphere, are much less likely to succeed. This rather undesirable result is further considered in the next chapter, dedicated to a normative analysis of the propriety of fuzziness.

[57] See Michael Foley, *The Silence of Constitutions* (Routledge 1989); Stephen Holmes, 'Gag Rules or the Politics of Omission,' in Jon Elster and Rune Slagstad (eds), *Constitutionalism and Democracy* (CUP 1988) 19.

[58] See ch 1.

2. The Rise and Retention of Fuzziness: Mapping the Explanatory Factors

I begin with the literature on 'soft law', discussed in Chapter 3. In that chapter, I rejected the possible reliance on this term as a synonym for fuzzy law. Recall, that soft law is defined as a written but not formally binding rule, introduced through consensus, which is nevertheless considered as directing an arrangement, though it cannot be directly enforced. In that chapter, I rejected the adoption of this synonym for two reasons. First, soft law refers to rules that are not formally made, while fuzziness features in legally binding rules. Secondly, soft law may be fuzzy in terms of its origin and status, but need not be fuzzy in its content.[59] However, the extensive study of this feature of legality, mainly in the field of international law, offers a useful starting point for the analysis offered in this chapter.

The reasons or utilities for the choice of soft law in Dinah Shelton's definitive account of the place of soft law in international law was garnered from the rich literature. Nine answers were offered to the question 'why are states adopting soft law texts?' Listed without ordering, they included the following: (1) crises may require rapid response; (2) soft law can be more effective in garnering the acceptance of reluctant states; (3) it can be useful for addressing new fields; (4) it enables non-state actors to participate; (5) it can be adopted as useful adds-ons to formally made treaties; (6) soft law can be offered as a less onerous alternative as a form of 'deregulation'; (7) it can be used in social policy issues that are critical to states and are traditionally in the exclusive domain of their legislatures; (8) it can serve to avoid political battles in contested fields due to the removal of the ratification process required for the adoption of a formal treaty; and (9) it can provide an appearance of states' responsiveness while no obligation is introduced.[60]

Some of these answers are not directly applicable to the context of fuzziness in domestic law. Reasons (2), (4), and (7) (garnering the acceptance of reluctant states; availability to international organizations and other non-state bodies lacking the power to make binding law; and treatment of issues traditionally left to state legislatures) are linked with distinct features of transnational law, although they can still be translated to apply in domestic legal arenas.

More central to the structure of my analysis is the need to distinguish between two types of justifications. First, some of the reasons offered concern the requirements of governance, echoing the traditional account of the need for flexibility due to complexity, fast-changing conditions and the need for expert decision-making, mentioned at the beginning of this chapter as factors to be taken into account by rule-makers and policy-implementers keen to improve the quality of governance

[59] See ch 3.

[60] Dinah Shelton, 'Soft Law' in David Armstrong (ed), *Routledge Handbook of International Law* (Routledge 2009) 68, 75–77. Numbering added. For additional studies see ch 3.

in the modern state. Reasons (1), (3), (5), and possibly (4) belong to first group of factors. In such cases, fuzziness is internal to the husbandry of the modern state, and is introduced as a bona fide attempt to answer its contingencies.

As for exogenous reasons, reasons (2), (7), and (8) are concerned with the insertion of fuzziness in cases of disagreement, either disagreement regarding the identity of the institution that is to regulate the issue or, more often, disagreement over the rules themselves, and are thus classified as exogenous. The analysis of these two groups of factors, offered below, identifies some additional factors. This extended analysis contributes to a well-rounded overview of the political economy of fuzziness.

Still within the group of exogenous rationales, reasons (6) and (9) link to the value of appearances, an aspect that is central to some forms of fuzziness. Beyond the ways they are presented in Shelton's account, appearances are crucial, for example, in the existence of a 'dead-letter' law that was introduced due to external pressure but never or rarely applied, or when agencies consistently and selectively under-implement a formal arrangement due to agency disagreement with the framework forced upon them.[61] My analysis of exogenous reasons, offered below, is based on their classification to four groups. All of these are discussed below.

3. Endogenous Reasons for Fuzziness

This group of factors is organized around the understanding that some features of law and legal culture are likely to engender fuzziness. As above, I am less interested with types of open-endedness that do not reach a degree of fuzziness that renders an arrangement unintelligible, offers a mere façade of legality, or otherwise does not in fact direct executive action. In addition to Shelton's three (or four) reasons, which are all concerned with utility and flexibility,[62] in this section I address two additional endogenous reasons for fuzziness: the need to introduce open-ended constitutional frameworks, and the retention of historical structures that maintain their force due to institutional 'stickiness'.

Traditionally, constitutions are presented as necessarily open-ended and flexible. The art of constitutional drafting requires the achievement of a proper balance between stability and sufficient flexibility. Establishing a workable framework for the operation of the state over time and in changing conditions, without the introduction of recurring, frequent amendments that themselves challenge stability, necessarily leads to ambiguity. This argument echoes the arguments for expertise and utility in the administrative state, as it too draws on the assumption

[61] For analyses of these types of fuzziness see Chaps 3, 8.

[62] As mentioned above, these refer to the need to act rapidly during a crisis, to address new, uncharted fields, to be added onto existing formal rules, and, perhaps, to enable participation.

that constitutional drafting and maintenance are motivated by drafters intent on achieving the best-working framework for the polity.

Consider, for example, the presentation of the US Constitution in the US Supreme Court website, which states that

> ... it is evident that constitutional interpretation and application were made necessary by the very nature of the Constitution. The Founding Fathers had wisely worded that document in rather general terms leaving it open to future elaboration to meet changing conditions. As Chief Justice Marshall noted in *McCulloch v. Maryland*, a constitution that attempted to detail every aspect of its own application "would partake of the prolixity of a legal code, and could scarcely be embraced by the human mind ... Its nature, therefore, requires that only its great outlines should be marked, its important objects designated, and the minor ingredients which compose those objects be deduced from the nature of the objects themselves."[63]

These well-established views of constitutions as essentially endogenously fuzzy should be challenged from at least two directions. First, constitutions vary in their length and depth. Tom Ginsburg's study of the texts of 501 constitutions, conducted in 2010, identified some extremely short constitutions—mostly non-democratic—such as China's 1975 constitution (2,923 words long). Among the lengthier ones, the champion at that time was India's constitution, which swelled to 117,820 words, counting its schedules.[64] While somewhat indicative of the degree of open-endedness, it should be noted that length in words doesn't necessarily indicate a high level of detail that renders the text less open to interpretation. Lengthy texts do not necessary offer highly detailed and less-interpretable arrangements. In fact, lengthy constitutions may just as well contain *more* open-ended clauses open to interpretation.[65] Still, the link drawn between constitutions and open-endedness is sometimes made too hastily.

Another aspect concerns the tendency of some scholars to address the drafting of a constitution as a conscious process designed to reach an optimal arrangement. The above reference to the 'wise' wording of the US Constitution echoes yet another example of what I called above 'bona fide intent to ensure optimal governance'. Such processes may be part of the drafting of a constitution: as Rosalind Dixon argues, higher detail may be the outcome of lesser trust in the courts as interpreters

[63] Supreme Court website <https://www.supremecourt.gov/about/constitutional.aspx>. Citing *McCulloch v Maryland*, 17 US 316, 407 (1819).

[64] Tom Ginsburg, 'Constitutional Specificity, Unwritten Understandings and Constitutional Agreement' in A Sajó and R Uitz (eds), *Constitutional Topography: Values and Constitutions* (Eleven International Publishing 2010) 69, 71.

[65] Ginsburg's attention to preambles (ibid 71) is but one aspect of this possibility, since generally, preambles do not contribute to tight arrangements.

of the constitution.[66] Yet political exigencies may be prime reasons for the adoption of a fuzzy constitution; this aspect is discussed below as an exogenous factor.

History and institutional stickiness operate as another type of endogenous force. When an arrangement is initially fuzzy, as in the case of the Royal Prerogative in the UK, its transformation into a clear, accessible, and formal arrangement is likely to be difficult, if at all attainable.[67] This possible endogenous factor, which emphasizes the force of past arrangements and the aversion to their reform, has been discussed for several decades by new institutionalist scholars. Following the concepts of 'path dependency' and 'institutional stickiness', this stream of research originated in economics.[68] The idea that 'institutions matter' was subsequently adopted as a school of study in politics and governance studies. The insight was simple and compelling: institutions (broadly defined, and unquestionably including law and legal arrangements) tend to be 'sticky'. The costs of change and the uncertainty of the outcome of change, as well as human tendency to stick with known structures, all contribute to relative equilibrium and constancy of any given institution.[69] The 'stickiness' of institutions and their aversion to change is thus central to this group of theories, especially its historical variant. Philipp Genschel succinctly analysed the main reasons for institutional tendency towards stability. Costs involved in the formulation and implementation of reform, uncertainty as to the actual effect of an achieved reform, and political conflicts inherent in reforms, all put a premium on maintaining the status quo. Indeed, straining a regulatory programme through the legislative sieve requires extensive mobilization of resources. This move is a risky one, as the preferred legislative outcome is not assured to survive the power-game preceding legislation. The legislative process introduces additional interest groups into the debate over the reform. Opening the issue to wider public debate enhances the risk of opposition and of possible engineering of the framework during its process of formalization, in ways that do not accord with the original intent of the policy designers.[70] Change, the least explained element, can 'punctuate the equilibrium'; such critical junctures may be the outcome of extreme political pressure, or, for some, be more incremental, but the emphasis is still on 'stickiness'.[71]

[66] Rosalind Dixon, 'Constitutional Drafting and Distrust' (2015) 13 ICON 819.

[67] See ch 4 and below.

[68] For introduction in the field of economics see W Brian Arthur, 'Self-Reinforcing Mechanisms in Economics' in Philip W Anderson, Kenneth J Arrow, and David Pines (eds), *The Economy As an Evolving Complex System* (Addison-Wesley 1988) 9; Douglass North,

[69] For some of the central voices see James G March and Johan P Olsen, 'The New Institutionalism: O rganizational Factors in Political Life' (1984) 78 Am J Poli Sci 734; Sven Steinmo, Kathleen Thelen, and Frank Longstreth (eds), *Structuring Politics: Historical Institutionalism in Comparative Analysis* (CUP 1992); Peter A Hall, Rosemary CR Taylor, 'Political Science and the Three New Institutionalisms' (1996) XLIV Political Stud 936, 937–42.

[70] Philipp Genschel, 'The Dynamics of Inertia: Institutional Persistence and Change in Telecommunications and Healthcare' (1997) 10 Governance 43.

[71] See Frank Baumgartner and Bryan D Jones, *Agendas and Instability in American Politics* (2nd edn, University of Chicago Press 2009).

Under this tradition, law and the attitudes towards it are essentially stable; although this stability is the outcome of the play of political and psychological factors, stability is considered as internal to the law, and can thus be central to the longevity of fuzziness, once it emerges. Following the famous adage 'if it ain't broke, don't fix it',[72] rule-makers who have benefitted from previous fuzzy arrangements will need strong incentives for effecting any change in their practices. The examples discussed below refer to such incentives, but the general tendency to stick to the known is embedded in human nature, more so in the context of law, an exceptionally formal social structure that endorses the value of stability.

The retention of the Royal Prerogative, still part of the constitutional framework in the UK despite the removal of any link to the Crown as the source of those powers, effected decades ago if not centuries, serves as an excellent example. Discussed in detail in Chapter 4, I follow the main points of that analysis and supplement it with a consideration of the ways the prerogative, while abolished in some areas as a result of a long and rather tortuous processes, has not been removed.

The prerogative, as defined after the 1688 Glorious Revolution, pertains to those powers retained by the Crown that have not been taken away by Parliament, and was part of the compromise reached with (or forced on) the Monarchy at the end of the seventeenth century. For centuries, prerogative powers remained strongly tied with the eminence of the Monarch, but by the end of the nineteenth century, a clear constitutional convention recognized that, de facto, these powers were exercised by the government of the day.[73]

By its nature, then, 'prerogative' refers to a historical list of specific powers, largely acknowledged by courts but not dependent on their recognition. The legitimacy of their exercise remains a constitutional convention, one of the constitutional rules that are considered part of the unwritten constitution of the United Kingdom.

Dicey's still-influential definition supported the introduction of the residuality doctrine. Under this central limitation, no non-statutory powers, even lofty prerogatives, can be exercised when a statute governs the same field, although the extent and force of this rule are continuously debated.[74]

In Chapter 4 I traced the 'shrinking' of the prerogative due to the general expansion of legislation over the past two centuries, twinned with the subjection of such powers to judicial review. Here, attention to the statutory reforms that have removed some of these powers in favour of legislation, and the failure to fully eliminate the prerogative despite a series of attempts, at least tacitly opposed by

[72] This proverb is usually credited to Bert Lance, Jimmy Carter's Head of the OMB in 1977, in the context of his view on saving government expense. See 'Emphasizing the M in OMB' *Nation's Business* (May 1977) 27.
[73] See ch 4.
[74] ibid.

governments, serve to explain the allure of the retention of this fuzzy constitutional construct.

Some prerogatives have indeed been legislated: Chapter 4 chronologically addressed the introduction of legislation regulating areas that range from coinage to the setting of dates for parliamentary election. The fields still regulated under the prerogative, as shown there, are far from insubstantial, including the conduct of foreign affairs, the deployment of armed forces, and the passport regime.[75]

More than a few private members' bills were tabled, in recurring attempts to grandly reform the prerogative, to no avail.[76] The 'New Labour' programme, launched in the mid-1990s, marked a commitment to constitutional change, but the legislation of the prerogative was a lengthy and incomplete process. Tony Blair's grand manifesto, which led to several tectonic transformations in the first years of his office, namely the enactment of the Human Rights Act and the devolution legislation, did not include a commitment to the reform of the prerogative as such.[77] Recurring attempts to reform were made through the introduction of bills that were largely tabled by Labour left-wingers and members of the Liberal Democratic Party, the emerging challenge to Labour. These may have been crucial to the slowly turning, but still insufficiently strong, change in elite centre-left public opinion against prerogative.[78] Marking major steps in the rise of political attention to the matter, extensive hearings and debates held by three parliamentary committees that led to the publication of influential reports represent the mixed zeitgeist regarding reform.[79]

[75] ibid.

[76] For some of these bills see Crown Prerogative (House of Commons Control) Bill 1988 [HC 117]; Crown Prerogatives (Parliamentary Control) Bill 1999 [HC 123]; Prime Minister (Office, Role and Functions) Bill 2001 [Presented at HC as Bill 60]; Armed Forces Deployment (Royal Prerogative) Bill 2016–17 [HL 10]. For analysis of the politics surrounding the latter bill see next section.

[77] For a lament over this state of affairs voiced in the late 1990s see Keith Syrett, 'Prerogative Powers: New Labour's Forgotten Constitutional Reform?' (1998) Denning L J 111.

[78] For Bills introduced during that period see the Crown Prerogatives (Parliamentary Control) Bill 1999, HC Bill 55 (reintroduced by Tony Benn Labour MP); Parliamentary Control of the Executive Bill, 1999, HC Bill 123 (presented by Labour MP Tony Benn and an all-party group of MPs); Armed Forces (Parliamentary Approval for Participation in Armed Conflict) Bill, HC Bill 31 (2004–2005) (presented by Labour MP Neil Gerrard); Executive Powers and Civil Service HL Bill (2003–2004) (Lord Lester of Herne Hill, as a Lib-Dem member of the House of Lords); Armed Forces (Parliamentary Approval for Participation in Armed Conflict) HC Bill (2005–2006) [16] (Clare Short Labour MP until 2006, then independent).

[79] The House of Commons Public Administration Select Committee published its report in 2004, recommending that prerogatives pertaining to ministerial powers be comprehensively legislated. It also set a timetable for further action and appended a draft bill, the Ministers of the Crown (Executive Powers) Bill. The Bill addressed powers in the context of armed conflict and war, the ratification of treaties, and the issuance of passports. Three years later, and following the Government's Green Paper of 2007 (n 80), the Joint Committee on the Draft Constitutional Renewal Bill published a lengthy report that touched upon most of these, and other aspects of governance, omitting reference to the passport regime. See House of Commons Public Administration Select Committee, *Taming the Prerogative: Strengthening Ministerial Accountability to Parliament*, HC 422 (2004); Joint Committee on the Draft Constitutional Renewal Bill, *Draft Constitutional Renewal Bill*, HL Paper 166-I, HC Paper 551-I (2008). Finally, the Political and Constitutional Reform Committee's 2014 report, concerned with the powers of the prime minister, again offered a prescription for limiting power, this time by providing

A month after Gordon Brown's entry into office in 2007, a government green paper, a consultation document, declared that 'in general the prerogative powers should be put onto a statutory basis and brought under stronger parliamentary scrutiny and control', but the general intent, to ensure greater parliamentary involvement, was not necessarily to be achieved by the eradication of prerogative powers. Immediate recommendations, not all of them subsequently adopted, offered a variation of formal changes, ranging from a change of an existing convention to legislation.[80] Supplementing a list of prerogative powers that were to be regulated under the general intent to 'limit the power of the executive', the document contained a general declaration that the government will 'begin a modern, systematic reform of the scope and nature of the prerogative powers'.[81] Two of the specified topics, namely the regulation of the civil service and the laying down of treaties in parliament prior to their ratification, were indeed central elements of the statute that carried the grand title 'The Constitutional Reform and Governance Act 2010', which entered into force less than a month before Brown's resignation. The Fixed-Term Parliaments Act 2011, enacted during Conservative prime minister David Cameron's premiership, set fixed dates for polls for parliamentary general elections, and to date has ended the series of successful reforms. Since then, the emergence of Brexit has had nothing to do with such reform, although it has marked a watershed in the context of the interaction between prime ministers and parliaments, an issue partially discussed elsewhere in this book.[82] Other aspects, including the regulation of the passport regime and the deployment of armed forces, have not been touched.[83]

Instead of this tortuous, piecemeal, and partial movement for reform, all Prime Ministers at the helm who enjoyed majorities in parliament could have gone further, and followed more recommendations, at least those published by parliamentary committees. However, this did not happen.

Stickiness also applies when new arrangements are introduced. When the *Bancoult 1* decision signalled to the British government that it could not evacuate the population of an island under a territory constitution made in an order

an exhaustive list of powers to be exercised by the Prime Minister, presented in the form of an 'example Bill'. No governmental response to the report is documented. See Political and Constitutional Reform Committee, *Role and Powers of the Prime Minister*, First Report of Session 2014–2015, HC 351 (2014). See also Gail Bartlett and Michael Everett, *The Royal Prerogative*, House of Commons Briefing Paper 03861 (2017).

[80] *The Governance of Britain*, CM 7170 (2007) 17.

[81] ibid 23. The powers specified in Part 1 were the deployment of armed forces abroad, the ratification of treaties, the dissolution of Parliament, the recall of the House of Parliament, and the legislation of the Civil Service. ibid 16–23. For the treatment of the first power see analysis below.

[82] See ch 5, concerned with the impact of Brexit on air pollution law.

[83] For a recent list of existing prerogatives see Emily Haves, 'Prerogative Powers of the Crown', House of Lords Library Briefing, 13 December 2019, via <https://researchbriefings.parliament.uk/ResearchBriefing/Summary/LLN-2019-0156>.

in council, it did not legislate the provision, but reverted to a second use of the prerogative-based order in council, which initially remained undisclosed like the first. The repeated reliance on this type of measure was then explained by the need to maintain secrecy in this sensitive area (issues of national security and foreign affairs were of course raised), but the ease in which such an order could be made was a crucial element, available due to the Crown's retention of its prerogative power to make law in British territories, notwithstanding the existence of several delegating statutes in this field.[84]

This 'stickiness' can be explained in institutionalist tools, although I offer a second, political account in the next section. The unprecedented move for bold constitutional reform in the UK between 1997 and 2011, and later, the decision to withdraw from the EU, are marked exceptions to a rule that enshrines stability and continuity. Without attempting to discuss the origins of those tectonic shifts, the mixed results as far as the prerogative is concerned—some substantive reform alongside restraint—may best be explained as the product of politics, considered below as an exogenous factor. After all, transformation costs and political sensitivity, clearly part of any reform of the prerogative, were just as salient to the devolution reforms. It is quite likely, however, that the political prices to be paid by refraining from devolution were considered high enough to advance these reforms, while the reform of the prerogative, which carried a much lesser weight in political campaigns, could be sidestepped.

Institutionalism may offer a better explanation for the post-2011 absence of change. The absence of retraction from earlier legislation can be found, a possible example of the difficulties of change. Once introduced, governments have not moved towards the removal of reforms, for example the legislation concerning the civil service, which would have possibly offered them access to the 'abeyed' prerogative.[85]

4. Exogenous Reasons for Fuzziness

This section considers reasons for the adoption and retention of fuzziness that have little to do with bona fide intentions to achieve an optimal, flexible, but sufficiently contained arrangement. Four distinct political forces are addressed: power-accumulation, disagreement, pressure to act, and marginalization. All can have

[84] On the affair see Chap 4.

[85] The fate of a legislated prerogative power is still debated. For a proponent of the abeyance argument, under which a prerogative power is revived after legislation is removed, see Robert Craig, 'Casting Aside Clanking Medieval Chains: Prerogative, Statute and Article 50 after the EU Referendum' (2016) 79 MLR 1041. For another possible explanation for the subsequent absence of reform, that of marginalization, see below.

an effect on the process of rule-making and rule-application, which may lead to fuzziness.

a. Power-accumulation and retention

In the tradition of public choice theories, this part of the inquiry draws on three assumptions: (1) all government players act to enhance their relative powers (depending on the theory, their own and/or the interest groups they serve); (2) fuzziness is a form of power-enhancement, as it enables players to act under conditions of low visibility, and therefore, in the relative absence of robust constraints; and (3) fuzziness can enhance power in two opposing ways: by ensuring the retention of power, or by its revocable delegation to another branch. Such opt-out strategies are preferable in sensitive fields in which any decision is likely to generate opposition that could endanger the player's status; in other fields, the more fuzzy the authority, the higher the potential for the retention of power.

The generating of grey holes by executives is the easiest explained under these assumptions. In the relative absence of constraints and under weak transparency conditions, fuzziness offers executives relative freedom to aggregate their power. Hence, for example, the reluctance to legislate some of the classical prerogative powers, those concerned with the conduct of hostilities, foreign affairs, and, by extension, the passport regime.[86]

As for fuzzy constitutions, once again I set aside accounts that consider drafters to be motivated to introduce the best structure that could withstand time and provide answers to changing conditions, as in the presentation of the founding fathers who had 'wisely worded that document in rather general terms leaving it open to future elaboration to meet changing conditions', cited above;[87] instead, I address the interests that lead to the adoption and retention of excessive fuzziness.

Theories of power-enhancement in the drafting of a constitution identify different interest groups intent on benefiting from the constitutional structure, such as members of a political faction dominant at the time of the drafting to endangered elites who are able to seize the moment to minimize the danger of future threats.[88] For the purposes of this chapter, the question to be asked is whether fuzziness could best serve those who wish to enhance or retain their powers. Fuzziness may be attractive, as it enables these elites to proceed without spelling out their visions of grandeur.

[86] See text to n 83.

[87] See text to n 63.

[88] For accounts that focus on elite group interests see Ran Hirschl, *Towards Juristocracy: The Origins and Consequences of the New Constitutionalism* (Harvard University Press 2007); Michael J Klarman, *The Framers' Coup: the Making of the United States Constitution* (OUP 2016); Michael Albertus and Victor Menaldo, 'Constitutions and Elite Deal-Making' in Michael Albertus and Victor Menaldo, *Authoritarianism and the Elite Origins of Democracy* (CUP 2018) 63.

An entirely different account can be advanced in the analysis of the adoption of the proclamation, originally of English provenance, by early US presidents. As Samuel Huntington noted, '[t]he American Revolution removed the English Crown from the American scene [and] made history by establishing the people as the constituent power, but 'its political institutions did not undergo revolutionary changes ... the English colonists took ... late medieval and Tudor political ideas, practices and institutions across the Atlantic with them'.[89] This tradition instructed the creation of the independent state and, some argue, is still part of the ethos of the US, at least in the context of the presidency.[90] The proclamation, arguably first used by President George Washington in the Proclamation of Neutrality of 1793,[91] and all other unilateral measures employed by presidents, have served to empower and enhance presidents and prime ministers who have serially issued such measures.[92]

The link between unilateral rule-making and power-enhancement is clearly expressed in Moe and Howell's following observation, which links the enhancement of power with the structural features of the US constitutional framework:

> Presidents have incentives to expand this institutional power, and they operate within a formal governance structure whose pervasive ambiguities—combined with the advantages inherent in the executive nature of the presidential job—gives them countless opportunities to move unilaterally into new territory, claim new powers, and make policy on their own authority. Congress has only a weak capacity for stopping them, because its collective action problems render it ineffective and subject to manipulation. The Supreme Court is capable of taking action against presidents, but is unlikely to want to most of the time and has incentive to be sympathetic.[93]

In the same context, another example of the link between fuzziness and power-enhancement, discussed in Chapter 5, is the continuing ambiguity of the legal nature of British proclamations and orders in council and their equivalents in the US, proclamations and executive orders. In that chapter I noted that both systems use these titles when making rules that are either based on statute, or on constitution-based constructs, and often on both. The retention of this ambiguity is helpful in several ways. Formidable titles such as 'order in council' or 'presidential executive order' head two very distinct types of rules. The use of such mighty titles for

[89] Samuel P Huntington, *Political Order in Changing Societies* (Yale University Press 1968) 93, 96–97.

[90] See Cass Sunstein, 'An Eighteenth Century Presidency in a Twenty-First Century World' (1995) 48 Arkansas L Rev 1.

[91] *A Proclamation*, 22 April 1793 in James R Richardson (ed), *A Compilation of Messages and Papers of the President 1789–1897* (Government Printing Office 1896–1899) Vol I, 156–57.

[92] For these measures see Chap 5.

[93] Terry M Moe and William G Howell, 'Unilateral Action and Presidential Power: A Theory' (1999) 29 Pres Stud Q 850, 870 and throughout. See also William G Howell, *Power without Persuasion: The Politics of Direct Presidential Action* (Princeton University Press 2003).

delegated legislation has a clear political advantage. Those not versed in law and politics might consider them identical in status to powers that are based on the constitution.[94] The outcome—an elevation, at least as far as appearances, of some sorts of delegated legislation—could only be happily adopted by their promulgators.

Moving to legislatures, the analysis of the extent of delegation, discretion, and the other types of legislative-generated grey holes, discussed in this article, should take account of two overlapping groups of factors. Fuzziness may serve the legislature or be generated by an executive that dominates the legislative process. Under a different scenario, a zealous super-majority may introduce ambitious, politically beneficial statutes that are no more than pastiche law from inception. Shared government in presidential regimes and the size of the majority and coalition politics in parliamentary regimes structurally shape the dominance of the executive over the legislation and her ability to realize her preferences, at the point of the introduction of a statute and beyond.[95] The stronger the executive under this matrix, the freer it is to create grey holes when so expedient through the agency of the legislature. Other factors include the relative weight of the legislature's long-term and short-term preferences. Re-election, and the possible outcome of non-election and of post-election climates, are usually considered the central motivations of legislators, but long and medium-term considerations may be outshone by pressing current needs.[96]

In the context of multiple decision-makers, I argued above that the larger the number of holders of authority, the more likely the emergence of several, possibly competing, readings of an arrangement. Among other difficulties, consistency in application can therefore be weakened. The two forms of patchworking, piling-up and dispersion, equally challenge the proper operation of public power. In her examination of the 'piled up' Turkish emergency legislation, Questiaux noted that 'because of the growing complexity of this overlapping legislation, it has been extremely difficult in practice to contest the legality or constitutionality, as may be the case, of the state of emergency'.[97] Indeed, in the existence of a pile of legal measures, the coherence of an arrangement is compromised, and deciphering a legal arrangement requires a high level of legal expertise. When several routes of executive action are available, executives are granted a choice of sources, while other players in the public sphere may find it very difficult to plan ahead. In the absence of rules that limit patchworking, such fuzziness may grow in time. Similarly,

[94] See Chap 5.

[95] For a discussion of the spectrum of power configurations that cut across regime types, see Chap 1.

[96] Consider, for example, the British refusal to legislate the deployment of forces, studied inter alia in Fahrid Chishty, 'Reconfiguring the War Prerogative: How Executive-Legislative Tensions Continue to Determine, and Obscure, the Legal Basis on Which Armed Forces are Deployed to Overseas Conflicts Under the UK Constitution' (2018) King's Student L Rev and Strife J 14.

[97] Nicole Questiaux, Study of the Implications for Human Rights of Recent Developments Concerning Situations Known as States of Siege or Emergency, UN ESCOR, 35th Sess, Agenda Item 10, UN Doc E/CN.4/Sub.2/1982/15 (1982) 29.

fuzziness-by-dispersion renders any arrangement difficult to grasp and necessitates trawling through the entire legal system; easy access to the law, necessary for planning ahead, is seriously impaired. Various forms of reliance on unwritten law set similar dangers.

In sum, fuzziness enables all government players to enhance their relative powers in ways that do not incur the same costs paid when such enhancement of powers is attempted through the adoption of a clear, detailed rule or clear, detailed implementation policies.

b. Disagreement

Disagreement, both during the design of an arrangement and after its introduction, is likely to produce fuzziness: contested or undecided issues are likely to be fuzzied-up by the introduction of indeterminate, openly interpretable arrangements and by the adoption of patterns of application that are inconsistent with the formal rules.

(1) During the design stage

Disagreement leads to the adoption of compromises. Under this truism, some compromises may be clear-cut. Consider, for example, the better-known compromises made during the framing of the US Constitution, including those concerning state representation in the bicameral legislature, the 'three-fifths compromise' regarding the voting weight of slaves,[98] and, in the context of the president, the mode of his election by the electoral college.[99] Yet sometimes, in the face of disagreement that leads to inability to decide, issues are left open-ended, and are thus essentially fuzzy.

Underlying the final wording of Article II, discussed in Chapter 4 and further detailed below, lay deep ideological disagreement.[100] The battle between Federalists and Anti-Federalists, who pushed for distinctly different constitutional structures,[101] was waged alongside a parallel dispute within the Federalists. Both factions, led by Hamilton on one side and Jefferson and Madison on the other,

[98] For a short history of this 'Great Compromise' see Max Farrand, *The Framing of the Constitution of the United States* (Yale University Press 1913) ch VII, esp 94–104. See also Garry Wills, *Negro President: Thomas Jefferson and the Slave Power* (Houghton Mifflin 2003); Michael J Klarman, *The Framers' Coup: The Making of the United States Constitution* (OUP 2016) 265–77 (noting that this fraction was well-recognized as a proposed and applied amendment to the Articles of the Confederation).

[99] See Farrand (n 98) 160–76; Shlomo Slonim, 'The Electoral College at Philadelphia: The Evolution of an Ad Hoc Congress for the Selection of a President' (1986) 73 J American History 53.

[100] This is the dominant view, but see accounts that emphasize consensus, eg TE Cronin and MA Genovese, *The Paradoxes of the American Presidency* (OUP 1998) 2–3 (claiming that 'the founders purposely left the presidency imprecisely defined. This was due in part to their fears of both the monarchy and the masses, and in part to their hopes that future presidents would create a more powerful office than the framers were able to do at the time. They knew that at times the president would have to move swiftly and effectively, yet they went to considerable lengths to avoid enumerating specific powers and duties in order to calm the then widespread fear of monarchy').

[101] On the Anti-Federalists see eg S Cornell, *The Other Founders; Anti-Federalism and the Dissenting Tradition in America, 1788–1828* (University of North Carolina Press 1999).

supported an executive that could rise above normal law in emergencies, but the differences between the theories on the nature of the constitution at large, and executive powers in particular, were far from marginal.

The Virginia Plan, presented by the Virginia delegates as an opening gambit, was designed to grant limited powers to the President: he was to be appointed by Congress, and subject to it. A second proposal tabled by New Jersey further limited the presidency by adding an executive council and removing the president's veto power. Other delegates supported a stronger office. Denying rumours that monarchy was considered, Hamilton's vision was of a 'governor' that would have an absolute veto, extensive powers in foreign affairs, and the power to unilaterally appoint ministers and high-level officers. None of these visions reached fruition; the contribution of Gouverneur Morris and James Wilson, two Pennsylvania delegates with Federalist leanings, was much more central to the emergence of Article II and its fuzzy provisions concerned with presidential powers.

Countering the New Jersey Plan, Wilson offered a different plan, which could be seen as the blueprint for Article II, but his, and all other options, remained open for debate. Two months after the opening of the Convention, the question concerning presidential powers was transferred, with other unresolved issues, to the Committee of Detail, a four-member committee of which Wilson was a member. The draft constitution they prepared, largely based on the Constitution of the State of New York, contained clauses that are echoed in Article II, including a take-care clause, but no final version was agreed by the Committee. The issue was then moved to the 'Committee of Unfinished Portions', headed by Jonathan Brearly, a New Jersey delegate, which added several powers to the president. As a final twist, the Committee of Style, headed by Morris, was responsible for some of the changes that contributed to fuzziness: while the vesting clauses in Articles I and III, opening the sections listing their powers, were changed to connote a closed list of powers, Article II's vesting clause remained open-ended. This part of Article II was approved by an already exhausted convention, with little debate. The relegation of this issue to no less than three committees, and the final provision designed to appease all members of the debate, were clearly the outcome of the disagreements briefly discussed above.[102]

The ratification of the Constitution did not lay that disagreement to rest. The disagreement was fully exposed during the post-ratification era; the focus is usually on the 1793 *Publius-Pacificus* debate, held between Alexander Hamilton and James Madison, although other debates flared during the first years of the constitution.[103] The *Publius-Pacificus* debate was concerned with the constitutionality

[102] For historical accounts see Farrand (n 98); Klarman (n 98). On the element of disagreement see eg Martin S Flaherty, 'The Most Dangerous Branch' (1996) 105 Yale LJ 1725, 1790–91.

[103] The other early examples of disagreement were the debate in Congress over presidential removal power, and the debate on the constitutionality of a national bank, held in 1789 and 1791. See generally on the first, CC Thach, *The Creation of the Presidency, 1775–1789* (Johns Hopkins Press 1922) 140–65; on both, and other disagreements, NE Cunningham (ed), *Jefferson vs Hamilton: Confrontations that*

of President Washington's proclamation of neutrality in the conflict between Britain and France.[104] In this debate, and elsewhere, Hamilton strongly supported a powerful presidency: at an early point, he advocated the instatement of a hereditary monarch, a suggestion removed later, but his general support of a strong president remained.[105] In the debate over George Washington's neutrality proclamation, Hamilton found both functional and textual bases for his support of the legality of the proclamation, arguing inter alia that the enumeration of presidential powers in Article II did not derogate from the broad authority granted in the vesting clause; therefore, 'the *executive power* of the nation is vested in the president; subject only to the *exceptions* and *qualifications*, which are expressed in the instrument'.[106] Madison's opposing, clause-bound interpretation led to the rejection of unilateral presidential power in the issues at stake, the signing of treaties and war powers; if at all, they could have been linked with prerogative, which was clearly not part of the constitutional framework.[107] Jefferson's strict views on the construction of the constitution were equally opposed to Hamilton's political theories.[108]

Nothing in these early debates has since been resolved. As discussed earlier in this book, opposing factions regarding the nature of presidential power have been able to rest their arguments on the text of the constitution; disagreement has not been resolved, and the continued fuzziness has only assisted in fuelling the debate.

(2) After introduction

Measures introduced due to external pressures may be unpopular from inception. A well-known example, the War Powers Resolution, offers a typical example. The statute requires presidential consultation with Congress before introducing United States armed forces into hostilities, and sets further consultation and reporting requirements; in certain cases, reporting can trigger a sixty-day time limit on the use of US forces in the absence of Congressional approval. Supported by claims of the unconstitutionality of the resolution, presidents have at best generally submitted ex-post reports, citing that they are 'consistent' with the WPR: only one of

Shaped a Nation (Bedford St Martin's Press 2000); Clement Fatovic, 'Constitutionalism and Presidential Prerogative: Jeffersonian and Hamiltonian Perspectives' (2004) 48 Am J Pol Science 429.

[104] For an edited compilation see Alexander Hamilton, James Madison, and Morton J Frisch (ed), *The Pacificus-Helvidius Debates: Towards the Completion of the American Founding* (Liberty Fund 2007).

[105] Brief of Speech on Submitting His Plan of Constitution, *The Works of Alexander Hamilton* (HC Lodge ed, Putnams 1904) Vol 1 370, 376. See also eg Thach (n 103) 92–94; Farrand (n 98) 87–89.

[106] Italics in the original. Pacificus I in Alexander Hamilton (Pacificus) and James Madison (Helvidius) *Letters of Pacificus and Helvidius on the Declaration of Neutrality* (Gideon 1845) 9–10. The argument was both functional and textual, the latter referring to the language of the vesting clauses of Articles I and III, which were both explicitly defined the enumerated powers as a closed list: '[t]he difficulty of a complete enumeration of all the cases of executive authority, would naturally dictate the use of general terms ... The different modes of expression employed in the constitution, in regard to the two powers, the legislative and the executive, serves to confirm this inference'. ibid 10.

[107] Helvidius I–IV, ibid 53–92.

[108] See eg Fatovic (n 103) 433–39.

136 reports submitted before February 2012 cited the statute that set the reporting duty.[109]

c. Pressure to Act

In some cases, external pressure to make a legal arrangement may lead to its adoption despite the reluctance of rule-makers to fully implement it. Such pressures may arise due to the existence of transnational commitments to act, may be the outcome of domestic pressure to answer a perceived need, or may be the result of government perceptions that a formal introduction of a rule may be beneficial politically. In all such cases, a rule, either statutory or under delegated power, may be added to the rule-book without having actual impact. Pressures may also change over time. On its inception, a rule may be welcomed by all, but changing conditions may give rise to changes in government attitudes towards the rule. Unable to strike it down, again for political reasons, the rule, which may have been highly detailed and anything but fuzzy, may transform into pastiche law, a form of fuzziness discussed in Chapter 8. This may occur even when the law was originally welcomed by all participants in the public sphere.[110]

d. Marginalization

I end with a less-recognized exogenous factor. An arrangement may be fuzzily designed due to the existence of other pressing needs conceived as more important, either due to their content or to their political implications. Paraphrased, the maxim 'when the cannons are heard, the muses are silent' captures the essence of the classical argument about the inability to make a detailed emergency law in wartime. This state of affairs is not limited to a single extreme context.

Returning to the drafting of the US Constitution by the 1787 Philadelphia Constitutional Convention, I have noted above that the details concerning presidential powers were relegated to several committees and were not discussed extensively by the Convention itself. This does not imply that the Convention was entirely uninterested in this aspect or in the nature of the presidency; however, priorities lay elsewhere. Much of the time allocated to the discussion of Article II was dedicated to issues concerning methods of the election of the president. Time constraints didn't enable extensive debate on other matters, which objectively carried at least similar weight, but were deemed less urgent in the eyes of representatives

[109] Richard E Grimmett, *War Powers Resolution: Presidential Compliance*, Congressional Research Service, 7–5700 (2012), summary page; for general analyses, see Curtis A Bradley and Jack L Goldsmith, 'Congressional Authorization and the War on Terrorism' (2005) 118 Harv L Rev 2047; Mariah Zeisberg, *War Powers: The Politics of Constitutional Authority* (Princeton University Press 2013). For further details see Chap 8.

[110] In addition to the case of the War Powers Resolution discussed above, see the example of the annual riders in US Appropriations Acts, prohibiting funding of the introduction of a permit regime concerning emission of gases from biological processes associated with livestock production, discussed in Chap 8.

of smaller states who wished to secure their state's interests. Disagreement was discussed above as an explanation, but the issues that did reach the plenary and discussed in detail were subject to just as much disagreement. The lesser time spent on other issues may have also contributed to their eventual fuzziness.

This case can thus be presented as an example of 'marginalization'. During the design stage of a regulated issue, attention to clarity may be limited, not necessarily due to its complexity or the existence of deep disagreement, but due to a perception of the priority of other pressing matters.

A similar tale can be told in the context of post-design limitation of fuzziness. The tidying up of messy law is not likely to be highly prioritized politically; legislatures and executives are constantly under pressure to address more urgent issues, and, as discussed above, the attractions of fuzziness are many. The persistent pattern of piling-up, discussed in Chapter 7, is one such example. The introduction of a statute could be the opportunity for streamlining the field, but in many cases, parallel arrangements have remained in force, leading to further fuzziness in that area of action.

Calls for 'reform' may escalate on the political agenda—a good example is Tony Blair's political platform presented before his election in 1997—but such calls are generally concerned with change of content, not with mere legal ordering. This example also shows that exceptions exist: a few years after the enaction of the 1997 devolution acts and the 1998 Human Rights Act, some reform of the prerogative was introduced by the British parliament.[111] Of course, as this book has argued, the whittling-down of fuzziness is not only a matter of introducing orderliness, but priorities usually direct energies elsewhere.

As a final example, the absence of British reform of the prerogative in recent years, discussed above in the contexts of institutional stickiness and power-retention, may also be explained under this rubric. Attention to Britain's exit from the European Union was a constant feature of high constitutional politics since 2015; other issues faded into the background.

D. Concluding Remarks

This chapter addressed two aspects that should be part of any normative analysis of the propriety of executive reliance on fuzzy law as a tool for maintaining its political dominance over law without moving into the zone of illegality. Setting the discussion under two theoretical constructs—the rule of law and participatory democracy—it is argued that the retention of patterns of fuzzy law directly endangers proper democratic governance.

111 See above text to n 76 and Chap 4.

Although fuzzy nodes of power may be employed for the public good just as much as they can be sources for abusive government action, and excessive, abusive power may be authorized by a detailed statute—after all, statutes can grant extensive power and refrain from setting limits on its exercise. However, the lesser the detail set on the exercise of power, the greater the danger of employing power in ways that escape processual systemic constraints designed to promote legitimacy.

In their design stage, fuzzy rules are more likely to suffer deficits in participation, deliberation, and representation. The multi-player interaction inherent to the legislative process can be replaced by single-player rule-making by bodies that lack the proper attributes of representation. Once embedded within the legal or semi-legal spheres, the opacity of fuzzy rules severely constrains citizens' reliance on them when planning ahead, and facilitates the inconsistent application of rules. Further, accountability and review processes, when available, are weakened: under conditions of less accessibility and clarity, a properly detailed challenge to a fuzzy arrangement may be difficult, if not impossible. Fuzziness may also render reporting and other post-implementation review no more than a charade: when access to the data is largely limited to the government, the assessment of reports is just as difficult.

The second part of this chapter provided a tentative list of factors that push towards the retention and extension of fuzziness. In addition to the existence of endogenous factors that derive from the indeterminacy of text and institutional aversion to change, the political benefits garnered by both the legislature and the executive virtually ensure the flourishing of fuzziness. These exogenous factors were classified under four heads: power-accumulation, disagreement both in the design stage of an arrangement and its subsequent application, external political pressure to 'deliver' an arrangement, and the marginalization of issues concerned with the removal of fuzziness.

In sum, although I join those who argue that fuzzy law is an unavoidable feature of governance, I disagree with the forging of a normative link between this inevitability and the well-being of society. This chapter advances the opposite argument, and considers the prices paid by retaining fuzzy law to the central values of a well-functioning, citizens-focused democracy. Here, I join forces with some of the critics of the growth of the administrative state, but only to a certain degree. Those who call for the eradication of fuzziness through the adoption of a renewed vision of the state, of its government and its legislature, or by prompting the takeover by the judiciary, at least in some fields of government action, are just as misguided as their opponents; they assume (or at least are ready to hope) that these counter-forces could eliminate open-ended forms of law. All that can be expected is interstitial reduction of fuzziness by the enhancement of counter-forces.

Accordingly, in light of both the problematics of fuzzy law and its undeniable attraction for decision makers, the next, and final chapter is dedicated to a normative exploration of the power of review mechanisms. I fully support the enhancement of review, and focus on judicial review due to the existence of current attacks over this form of collective decision-making. I will not assume that such mechanisms, even the strongest and most efficient, are likely to assist in the eradication of all fuzziness, but the recognition of both problems and interests for preservation, which was the central aim of this chapter, is of ultimate importance for the achievement of a maximum degree of flattening the inevitable tension that is explored in this book.

10

Keeping the Internal Tension Under Check

The Role of the Judiciary in a Multiple-Fora Participatory/Deliberative Democracy

A. Introduction 289
B. In Search of Normative Integrity 293
C. The Role of the Judiciary: A Critical Overview 295
D. Enhancing Judicial Review: Arguments from Democratic Theory 306
1. The Rule of Law 306
2. Participatory/Deliberative Democratic Theory 308
3. But Why the Courts? 312
E. Addressing Counter-Arguments 313
F. Concluding Remarks 319

A. Introduction

Under the central theme of this book, the need to grant powers to the executive branch necessarily engenders the risk of abuse of power. The question discussed in this chapter is deceptively simple: assuming that abuse of executive power is a constant potential, how far, and how deep, should the judiciary's review of executive powers go? Under the normative argument offered in this chapter, the judiciary should be a central, albeit not the single or even necessarily dominant, checking force of all types of executive action.

First, an initial question about the role of the judiciary should be set aside. The model advanced in this book identified three generators of fuzziness: constitutions (and constitutional constructs), legislators, and executives. Shouldn't the judiciary be added as another generator of fuzziness? After all, haven't courts contributed to this widespread feature, as many decisions discussed in the previous chapters attest?

While courts have clearly done their share, by recognizing and upholding certain fuzzy practices, this is exactly what they have done: they have upheld fuzziness. At least in common-law systems, courts decide on the basis of arguments brought

A Theory of the Executive Branch. Margit Cohn, Oxford University Press (2021). © Margit Cohn.
DOI: 10.1093/oso/9780198821984.003.0011

forth by the parties to a case. Rare will be the case in which a court develops a new form of fuzziness.

Justice Sutherland's sole-organ doctrine, discussed in Chapter 4, may be one possible exception. The main argument in *Curtiss-Wright*, the 1936 decision on the indictment of military aircraft exporters for contravening the prohibition set in a Joint Resolution, a form of legislation shared by two Houses of Congress, was that the statute improperly delegated power to the president, who was authorized to set such embargos by proclamation. A relatively lengthy portion in Justice Sutherland's opinion was dedicated to the development of a theory under which the president held plenary and sole powers.[1] Alongside the debate over the propriety of this ground for the recognition of this source of fuzziness, commentators have provided different accounts of the factual question of whether parties, mainly the appellants at the Supreme Court (the Solicitor General), included the argument for the president's sole power in their briefs. Accounts that '[n]one of the briefs on either side discussed the availability of independent or inherent power' do not settle well with remarks such as 'the foreign relations power was only fleetingly and vaguely suggested on brief';[2] still, the shared message is clear: this doctrine was at least largely an independent judicial contribution.

This exception does not belie the general rule: courts have not been actively involved in shaping novel forms of fuzziness, at least not those from the US and the UK; generally, the decisions discussed in this book in which courts were ready to accord some form of legality to a challenged action upheld existing fuzzy forms of law, defended by one of the parties to the case. This insight leads us to normatively consider the role of courts as setting constraints on fuzzy executive power, rather than on upholding it.

This chapter does not use the term 'judicial review', often employed by participants in the extensive debates over the legitimacy of judicial output, as the term carries different meanings and can thus cause confusion. In the US, 'judicial review' usually connotes the power of courts to invalidate statutes for unconstitutionality, while the British have traditionally applied the term in their discussions of review of administrative acts, usually under administrative law grounds. To ensure that my discussion is not limited to the question of the legitimacy of review of a single stratum of law, the analysis in this chapter is framed under the general question of 'the role of the judiciary'—a phrase that aptly ensures that all types of judicial output are considered.

Concerned with the role of the judiciary as a constraining agent of fuzzy law, the chapter is laid out in two layers. First, in light of the special problems attached

[1] *US v Curtiss-Wright*, 299 US 304, 317–18 (1936). On the doctrine see ch 4.

[2] See, respectively, Louis Fisher, 'The Staying Power of Erroneous Dicta: From *Curtiss-Wright* to *Zivotofsky*' (2016) 31 Con Commentary 149, 166; Charles A Lofgren, '*United States v Curtiss-Wright Export Corporation*: An Historical Reassessment' (1973) 83 Yale LJ 1, 11.

to reliance on fuzzy law, I advance arguments that call for enhanced review in this context. The chapter offers more: each of the arguments brought forth with regard to the constraint of fuzziness is developed into a contribution to the ongoing general debate over the role of the judiciary in the shaping of the public sphere. Several reasons justify the expansion of the discussion. It is impossible to address the particular question of the constraint of fuzziness without relying on the general normative issue, and, hence, normatively assessing its aspects; fuzziness itself is fuzzy, and an overarching theory is required to explicate the particularities of this context. Finally, the insights gained in the context of review of fuzziness are of importance to the debate over the role of the judiciary in the public sphere, and could thus not be removed from the discussion. Hence, the overviews of the literature are concerned with the general question; little has been offered in the context of action under grey holes or fuzzy nodes. As for the normative parts, the sections concerned with the two theories used to support active participation, open with arguments directed to the review of fuzziness, then turn to the general layer.

Most of the general debate, parts of which are discussed in the chapter, and not only in the US, has been concerned with review in constitutional-law aspects. The protection of rights by the judiciary is a dominant feature, as is the question of the legitimacy of the invalidation of statutes by judiciaries. These are of course central issues, but I am also concerned with review of administrative action, those seemingly 'mundane' areas of agency discretion, policy-making, and the like. Only two of the surveyed contributions have focused on the latter, with the addition of a third participant who has introduced a philosophy of judging in these areas in his contribution as a judge.

The general debate over the role of the judiciary is instructed by two different understandings on the nature of adjudication in the public sphere. For some, the main function of the court is to resolve specific disputes, mainly between two members of society, and, by extension, between an aggrieved member and a public officer or body. The focus under this view is on the ability of the aggrieved to receive justice through courts, when other venues do not deliver. A different wide-lens analysis considers the judiciary in the broader context of decision-making in the public sphere. Both analytic bases are valid in common-law systems, and do not exclude each other, yet it is important to understand that the choice between these two foci, often intuitively made, may impact on the normative argument made by participants in this debate.[3]

In sum, this book focuses on the executive branch and executive action, and specifically addresses forms of fuzziness; my case for an active judicial role could

[3] This distinction roughly corresponds to Lon Fuller's distinction between adjudication as a means for the settling of disputes and adjudication as a form of social ordering, but Fuller's idea of 'social ordering' is not linked with the argument developed here, and his account of the limits of adjudication is substantively different from mine. Lon L Fuller, 'The Forms and Limits of Adjudication' (1978) 92 Harv L Rev 353, 357. For other views on the nature of the function of the judiciary see below.

have been made only in the context of the exercise of fuzzy forms of governance. However, the argument regarding the role of the judiciary, offered here, is more expansive. Beyond the main themes of the book, statutes may be invalidated for incompatibility with constitutional provisions that have nothing to do with executive exercise of power; for example, issues concerning the electoral process or federalism may have little to do with the executive. Secondly, and in the context of review of executive powers, some such powers are squarely exercised under a framework that is relatively non-fuzzy. The general argument made here is designed as a contribution to the general debate over the proper role of the judiciary in the context of public law at large, with special attention granted to the question of review of administrative policy, an aspect sometimes overlooked by those who target rights and the invalidation of statutes for non-constitutionality.

In addition to reliance on the 'rule of law' as instructing the proper stance, my argument draws on a vision of governance that is the product of continuous political interaction between a large number of players in the social and political spheres. This version of participatory/deliberative democracy moves, in line with deliberative systems theory, from the emphasis on a two-player game towards a form of polyarchic governance. In the tradition of participatory/deliberative democracy, I argue that the polity should enable and encourage vigorous debate and interactive checking-and-balancing through the establishment of a variety of mechanisms that operate as intermediators between individuals and decision-makers, one of them being the judicial system. In this way, the question of the representative nature of the judiciary, in itself addressed in the chapter, is transformed to an argument of the court as a venue of representation of individuals.

The chapter opens with a commitment to the presentation of an ideologically neutral theory. Here, I set some question-marks over the neutrality of some of the participants in the general debate on the role of the judiciary, pointing at a possible correlation between their normative stance and their politics, exemplified by readiness to shift their normative claim when judiciaries experience an ideological shift. In this context, I argue that within the democratic framework, theories concerning the role of state bodies should remain constant under different general leanings of the judiciary at any time; attitudes presented as normative should not be swayed by participants' positions on the rulings of either conservative or liberal courts.

Part C is dedicated to an overview of some of the main participants in the debate. I critically address theories that consider the judiciary redundant for the maintenance of a healthy polity that self-checks possible abuse of executive power, as well as calls for the limiting of active intervention to so-called 'constitutional' issues that involve alleged breaches of human rights. Part D turns to my normative argument, which draws on two distinct strands of democratic theory, the rule of law and multiple-player participatory/deliberative models of democracy. The latter path, a road rarely taken by legal philosophers and public law theorists, draws its insights from a view of the judiciary as intermediator and promoter of active citizen participation and deliberation, which should involve vigorous judicial involvement in steering the decision-making process.

In the following part, I critically assess the main arguments against judicial participation. Rejecting the assumption that courts are necessarily the 'bearers of the last word', I address the 'democratic deficit' argument, which focuses on the issue of the representative nature of this branch, arguments concerned with the expertise and knowledge held by courts, and arguments that brand active, participation-inducing judiciaries as the main culprits responsible for some cases of deterioration of democratic processes.

In sum, the argument promoted in this part is based on two claims. I reject the assumption of the omnipotence of the judiciary as the 'bearer of the last word' and the ensuing hierarchical model of decision-making in the public sphere. Instead, the judiciary is presented as a key, but not necessarily supreme, player in a multi-participant arena concerned with both authorizing and checking against abuse. Under this theory, the infamous argument regarding the judiciary's 'democratic deficit' transforms into a claim that emphasizes the role of courts as participation-enhancing fora, by offering members of society, particularly the weak, who have less or no access to the decision-making and power-allocating processes, the opportunity to bring forth their grievances and thereby contribute to these processes.

B. In Search of Normative Integrity

Too often, scholars have normatively addressed contested issues, constructing arguments that are presented as universally applicable on the basis of their political views. Sometimes, normative views undergo change with the shift in governing politics, a transformation that raises questions over the true universal nature of these views. In a different context, that of the freedom of speech, Jack Balkin discussed this 'ideological drift', pointing at the tendency of some leftists to abandon their earlier liberal positions when the freedom of speech was cited to support rightist, conservative speech or action. Balkin showed that in some cases, normative attitudes towards this aspect of governance were transformed following a move from one pole of the political-ideological spectrum to the other.[4]

A similar tendency can be found in some of the scholarship concerned with the role of the judiciary. Core democratic values such as democratic representation, the protection of civil rights, human dignity, and equality, can be interpreted and applied under different political flags. More so are social/economic ideological platforms that are distinctly ideologically driven. Such platforms range, within the

[4] Jack Balkin, 'Some Realism about Pluralism: Legal Realist Approaches to the First Amendment' (1990) (3) Duke LJ 375, 383.

democratic framework, from so-called 'right-wing' market-liberalism to 'leftist-leaning' social democratic visions of state involvement.

Programs designed under a distinct ideology, whatever its color, have serially reached courts during the political struggles that preceded their introduction and continued during their implementation. Suffice to mention, in the US, the New Deal court that succumbed to President Roosevelt's market reforms, the expansion of the protection of civil rights by the Warren court, and the libertarian attitudes taken by the majority in the Rhenquist and post-Rhenquist Supreme Courts. If most 'leftist' scholars lauded judicial activism in the 1960s and 1970, during the eras of the liberal court, a new generation of post 1980s scholarship, writing on courts that turned much more conservative in their leanings, has moved to support judicial restraint. To date, twenty-first century scholars who follow a similar path sometimes denigrate 'activism', and, like their predecessors, couch their arguments in universally applicable normative claims. In other words, during periods of judicial decision-making that seem to deliver and promote some scholars' views, judicial involvement is lauded; not so when courts seem to push for the opposite ideology.

Some scholars have not fallen into this trap. In his call to abolish judicial review of legislation in the US, Mark Tushnet's call for terminating judicial ability to invalidate statutes for unconstitutionality, argues that the question 'whether liberals or conservatives benefit from judicial review' should be replaced by an evaluation of judicial review 'in a principled rather than political way'.[5] Practicing what he preaches, Tushnet's normative call has nothing to do with the content, ideological or other, of US courts' decision-making: it is more of an institutional argument. Some critics of Tushnet's stance (which I contribute to below) are aware of the importance of neutrality, as in the case of Mark Graber's scathing review of Tushnet's move to populism, supported in the same book. In a seemingly casual comment, Graber notes that ' [j]udicial review looks pretty good to liberals when the choice is between Earl Warren and Joe McCarthy'—a hint that political preferences may stand at the basis of arguments couched as universal.[6] Similar insights may be gleaned from US administrative law scholarship. The continuous debate over the role of courts as reviewers of agency decisions, which revolves around the famous *Chevron* ruling regarding levels of deference to agency interpretation, is presented as a universal institutional argument that has nothing to do with content; whether all participants' views are indeed devoid of prior assessments of the politics of agency requires further attention elsewhere.[7]

[5] Mark Tushnet, *Taking the Constitution Away from the Court* (Princeton University Press 1999) 152.
[6] Mark A Graber, 'The Law Professor as Populist' (2000) 34 U Rich L Rev 373, 402.
[7] *Chevron v Natural Resources Defense Council*, 467 US 837 (1984). For an overview see Valerie C Brannon and Jared P Cole, *Chevron Deference: A Primer*, CRS Report No R44954 (2017).

The insight that normative arguments may sometimes be instructed by the politics of their proponents serves here as a cautionary element. Normative views are usually presented as universal and neutral, but when a shift in theory occurs alongside an ideological-political transformation, the universal validity of the theory should at least be questioned. Alternatively, openness is a better form.

If indeed the normative debate over the role of the judiciary, at least in the US, is shot with an underlying political agenda, this state of affairs does not only challenge the question of normative integrity in its home setting. A seemingly neutral theory, developed against the particularities of one system, may be implanted onto the theoretical debate in other systems, which are distinctly different from the social, economic, and legal particularities of the US, and share little of the political leanings of their judiciaries.

In sum, the pro-judiciary argument advanced here is designed under the principle labeled 'normative integrity', pointing at the difficulties that may emerge due to theorists' views on the content of decisions in an area posited as an institutional one. Adhering to this recommendation for normative integrity, my argument strives to be universally applicable. Unconnected, as much as possible, from the distinct set of values I espouse, I find that heightened judicial review offers better promise for a properly administered democratic polity.

C. The Role of the Judiciary: A Critical Overview

The dispute over the role of the judiciary has been raging for decades. As mentioned above, in US-lingo, 'judicial review' is dedicated to judicial invalidation of statute law due to inconsistency with the Constitution; the same term was traditionally applied in the UK mainly in the context of review of administrative action. Most general theories on the role of the judiciary, however, have focused on the constitutional aspects, considering both the role of this branch in the constitutional framework and the democratic legitimacy of striking out statutes, an issue that has always concerned US theorists, and has risen in importance after the entry into force of the unique framework introduced in the UK in the Human Rights Act. In the frame of this book, I focus on the review of executive action, rather than on legislation. Discussion of constitutional-type review is however not set aside, as executive action often implicates on areas considered constitutional, mainly when the action involves alleged breaches of recognized and protected human rights or is firmly embedded in legislation. Yet, important to the assessment of the theories reviewed in this section, my interest lies in prising out, in addition to the normative views on judicial review in constitutional contexts, also the possible stances of such theorists regarding review under administrative law, when policies and exercise of powers are challenged under traditional administrative law grounds. I show below that many of these theories are essentially directed to the constitutional, although a large number of these, especially the ones I describe as 'middle-ground' theories, reject extensive review when constitutional issues are absent. Very few squarely direct their attention to review of administrative action as such and argue for its enhancement; I join them in the next section of this chapter.

A second introductory comment is in place. As mentioned in the introduction, the message of this chapter extends beyond the question regarding the proper judicial stance towards fuzzy forms of executive action. All of the theories reviewed in this section, and some of my subsequent arguments, are concerned with the general inquiry into the ways courts should contribute (or interfere, depending on one's position) with the ways society and politics shape the public sphere.

This overview, then, is concerned with both levels of adjudication, review of statute law and review of administrative action, as long as they are directed by the executive, but its main thrust is not the sanctity or superiority of the constitution. Rather, I ask whether any features of the judiciary, or other features of the polity, should support a call for the ejection of the judiciary from the arena of review of executive power—a direction I do not take.

Several scholars advocate such an ejection. Mark Tushnet's call to 'take the constitution away from the court' was mainly concerned with judicial review of legislation.[8] Eric Posner and Adrian Vermeule's focus on administrative law still carries a constitutional flavor, as presidential action, with which they are mainly concerned, tends to be at least partially based on the Constitution. Focusing mainly on the US, theirs is a true call for the elimination of judicial review of executive action.[9] First, they argue that judicial oversight over the executive has generally failed, despite some evidence to the contrary. Judges are generalists rather than experts in particular fields; the geographical dispersion of US courts leads to inconsistency; and, finally, judges suffer from a 'legitimacy crisis' in a sociological sense, which in their view stems from their being 'legal technocrats appointed for their expertise rather than elected on a partisan basis'.[10] Secondly, they argue that politics and public opinion successfully substitute the failed reliance on judiciary as a checking institution. Elections, the party system, and the political culture of the US, including its endemic culture of 'tyrannophobia', sufficiently cabin presidents from overusing their powers.[11]

This reliance on the force of politics as singlehandedly capable of eradicating excessive executive power is overly optimistic. Even if we accept that politics, social

[8] Tushnet (n 5).

[9] For a discussion on constitution-based authorization see ch 5.

[10] Eric A Posner and Adrian Vermeule, *The Executive Unbound: After the Madisonian Republic* (OUP 2011) 10, 29–30 and *passim*. Citation at 30. As support for the latter argument, Posner and Vermeule cite Richard Fallon's article on 'legitimacy'. Fallon addresses 'sociological legitimacy' as one aspect of legitimacy; the article is not concerned with the question of the legitimacy of courts as such. See Richard H Fallon Jr, 'Legitimacy and the Constitution' (2005) 118 Har L Rev 1787, 1795.

[11] Posner and Vermeule (n 10) esp chs 4, 6. See ch 1 for further analysis.

forces, and political cultures operate in a non-arbitrary, indiscriminate, and reasoned way—an assumption that is at least highly questionable—such social and political checking mechanisms are picky. First, they are more accessible to strong interest groups: weaker members of society and minorities are more likely to be underserved by these channels. Secondly, the political sphere is usually less concerned with so-called mundane cases of abuse, which can severely affect members of society. Executives must be aware of the limited interest of politicians and shapers of public opinion in 'lesser' fields of action; thus, the argument for self-constraint fails in these cases. The search for a checking mechanism that operates in a steady, continuous, and non-arbitrary fashion must look elsewhere. Furthermore, the authors of *The Executive Unbound* seem to support politics as a means of mediation between the public and government, an argument that implies that politics enhances participation and deliberation; at the same time, they fail to grasp the function of the judiciary as an inducer of participation/ deliberation, an aspect further addressed below.

'Middle-ground' theories call for different forms of reserved, constrained, or otherwise deferent judicial output. Most belong to two camps. Some call for overall limitation of the extent and depth of judicial decision-making, subject to rare exceptions; others carve out areas in which the courts are required to make substantive decisions, usually in the case of issues involving breaches of human rights and relegate all other issues to the zones of deference or restraint.

Within the first camp, Cass Sunstein's *One Case at a Time* argues that the US Supreme Court, in fact all courts, should make 'shallow' and 'narrow' rulings that apply only to the dispute before them. This stance, labeled 'minimalism', is generally justified, as judges often lack adequate information and cannot foresee all consequences of a decision. The judges' cognitive limitations, and the possible costs (or effects) of error, are joined by the argument that minimalist decision-making, which grants latitude to other branches of government, offers better space for decision-making under the political process, and thus promotes democracy.[12] Yet, Sunstein continues, this is no call for overall minimalism: in some cases, the opposite stance, 'maximalism', is in place. Rulings based on substantive reasoning, designed to apply broadly, may be suitable when the merits of the solution seem clear to the judges, rather than inconclusive, when such ruling is likely to reduce costly uncertainty for future parties, promotes advanced planning, or promote democratic goals, that is, process and uncontested values.[13]

Conceding that he does not argue for a 'full-scale argument for minimalism', Sunstein's middle-ground theory is confusing. Beyond questions regarding the application of these exceptions (for example, how would a court assess the

[12] Cass Sunstein, *One Case at a Time: Judicial Minimalism on the Supreme Court* (Harvard University Press 1999) 46–57.
[13] ibid 57–60.

contestability of the issue they are required to address)—an element that exists whenever an open-ended exception is set—it is unclear whether courts should indeed refrain from entering a field that is truly under debate. Sunstein seems to choose easy examples to test these exceptions: for him, *Brown v Board of Education* and *United States for Virginia* were rightly wide and deep, respectively, since, in the first case, 'the court had confidence in a flat ban of segregation', and 'by 1996 the Court had a good understanding of what underlies the prohibition on sex discrimination'.[14] Yet, assessing a decision in hindsight is tricky, and, in any case, cannot fully convince those who wish to consider the proper judicial stance in an ongoing controversy. At its time, *Brown* was not a simple case of a decision under consensus. In a separate piece, Sunstein discussed the serious initial differences of opinion between the Justices during the earlier stages of deliberation; some of the Justices were set to dissent, and an agreement was achieved only after Earl Warren replaced Fred Vinson as Chief Justice.[15] This, then, was no easy case of consensus. More problematic is the fact that *US v Virginia* was not unanimous; the existence of a dissent sets a serious challenge to the argument for the existence of clear judicial consensus, or, at least, removes such decisions from inclusion.[16] And in both cases, social consensus was far from evident. It would seem that these examples were chosen for their incontestability in 1999, the year of Sunstein's publication, but judges are required to decide on a difficult issue with no benefit of foresight. The argument may be valid, but the examples do not make it service. At least one other exception set by Sunstein is just as open to criticism.[17]

Next in this 'middle-ground' group is Alon Harel. His argument echoes Sunstein's but is cushioned in constitutional theory and is disconnected from any single national structure. Similar to most theorists, including the two scholars to be discussed next, Harel is essentially concerned with the protection of fundamental rights; issues pertaining to other contexts in which a dispute between an individual and a public body are not of direct concern.

Harel identifies the court's role as essentially providing a hearing for the aggrieved. For him, hearing consists of three components: the voicing of a grievance,

[14] ibid 59–60.

[15] Cass R Sunstein, 'Did *Brown* Matter', The New Yorker (26 April 2004) <https://www.newyorker.com/magazine/2004/05/03/did-brown-matter>. For the first decision, restoring the case to the docket, see *Brown v Board of Education*, 345 US 972 (1953). For the final decision, which was famously difficult to apply, see *Brown v Board of Education*, 349 US 755 (1954).

[16] The dissenting Justice in that case, Justice Scalia, receives a scathing criticism in Sunstein's work as a staunch maximalist of the formalist breed (ibid, *US v Virginia*, ch 9), raising questions whether the anti-maximalist argument was at least somewhat influenced by the author's criticism of the judicial and political views of that Justice.

[17] The likelihood of reducing uncertainty, it may be argued, will only be enhanced by minimalist rulings; under this exception, it seems that all cases that have broader implications would be included as exceptions to the rule of minimalism, an outcome that is not likely to be adopted by Sunstein. As for democracy-enhancing, this exception, which resonates with John Hart Ely's views on judicial review, this seems to me to be the gist of the argument, which ties in with other middle-ground theorists, discussed below.

the reception of a reasoned justification for the challenged action, and the duty that may be set on the decision-maker to reconsider the initial decision.[18] Regardless of the decision on the matter, the opportunity to be heard offers, for him, a non-instrumentalist justification of judicial review.[19]

Harel's argument for 'hearing' as the rationale for review is twinned with a call for judicial review that is 'constrained' and 'case-specific'. Having identified the essential role of courts as providing a hearing to the aggrieved, the necessary outcome for him is that courts should not extend their sights beyond the fulfillment of this limited function.[20] Harel rejects what he calls 'judicial supremacy', that is, the state of affairs in which courts authoritatively interpret constitutional meanings and that requires other bodies to defer to such interpretations. Instead, courts should narrowly decide the case brought before them: Tushnet, Gardbaum, and others' treatment of 'populist' and 'weak forms' of judicial review are cited as support.[21] Still, constraint is not categorical: central considerations, such as certainty, predictability, and co-ordination, may pragmatically justify courts' decision-making that, in some cases, normatively applies beyond the particular case.[22] This, then, is a type restraint theory that is relative rather than absolute.

In his argument, Harel explicitly rejects teleological arguments, or 'instrumental' theories that justify judicial review.[23] As such, his is also a process-oriented argument, which focuses on the benefits of the hearing process incurred by the aggrieved person. Despite his insistence that the hearing process, and its three components, suffice as justification, those aggrieved are necessarily after a result; mere hearing cannot satisfy them. Hence, the argument for marginalization of the outcome may be workable as a theory, but may disserve the idea that judicial review should be preserved. If the courts merely function as hearing-boards, their promise for the aggrieved is likely to quickly fade. Harel's second argument, the argument for constrained review, is subject to my general critique of all such middle-ground theories, which will be addressed after consideration of two additional calls for relatively constrained/deferent/narrow review.

In a more recent contribution to the debate, Harel supplements this argument by calling for 'robust deference' owed by the legislature to the judiciary, alongside the

[18] Alon Harel, *Why Law Matters* (OUP 2014), 202–16.

[19] ibid.

[20] ibid, esp 194 n 6, 210–20. See also Alon Harel and Adam Shinar, 'Between Judicial and Legislative Supremacy: A Cautious Defense of Constrained Judicial Review' (2010) 10 Intl J Constl L 950.

[21] See eg Tushnet (n 5); Stephen Gardbaum, *The New Commonwealth Model of Constitutionalism: Theory and Practice* (CUP 2013); Rosalind Dixon, 'The forms, Functions, and Varieties of Weak(ened) Judicial Review' (2019) 17 Intl J Constl L 904. Note that these bodies of scholarship are concerned with judicial power over the legislation, rather than on the role of the courts in all aspects of review, including administrative-law judicial review. This is but one example of the tendency to join both aspects without attending to the difference between them that may justify distinct argumentation.

[22] Harel (n 18) 215–16.

[23] ibid 194–202.

duty of courts to generally defer to the legislature.[24] This call could be interpreted as one that makes one step towards the understanding of the decision-making process as a collaborative process. However, this addition to the debate may be interpreted as a recipe for the introduction of a system that applies a rule of universal restraint. The result of curbing both the legislature and the judiciary may produce a stilted political arena, a result that is anathema to theories of active participation and deliberation, discussed in the next part.

Turning now to the camp that openly distinguishes between the protection of rights and other contexts, I open with David Dyzenhaus' work on the rule of law during emergencies. Dyzenhaus is not usually considered a middle-ground theorist, as he retains faith in the judiciary despite its patchy record during emergencies, and emphasizes its potential as a protector of a substantive version of the rule of law.[25] Yet, regarding review in other contexts, that is, in cases defined as pertaining to administrative law, Dyzenhaus advances the type of deference theory that draws on variegated contextual standards. [26]

Writing in the context of the UK, Aileen Kavanagh retains the contention for deference (albeit relative) in contexts that do not involve the protection of human rights. Taking a stance similar to Dyzenhaus', her argument draws on a distinction between 'constitutional' and 'normal' politics. The first category concerns the protection of human rights, in the UK, essentially under the Human Rights Act (HRA). The second province of 'normal politics' is not directly defined; it is seemingly residual, concerned with matters *not* involving a human-rights claim.[27] As far as the protection of human rights, the framework of the HRA and its review mechanism justify and require active judicial review, under a 'participatory' model that is addressed below. At this point, attention to the second province of action, roughly corresponding to administrative policy-making and its application, reviewed under administrative law grounds, is due.

Linking this issue with the concept of 'deference', Kavanagh refrains from accepting a strong, a-contextual rule for judicial restraint. For her, such 'substantive deference' is misguided. Nor can the 'polycentricity' of an issue, as promoted by Lon Fuller,[28] be the defining feature for discerning whether deference/restraint be practiced. In the end, deference is contextual; rather than 'spatial', its proper extent is 'a matter of degree'. Still, in this 'collaborative enterprise', courts should retain their roles as 'junior partners', showing respect to the legislature and to the

[24] Alon Harel, 'Why Legislatures Owe Deference to the Courts' (2019) 38 Revus 9.
[25] David Dyzenhaus, *The Constitution of Law: Legality in a Time of Emergency* (CUP 2006).
[26] ibid eg 143–44.
[27] For the distinction see Aileen Kavanagh, *Constitutional Review Under the UK Human Rights Act* (CUP 2009) 9, 340–41.
[28] Fuller (n 3).

executive, respect that can be traced to three arguments: relative institutional competence, expertise, and constitutional legitimacy.[29]

The last middle-ground theory discussed here is Jeff King's study of the adjudication of social rights. In *Judging Social Rights*, the expansion of the analysis beyond the focus on civil and political rights and the call for the constitutionalization of social rights is twinned with a second theme, concerned with the role of courts as adjudicators of social rights claims. Within this enlarged zone of reviewable cases, King takes a middle path. Opening with an assessment that courts are to be valued as a conduit for the promotion of accountability, as alternative processes such as tribunals, ombudsmen, and ADR are inadequate when in the absence of judicial review, King argues that in adjudicating social rights (and perhaps, by extension, in general), judges should be instructed by four principles that operated on a contextual basis. A binary solution is not offered here; generally, the particularities of the claim and the claimants will be decisive in the application of these interpretative principles. The default choice, in King's words, is 'incrementalism' in the review of social rights, although departures are appropriate where his principles of restraint do not apply, a stance that echoes, but certainly does not follow, Sunstein's call for small-step advancement, which opened this review of middle-ground theories.[30]

King is still concerned with judicial review of rights-claims, albeit under an expanded view of the nature of the rights to be protected. This may be explained by the focus of his study, which after all is concerned with the recognition and protection of social rights. It would appear that here, too, his argument could have purchase in other areas, including matters of so-called 'pure' policy, but this is not part of King's message.

I welcome the adoption of the call for active review in the human rights context. Clearly, government action that interferes with established rights of individuals must be subject to review of the most 'anxious' kind. However, the limitation to

[29] See Aileen Kavanagh, 'Deference or Defiance?: The Limits of the Judicial Role in Constitutional Adjudication' in Grant Huscroft (ed), *Expounding the Constitution: Essays in Constitutional Theory* (CUP 2008) 184; Kavanagh (n 27), esp Chapter 7; Aileen Kavanagh, 'The Role of Courts in the Joint Enterprise of Governing' in Richard Ekins, Paul Yowell, and NW Barber (eds), *Lord Sumption and the Limits of Law* (Hart 2016) 121. For Fuller's argument see (n 3). For the claim that polycentricity is 'pervasive', evident in all matters addressed in the public sphere, see Jeff A King, 'The Pervasiveness of Polycentricity' [2008] PL 101; Jeff A King, *Judging Social Rights* (CUP 2012) 189–210.

[30] Under the principle of democratic legitimacy, the first of these four interpretative principles, reticence to intervene may be proper when rule-makers properly exercise their roles, with exceptions concerned with the particularities of the claimants and the political set-up. Next, Fuller's argument for judicial restraint in polycentric areas is redesigned to include factors that attenuate deference. The third principle, the expertise of decision-makers and their actual exercise of it, weighed against the benefits of oversight and accountability, and the fourth, concerned with the importance of retaining flexible government action as weighed against claims for individual justice, both contribute to the construction of a framework that upholds judicial participation, but only to the extent prescribed. Jeff King, *Judging Social Rights* (CUP 2012), esp chs 6–10. For King's analysis on Sunstein's *One Case at a Time* see ibid 303–06.

that context is open to criticism. First, the distinction between 'constitutional' and 'normal' politics is not only porous—most distinctions are—but also questionable. As Kavanagh admits, some issues concerned with the allocation of resources touch upon, if not directly impact, on the rights of those receiving or being denied these resources.[31]

The different accounts offered by these scholars share a view of constrained review, to different extents and in different forms. In my view, the emphasis on restraint is problematic. Restraint is not only a matter of degree; its exercise may support a growing culture of restraint/deference, and contribute to a process of gradual decline of judicial readiness to decide in a case-specific mode. Under such a slippery-slope scenario of gradual decrease of intervention, trust in the judiciary as an aide in deciding grievances may be compromised, and could whittle down the very rationale for review by courts.[32]

Furthermore, the tendency to view human-right issues as high-level politics, to be granted special protection against abuse, twinned with a slightly disparaging attitude towards so-called mundane issues of 'low policy', should be criticized. As any person living in any modern state can attest, many of such 'low policies' can have an immense impact on a person's daily life. Policies consciously designed to avoid direct interference with equality, privacy, and the like, can still severely constrain the ability of individuals to freely plan their life; some government decisions that are essentially irreversible, as in the case of allocation of land and the neglect of the environment, cannot be attached to the rights of an individual. When social rights, more so broader societal interests that do not directly impact on a specific person, do not receive sufficient recognition, presenting them as 'normal politics' subject to diluted review, the possible beneficiaries will be those who had the benefit of directly influencing the decision-makers.

Moving towards those who invite courts to intervene, TRS Allan, known for his support of courts, still doesn't call for enhanced review in all fields of government action, but his view takes an additional step towards this position. Essentially, for him, all pre-designed doctrines, such as a doctrine of deference, should be eschewed in favour of a sensitive contextual stance. Justices must exercise caution before intervening with policy decisions, but, under an assumption that government bodies act in good faith for the public good, this argument does not support the adoption of any doctrine for self-control, such as 'due deference', a version of deference theory that is contextual, as adopted, inter alia, by Murray Hunt and Aileen

[31] See eg Kavanagh (n 27) 224.

[32] One may argue that the danger of escalation operates in both directions. Under this alternative argument, courts that tend to intervene in certain issues are likely to gradually expand and deepen their activism. While not analytically incorrect, courts do not easily step too far from social consensus: social and political forces limit this escalation much more than the opposite potential reduction of judicial participation.

Kavanagh.[33] For Allan, such attempts to ground the difficult exercise of judicial review are misguided, as the result of each case is essentially determined by the substance of the issue brought before the court. Attempts to clothe this exercise with similes of doctrine and principle may lead to a misconception under which issues can easily be classified either within or outside the remit of review; it might lead to excessive emphasis on restraint in cases considered 'political', when review is required; and it carries the risk of marginalizing what he considers the central criterion, that of substance.

Under Allan's account, courts should not be reluctant to intervene when rights are breached or when a government body acts illegally; it should be more reticent to intervene in matters of policy. On first glance, this argument seems to tally with other middle-ground theories of the type discussed above. However, the reluctance to adopt this deceptively workable neutral doctrine, or the sister doctrine of variable intensities of review, offers, for Allan, a better path for ensuring that decision-makers do not escape review in all proper set-ups.[34]

It is unclear whether Allan would recognize that some challenges to policy should be entertained even when a direct right is not breached, or whether his conception of 'rights' is broader than that adopted by others. In his discussion of the review of policy decisions involved with the allocation of scarce resources, he argues that '[i]f it is alleged that financial resources are so unevenly distributed between competing claimants that the unfairness amounts to the breach of constitutional rights, the distribution must be judicially considered in the context of the rights at issue'.[35] Indeed, Allan concedes that 'the any unfairness would have to be grave in order to amount to a constitutional wrong', but continues that 'the court would have to confront the relevant questions of law'.[36] Minimally read, then, little support is found here for carving out entire spheres of state action from the sphere of review.

Placed furthest in this continuum are theorists who directly oppose categorical limitation of the judiciary. Ronald Dworkin clearly considers courts as important players in the public law field: they should act with an intent to protect core moral values, the protection of which is the main reason for the existence of a well-working democracy.[37] I set aside the examples of Judge Hercules and of his lesser colleague Judge Herbert, analytically used to explicate the proper form of judicial

[33] For Murray Hunt's view, which is not presented here, see Murray Hunt, 'Sovereignty's Blight: Why Contemporary Public Law Needs the Concept of "Due Deference"' in Nicholas Bamforth and Peter Leyland, *Public Law in a Multi-Layered Constitution* (Hart 2003) 339. For Kavanagh, see eg Kavanagh (n 27); Kavanagh, 'Deference or Defiance?' (n 29).

[34] See eg TRS Allan, 'Human Rights and Judicial Review: A Critique of "Due Deference"' (2006) 65 CLJ 671; TRS Allan, 'Deference, Defiance, and Doctrine: Defining the Limits of Judicial Review' (2017) 60 U Toronto LJ 41.

[35] Allan (n 34) 693.

[36] ibid.

[37] Ronald Dworkin, *Taking Rights Seriously* (Harvard University Press 1977); Ronald Dworkin, *Law's Empire* (Belknap Press 1986).

reasoning, in favour of dealing with the question of whether Dworkin's forceful arguments for morality-based unfettered adjudication applies in cases considered less laden with constitutional law.

Most of the examples provided across Dworkin's œuvres are largely concerned with constitutionally protected rights, but there is sufficient evidence of his readiness, to some degree, to apply his call in some so-called lesser contexts. His claim that in the absence of a settled rule, judges should decide on the basis of principles (which also inform all rules), is based on a 'rights thesis', under which courts decide on concrete rights.[38] 'Rights', here, are distinguished from policy decisions, or rules that are intended to achieve a collective goal,[39] but the term 'rights' still carries a broad meaning, connoting any action that is not prohibited.[40] Dworkin's distinction between 'legal' and 'constitutional' rights[41] can support a reading under which any action that impacts on an individual should be actively reviewed by judges. Still, even under this expansive reading of what is in essence a call for protecting equal concern, missing here are cases concerned with overarching communal policies that are likely to impact on society-at-large despite the impossibility of attaching damage to particular individuals, an aspect that may be challenged in courts on administrative law grounds.

Aharon Barak, the professor of law who served as a Justice in Israel's Supreme Court and was its president for eleven years, has offered a strong version of this type of theory, couched in a theory of democracy that is distinctly substantive. Alike others in this camp, Barak advocates judicial protection of democratic values and human rights, and attention is granted to the question of democratic legitimacy of the repeal of laws for unconstitutionality.[42] However, his is not a theory that is directed merely to the rights contexts. Barak has also developed a rich jurisprudence that opened the gates of the courts and enabled in-depth review of policy decisions and issues concerning the continuing terms of office of indicted high-level politicians, inter alia through a development of a more relaxed standard of reasonableness and the virtual abolition of standing. These developments were introduced under a distinct vision of the nature of the administration as a public trustee, twinned with an emphasis of the role of the courts to ensure that no abuse of power occurs. While those transformations were the product of collective judicial efforts,

38 Dworkin *Taking Rights Seriously* (n 37) 82–90.

39 See eg ibid 90–92.

40 ibid esp 186–97.

41 See eg ibid 191.

42 Aharon Barak, *The Judge in a Democracy* (Princeton University Press 2008). In a short article that condenses much of Barak's arguments, he wrote that '[the court's] role is to give effect to the deep values of their society as expressed in its basic documents, its traditions, and its history. Their role is not to express the mood of the day. Judges should not be defensive in the face of the countermajoritarian arguments. When judges declare a statute unconstitutional, their declaration fits democracy fully, because they get their review power from the democratic constitution, and because democracy is riot simply majority rule, but also the protection of rights and freedoms of every individual'. Aharon Barak, 'The Role of a Judge in a Democracy' (2005) 88 Judicature 199, 199.

Justice Barak was clearly a strong force in introducing and, at least temporarily, sustaining these transformations.[43]

The final theorist belonging to the group that upholds an active judiciary discussed here directly, and uniquely, targets administrative law. Philip Hamburger's denigration of the 'administrative state', motivated by a harsh critique of its rise and expansion, is coupled by a call for judiciaries to reject the doctrine of deference, which 'has crawled back to the surface and returned to life' after its burial in nineteenth century England.[44] Offering the strongest support of review of administrative action, Hamburger views Justice Coke's valiant battle against Crown absolutism, fought in England in the early seventeenth century, to be a guiding light in current-day United States.[45] Delegation and deference, both deeply embedded in the canons of US administrative law, are then the two main doctrines challenged by Hamburger and other proponents of 'the new Coke' movement (a term coined by two of its opponents).[46] Alongside some support of Hamburger's thesis,[47] and the growth, in number and force, of supportive judges who call for the reconsideration of deference to the administration,[48] the academia has mainly responded critically.[49]

Some of the participants in this debate have not embedded their normative calls in a detailed and developed theory of democracy of the types discussed in the next section. General references to 'the rule of law', the 'failure' of the judiciary, and 'extralegality', to name a few, sometimes feature as elements that instruct the proper role of the courts.[50] More is needed here; theories that draw on the rule of law ideal,

[43] For an overview of these transformations see Rivka Weill, 'The Strategic Common Law Court of Aharon Barak and its Aftermath: On Judicially-led Constitutional Revolutions and Democratic Backsliding' (forthcoming 2020) L and Ethics Hum Rgts (analysis includes the assessment of the post-Barak era).

[44] Philip Hamburger, *Is Administrative Law Unlawful?* (University of Chicago Press 2014) 298.

[45] See eg ibid 45–47, 319–20.

[46] Cass R Sunstein and Adrian Vermeule, 'The New Coke: On the Plural Aims of Administrative Law' (2015) Sup Ct Rev 41.

[47] Gary Lawson, 'The Return of the King: The Unsavory Origins of Administrative Law' (2015) 93 Texas L Review 1521.

[48] See Chapter 9.

[49] In addition to direct critiques on the historical and other elements of the book (see eg Adrian Vermeule, 'No' (2015) 93 Texas L Review 1547), substantive critique addresses both foci. Adrian Vermeule finds that deference, as embedded by courts, is a complex multilevel doctrine built on precedents, that does not equal judicial exit; this 'voluntary and unilateral surrender' is entirely within the limits of constitutional legality (eg Adrian Vermeule, *Law's Abnegation* (Harvard University Press 2016); for Gillian Metzger, the very structure of the administrative state is not only constitutional, it is 'constitutionally obligatory', given the existing broad delegations of discretionary power, and the (re)entrance of courts as active participants would only risk their own constitutional status: Gillian E Metzger '1930 Redux: The Administrative State under Siege' (2017) 131 Harv L Rev 1. See also Jack M Beermann, 'The Never-Ending Assault on the Administrative State' (2018) 93 Notre Dame L Rev 1599 (questioning some of Hamburger's historical accounts, the viability of judicial departure from deference towards higher levels of intervention, suggesting, at best, the possibility for a thinner version of deference lite, and concluding that the administrative state is politically likely to endure).

[50] This is far from a universal failing. See, eg, Barak's consistent reliance on democratic theory, and King's work, which is embedded in theories of deliberative democracy, further developed beyond ch 9 in Part D.

and theories of multi-participatory democracy, discussed in the next section, offer a basis for the normative argument to be now unfolded.

D. Enhancing Judicial Review: Arguments from Democratic Theory

The previous chapter, which identified the innate problems set by fuzzy law to proper governance, embedded the analysis of these problems in two strands of democratic theory: the rule of law ideal and participatory/deliberative theories.[51] This part develops my normative call for heightened judicial role under both these theories. I end this part with a contribution to the discussion of the question 'why courts', tying in these theories with the grant of review power to courts rather than other bodies.

1. The Rule of Law

The concept of the rule of law, which is used in many a theory concerned with the advancement of a proper model of democracy, was discussed in Chapter 9. Here, I rely on the distinction between 'thick' and 'thin' theories, to show that in the context of the review of fuzzy legality, even thinner versions support heightened review.

In an earlier article on the royal prerogative (considered in this book as one form of constitution-generated fuzziness), I argued that reliance on that historically based source of power that enables executive action in the absence of an empowering statute should be subject to strict, or 'anxious' scrutiny, a British doctrine, adopted in the context of challenges of government interference with a human right, which resonates, to a degree, with US variegated standards of review.[52] The same argument should apply to all forms of fuzziness, in light of their direct threat to the rule of law, even in its thinner versions that emphasize processual values: in the absence of clarity, accessibility, and consistency, all types of review should be enhanced, including the review meted out by the judiciary.

By extension, this argument applies to the general question of the role of the judiciary, but further attention is in place.

[51] See ch 9.

[52] Margit Cohn, 'Judicial Review of Non-Statutory Executive Powers after *Bancoult*: A Unified Anxious Model' [2009] PL 260. For the US doctrine see *United States v Carotene Products* 304 US 144, 152 n 4 (1938), and, eg, Lewis F Powell Jr, '*Carolene Products* Revisited' (1982) 82 Col L Rev 1087.

Some theorists explicitly weave 'the rule of law' into their theories on the role of the courts. Discussing the propriety of judicial decision-making in politically laden contexts, Ronald Dworkin's distinction between the 'rule-book' and the 'rights' conceptions of the rule of law, essentially the ancestor of the distinction based on thickness, does forge this link, by arguing that 'the two conceptions of the rule of law offer very different advice on the question of whether judges should make political decisions in hard cases'.[53]

Indeed, thicker visions of the rule of law ideal support judicial participation in several ways. The emphasis on the existence of an independent judiciary and the allocation of the role of review to this government branch, important features in such theories, offer a vision that supports my argument.

David Dyzenhaus' notion of the rule of law, developed in his work on legality in times of emergency, is self-declared as 'rather bare', but is subsequently described as an ideal that 'links procedural constraints to substantive values', should, in my view, be located at the middle of the thin-thick spectrum.[54] His is an argument that awards the judiciary an important, if not crucial role in the protection of the rule of law; for him, requirements for due process, fair and reasonable action that respects equality, are to be fulfilled by the subjection of government action to review by independent judges.[55]

Calls for active judicial contribution can also be made under 'thinner', more processual versions of the rule of law ideal. As in the case of their sister theories, not all, if not most, of those who participate in the general question regarding the role of the judiciary have set a premium on the rule of law as a basis for their arguments. For example, Fuller's influential work on the rule of law, prominently featured in the previous chapter, was concerned with the values to be protected rather than with the means for their protection.[56] Still, an argument for judicial involvement can easily be made under a vision of the rule of law that mainly supports processual values, as discussed above.

Dworkin, Dyzenahus and others that based their arguments on this ideal, have, as noted above, focused on human rights contexts. Yet, the values encapsulated in the rule of law, be they moral understandings, fairness or mere clarity and accessibility, could all inform review of administrative discretion and government policy-making. Still, the marginalization of the latter element of public law deserves further substantiation of the normative argument advanced here. The second set of democratic theory, now discussed, offers further support for a vision of the judiciary that has much less to do with morality, rights, or other principles considered part of the rule of law.

53 Ronald Dworkin, *A Matter of Principle* (Harvard University Press 1985) 13. In this context see also Ronald Dworkin, *Taking Rights Seriously* (n 37) esp 131–49; *Law's Empire* (n 37).

54 Dyzenhaus (n 25) 12, 14. See further, ch 9.

55 ibid 12–13 and throughout the book.

56 Fuller (n 3) and the discussion above.

2. Participatory/Deliberative Democratic Theory

The second vision of democracy that drives my normative claim is based on a development of theories of participatory democracy, deliberative democracy, and its offshoot, deliberative systems theory. As in the case of the above analysis on the impact of the rule of law, an introduction to these theories and their contribution to the assessment of the dangers posed by fuzzy legality was offered in Chapter 9. Here, I consider their application in the context of the role of the judiciary.

First, let us consider the impact of such theories on the review of executive creation or application of fuzzy law. Several forms of fuzziness cancel deliberation and eliminate all elements of participation. The main culprit is unilateral rule-making. When presidents and prime ministers revert to the use of executive orders, introduced under a general reference to the constitution and laws of the country, or rely on the British prerogative, they are able to move forward in the absence of legislative involvement. Here is a case of action that requires anxious scrutiny, not unlike the argument made above in the context of reliance on the rule of law. Similar claims can be made with regards to other forms of fuzziness. Open-ended statutes essentially marginalize the participation inherent in the legislative process, and offer the executive a broad interpretational discretion, as do extensive grants of discretion and permissions to delegate. Furthermore; executives who refrain from implementing a statute, turning it to mere pastiche, are responsible for a distinct type of single-handed decision over the force of the law. Similar arguments can be made with regards to all forms of fuzziness .[57]

Moving now beyond the focus on fuzziness, which is not treated as such in this literature, it is important to note that the rich literature on participation and deliberation, which supplements elections by an additional deliberation-inducing process is generally not directly concerned with the judiciary. Fishkin's call for the addition of a single formal-type mechanism of 'deliberative polls' could offer one example.[58] Some of the more expansive accounts in these groups of theories have granted a certain, if limited, attention to the courts as foras for deliberation. Courts have been cited as one of the many institutional sites of contestation;[59] Donald Bello Hutt's attention to their role under the deliberative endeavor may mark a rising interest in the role of the judiciary, although Hutt sets doubt on the suitability of courts as performing a deliberative function, an issue I further discuss

[57] For a general schema see ch 3 Table 1.

[58] Introduced as a practical solution to the problem of direct democracy in large communities, these are organized events, institutionalized if not formalized, enabling participants to voice their views and ensuring that they are heard. See James S Fishkin, *Democracy and Deliberation* (Yale University Press 1991).

[59] Jane Mansbridge and others, 'A Systemic Approach to Deliberative Democracy' in Jane Mansbridge and John Parkinson, *Deliberative Systems: Deliberative Democracy at the Large Scale* (CUP 2012) 1, 2.

below as one of two convoluted understandings of participation and deliberation.[60] For now, I argue that there are no strongly convincing reasons for the limitation of the number of such deliberative and participation-inducing processes.[61] Instead, asserting the crucial role of active citizen deliberation, systems should strive to establish multiple institutions and structures promoting participation.

Within this framework, the function of courts as intermediary institutions, rather than supreme fora that strike down the output of all other decision-making bodies requires more attention. A variety of institutions acting as intermediaries would empower those whose resources are limited. Those who most need to participate, due to their inability to directly interact with the political decision-makers, are most likely to be limited in their time, organizational capabilities, and financial resources. Melissa William's insistence on granting 'voice' to marginalized groups echoes the importance of the existence of heightened representation, although she focuses on the representation of women in the legislative decision-making process, and is less concerned with the number of available fora.[62] In this context, I argue that courts play an important (but not a single and final) role as an intermediary forum.[63]

The third relatively neglected aspect of multiple-fora deliberative democracy can be instructed by the image of 'the marketplace of ideas'. This image has coloured the debates over the utility of free speech. Attributed to John Stuart Mill's call for free speech as an avenue for a search for the truth,[64] due to the infallibility of single enforced positions and John Milton's claim that truth is most likely to achieved in a 'free and open encounter',[65] the idea was adopted in countless considerations of the freedom of speech, both in scholarship and courts.[66] In a similar vein, it is argued that the passing of policy decisions through several fora, not only

[60] Donald Bello Hutt, 'Deliberation and Courts: The Role of the Judiciary in a Deliberative System' (2015) 64 Theoria 77. See also Donald Bello Hutt, 'Measuring Popular and Judicial Deliberation: A Critical Comparison' (2018) 16 I.CON 1121, 1138–46.

[61] The possible arguments for containing the number of fora rely on considerations of utility and finality. Under the first, the costs of providing multiple fora may exceed their contribution; the second argument focuses on the importance of reaching a stable arrangement, which would thus enable reliance and thereby improve trust in the government. In my view, and following deliberative systems theorists, both arguments are troubling if taken to their extreme. Utility cannot, in itself, justify the removal of a forum that contributes to the improvement of governance. At most, one can argue that some fora may be rejected, but the judiciary, with its record of correcting governance flaws, should not be one of them. As for finality, my view on governance as a continuous process does not conform with excessive reliance on the importance of reaching a final framework. Constant changes occur, and must continue to be part of a healthy polity; attempts at curbing change directly compromise the vitality and flexibility of government action.

[62] Melissa S Williams, *Voice, Trust, and Memory: Marginalized Groups and the Failings of Liberal Representation* (Princeton University Press 1998) ch 4. See also the analysis in the following section.

[63] For another reconsideration of the role of courts, this time pointing at their function as monitors and co-ordinators, the latter closer to the argument advanced here, see David Law, 'A Theory of Judicial Power and Judicial Review' (2009) Geo L J 723.

[64] John Stuart Mill, *On Liberty* (Osgood and Co 1871), ch 2, esp 35–36.

[65] John Milton, *Areopagitica* (Jebb Ed) (CUP 1918) 58.

[66] For decisions of the US Supreme Court that adopted the image see eg *Abrams v US*, 250 US 616, 620 (1919) (per Justice Holmes, dissenting) (considering 'free trade in ideas' as 'the best test of truth is the power of the thought to get itself accepted in the competition of the market'); *US v Rumely*, 345

enhances participation; it also enables a well-rounded examination of the decision under consideration.

Some indication that courts can, and do, perform this function is still found in the literature. Mark Graber's 'The Law Professor as Populist' was a direct diatribe against Mark Tushent's call for 'taking the constitution away from the court', discussed above. Questioning the validity of the calls of elite academics for the adoption of a 'populist' democratic structure, Graber notes that judicial review 'may facilitate public participation in constitutional decision-making because litigation is a form of political participation'; being a 'particularly cheap form of political participation', litigation serves to expand participation.[67] This is not always the case: even in systems that require relatively low filing fees, litigation costs may be prohibitive, unless covered by a third party.[68] Still, these costs cannot compare with the costs incurred in the creation and maintenance of a strong political interest group, able to exert direct pressure on legislators and policy-makers.

The point here, as Graber claims, is that choosing this forum 'may increase public control over constitutional meanings when elected officials have not and will not resolve those controversies presently resolved by courts'.[69] His argument echoes earlier calls, for example political scientist Terri Peretti, who argues that

> … there are a variety of forms of political representation and responsiveness, none of which needs be regarded as superior to or more democratic than another. Rather, each has instrumental or systemic value. By employing redundant and diverse forms of political representation and arranging them nonhierarchically, two objectives can be achieved. First, the opportunities for groups to gain access to and an effective voice in government policymaking are greatly expanded. Second, the political system as a consequence will possess a greater capacity to discover, with more certainty and reliability, the stable and enduring bases of political consensus.[70]

US 41, 56 (1953) (per Justice Douglas) (using the term). For the literature see eg Stanley Ingber, 'The Marketplace of Ideas: A Legitimizing Myth' (1984) Duke LJ 1.

[67] Mark A Graber, 'The Law Professor as Populist' (2000) 34 U Rich L Rev 373, 404.

[68] See, in the context of UK, Tom Hickman, 'Public Law's Disgrace', UK Constitutional Law Association, Constitutional Law Group (9 February 2017) <https://ukconstitutionallaw.org/2017/02/09/tom-hickman-public-laws-disgrace/>; Tom Hickman, 'Public Law's Disgrace: Part 2', UK Constitutional Law Association, Constitutional Law Group (26 October 2017) https://ukconstitutionallaw.org/2017/10/26/tom-hickman-public-laws-disgrace-part-2/.

[69] Graber (n 67) 406.

[70] Terri J Perretti, *In Defense of a Political Court* (Princeton University Press 1999) 219. See also Susan E Lawrence, *The Poor in Court: The Legal Services Program and Supreme Court Decision Making* (Princeton University Press 1990) 151–59 (still noting that success is conditional on garnering support in the political arena). If at all needed, additional support may be found in Christopher Peters' 'Adjudication as Representation', although this article is mostly concerned with the features of common-law adjudication that essentially offer parties the power to frame the issues to be decided by the judge. In itself, this analysis is only tenuously linked with the argument advanced here, but claims such as that 'adjudicative lawmaking can, under certain conditions, claim democratic legitimacy by ensuring

Indeed, minorities and other weaker groups may find an application to the judiciary an alternative, sometimes a better alternative, to gain direct access to government corridors; removal of this channel is likely to enable only stronger society members to be represented.[71] This is not always the case: even in systems that require relatively low filing fees, litigation costs may spiral, unless covered by a third party.

Yet another aspect of judicial involvement that invigorates participation and deliberation is its function as a venue for moving issues upwards on the public agenda. Courts may be referred to in highly debated contexts that are otherwise likely to be shunted by politics, as in the cases of racial segregation and abortion in the US during some periods.[72] Debate, even when unsuccessful in court, may raise public consciousness and lead to later success, as these examples attest.

Furthermore, consider the utility of multiple testing in different fora, generally discussed above. Even in cases in which a lively debate over a contested issue exists, the addition of another layer of discussion, this time relatively divorced from politics, contributes to the development of a well-rounded discussion over all aspects of the issue. The testing of an issue in multiple fora, including under a separate, a-political set of rules, promotes healthy debate and enhances the likelihood of reaching a better solution. Decisions such as British Prime Minister Boris Johnson's prorogation of parliament in the UK at the cusp of the Brexit process, and the line of decisions concerned with President Trump's construction of the wall between Mexico and the US, serve as sufficient examples.

In sum, drawing a multi-player deliberative theory of democracy, I argue that active multiple fora engender participation in different venues, inter alia by acting as intermediaries between the aggrieved and the wielders of power. Active fora also promote the potential for reaching a well-rounded policy decision through multiple testing of an issue in several institutional formats and under various sets of rules. Courts, which are neither supreme nor omnipotent, offer promise as generators of both types of utility—an argument further discussed in the following section.

constructive participation through interest representation' could support the argument discussed here. See Christopher J Peters, 'Adjudication as Representation' (1997) 97 Colum L Rev 312, 320. Such accounts should be distinguished from calls for collaborative decision-making, which are mainly concerned with the dialogue between the judiciary and the legislature.

[71] This point is forcefully made in Kavanagh (n 27), but, as discussed above, this argument for judicial participation is centred on 'constitutional politics' under the HRA.

[72] Suffice to note Alexander Bickel's skepticism in his famous 1962 *The Least Dangerous Branch*, written during a period in which the impact of *Brown v Board of Education* was under question (*The Least Dangerous Branch: The Supreme Court at the Bar of Politics* (Bobbs-Merril 1962)). On abortion see eg Mark A Graber, *Rethinking Abortion: Equal Choice, the Constitution and Reproductive Politics* (Princeton University Press 1996).

3. But Why the Courts?

The previous two parts have offered a multi-layered argumentation regarding the importance of active review over executive action. The linked question, grappled by theorists involved in this debate, is then 'why the courts?' Nothing in this following section is novel, but a short exposé is still required to wrap up the argument.

Harel's work, more recent than the others' discussed below, is a useful starting point, despite his call for limited intervention of courts, based on the value of a mere hearing, two aspects criticized above. Harel argues that considering the nature of judicial decision-making, 'courts are especially suited to facilitate a hearing': the judicial process offers an individual the opportunity to voice a grievance; respondents are required to justify their challenged action; and courts are required to decide on the matter brought before them. However, for Harel, any body that is assigned with a similar task essentially performs a judicial function: the process of reasoning that is the product of the above stages is *judicial*; the identity of the decider, and its institutional status, seemsecondary.[73] This argument may seem circular ('the courts/judiciary should decide because they act judicially'), but knowledge of the judicial process supports this argument, and holds purchase well beyond the existence of hearing; furthermore, the attachment of this role to the judiciary, and not to other hearing bodies, is crucial, as claimed below.

Beyond their ability to hear, several aspects have been discussed as justifying review by courts. I focus on two of these.[74] First, the question of 'why judges?' has often been answered by reference to judges' professional expertise (judges are after all trained as persons who must decide between competing arguments under an ethos of neutrality and fairness) and their institutional detachment and independence.[75]

Furthermore, the judiciary is part of the framework of government; even without holding the power of the purse, it does have the power to issue decisions that bind the parties before them. The enforcement power of courts is contested (hence the reference to the sword, which Hamilton famously found courts in no possession thereof),[76] but its edicts still carry the imprimatur of the state. If hearing were indeed the only aspect, one could have granted the role to psychologists and counsellors, who are arguably better as listeners and interpreters of complaints. Challengers of government

[73] Harel (n 18) 213–14.

[74] For Harel's overview of these, and other theories he considers as 'instrumentalist' see ibid 194–202.

[75] For the expertise argument see eg Charles Lund Black and Philip Bobbitt, *A New Birth of Freedom: Human Rights, Named and Unnamed* (Yale University Press 1999) 125 (focusing on review in human rights contexts). For the second argument see eg Owen M Fiss, 'Foreword: The Forms of Justice' (1993) 93 Harv L Rev 1, eg 13, 34, 45 (supplementing the argument relying on independence with 'the judge's obligation to participate in a dialogue', a process-based argument that in itself extends beyond Harel's).

[76] See 'Federalist 78' (Hamilton), in Benjamin Fletcher Wright (ed), *The Federalist Papers* (Belknap Press 1961) 490; reiterated inter alia in *Baker v Carr*, 369 US 186, 267 (1962).

power appeal to the judiciary due to its power to bind, embedded in the constitutional framework they work under.[77]

E. Addressing Counter-Arguments

In the previous parts I argued that the promotion of heightened participation and deliberation requires the development of various institutions and frameworks that empower such involvement through their function as intermediatory bodies, and that they contribute to the process of multiple-testing of issues to be decided in the public sphere. I argued that courts are perfectly suitable to exercise both functions. A well-rounded argument must address other claims brought forth by those who advocate limited, constrained judicial involvement.

These arguments are generally made under the assumption that courts are unduly dominant, by holding the 'power of the last word': under this argument, courts should be feared due to the fact that each and every case brought before them receives a final edict, after which no other member or body in the public sphere can challenge the ruling and its impact. Chief Justice Marshall's holding in *Marbury v Madison*, '[i]t is emphatically the province and duty of the judicial department to say what the law is'[78] was classically translated to connote that a judge's ruling on 'what the law [was]' was final, binding, and, at least when 'it [was] the constitution [the court was] expounding',[79] the ruling could only be overridden by a constitutional amendment.

Such visions are based on a hierarchical notion of the decision-making arena and require retuning. Courts are indeed influential in many fields of political decision-making, but they cannot be considered the holders of absolute power. Political scientists and legal scholars have provided ample empirical proof from the United States and elsewhere that supports the latter proposition. According to one of these studies,

> ... if we can say nothing else with certainty, we can say that there is no 'last word' in politics. No person or individual ever gets to say what the law is finally; Congress can and often does react to court decisions, as can agencies and the president. Each actor in the political and legal setting – president, agency, Congress, litigants, court – can take new courses of action, devise new interpretations or enact new statutes. This capacity to react is a fundamental feature of the political process.[80]

[77] For a more sophisticated account of the dynamics of compliance with judicial output see Law (n 63). For my purposes, the argument from formal legitimacy could suffice; further development of this point is relegated to future work.

[78] *Marbury v Madison*, 5 US 137, 177 (1803).

[79] *Mculloch v Maryland*, 17 US 316, 407 (1819).

[80] John Ferejohn and Barry Weingast, 'A Positive Theory of Interpretation' (1992) 12 Intl Rev L and Econ 263, 263. See also, eg, William N Eskridge, 'Overriding Supreme Court Statutory Interpretation Decisions' (1991) 101 Yale LJ 331; Keith E Whittington, 'James Madison Has Left the Building' (2005) 72 Chi L Rev 1137.

Indeed, rare is the decision that is fully implemented when met with strong political and social opposition. Post-decision dynamics of so-called ground-breaking decisions link the social and political internalization of the judicial ruling with overt and covert social and political support over time. The claim that courts enforce their rulings on unwilling polities is too crude; a more nuanced assessment of the interaction between courts and societies is required.

First in the series of arguments presented and criticized here is the argument regarding the 'democratic deficit' of the judiciary. Since justices are not popularly elected, the argument goes, this dominance cannot be sustained: courts lack the legitimacy deriving from the democratic process. The so-called 'democratic deficit' of the judiciary, or the counter-majoritarian difficulty, have been relied upon by many an opponent of judicial active decision-making.[81] Its proponents argue that since judges are un-elected and belong to a small elite, they do not represent society-at-large. Yet there are strong counter-arguments that refute, or at least minimize, the force of such claims.

The argument for elite membership could be rejected simply by arguing that the elite is over-represented in all government bodies.[82] In addition, arguments for professional expertise and dedication to neutrality offer further support.

Beyond this, this school of argument fails to recognize that 'representation' features in two contexts. The first, internal aspect, pertains to the nature of the judiciary itself as representative, while the second is related to the decision-making process in its entirety. Most arguments made under the title 'democratic deficit' are concerned with the first aspect: critics address the democratic legitimacy of unelected judges and their capacity to represent society. Under the second aspect of representation, the question of representative capacity concerns the ability of courts to represent the public. The contribution of courts as representing the public, an important feature that is less discussed in this context, may cancel out some of the problems arising from the non-election of judges.[83]

Hanna Pitkin's contribution in *The Concept of Representation* considers both aspects. For here, 'representation' is a multifaceted concept: representation bears

[81] Since Bickel's seminal contribution (n 72), thousands of pages have been dedicated to the argument that unelected judges cannot and do not represent their society. On this argument see eg Matthew D Adler, 'Judicial Restraint in the Administrative State: Beyond the Contermajoritarian Difficulty' (1997) 145 Uni Penn L Rev 759; Barry Friedman, 'The Birth of an Academic Obsession: The History of the Birth of the Countermajoritarian Difficulty, Part V' (2002) 112(2) Yale L J 153 (last in a series of articles); Kavanagh (n 27) 190–96.

[82] For some of the parents of elite theory see Gaetano Mosca, *The Ruling Class (Elementi di Scienza Politica)* (Hannah F Kahn trans, McGraw-Hill 1939); Elmer Eric Schadttschneider, *The Semisovereign People: A Realist's View of Democracy in America* (Holt, Reinhart and Winston 1960).

[83] A parallel distinction exists in discussions of deliberation. Two distinct issues may be addressed, the first concerning the nature of the judicial process as deliberative, that is, the capacity of courts to maintain deliberation within the courtroom. For an example of such an analysis see Conrado Hübner Mendes, *Constitutional Courts and Deliberative Democracy* (OUP 2013), esp ch 4. The second issue relates to the role of courts as promoters of deliberation across the system, a direction taken by most followers of deliberative systems theory.

different meanings, each of which can be linked with a distinct function of the democratic framework. Under an open-ended definition of 'representation', 'the making present *in some sense* of something which is nevertheless *not* present literally of in fact',[84] the first meaning, 'formalistic' representation, emphasizes action of the agent (the representative) under authorization of the represented, subject to accountability mechanisms. For some, 'the crucial criterion becomes elections', being a grant of authority, although under this vision, representation-under-authorization does not necessarily link representation with election. Within this group of theories, accountability, or the requirement that the representative is held to account and answers to those whom he represents, is considered another aspect of formalistic representation.[85] Up to this point, representation could tally with the so-called 'contemporary theories of democracy', at least with those who link representation with the political act of elections.

Under Pitkin's second understanding, that of 'descriptive representation', the degree of representativeness derives from the degree of resemblance of representatives to the represented. Finally, 'symbolic representation' occurs when an object, physical, rendered, or conceptual, comes to 'stand for' the represented, as in the case of the flag or the King representing the nation.[86] This unpacking of the concept of representation clearly supports a departure from visions that insist on formal authorization to represent via formal political structures.

For Pitkin, then, representation carries multiple meanings and can be effected in a variety of ways. Bodies can 'stand for' others even when they are not elected, as are heads of state, symbols of sovereignty, and, indeed, judges. Discussing the judiciary as but one example of her general conceptual exercise, she notes that

> [E]ven appointed judges have been called unelected judges can still be considered representatives ... from a formalistic standpoint, a judge is an agent of the state like all government officials. His pronouncements are not private expressions of opinion, but official utterances of the state. In a democracy where all agencies of the government are servants of the people, the judge might be said to represent the people. From the "standing for" interpretation, he may represent by embodying the values of a society; he may be a symbol representing the society. From the doctrine that anyone whose commands are obeyed and whose leadership is accepted

[84] Hanna Fenichel Pitkin, *The Concept of Representation* (University of California Press 1967) 8–9. Italics in the original. Another recurring idiom in this context is the relationship in which the representative 'stands for' the represented; see eg 60, 92.

[85] ibid 38–59; for citations see ibid 43.

[86] A fourth meaning, 'substantive representation' derives from Pitkin's chapter titled 'political representation'. For these meanings see ibid 60–91, 92–111, 209. For an analysis that also extends to additional contributions to the study of representation see Jeffrey Kurebwa, 'A Review of Hanna Pitkin's (1967) Conception of Women's Political Representation' (2015) 5 (11) Intl J Scientific and Research Publications 50.

as a representative, a judge certainly represents. In this sense it can even be argued that the judge may be "less representative" if elected than if appointed.[87]

Further development of the concept of representation can be found in the growing number of studies of the representative quality of transnational and non-elected bodies, as well as figures that represent a social agenda: in such climates, even Bono may make a successful claim for representing Africa.[88]

Of course, opponents of an active judiciary are likely to make two counter-arguments against these accounts of 'representation'. First, they may argue that in a democracy, true representation is achieved only by direct elections: all other 'meanings' may be valid in other fields, such as literature, film, and business, but not in politics. While this type of argument is not false, it still represents a stilted, formalistic vision of the value-base of democracy. The focus on elections is akin to the equation of democracy with the majority rule. A more nuanced presentation of representation enriches the understanding of the structural nature of a polity, by recognizing sets of processes that operate to ensure different ways of representation of the people by a variety of techniques.

Secondly, even under the adoption of an expanded account of 'representation', opponents may argue that the issue is not whether judges *can* be considered representatives of society, of the rule of law, of justice, or of any other value. The question is normative: *should* courts act as representatives of the people when they are not elected?

Such scholars focus on one aspect of representation, linked with the appointment of judges, and marginalize the other important aspect of representation, addressed above. After all, courts are usually activated by aggrieved persons: as discussed above, the judicial process itself is a form of representation; tying in with theories of participation and deliberation, the 'democratic deficit' argument should lose some of its force.

This leads to further consideration of the argument on participation, so dear to some populists who seem to reject the judiciary. It is unclear why the judiciary, and the judiciary alone, should be excluded from the participatory framework celebrated by these theorists. The record of the judiciary, if expected to save a society from all its woes, is indeed inescapably imperfect, but other modes of

87 Pitkin (n 84) 116–17. As support for the last claim, Pitkin cites Carl Friedrich's entry on 'representation' in the *Encyclopaedia Britannica* (1960), where he claims that had Supreme Court justices been elected by the people, they would seem to be, for most people, less representative, since 'all representation involves ideas; for only through an idea can the making present of one thing or person by another be conceived'. Cited ibid, 116 n 7. See further ibid 118.

88 See eg Joseph P Witherspoon, 'The Bureaucracy as Representatives' in James R Pennock and John W Chapman (eds), *Nomos X: Representation* (Atherton Press 1968) 229 (considering one form of an 'extra-elective' political representation). See also Ruth W Grant and Robert O Keohane (2005) 'Accountability and Abuses of Power in World Politics' (2005) 99 Am J Poli Sci 29, esp 33; Michael Saward, 'Authorization and Authenticity: Representation and the Unelected' (2009) 17 J Pol Philosophy 1.

decision-making carry their own imperfections.[89] In a simplified conclusion of his argument, Mark Tushnet claims that '[l]egislative and executive officials charged with interpreting a constitution can do an "OK" job'.[90] This is clearly a possibility, but so is the possibility that courts can do some good sometimes, as history has amply showed. Further, under any form of checks and balances, the impact of some of these flaws may be minimized by other participants' contributions; it simply makes little sense to eject one potential checking power and consider the outcome as promising better potential for the limitation of abuse. Heightened participation in both political and legal fora could act to correct some of these failings.

The next argument concerns the expertise and knowledge of judges. For some, these are two distinct arguments, brought as possible justifications for deference, at least in so-called 'mundane' areas. The knowledge deficit, it is argued, first and foremost stems from the institutional framework in which courts operate: resolving a dispute, the courts only have the material brought before them by the parties to the litigation. The nature of adjudication precludes judicial reliance on external knowledge that is not provided during the process; hence, attempts to make sweeping rules should be abandoned.

A linked argument weighs the ability of courts to decide on human rights issues against their capability to decide on broader policy. In this context, it is argued that courts are experts in deciding concrete disputes involving claims of rights, and are not well-equipped to decide upon polycentric issues, which require complex balancing of competing claims involving policy, resource-allocation, and social preferences.[91]

These sub-arguments are misguided if taken to their logical end. The argument for expertise in human-rights issues ignores the unavoidable porous nature of the distinction between this and other 'mundane' fields, a point discussed above. Human rights issues often raise questions of policy, and courts are unavoidably required to weigh social interests in their decision-making,

As for the argument for insufficient information provided during a judicial process: this fetching idea of the 'bivalent form' of the adjudicatory process[92] should be contrasted with the ways courts conduct their proceedings, especially in contested issues. The assumption that parties select the data that suits their agenda cannot be refuted, but the very nature of the adversary process promotes the provision of well-rounded accounts on the basis of which the courts may be able to decide. The addition of *amici curiae* to a process further contributes to the quality and quantity of the information provided to the courts. Despite the trappings of the adversarial

[89] See Fuller (n 3) 394–404. See also, presenting different points of view, TRS Allan, 'Common Law Constitutionalism and Freedom of Speech' in Jack Beatson and Yvonne Cripps (eds), *Freedom of Expression and Freedom of Information: Essays in Honour of Sir David Williams* (OUP 2000) 17, 22.

[90] Tushnet (n 5) 156–57.

[91] See Fuller (n 3); Kavanagh, 'Deference or Defiance?' (n 29).

[92] For the term see Timothy Endicott, 'The Impossibility of the Rule of Law' (1999) 19 OJLS 1, 15.

process, the conclusion that courts are ill-equipped to operate as promoters of participation is misguided. At least, it should be considered as another imperfection, which, as argued above in the context of the exclusion of the judiciary by populists, should be weighed against the imperfections of other players as well as the understanding that courts are not omnipotent, and, thus, errors, misdirected decisions or plainly unpopular judicial edicts are likely to be changed after delivery.

A different, possibly stronger argument against the enhancing of the judiciary as a check on the government focuses on the social prices paid in the so-called era of judicial supremacy. In his classic critique of the power of US courts to invalidate statutes, James B Thayer supplemented his rich historical analysis with the argument that the outcome of such a practice is the diminishing responsibility of decision-makers. In the face of judicial review of legislation, he argued, governments 'have felt little responsibility; if they are wrong, they say, the courts will correct it ... the checking and cutting down of legislative power, by numerous detailed prohibitions in the constitution [applied by courts], cannot be accomplished without making the government petty and incompetent'.[93] This argument has been forcefully advanced in Israel: Ruth Gavison argues that enhanced judicial review has contributed to the deterioration of other forms of public decision-making and to the gradual deterioration of civil society at large, for two (somewhat opposing) reasons. First, in this climate, political actors tend to desist from action; under the understanding that the court would eventually shape the final arrangement, there is no political utility in decision-making that might be overturned. Secondly, judicial involvement has weakened self-correction processes; actors now assume they can act freely as long as the court does not rule otherwise. The negative impact is exemplified by the fact that few politicians step down from office following the initiation of criminal investigations against them, since the court-created rule ordering suspension applies only after formal indictment.[94] The outcome, it is argued, has warped the principles of political responsibility, 'juridified' the public sphere at the expense of other self-correcting mechanisms, and minimized the beneficial impact of politics.[95]

Yet, an equally strong argument can be made for the opposite causal connection. In a chicken-and-egg style, one can posit that courts have self-enhanced to fill voids left by weak governments that prefer not to bear the brunt of decision-making, especially in sensitive and difficult contexts.

[93] James B Thayer, 'The Origin and Scope of the American Doctrine of Constitutional Law' (1893) 7 Harv L Rev 129, 155–56. See also Mendes (n 83) 86, citing Sunstein ('the cost of maximalism is the consequent impoverishment of deliberation in the public sphere with respect to these judicially bared issues').

[94] HCJ 3094/93 The Movement for Quality in Government v State of Israel, English trans via www.court.gov.il.

[95] Both aspects are developed in Ruth Gavison's forceful argument against judicial activism, voiced inter alia in Ruth Gavison, 'The Court in Rifted Democracies' (1999) 33 Isr L Rev 216; Ruth Gavison, 'Legislatures and the Quest for a Constitution: The Case of Israel' (2005) 11 Rev Const Stud 345.

Furthermore, blaming the courts and only the courts for all society's woes is way too simple. Empirical studies, or other forms of robust proof, are required to substantiate such a claim. Existing qualitative studies do not establish a correlation between strong courts and weak governments. Other forces seem to be better candidates as bearers of responsibility, or at least deserve to share the blame. Moreover, this argument implies that indeed, courts can, and have, achieved the status of ultimate decision-maker, an assumption challenged above.

In sum, under an enhanced theory of participatory/deliberative democracy that expands the arena to include various fora of discourse in formal and informal venues, I join calls for the continued involvement of the judiciary as a check on the executive in all its fields of action. Courts play an important, but not omnipotent role in the public arena. They operate as intermediators between members of a society and its decision-makers, operating as an alternative for those who have less access to the latter. Courts also contribute to the quality of decisions by supporting and expanding multi-level discussion. This form of review, alongside others—political and social—is required if today's society wishes to maintain some measure of balance under the internal tension model described in this book. The executive will continue to self-empower: this is not only inherent to its own structure, but is also often required under the exigencies of current reality. Yet executive dominance can only be supported when several robust checking mechanisms operate in tandem to alleviate at least part of the potential for abuse. The utilities of the retention and enhancement of the judiciary's checking role outweigh the dangers endemic to judicial participation-enhancing that have received undue emphasis.

F. Concluding Remarks

This chapter ends a book that is mainly analytical and descriptive. An important part of the essay, which should not be overlooked, the chapter was designed to quell arguments that deduce that since fuzziness of law is an inevitable feature of governance, it should be welcomed or at least accepted, for lack of a better option. No such defeatism is in place. The crucial role of review mechanism in suppressing excessive fuzziness, as much as possible, requires attention.

Rather than merely focus on the proper degree of review of action that directly affects protected rights, an undoubtedly important aspect, the chapter takes two steps forward, following one of the themes of this book, which puts a premium on all sub-chapters of public law, blending constitutional and administrative law. First, in the context of fuzziness, the main focus of the book, I argue that the problems created by all such forms of grey holes more than justify enhanced review; the high prices paid by societies in which fuzzy law enhances executive power more than justify the augmentation of all forms of review, including the judicial. Rather than stop here, the chapter was also intentionally devised as a contribution to the general ongoing dispute about the role of the judiciary as a constraining agent. In this part of the chapter, and following the previous one, I base my argument for active review, not only on the principles reflected in the rule of law ideal, but also on an argument from governance. Setting judicial review in a framework that seeks to enhance participation, the judiciary, stripped from accusations of supremacy over all other forms of decision-making, operates as an intermediator by offering members of society, especially those that do not have direct access to government corridors, an additional forum for voicing their concerns and thereby contributing to public deliberation over all contested aspects of social and political life.

In my view, this chapter is a proper ending to a focused consideration of the nature of the executive branch. Never acting alone in the public sphere, executives should not be granted political ascendancy over all other branches of government, even in times in which the case for dominance seems to gain a higher level of support. Addressing the calls for such domination against other arguments for cabining such power, the chapter has relied on a vision of a judiciary that is an important, but never supreme, player. This joint rule of law or political project, depending on the arguments brought forth, should inform all assessments of the role of the executive in democratic societies.

Conclusion

The state of Utopia (or Ruritania, take your pick) is a functioning democracy. Elections are held periodically, and citizens, regardless of gender, wealth, or area code, are each granted a vote. Initially, this was a parliamentary regime; political instability led to a regime change through the introduction of direct elections to the newly established presidency, held alongside elections to parliament, but ensuing tensions between the two branches led to the reinstatement of the former regime. Throughout these periods, President Hercules and Prime Minister Herbert, both heads of the executive branch during the respective periods, retained dominance, if not supremacy, in the political sphere.[1]

That political dominance was never considered to have shaken the foundations of the state's democratic character. The government generally followed the laws of the state, that is, the output of a duly elected legislature. This was no corrupt regime, or at least one that could profess its general commitment to law-abiding action. Political dominance was not only the direct result of legislation which explicitly granted such dominance; Hercules and Herbert gained much of their powers through reliance on a variety of constructs that enabled them to act in the shadow of the law, inter alia by issuing unilateral declarations of policy relying on vague references to the spirit of the constitution or the laws, introducing programmes through contracting, and refraining from enforcing some laws they were opposed to. Whenever challenged (a rare case), they justified their action not only by the fact that nothing they had done was contrary to law, but also on their role as protectors of the well-being of society.

The rarity of challenges in court was not necessarily explained by general social support of the entire action, but largely due to the virtual impossibility of tracing some of the measures taken by the heads of the executive. Some unilateral declarations, and all government contracts, were never formally published, nor were they easily traceable. Information about enforcement practice was likewise not easily discovered by those who wished to assess them.

The state may have flourished during these decades, although the degree of success of any society is generally measured in line with the politics of those evaluating the outcome of government policy. Prices were however paid: while seemingly

[1] Apologies to Ronald Dworkin are due; the pull was difficult to resist.

A Theory of the Executive Branch. Margit Cohn, Oxford University Press (2021). © Margit Cohn.
DOI: 10.1093/oso/9780198821984.003.0012

remaining an organizing social tool, the actual function of law as a means for grasping political action was substantially reduced.

Utopia (or Ruritania) is not alone. This book has traced the ways two central Western democracies, the United Kingdom and the United States, have developed and retained fuzzy modes of law that were relied upon by aggrandized heads of the executive branch. Viewed as an unavoidable feature of governance, the resulting argument for a similar aggrandizement of review by courts, designed to curb some of the ensuing abuse of power, is central to the rounded model offered in the book.

This book should be considered as an invitation to the further development of theories of the executive branch that apply to more than one democratic system. In the comparative context, the insights gleaned from detailed analyses of two common-law systems should be tested not only on other common-law systems but also on systems that belong to other families of law. On the normative level, there is a pressing need to better assess the inevitable reality of executive dominance in the shadow of the law, to be checked under developed review mechanisms, primarily, but not singly, by an empowered judiciary.

Index

For the benefit of digital users, indexed terms that span two pages (e.g., 52–53) may, on occasion, appear on only one of those pages.

Tables are indicated by *t* following the page number

Ackerman, Bruce, 18
administrative state, the, 18–20
AG v De Keyser Royal Hotel, 75n.48, 110n.31, 123–24, 124n.102, 128, 175
agencies, independence of, 14, 37–39
UK, in the, 36–37
US, in the, 31–36
air pollution law
England, in, 188–89
domestic legislation 177–78
Clean Air Act 1993, 193
Environment Act 1995, 84, 192n.93, 193
Environmental Protection Act 1990, 81, 83, 190, 192, 214–16, 245–46
Pollution and Prevention Act 1999, 82n.74, 192n.91, 192, 193, 215–16, 245nn.83–84
EU law, 190–92
international law, 189–90
layers of law 189–93
US, in, 194
agencies and bodies
Council on Environmental Quality, 206
Environmental Protection Agency *see separate entry*
layers of law
constitutional law, 194–97
federal domestic legislation, 196–97
Clean Air Act *see separate entry*
Comprehensive Environmental Response, Compensation, and Liability Act, 205
Federal Power Act, 216–17
National Environmental Policy Act, 206
Pollution Prevention Act 1990, 205
international and transnational law, 195–96
riders, in appropriations acts *see separate entry*
unilateral executive measures, 206–7
US Code (USC), 197, 206
treaties, 189–90
Allan, TRS, 302–3
Aristotle, 43–44, 45, 258
Article II, US Constitution, 72–73, 112, 113–14

Bancoult affair, 103–4, 277–78
ICJ Advisory opinion (2019), 103–4
Mauritius v UK, 104n.6
orders in council *see separate entry*
R (on the application of Bancoult) v Secretary of State for Foreign and Commonwealth Affairs, 129–30, 143n.23, 145n.29
R (on the application of Bancoult) v Secretary of State for Foreign and Commonwealth Affairs (No 2), 103–4, 128n.113, 128–29, 131, 142–43
R (on the application of Bancoult No 3) v Secretary of State for Foreign and Commonwealth Affairs, 104n.6
R (on the application of Hoareau and Bancoult) v Secretary of State for Foreign and Commonwealth Affairs, 104n.6, 128n.113, 131n.130
UN resolution A/ RES/ 73/ 295 (2019), 104n.6
Barak, Aharon, 23n.80, 304–5
Bardach, Eugene, and Robert A Kagan, 91nn.99–100, 227n.9, 249–50, 266n.51
binary thinking *see* executive branch, models: bipolar model, the; hierarchical thinking, rejection of
black holes, 64–65, 256
Blackstone, William, 108
Brexit, 177–78
legislation, 203–4
European Union (Withdrawal) Act 2018, 143n.24, 177–78, 203–4
European Union (Withdrawal Agreement) Act 2020, 177–78, 203–4
Burmah Oil v Lord Advocate [1965] AC 75, 124n.102

Chandler v DPP [1964] AC 763, 128n.115, 131nn.126–128

Clark, Justice Tom C, 50n.34–51, 133n.137
Clean Air Act, US, 35, 79, 89, 194, 196, 205, 206–7, 217, 233–35
ambiguity, 114–15
and delegation, 83–84
Clinton, William J (Bill), 29n.93, 33–34, 153–54
Cohn, Margit, 20n.68, 26n.87, 66n.28, 69n.35, 104n.8, 117n.69, 119n.84–20, 251n.106, 306n.52
Coke, Lord Edward, 20
Commander-in-Chief clause, 113
commencement of statutes, 192, 239–40, 242–47
Constitution, the US
Article II, 113–14
drafting of, 272–74, 279, 282–84, 285–86
constitution, unwritten, 107–8
Fuzziness, and, 73–75
constitutional conventions, 73–74
constitutional doctrines and principles, 75–78
history-based, 77
constitutionalism, 22–24
Corwin, Edward S, 11, 14n.24, 16n.34, 55–56
Council of Civil Service Unions v Minister for the Civil Service (GCHQ), 128–29, 131n.126, 131, 142–43, 260–61
courts, role of, why *see* judiciary, why
Craig, Paul, v, 8, 9n.4, 10, 11n.13, 22, 45n.12, 108n.23, 177n.29, 259n.14, 259n.20
Craig, Robert 124n.102, 278n.85
creative compliance, 91–92, 224, 225–39, 252
Criminal Injuries Compensation Board ex parte Lain, 75, 105n.9, 116n.58, 128n.115, 246n.87

Dames & Moore v Regan, 16n.32, 51n.36, 77n.59, 102n.1, 121n.89, 125–26, 133n.142, 160n.77
deference, judicial, 17–18, 20, 26n.87, 134, 135–36, 295, 297, 299–301, 302–3, 303n.34, 305, 317, 317n.91, *see also* judicial review: normative theories
De Smith, Stanley, 147–48, 260–61
delegation, 60–62, 82–85
deliberative theory of democracy *see* participatory theory
democratic deficit, 293, 314–16
and participation, 316–17
and representation, 314–16
Department of Energy (US), 217
Dicey, Albert Venn, 46, 108–9, 110, 258, 275
dichotomy-based thinking, rejection of, 24
discretion, 60–62, 80–82
Dixon, Rosalind, 273–74, 299n.21
dominance, of the executive, 4, 7, 13, 16–17, 22, 30–31, 48, 49, 52, 65–66, 113, 162, 175, 184, 255, 281, 286, 319, 321
and agencies:
compared, 37–39
UK, in, 36–38
US, in, 32–36, 41
and judicial review, 57–58, 289–320, 322
political reality, in, 115–16
see also executive branch, models: imperial executive
Dworkin, Ronald, 23n.80, 259n.16, 303–4, 307, 321n.1
Dyzenhaus, David, 2, 52n.40, 64, 170n.6, 256n.4, 257nn.8–9, 259–60, 268n.53, 300, 307

emergency, declaration of national, 169
emergency law, 78–79, 169–71
UK, in the, 171–73
anti-terrorism law, 200–3
layers of law
constitutional law, 175
customary international law, 173–75
domestic legislation, 179–80
Prevention of Terrorism Act, 180, 200n.6, 202
US, in the, 180–81
layers of law
constitutional law, 181–82
customary international law, 182–84
domestic legislation, 185
EU law, 177–79
international treaties, 176, 184
UN measures, 177, 185
USC, 210
see also terrorism, counter measures
enforcement, 224
informal, 226–32
law as last resort, 226
pyramid, 227
see also creative compliance
Environmental Protection Act, UK, 81, 83–84, 190n.83, 192, 214–16, 245–46
and discretion, 81–82
Environmental Protection Agency, US (EPA), 194–95
History, 233–35
European Convention of Human Rights
derogations and reservations, 179
and terrorism, 179
executive agreements, 155–56

executive branch:
 definition, 8
 and separation of powers *see* separation of powers
 see also agencies, independence of; executive branch, models; executive branch, theories
executive branch, models:
 bipolar model, the, 53–55
 exception-based theories 49–52, *see also* executive branch, theories: managerial theories
 imperial executive, the, 47–52, *see also* executive branch, theories: managerial; executive branch, theories: exception-based
 internal tension model *see* internal tension theory
 managerial theories, 47–49, 52
 subservient executive, the, 43–47
executive branch, theories
 ambiguity/ambivalence, 10–11, 53
 dominance, of the executive *see separate entry*
 exception-based, 49–52
 inherent powers, 15
 managerial, 47–49, 52
 paradox, 10–11, 42–43, 56
 personal presidency, 11–12
 personification, 75–76, 117–20
 public choice, 12–13
 stewardship theory *see separate entry*
executive orders, 17–18, 33–34, 102, 105–6, 149–50, 151–52, 156–57, 162, 194–95, 213
 and fuzziness, 70*t*, 268, 280–81, 308
 history, 151–52
 judicial review, of, 50, 77, 125–26, 127n.110, 131–34, 159–60
 legal status, of, 158–60, 162–63
 mixed authority, 94–96, 102, 122–23, 127, 156–58, 209, 210–11
 numbered
  1, 151–52, 156n.66, 208
  9066, 18n.48, 89–90, 107n.18
  9102, 89–90
  10244, 33n.108
  10340, 122, 132–33, 156n.66
  10925, 159n.76–60
  11246, 152n.49
  11821, 133n.141
  12072, 159n.76–60
  12088, 33n.109–34, 195n.103, 195n.105, 207n.33
  12174, 33n.108
  12294, 16n.32
  12333, 209
  12866, 33–34, 106n.16, 207
  12291, 33n.108, 73, 113–14, 132–33
  12947, 209n.40
  12957, 157
  13371, 33n.109–34, 34n.111–35, 152n.50, 194–95, 207, 247–48
  13432, 33n.109–34, 34n.110, 194–95, 207n.33
  13526, 160n.80–61
  13645, 210–11
  13765, 102n.2
  13766, 102n.2
  13767, 102n.2, 236
  13768, 102n.2, 152n.53
  13769, 132
  13771, 33n.109–34, 34n.111–35, 194–95
  13777, 33n.109–34
  13783, 207n.33
  13846, 95n.114, 152n.51, 157n.67
  13856, 156–57
  13886, 209n.40
  13928, 152n.51
 numbering, 152
 publication of, 160–61
 unnumbered, 151n.46

Farber, Daniel, 227, 228n.14–29, 232, 250
Farrand, Max, 112n.44, 113n.47
Fisher, Louis, 14n.26, 15n.28, 117n.65, 117n.67, 290n.2
Foley, Michael, 30n.97, 49n.27, 270n.57
Frankfurter, Justice Felix, 15–16, 77, 121
Fuller, Lon, 259–61, 262, 291n.3, 300–1, 301n.30, 317n.89, 317n.91
funding
 and appropriations Acts *see* riders, in appropriations acts
 under-funding, 218–22
fuzziness, prices paid, 287
 and the rule of law, 260–62
 benefits, consideration of, 265–68
 executive-generated, 249–51
 statute-generated, 212–22
fuzziness, why, 286, 287
 endogenous factors, 274–78
 exogenous factors, 278–86
 inevitability, 269–70
 marginalization, of issues, 285–86
 power-accumulation, 279–82
  constitutions, by
  after entry into force, 284–85
  drafting of, 272–74, 279, 282–84, 285–86

fuzziness, why (*cont.*)
executives, by, 279, 280–81
legislatures, by, 281
pressure, external, 285
public choice analysis, 279–82
fuzzy law, 60–68
executive, generated by *see* fuzzy law types: executive-generated
judicial review of, 3, 57–58, 306
judiciary, generated by, 68, 289–90
legislature, generated by *see* fuzzy law types: statute-generated
problems, created by *see* fuzziness, prices paid
fuzzy law types, 69, 70*t*
constitution-generated, 72
open-ended provisions, 72–73
executive-generated, 91–96, 223–52
extra-statutory parallel arrangements *see* unilateral executive lawmaking; unilateral executive measures
multiple mixed-sources, 94–96, 140–41
pastiche law, 92–93, 239–49, 252
floating statutes *see* commencement of statutes
non-commencement *see* commencement of statutes
prices paid *see* fuzziness, prices paid
selective enforcement, 224, *see also* creative compliance; implementation; enforcement
under-funding, 240, 247–49
under-implementation, 240–41
statute-generated, 218–22
delegation *see* delegation
discretion *see* discretion
lopsided statutes, 89–90
multiple and indeterminate decision-makers, 86–89
open-ended provisions, 79–80
patchwork legislation *see separate entry*

Gavison, Ruth, 319
GCHQ see *Council of Civil Service Unions v Minister for the Civil Service*
Ginsburg, Tom, 273–74
gloss, historical, 16–17, 77
Graber, Mark, 294, 310, 311n.72
grey holes, 2, 60, 64–66, 68–69, 85, 256, 269, 279, 281, 291, 319–20
Gross, Oren, and Fionnuala Ní Aoláin, 54–55, 78n.64, 170n.6

Hamburger, Philip, 20, 305
Hamdan v Rumsfeld, 95, 102n.1, 126, 132, 183–84
Harel, Alon, 298–300
Hawkins, Keith 67n.31, 91, 226, 266n.51
hierarchical thinking, rejection of, 24–25
see also executive branch, models: bipolar model, the
Hoffmann, Lord, 129
Holmes, Stephen, 271
Howell, William G, 149, 282

implementation, of statute, and fuzziness, 225, 262
see also fuzzy law types: executive-generated; fuzzy law types: executive-generated, pastiche law
institutionalism, new, 274–75, 277–78
internal tension theory, 25–26, 55–56, 57–58
executive, related to the, 26–27

Jackson, Justice Robert, 16, 77, 122, 125–26, 132–33
judicial action and diminishing government influence, 289, 318
judicial expertise, arguments regarding, 317–18
judicial omnipotence, arguments regarding, 293, 299, 313–14
judicial review
counter-arguments
democratic deficit *see separate* entry
weakened government accountability
normative integrity, of theories, 292, 293–95
normative theories
enhancement theorists
Barak, Aharon 23n.80, 304–5 *see also separate entry*
Dworkin, Ronald *see separate entry*
Hamburger, Philip *see separate entry*
middle-ground theorists
Allan, TRS *see separate entry*
critique, of, 297–98, 299–300, 301–3
Dyzenhaus, David *see separate entry*
Harel, Alon *see separate entry*
Kavanagh, Aileen *see separate entry*
King, Jeff *see separate entry*
Sunstein, Cass *see separate entry*
restraint theorists
critique, of, 296–97
Posner, Eric, and Adrian Vermeule *see separate entries*
Tushnet, Mark *see separate entry*
rights-based theories *see* Dyzenhaus, David; Kavanagh, Aileen; King, Jeff; middle-ground theories
judiciary, function of

agenda-raising, 311
decision-making in public arena, 291
deliberation/participation-enhancement, 308–11, 319
dispute-resolution, 291
intermediation, 292–93, 309, 313, 319–20
representation-enhancement, 307
rights-protection, 291, 297, 298, 300–5, 307, 317
rule-of-law protection, 307
judiciary, why, 312–13

Kagan, Robert A, *see* Bardach, Eugene, and Robert A Kagan
Kavanagh, Aileen, 300–1
King, Jeff, 301

Laker Airways v Department of Trade, 123–24, 127, 128n.115
Lawson, Gary 18n.54, 19n.55, 305n.47
legislative mandate, 66–68
Lester, Lord Anthony, 78n.62, 276n.78
Lincoln, Abraham, 51, 75–76, 151–52, 169–70, 181n.46–82, 208
Locke, John, 11, 43–44, 258
Lord, Clifford L, 149n.39, 152n.47
Loughlin, Martin, 24–25

Malone v Metropolitan Police Commissioner, 86n.81, 117–19, 120
Mansfield, Harvey, 53, 56
Marshall, Chief Justice John, 116–17, 273, 313
memoranda, 152–53
see also torture memos
Moe, Terry, 48–49, 149n.39, 280

Neustadt, Richard, 48
New London College v Secretary of State for the Home Department [2012] EWCA Civ 51 77n.61, 119–20
non-statutory executive powers, 106–7
and sovereignty, 116–17
see also unilateral executive law-making; unilateral executive measures

Obama, Barack H, 29n.93, 33n.109–34, 39n.127, 134n.147, 150n.40, 151–53, 155n.63–56, 217n.72–18, 241
Office of the Management of the Budget (OMB), 33n.105, 33–34, 238
orders in council, 103–4, 105–6, 110–11, 139, 141, 142–45, 172–73, 200n.7, 277–78
and fuzziness, 280–81
judicial review of, 128–30, *see also* fuzzy law: judicial review; prerogative, Royal, judicial review of
legal status, of, 144–46
publication of, 142–43, 146–48, 203, 260–61
source of authority, 138
mixed-authority, 141, 144, 149
prerogative-based, 142–44
statute-based, 142–44

parliamentary and presidential regimes, comparison, 27–31
participatory theory of democracy, 262–65, 308
and fuzziness, 265
and judicial review, 308–11
passport regime, UK, 74–75, 104–5, 109, 111, 131, 142–43, 148, 276, 276n.79–77, 279
patchwork legislation, 85–86
contradicting provisions, 216–17
dispersion, 85, 198–99, 204–12
funding, under- as patchworking *see* funding: under-funding
and fuzziness, 85–86, 212–22, 261–62
piling-up, 85, 198–204
consequences of, 212–16
prices paid *see* fuzziness, prices paid
Perretti, Terri, 310
Philadelphia Convention, 112
and Article II, 112–13
Pildes, Richard, 52
Pitkin, Hanna, 314–15
Plato, 23n.77, 45
Posner, Eric A, 9n.4, 16–18, 48, 49, 50, 51–52, 54, 64, 65–66, 68, 82n.76–83, 155n.62, 256, 265–66, 296
Prakash, Saikrishna B, 10n.27, 56n.51, 117n.64
prerogative, royal, 20–21, 74–75, 108–12, 275
and fuzziness, 70*t*, 75
judicial review of, 74–75, 103–4, 128–31, 135, 140n.6, 246–47, 275–76
reform, of, 276–77, 286
proclamations, UK, 139–41
definition, 139
history, 139–42
source of authority, 141
prerogative-based, 141–42
statute-based, 141–42
see also Statute of Proclamations
proclamations, US, 151
history, 150–51
proclamations, US, named
emergency, declaration 2019, 169n.1, 209n.40, 237n.48

neutrality 1793, 151n.43, 208, 280n.91
proclamations, US, numbered
1, 150–51, 156n.66
4, 151n.43, 208, 280n.91
179, 158n.71
9844, 169n.1, 209n.40, 237n.48
9852, 151n.44
9891, 151n.44
9892, 151n.44

Questiaux, Nicole, 54–55

R (Hooper) v Secretary of State for Work and Pensions [2005] 1 WLR 1681, 116n.58, 118–19, 121–22
R (on the application of Bancoult) see Bancoult affair
R v Secretary of State for Foreign and Commonwealth Affairs, ex parte Everett [1989] QB 811, 105n.10, 131n.128, 143n.22
R v Secretary of State for the Home Department, Ex Parte Fire Brigades Union, 246–47
R (Miller) v Secretary of State for Exiting the European Union, 109n.30, 124n.102, 130
R (Miller) v The Prime Minister and Cherry v Advocate General for Scotland, 130
Ram doctrine, 77–78, 119–20, *see also* executive branch, theories: personification; third source powers
Raz, Joseph, 259n.14, 259–60, 260n.22
representation, 25, 263–64, 314–16
and fuzzy law, 101–2, 268, 287, 292, 309, 310
see also Pitkin, Hanna
residuality doctrine, 109–10, 121, 123–27, 130, 132–33, 135, 175, 275
override of, 126–27
riders, in appropriations acts, 35–36, 40–41, 206–7, 238–39
Roosevelt, Franklin D, 9, 50, 76, 122, 294
rule of law, the, 3, 22–23, 45–47, 56, 57, 60, 63–64, 65, 110, 222, 250, 257–62, 267, 268, 300, 305–7

Scheppele, Kim Lane, 51n.38, 54
Schlesinger, Arthur, 14n.26, 49–50, 52, 54, 180n.43
Schmitt, Carl, 16–17, 49–50, 52
selective enforcement *see* creative compliance; fuzzy law types: executive-generated
separation of powers, 43–45
Shelton, Dinah, 62–63, 271, 272
Shklar, Judith, 45n.10, 258
signing statements, 153–55, 211–12, 236–37
soft law, 62–64, 271
and fuzzy law, 63–64, 66, 271–72
Statute of Proclamations, 140–41
stewardship theory, 15, 50, 70*t*, 76
Strauss, Peter 10n.9, 14n.25, 31n.100, 56n.51, 134n.39
Sunstein, Cass, 48, 260, 297–98
Supplemental Environmental Projects (SEPs), 228–32
and fuzziness, 232–33
legality, of, 230, 231
Sutherland, Justice George, 15n.28, 50n.33, 116–17, 290

take-care clause *see* US Constitution: take-care clause
Tamanaha, Brian Z, 45n.11, 258n.11, 259n.14
terrorism, counter measures, 178–79
UK legislation
Anti-Terrorism, Crime and Security Act 2001, 180, 201–2
Civil Contingencies Act 2004, 179, 202, 262
Counter-Terrorism Act 2008, 180, 202
Counter-Terrorism and Security Act 2015, 63, 180, 202–3
Prevention of Terrorism Act 2005, 180, 200n.6, 202
Prevention of Terrorism Act 2006, 178n.35–79, 180, 202
Terrorism Act 2000, 173n.10, 180, 243–44
Terrorism Prevention and Investigation Measures Act 2011, 180, 202
Terrorist Asset-Freezing Act 2010, 180, 200nn.6–7, 202
US legislation
Intelligence Authorization Act, 211
International Emergency Economic Powers Act 1970, 156–57, 185, 210–11
National Emergencies Act 1976, 156–57, 169, 185, 209, 210–11, 236–37
USC, 185, 210, 212
War Powers Resolution 1973, 92, 185, 209, 222, 240–41, 284–85, 285n.110
Thach, CC, 112n.44, 112n.45, 283nn.103–105–84
Thayer, James B, 318, *see* judicial action and diminishing government influence
third source powers, 75, 77–78, 115–16, 118–19
see also executive branch, theories: personification; Ram Doctrine

Tomkins, Adam, 8, 9n.4, 10, 11n.13, 21n.71, 22, 36n.115
torture memos, 50, 152–53, 208
Trump, Donald, 19, 29–30, 33n.109–34, 34n.111–35, 94–95, 102–3, 132, 149–52, 152n.53, 154–55, 156–57, 169, 183n.52, 195–96, 207, 217n.72–18, 235–39, 241, 247, 311
Tushnet, Mark, 23n.77, 294, 296, 299, 316–17

unilateral executive law-making, 93–94, 223–39
unilateral executive measures, 137
  comparatively, 104–5, 137–38, 161–63
  executive agreements, 155–56
  history, compared, 162
  impoundment of funds, 153–54
  informal measures, 227–28
    as alternative to enforcement, 232–33
  judicial review of, 131–34
  legal status, 138, 162–63
    UK, in the, 145–46
    US, in the, 158–60
  line-item veto, 153–54
  memoranda *see separate entry*
  presidential directives, 156
  publication of, and access to, 138
    UK, in the, 146–48, 260–61 *see also* orders in council: publication of
  US, in the, 149–56, 160–61, *see also* executive orders: publication of
  signing statements *see separate entry*
  source of authority:
    mixed authority, 156–58, 163–64, 169, 194–95, 209, 210–11
    statute-based, 140–44, 146–47, 147n.34, 149, 156, 157, 172–73, 175
    see also executive orders; proclamations, UK; proclamations, US
unitary theory, 14–15
US Constitution
  commander-in chief clause, 50, 70*t*, 72, 89n.95–90, 113, 122, 125, 182, 208
  take-care clause, 70*t*, 72–73, 113–14, 122, 125, 194, 283
US-Mexico wall, 132, 134, 169
  funding of, 235–39, 249, 311
US v Curtiss-Wright, 15n.28, 16n.33, 77n.60, 116–17, 133, 290
US v Midwest Oil, 15–16, 77, 102n.1, 105n.15, 121, 126, 152n.47

Vermeule, Adrian, 9n.4, 16–18, 31n.100, 38n.122, 48, 49, 50, 51–52, 54, 64, 65–66, 68, 82n.76–83, 155n.62, 256, 265–66, 296
veto players, 28
Vile, Maurice, 43–45
Vinson, Chief Justice Fred M, 77–78, 122
Weingast, Barry, 61n.7, 92n.101, 225n.5–26, 233, 313

Youngstown Sheet & Tube v Sawyer, 15–16, 63, 77–78, 94–95, 121, 122, 125–26, 132–33, 156